FEVER AND AGUE CURED.

THE

TRAPPERS' REMEDY,

OR

OREGON AGUE POWDERS,

PREPARED BY

JOHN M. SMITH, late of Multnomah, O. T.

SOLD BY

SMITH & ATKINSON, 288 Baltimore street, Baltimore.

This Preparation has been used with eminent success, and being safe and speedy in its operation, has established for itself a high reputation in those quarters where its worth has beeu made known by experience

Being in a portable form it is very convenient for persons going into districts where Ague and Fever may prevail, as it can be carried without danger of soiling anything it may be packed with. By attending strictly to the directions, relief may be confidently calculated upon. No person afflicted with Ague and Fever should neglect to avail themselves of its virtues.

The attention of dealers is earnestly directed to this article, as it is one which they can recommend to their customers with confidence, and upon which they can realize a handsome profit.

FOR SALE BY

SMITH & ATKINSON,

SOLE PROPRIETORS,

288 BALTIMORE STREET, BALTIMORE,

And by Storekeepers and Druggists generally throughout the Country.

WM. LINTON,

MANUFACTURER OF

STONE & EARTHEN WARE,

ALSO,

FIRE AND STOVE BRICKS, &c.

POTTERY AND SALES ROOM

Corner of Lexington and Pine streets,

BALTIMORE, MD.

I am prepared to furnish the Trade with the above articles of a superior quality, at the lowest market prices.

☞All Orders addressed to me will be thankfully received and promptly attended to.
☞Delivered to any part of the city free of charge.

C. LEVERING. M. LEVERING.

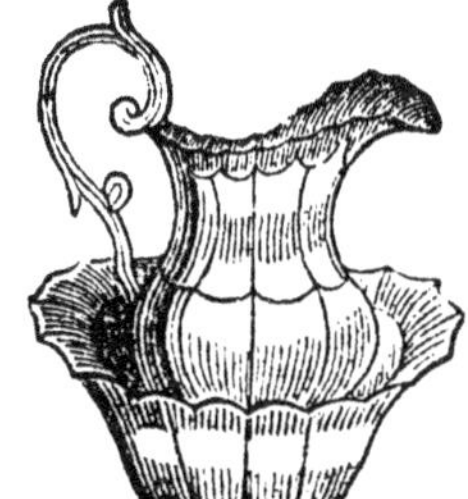

LEVERING & BRO.

IMPORTERS OF

CROCKERY,

CHINA AND GLASS,

Nos. 118 and 120 LOMBARD STREET, BALTIMORE.

A. P. SHARP,

CHEMIST AND DRUGGIST,

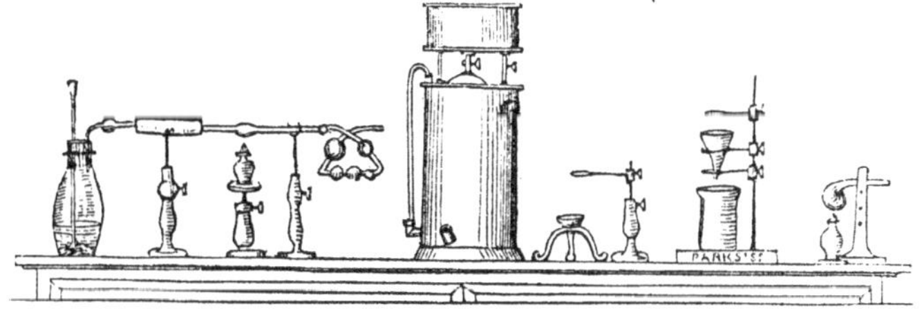

CORNER OF HOWARD AND PRATT STREETS,

BALTIMORE.

Importer of Chemical Apparatus of all kinds, Superior Microscopes, Blow-pipes, Reagents, chemically pure; Mineralogists supplied with every thing necessary to test Ores, Metals, &c. Fine Berlin Balances, Hydrometers of superior make for Acid, Leys, Syrups, &c. Porcelain dishes of all sizes. Stockhard's Apparatus complete, with a general assortment of every thing needed in Analytic or Experimental Chemistry.

BRASS GAS FITTINGS,

SUCH AS

Drop T. S., Drop L. S.

REDUCING SOCKETS AND CROSSES,

Of all the various sizes.

Brass Solder, Brass Casting and Brass Work of all kinds, manufactured at Eastern prices. Old Copper and Brass bought or taken in exchange.

ENGLISH & McSHANE,

No. 119 FRONT STREET, BALTIMORE,

BETWEEN GAY AND HILLEN STREETS.

LANSDALE & BRO.

OYSTER PACKERS,

No. 3 Balderston Street, Baltimore.

J. & W. GOSHORN,

COMMISSION MERCHANTS,

Wholesale and Retail Dealers in

GROCERIES AND HARDWARE,

Main Street, Charleston, Va.

Always on hand, a large assortment of Carpenters, Farmers, Blacksmiths, Lumbermen, Coopers' and other kinds of Tools, with a general supply of everything usually kept in Grocery houses.

MISCELLANEOUS ADVERTISEMENTS.

[ESTABLISHED IN 1837.]

CHARLES D. DE FORD & CO.

TOBACCO
COMMISSION MERCHANTS,
AND IMPORTERS OF
HAVANA CIGARS
AND
LEAF TOBACCO

No. 37 S. GAY STREET,

BALTIMORE.

Mr. George T. De Ford, our Agent, resides in Havana, and devotes his personal attention to the selection of Cigars for our sales.

We are prepared to execute orders to any extent, for all styles and qualities.

WATCHES
AND
JEWELRY,
AT WHOLESALE ONLY.

McCLEES & HAM,

No. 211 Baltimore street, (second story,)

BALTIMORE, Md.

Call the attention of Dealers to their Establishment, the only one in the above business, in Baltimore, devoted

EXCLUSIVELY TO THE WHOLESALE BUSINESS.

WATCHES

From all the most celebrated European Makers, and in every variety of case.

JEWELRY

Of every style and quality, and in all instances at Manufacturers' Prices.

☞ We beg to assure the Southern Trade, that our stock is as desirable, our prices as low, and our terms as accommodating as those of the best houses.

PAGE'S

IMPROVED PATENT CIRCULAR

SAW MILLS.

S. GANS, M. GANS, } { D. GANS, L. J. LEBERMAN.

GANS, LEBERMAN & CO.

WHOLESALE

Clothing Emporium,

No. 16 N. THIRD STREET,

PHILADELPHIA.

The Oldest exclusively Wholesale Clothiers in Phila.

Desire to draw the attention of the Dealers to their stock of

READY-MADE CLOTHING,

(Manufactured under the superintendence of two of the proprietors, who are Practical Tailors,) which for Cut, neat Fit, Style, Finish, Elegance, Uniformity and Low Prices, cannot be surpassed by any other Establishment. Their new and capacious Warehouse contains a complete assortment of all articles required by the Trade, and Merchants would derive great advantages by examining it before purchasing elsewhere.

1855. PHILADELPHIA. 1856.

HARDWARE, CUTLERY,

AND

Gun Warehouse,

No. 181 Market and 16 Commerce Streets.

MOORE, HENSZEY & CO.

Are now located at the above large and spacious warehouses, and keep constantly on hand, one of the largest and most magnificent stocks of

HARDWARE,

CUTLERY, GUNS,

TRACES,

Axes, &c.

Ever offered for sale in this country, to which they invite the attention of all that wish to make their purchases at a LOW RATE, our facilities for obtaining goods being such, that we can and will sell at such rates that the *closest buyers* shall not go away dissatisfied.

Prompt six months and cash buyers, will find it much to their interest to call and look through our immense stock of Foreign and Domestic Hardware, Cutlery, &c., our new warehouses,

No. 181 Market Street,

AND

No. 16 Commerce-st.,

PHILADELPHIA.

STATISTICAL GAZETTEER

OF THE STATE OF

EMBRACING

IMPORTANT TOPOGRAPHICAL AND HISTORICAL INFORMATION

FROM RECENT AND ORIGINAL SOURCES,

TOGETHER WITH THE RESULTS OF THE LAST CENSUS POPULATION,
IN MOST CASES, TO
1854.

EDITED BY

Richard Edwards.

RICHMOND:
PUBLISHED FOR THE PROPRIETOR.
1855.

FR

PREFACE.

I have been induced to prepare and publish this volume in accordance with a conviction that the business interests of the community demanded just such a publication. I am well aware that it is considered by Critics an unpardonable offence to bring a work to public notice and then apologize for its imperfections. This is not intended for such, and I hope they will give themselves no trouble on its account. The Editor claims no literary attainment—he only claims the merit due to enterprise and unconquerable perseverance in producing out of so varied, and from such numerous sources, this his first attempt to show forth in a neat and useful form the greatness of the State in her mercantile, manufacturing, commercial, and agricultural resources. One great perplexity in a work of this kind consists in the difficulty, if not impossibility of putting it into a form to suit the various classes of readers. If some trifle has been omitted in which an individual has a pecuniary interest—he will be like the Dutchman, who not finding his name in a Directory—calling at the Office for satisfaction inquires, "Vy you not put my names in the Correctory? Vy your Correctory is not vorth von cent. How do peoples knows vere he kets his Sour-krout?" To represent correctly the present condition of the State—so vast in extent and so various in feature, is a task of great difficulty as will readily be perceived. Owing to the endless number of topics and the changes that are continually taking place in every County, City, Town and Village throughout the land; there cannot but be great imperfection in the work. In the performance of this arduous task, every available means through which recent and authentic information could be obtained has been carefully consulted. So large a number of descriptions must necessarily be brief. It will, however, be perceived that notices of Counties and all important places are full and comprehensive. The aim has been to sum up in a small compass all the more important facts, and the most interesting points in the statistics of the census of 1850. I feel myself no less indebted to numerous gentlemen throughout the State whose names, were I authorized, it would be a pleasure to make known. But if my acknowledgments are due to such as gave important assistance, then, indeed I owe my heart-felt thanks to the merchants and manufacturers whose cards will be found within these pages, and for whose benefit I have endeavored to present them in conjunction with that which will attract not only the attention of the commercial community, but the public generally. If this has been happily effected, then am I content, and hope the present volume will approve itself to my advertising patrons, inducing them to continue the very liberal encouragement bestowed thus far upon my effort; and trust before the publication of a 2d volume many more may be induced to avail themselves of the benefit of such a circulation as this book will have. In presenting my efforts to the public, I am encouraged to think that those whose criticism is most to be valued, will be most capable of appreciating the difficulties of the undertaking. With these few remarks I commend it to the favorable regard of the Public. RICHARD EDWARDS.

GENERAL INDEX.

INDEX TO THE
CARDS AND ADVERTISEMENTS

OF THE LARGEST AND MOST RELIABLE MERCHANTS, MANUFACTURERS AND BUSINESS MEN OF RICHMOND, NORFOLK, PETERSBURG, LYNCHBURG, ALEXANDRIA AND WHEELING.

Hardware, Guns, &c., &c.

Hats, Caps and Furs.

Hotels and Restaurants.

Hotels.

Insurance Companies and Agents.

Iron Railing and Grating, &c.

Iron Nails and Steel Works,

Lumber Merchants.

Leather, Saddles, &c,

Marble Works.

Ornamental Work.

Painters & Blind Makers.

Paper Hanging and Upholstery.

Papers, News and Magazines.

Rail Road Car Factory.

Surgical Instruments.

Saw Manufacturers.

Sash, Doors, Builders, &c.

Stoves, Tin and Copper Ware.

Tobacco Manufacturers and Dealers.

Trimmings, &c.

Wagons, Carts, Dray Manufacturers.

Watches and Jewelry.

Wines, Liquors, &c.

RICHARD'S
Ladies' Furnishing
AND
TRIMMING STORE,
97 King St., & 3 Exchange Block,
Alexandria.

Toilet Articles, Perfumeries, Fancy Working Materials, Port-Monnaies, Work Laces, Writing Desks,

AND FANCY GOODS GENERALLY.

L. E. SWARTZWELDER,
DEALER IN ALL KINDS OF
ENGLISH AND AMERICAN HARDWARE,
EMBRACING
Saddlery, Cutlery, Guns, Shoe Findings, Hollow-ware Castings, Iron, Nails, Spiral Springs, Steel, &c.; House Joiners' Tools, &c.

LOUDON STREET,
WINCHESTER.

WILLIAM WELLS,
UPHOLSTERER & FASHIONABLE TRIMMER,
Loudon Street, nearly opposite Court House,
Winchester, Va.,

Keeps constantly on hand for sale, COTTAGE FURNITURE, in sets for Chambers; SOFAS; LOUNGES, spring seat and common; MAHOGANY CHAIRS, with spring and plain seats; Spring, Hair and Husk MATTRESSES; FEATHER BEDS, BOLSTERS, PILLOWS, &c., at city prices.
☞UPHOLSTERING done to order, and all kinds of Furniture Repaired at the shortest notice.
☞HAIR, FEATHERS, HUSHS, SPRINGS, &c., for sale, wholesale or retail, at low prices.
ORDERS thankfully received and promptly attended to.

CLOCKS, WATCHES AND JEWELRY.

JESSE BROWN,

LOUDON STREET,
Opposite the Taylor Hotel,
WINCHESTER, VA.

Keeps constantly on hand a Large assortment of FINE WATCHES AND JEWELRY of all kinds and patterns, which he will sell low for Cash, to suit purchasers.
☞All kinds of WATCH-WORK done in the best manner and with promptness, and warranted for twelve months.

LIST OF SUBSCRIBERS

IN BALTIMORE, PHILADELPHIA AND NEW YORK,

WITH INDEX TO THEIR CARDS AND ADVERTISEMENTS.

WILLIAM S. BURR. WILLIAM ETTENGER.

BURR & ETTENGER,

CARY STREET,

BETWEEN 15TH & 17TH STS.,

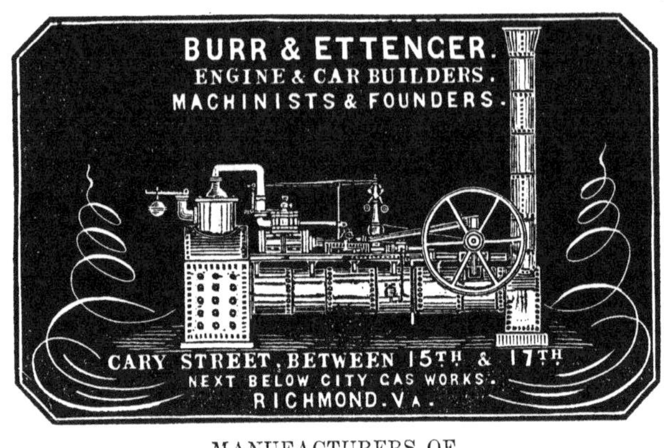

NEXT BELOW CITY GAS WORKS,

RICHMOND.

MANUFACTURERS OF

AND ALL DESCRIPTIONS OF

WOOD AND IRON WORK FOR RAILROADS.

ALSO,

PORTABLE & STATIONARY

STEAM ENGINES,

Circular Saw Mills, &c.

CASTINGS AND FORGED WORK

MADE TO ORDER FOR

SAW AND GRIST MILLS, MINES, AND OTHER PURPOSES.

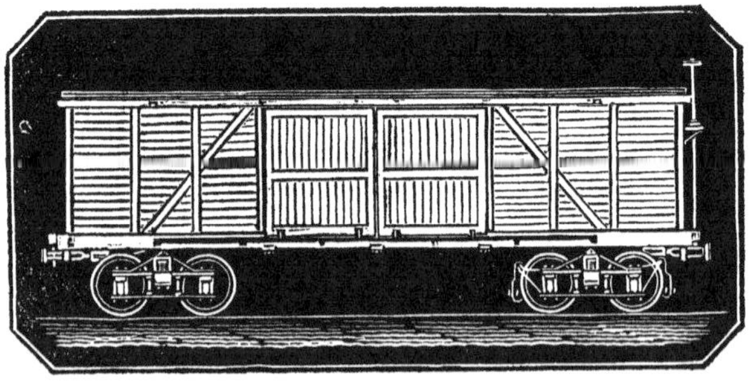

Engravers, Surgical Instruments, &c.

French Burr Millstones.

Flour Merchants.

Foundries, Machine and Iron Works.

Fancy Goods, Notions, &c.

Furniture and Chairs.

Fishing Tackle, Needles, &c.

Glass Ware, &c.

Hardware, Guns, &c.

Hats, Caps, Furs, &c.

Hotels.

House-Keeping Goods.

India Rubber Goods, &c.

Looking Glass, Frames and Show Cases.

Marble Works.

Oyster Packers.

Piano Forte Establishments.

Pump Block.

Printers' Materials.

Sewing Machines.

Scales, Safes, &c.

Soap.

Saddles, Harness, Hide and Leather,

Tin, Copper and Iron Ware.

Umbrellas, &c.

Wines, Liquors, Alcohol, &c.

White Goods,

Watches and Jewelery and Regalia.

GROSHONG, TUPMAN & CO.

110 MAIN STREET.

NEXT DOOR TO MITCHELL & TYLER'S,

RICHMOND.

LIST OF STOCK.

COATS!

COATS!! COATS!!!

Cloth Dress Coats,
Cloth Frock Coats,
Beaver Frocks,
Colored Cloth Frocks,
Pilot Hunting Coats,
Fancy Cassimere Frocks,
Tweed Business Frocks,
Satinett Business Frocks.

VESTS!

VESTS!! VESTS!!!

Fine Satin Vests,
Cheap Satin Vests,
Black Figured Silk Vests,
Fancy Silk Vests,
Black Velvet Vests,
Fancy Cassimere Vests,
Cheap Tweed Vests,
Black Alpaca Vests,
Mattesea Silk Vests,
Farmer Satin Vests,
Rich Velvet Vests,
Black Cassimere Vests.

PANTS!

Pants!! Pants!!!

Fine Black Doeskin,
Medium Black Doeskin,
Beaver Doeskin,
Coarse Black Doeskin,
Mixed Doeskin Cassimeres
French Tri-co'd Cassimeres
Fancy Ameri'n Cassimeres
Fine Black Satinetts,
Fancy French Cassimeres,
Fine Blue Satinett.

OVER CAOTS!

OVER COATS!!

Over Coats!!!

Fine Castor Beaver,
Napoleon Beaver,
Devonshire Kersey,
Ribbed Beaver,
Melton Beaver,
Lamb's Wool,
Petersham,
Black Pilot,
Whitney,
Lyon Skin,
Reversille,
Talmas.

CONSTANTLY ON HAND

A FULL AND COMPLETE ASSORTMENT

OF

Gentlemen's Furnishing Goods.

☞ We respectfully solicit of Strangers and Citizens a visit before purchasing elsewhere, as our motto is, Quick Sales, Small Profits, and Full Satisfaction to Customers.

GROSHONG, TUPMAN & CO.

Hor[illegible] Kent. William G. Paine. Robert A. Paine. William A. Thomas.

KENT, PAINE & CO.

Successors to Kent, Paine & Kent,

163 & 165 Main Street,

OPPOSITE THE EXCHANGE BANK,

RICHMOND,

IMPORTERS AND WHOLESALE DEALERS IN

FOREIGN & DOMESTIC

DRY GOODS.

The attention of Merchants from North Carolina, Tennessee and Virginia, is respectfully solicited to our very extensive Stock of

BRITISH, FRENCH AND GERMAN

DRY GOODS,

Which is imported direct, and purchased for Cash under the most favorable circumstances. We have also constantly on hand, and are receiving daily, a complete assortment of

AMERICAN FABRICS,

The whole comprising one of the largest Stocks, and as attractive as any in the United States. We are also prepared with a large and splendid Stock of

READY-MADE CLOTHING,

Manufactured in Richmond, and which will compare favorably in style and price with any Northern-Made Goods.

We particularly solicit Merchants visiting this Market, to call and examine our Stock, pledging ourselves to sell our Goods as low as they can be bought in any Market in this country.

☞ ORDERS respectfully solicited and promptly attended to.

KENT, PAINE & CO.

THE STATE OF VIRGINIA.

VIRGINIA, perhaps, in natural resources, as well as in geographical position, one of the most important States of the Union, lies generally between the latitudes 36° 30′ and 39° 43′ north, and extends east and west between longitudes 75° 40′ and 83° 33′ west, and is bounded on the north by Pennsylvania and Maryland, on the east by the Atlantic Ocean and Chesapeake Bay, on the south by North Carolina and Tennessee, and on the west by Kentucky and Ohio. With the exception of the long tongue of land between Pennsylvania and the Ohio River, and the peninsular projection between the Chesapeake Bay and the ocean, the State has an average length of 355 miles, and a breadth of 218 miles, and comprises an area computed at 61,352 square miles.

Virginia is naturally divided into east and west by the Blue Ridge, a division which obtains also in the distribution of the federal judiciary; but according to the State constitution, it is divided into four districts or sections—the *Tide Water*, below the lower falls of the rivers; the *Piedmont*, between those falls and the Blue Ridge; the *Valley*, between the Blue Ridge and the Allegany; and the *Trans-Allegany*—the latter comprising all the country west of the mountain ranges. The first mountains are found in the Piedmont section, which is traversed by

a low ridge, under the local names of White Oak, Southern, etc., and running nearly parallel with the Blue Ridge, at a distance of 25 or 30 miles. The Blue Ridge, although pierced by the Potomac, James, and Staunton rivers, constitutes a well-marked and continuous chain of more than 250 miles in length. In general, it forms rounded, swelling masses, but in several places, and especially the Peaks of Otter, shoot up in projecting summits to the height of 4,260 feet. The Kittatiny, or Blue Mountain, enters the State farther west, under the name of Great North Mountain, and forming the centre of the great plateau or table-land of Virginia, is continued, under various local names, until it takes the name of Iron Mountain, and enters North Carolina. It is pierced by the Potomac and James rivers running eastwardly, and by the New River running westwardly. West of this great ridge lie several detached masses, bearing the local names of Sideling Hill, &c. Still farther west is the great Allegany chain, which is broken through by New River and other streams to the north. Powell's Mountain appears to be an out-lier of this chain, and reaches to the height of 4,500 feet. Westward of the Allegany there is a general slope toward the Ohio; but several other considerable chains traverse this section, the principal of which is Laurel Mountain, of which Greenbrier, Great Flat Top, and the Cumberland Mountains appear to form a part. With the exception of Pennsylvania, Virginia is the only other State of the Union that has territory on both sides of the Allegany Mountains.

Virginia has noble rivers and streams, useful as channels of commerce or for industrial purposes. With few exceptions, the Ohio River west, and Chesapeake Bay east of the mountains, are the recipients of the waters of the whole State: those of Eastern Virginia flow, with an almost uniform south-easterly course, into the bay, carrying with them also the waters of the great valley, excepting only those of New River and the Holston, on the extreme southern part.

The Potomac rises in the Great Back Bone, but a few miles from the Youghiogeny, and pursuing a devious course, forces its way through the several intermediate mountain chains to the Piedmont section, where it is broken by falls nine miles above Georgetown, at which place it meets the tide-water, and

about 100 miles below, after a course of 350 miles, it reaches the Chesapeake. At Alexandria, 290 miles from the ocean, it is $1\frac{1}{4}$ miles wide, and below the city gradually expands, till at its mouth it forms a broad estuary, 10 miles in breadth. Ships of the line ascend to the navy yard at Washington; above this it is obstructed by numerous falls and rapids. The principal tributaries of the Potomac are its South Branch, which rises near the head-streams of James River, the Great Cacapon, and the Shenandoah, the latter of which flows about 120 miles along the western base of the Blue Ridge, and joins the main river at Harper's Ferry. "The passage of the Potomac through the Blue Ridge," says Mr. Jefferson, "is perhaps one of the most stupendous scenes in nature."

The *Rappahannock* rises in the Blue Ridge, and receives the Rapid Ann from the same ridge, and falling over the primary ledge of Fredericksburg, 100 miles from its mouth, there reaches tide-water. Vessels of 140 tons ascend it to this point. York River, formed by the union of the Pamunky and Mattapony, partakes rather of the character of a long narrow bay than of a river; to the junction, 40 miles from the bay, it is from two to four miles wide, and large vessels pass to Yorktown—smaller ones ascend some distance above the bifurcation.

James River, the principal river of Virginia, rises in the Allegany Mountains in several head-streams, of which Jackson's River must be considered the main constituent; after having received the Cow Pasture and the Calf Pasture rivers from the north, it forces its way through the Blue Ridge, and falling over numerous pitches, meets the tide 100 miles from its mouth at Richmond, which is accessible to vessels of 140 tons. The only considerable tributary of this river below the Blue Ridge is the Appomattox, which carries seven feet of water to Petersburg, 12 miles. The James River and Kanawha Canal, now complete to Balcony Falls, at the passage of the Blue Ridge, is constructed along the valley of the river, and is one of the most stupendous and important works in the United States.

The *Meherrin* and *Nottoway* are small rivers, which unite in North Carolina, and form the Chowan. The Roanoke is formed in Virginia by the junction of Dan River and Staunton River, two rapid mountain streams which rise, the former in the Blue

Ridge, and the latter in the North Mountain. The larger part of the Roanoke is through North Carolina, which State it enters about 40 miles below the union of its constituent rivers.

The great rivers of Western Virginia, flowing to the Ohio River, are—the Monongahela, one of the constituents of that river; the Kanawha; the Guyandotte; the Big Sandy, &c. The Monongahela is formed in Virginia by the junction of the West Branch and Tygart's Valley River, and beyond the Pennsylvania line it receives Cheat River, which descends from Greenbrier Mountain, and which is navigable for boats for a considerable distance. Little Kanawha River rises in the same district with the west branch of Monongahela River, and enters the Ohio at Parkersburg. The Kanawha, the principal river of Western Virginia, rises in the Blue Ridge, in North Carolina, and bears the name of New River until it unites with Gauley River, a small affluent from Greenbrier Mountain. The Greenbrier, above the latter, and the Elk and Coal rivers below it, are its principal tributaries. It is navigated by steamboats to Field's Creek, 75 miles from its mouth. The Covington and Ohio Railroad, and the James River and Kanawha Canal traverse the valley of this river. The Guyandotte and Big Sandy enter the Ohio below the Kanawha—the latter forming part of the boundary between Kentucky and Virginia. The Holston and Clinch, which drain the south-western section of the Great Valley of Virginia, pass into Tennessee, and, uniting at Kingston in that State, form the Tennessee River.

Virginia is an almost boundless field of mineral wealth, and within its limits, not only the useful, but also the precious metals are found in one part or the other. Gold, copper, lead, iron, coal, salt, lime, marls, gypsum, magnesian and alum earths, marbles, granites, soap-stones, and sand-stones are among the treasures, as yet for the most part lying unheeded in the bowels of the earth. Mining industry, however, has been commenced, and within the past few years has been wonderfully developed.

The first coal-field is found at the junction of the Tide-Water and Piedmont sections; and this extends from the Pamunky by Richmond to the Appomattox, a distance of about thirty-five miles, with a breadth of from one or two to eight miles. The coal is bituminous, in seams of enormous thickness, being 30,

EXTENSIVE BOOK STORE,

AND

PIANO FORTE WAREROOMS,

RICHMOND.

JAMES WOODHOUSE,

WHOLESALE AND RETAIL DEALER IN

BOOKS, STATIONERY, PIANO FORTES,

MUSIC AND FANCY ARTICLES.

ALL THE SCHOOL BOOKS IN USE.

LAW, MEDICAL, THEOLOGICAL, AND MISCELLANEOUS

Blank Books of every description, Letter and writing Papers, the best Ink of all kinds, in use, Globes, New Music, Drawing Materials, and Books on Drawing and Painting, Copying Presses, Mathematical Instruments, Gold and Silver Pencil Cases, Violins, Guitars, Flutes, Accordeons, and other Musical Instruments, Violin Strings, Pen and Pocket Knives, Diamond-Pointed Gold Pens, Surveyor's Compasses and Chains, Choice Books, and Fancy Articles—for Presents.

PIANO FORTES.

His supply of Piano Fortes is from the established and well known manufactories of *A. Stodart & Co.*, *J. B. Durham*, and *Jonas Chickering*, whose instruments can be relied upon for beauty of tone, great durability and elegance of finish.

The subscriber has participated in the sale of upwards of *one thousand* of these Piano Fortes, to some of the most respectable and well known families in Virginia and North Carolina.—They are warranted superior in all respects, and are offered at the Manufacturers' lowest Prices.

Books bound, and Blank Books of all kinds manufactured to order.

☞ Orders by letter faithfully and promptly attended to.

40, and even 60 feet thick, and of excellent quality. Coal has also been found on both sides of the Upper Appomattox. The coal of the Richmond basin is now extensively mined, and a railway to the principal mines has been built to facilitate its transportation to tide-water. Anthracite of great purity is found in the valley from the Potomac to the James River, south of which it contains a considerable portion of bitumen. Beyond the Alleganies there are some of the most extensive and valuable deposits of bituminous coal in the United States, which derive additional value from their being associated with not less important beds of iron and salt. At Wheeling, on the Ohio, and for fourteen miles down the river, the bank presents an uninterrupted bed of highly bituminous coal, upward of 16 feet thick. The Wheeling basin, indeed, extends for 30 miles up and down the river in Ohio and Virginia. Another vast field stretches above Clarksburg, on the Monongahala to Pittsburg, and far beyond to the north-east in Pennsylvania. There is also a valuable coal-field on the head-waters of the north branch of the Potomac. Thus we have five tiers of coal seams, with an average thickness of from 30 to 35 feet. There are also coal seams associated with salt springs on the Little Kanawha, and springs of petroleum, or rock oil, occur in the same tract. On the Great Kanawha is also a very rich and extensive coal-field: and on Coal, Gauley, and other rivers in this portion of Western Virginia, the beds of this mineral are frequently brought to view, and in fact no better general description can be presented of its extent than that it is almost continuous with the vast beds of sandstone which spread in nearly horizontal planes over nearly the whole of this broad region.

The salines of Virginia are almost wholly in the west. Salt-springs occur on the Holston, on the New River, and on the Greenbrier; but the most important works are on the Great and Little Kanawha rivers. The brine is raised by steam-power, and evaporated in large cast-iron pans over furnaces. The brine of the Kanawha wells contains very little gypsum or sulphuret of lime, and the process of crystallization is therefore attended with fewer difficulties than usual. The average yield of salt is about one bushel from every 65 or 70 gallons of brine.

The mineral springs of Virginia have long been noted for

H. M. SMITH,

CORNER MAIN and 19th STREETS,

RICHMOND,

MANUFACTURER OF

THRESHING MACHINES,

With and without Separators and Cleaners; Horse Powers, Portable and Stationary; Horse Rakes; Gleaners; Wheat Fans; Straw Cutters; Corn Shellers for hand, and for hand and horse-power; Hay Presses; Seed Drills; Land Rollers; Clod Crushers; Harrows; and the Michigan Double Plow.

Is Agent for Hussey and McCormick's Reapers and Mowers, and Pitt's Threshing Machines, and keeps at his Agricultural Warehouse a general assortment of Agricultural Machinery, Tools, &c. &c.

H. M. S. pays particular attention to repairing Threshers, Reapers and other Machines. Orders by letter will be promptly atended to.

WM. PALMER,

MANUFACTURER OF

AGRICULTURAL IMPLEMENTS,

AND DEALER IN SEEDS,

No. 20 MAIN STREET,

RICHMOND.

A HOME INSTITUTION.

FIRE, LIFE & MARINE INSURANCE CO.

THE RICHMOND FIRE ASSOCIATION

Are now prepared to issue policies of Insurance on the above descriptions of risks on as reasonable terms as any similar company, and respectfully ask a share of the patronage of the public. Applications will be received at the Office, **No. 223**, corner Main and 9th Streets, where the officers will cheerfully furnish all information that may be required. All losses promptly and liberally adjusted.

JAMES C. CRANE, Pres't.

J. H. BOSHER, Sec'ry.

their efficiency in numerous chronic complaints, and as the resort of the fashionable world in the summer season. The State abounds with these, but the best known are the White and Blue Sulphur Springs of Greenbrier county, the Salt and Red Sulphur and the Sweet, in Monroe county, Hot and Warm in Bath, Berkley in Morgan, Fauquier White Sulphur in Fauquier, Shannondale in Frederick, Alum in Rockbridge, Jordan's White Sulphur in Frederick, Red in Allegany, Grayson in Carroll, Botetourt in Roanoke, Holston in Scott, Augusta Springs and Daggus Springs in Botetourt.

Of the metallic products of Virginia, gold is at present perhaps the most important. It is found on both the North and Rapid Ann rivers, of the North and South Anna near their sources, of the Rivanna, in the lower part of its course, and of James River, above and below the mouth of the Rivanna. Within the past few years, several rich mines have been opened and worked successfully in these and other sections of the State. We believe that Commodore Stockton was one of the first who introduced into Virginia effective machinery for reducing, on a large scale, the quartz rock, and demonstrating that a profitable business could be done in this branch of mining. The Stockton mines are located in Fluvanna county. Among other at present productive mines are those of William M. Mosely & Co., and of the Garnett Mining Company, in Buckingham county. There are also mines more or less productive in Spottsylvania, in Stafford, in Fauquier, in Culpepper, in Orange, in Louisa, and in Goochland counties.

"It is a matter of not less mortification," says a Report of the Manufacturers' Convention, 1851, "than astonishment that Virginia, with an area of coal measures covering not less than 21,000 square miles, very much of which lies on or near navigable waters, and capable of yielding all the varieties of British coal, and of equal quality, should be reduced to the actual production of less than 200,000 tons of the value of $650,000, while Great Britain, with little more than half the extent of coal measures, produces annually, 37,000,000 tons, of about the value of $37,000,000 at the mines, and $180,000,000 at the market of sale. And in regard to the iron-trade, while Virginia has an unlimited supply of the finest ores, easily accessible for use and transportation, with the greatest abundance of

coal, wood, and limestone for their manufacture, yet under the operation of the present revenue laws of the country, her production, in spite of all the efforts of the State to encourage it, has shrunk to an almost inconsiderable amount, and is in danger of utter ruin."

The soils of Virginia are naturally of a most fertile nature, but in the old settlements they have been exhausted by a vicious system of tillage. In many parts, however, a renovation has been effected by the application of proper fertilizers, and the adoption of a more scientific mode of culture. The Eastern and Piedmont sections are chiefly engaged in the production of Indian Corn and Tobacco, the latter of which is one of the great staples of the State. Cotton is also produced in these sections. In the valley the crops are much the same, excepting that wheat takes the place of cotton, and the system of agriculture is superior to that followed in the lower country. Beyond the mountains, and westward to the Ohio river, is a fine country, adapted in soil and climate to the successful culture of all the grains, roots, and products of the Middle States, and equally propitious to the breeding and rearing of cattle and other domestic animals. It is not only a great agricultural district, but it is alike rich in minerals and metals of the greatest importance and value, and will eventually become the workshop of the State, as it is now the granary.

Bold scenery is one of the distinguishing features of Virginia; and no other State presents so many or so magnificent results of Nature convulsed. At Harper's Ferry, where the Potomac breaks through the Blue Ridge, the disruption has left behind it indelible marks of its force. The "Natural Bridge" below Lexington, according to Jefferson, is the most sublime of Nature's works. It is an arch reaching across a narrow ravine, which extends for some distance above and below, at the height of 215 feet above the stream which flows under it, 80 feet wide and 93 feet long;" and again he says, "so beautiful an arch, so elevated, so light, and springing as it were up to heaven, the rapture of the spectator is really indescribable." These are but a moiety of the magnificent scenes of the country; every where in the Great Valley, and among its mountain borders, are found spectacles of grandeur and sublimity. Virginia has also numerous caves and caverns, of which Madison's cave

and Weir's Cave, both in the vicinity of Staunton, are those best known. Madison's Cave extends about 300 feet into the earth, branching into subordinate caverns and terminating in two basins of water, of about 30 or 40 feet in depth. Weir's Cave is much more extensive, and its numerous halls and chambers are pillared with an astonishing profusion of stalactites, which in some places resemble stiffened water-falls, in others hanging in rich festoons and folds like tapestry, or seem to rise from the floor like columns, thrones, towers or statues; it extends 1,260 feet into the ground, and contains upwards of 20 large rooms, besides numerous passages and galleries. One of these halls is 260 feet in length, 33 feet high and from 10 to 20 feet wide; and another is 153 by 15 feet, with a height of 60 feet.

Counties.—Virginia is divided into 140 counties, viz: Accomac, Alexandria, Albemarle, Allegany, Amherst, Amelia, Appomattox, Augusta, Barbour, Bath, Bedford, Berkeley, Boone, Botetourt, Braxton, Brook, Brunswick, Buckingham, Cabell, Carroll, Campbell, Caroline, Charlotte, Charles City, Chesterfield, Clarke, Craig, Culpepper, Cumberland, Dinwiddie, Doddridge, Elizabeth City, Essex, Fauquier, Fairfax, Fayette, Fluvanna, Floyd, Franklin, Frederick, Giles, Gilmer, Gloucester, Goochland, Grayson, Greenbrier, Greene, Greensville, Halifax, Hampshire, Hancock, Hanover, Hardy, Harrison, Henry, Henrico, Highland, Isle of Wight, Jackson, James City, Jefferson, Kanawha, King George, King William, King and Queen, Lancaster, Lee, Lewis, Logan, Loudoun, Louisa, Lunenburg, Madison, Marion, Marshall, Mason, Matthews, Mecklenburg, Mercer, Middlesex, Monongalia, Monroe, Montgomery, Morgan, Nansemond, Nelson, New Kent, Nicholas, Northumberland, Northampton, Norfolk, Nottaway, Ohio, Orange, Page, Patrick, Pendleton, Pittsylvania, Pleasants, Pocahontas, Powhatan, Preston, Prince Edward, Princess Anne, Prince George, Prince William, Pulaski, Putnam, Raleigh, Randolph, Rappahannock, Richmond, Ritchie, Roanoke, Rockbridge, Rockingham, Russell, Scott, Shanandoah, Smythe, Southampton, Spottsylvania, Stafford, Surry, Sussex, Taylor, Tazewell, Tyler, Upshur, Warren, Warwick, Washington, Wayne, Westmoreland, Wetzel, Wirt, Wood, Wyoming, Wythe, York. *Capital*, Richmond.

The whole number of dwellings in the State in 1850 was, 165,815; of families, 167,530; and of inhabitants, 1,421,661;

viz: whites 895,304—males 451,552, and females 443,752; free colored 53,829—males 25,843, and females 27,986, and slaves 472,528. Of the whole population there were, *deaf and dumb*—white 581, free colored 18, slaves 112—total 711; *blind*—white 536, free colored 121, slaves 339—total 996; *insane*—white 922, free colored 46, slaves 58—total 1,026; and *idiotic*—white 945, free colored 120, slaves 220—total 1,285. The number of free persons born in the United States was 925,795; the number of foreign birth 22,394, and of birth unknown 585. The *native* population originated as follows: Maine 271, New Hampshire 239, Vermont 231, Massachusetts 1,193, Rhode Island 100, Connecticut 556, New York 2,934, New Jersey 11,447, Pennsylvania 6,823, Delaware 542, Maryland 10,328, District of Columbia 1,184, *Virginia* 872,823, North Carolina 7,343, South Carolina 281, Georgia 93, Florida 26, Alabama 92, Mississippi 78, Louisiana 93, Texas 7, Arkansas, 150, Tenn. 1,501, Kentucky 2,029, Ohio 5,206, Michigan 33, Indiana 288, Illinois 126, Missouri 223, Iowa 37, Wisc. 11, California 4, Territories 3, and the *foreign* population was composed of persons from—England 2,998, Ireland 11,643, Scotland 947, Wales 173, Germany 5,511, France 321, Spain 29, Portugal 51, Belgium 7, Holland 65, Italy 65, Austria 15, Switzerland 83, Russia 8, Denmark 15, Norway 5, Sweden 16, Prussia 36, China 3, Asia 4, Africa 3, British America 235, Mexico 4, Central America 1, South America 7, West Indies 72, Sandwich Islands 1, and other countries 76.

The following table will show the decimal progress of the population since the first census of the State, taken by the United States authorities.

Census.	White	Colored Persons.			Total	Decimal Increase.	
Years.	Persons.	Free.	Slave.	Total.	Population.	Numerical.	Per cent.
1790	442,115	12,766	293,427	306,193	748,308	—	—
1800	514,280	20,124	345,796	365,920	880,200	131,892	17.6
1810	551,534	30,570	392,518	423,088	974,622	94,422	10.7
1820	603,087	37,139	425,153	462,292	1,065,379	90,757	9.3
1830	694,300	47,348	469,757	517,105	1,211,405	146,026	13.7
1840	740,958	49,852	448,987	498,839	1,239,797	28,392	2.3
1850	895,304	53,829	472,528	526,357	1,421,661	181,864	14.6

The aggregate statistics of the resources, wealth, productions, manufactures and institutions of the State, according to the cen-

HARDWARE AND SADDLERY.

SMITH & ROBERTS,

IMPORTERS AND DEALERS IN

HARDWARE, CUTLERY,

GUNS AND SADDLERY,

Keep constantly on hand an extensive assortment of GOODS in the above line, to which we respectfully invite the attention of Country Merchants and others visiting this market.

NAYLOR'S STEEL.

A large stock of Naylor's Cast and Shear Steel, flat, square and octagon bars; for sale by the ton at manufacturer's price, or in lots to suit purchasers.

"ANCHOR" BOLTING CLOTH,

Of the best Manufacture, all sizes constantly on hand.

PATENT SAFETY FUSE,

By the barrel, or in smaller quantities, also Wedge Steel for Blasting purposes.

sus of 1850, and other official returns referring to the same period of time, are as exhibited in the following summary:

Occupied Lands, etc.—Improved farm lands, 10,361,155 acres, and unimproved lands, 15,792,176 acres—valued in cash at $216,401,441. The whole number of farms under cultivation on the 1st of June, 1850, was 77,013—in the Eastern District, 87,741, and in the Western District 39,272. Value of farming implements and machinery, $7,021,772.

Live-Stock.—Horses, 272,403; asses and mules, 21,480; milk cows, 317,619; working-oxen, 89,513; other cattle, 669,137; sheep, 1,310,004; and swine, 1,830,743. The live-stock of 1840, and the comparison of that with the live-stock of 1850, exhibit the following results:

Description.	1840.	1850.	Movement.		
Horses........	326,438 h'd	272,403 h'd	*decr.* 32,555 head,	or 99	per cent.
Asses & Mules..		21,480 "			
Milk Cows....	1,024,148 "	317,619 "	*incr.* 52,121 "	or 5.1	"
Working Oxen.		89,513 "			
Other Cattle,..		669,137 "			
Sheep........	1,293,772 "	1,310,004 "	*incr.* 16,232 "	or 1.3	"
Swine........	1,992,155 "	1,830,743 "	*decr.* 161,412 "	or 8.1	"

In 1850 the total value of live-stock was estimated at $33,656,659.

Products of Animals.—Wool, 2,860,765 pounds; butter, 11,089,359 pounds; cheese, 436,298 pounds; and the value of animals slaughtered during the year was $7,503,006. The wool crop accounted for in the census of 1840 amounted to 2,538,374 pounds; and hence the increase in the crop of 1850 was 322,391 pounds, or in the ratio of 12.7 per centum. In 1840 the average clip per fleece was 31.4 ounces, and in 1850, 34.9 ounces, making an increase in 1850 of 3.9 ounces per fleece, or 12.4 per centum.

Grain Crops.—Wheat, 11,232,616 bushels; rye, 458,930 bushels; Indian corn, 35,254,319 bushels; oats, 10,179,045 bushels; barley, 25,437 bushels; and buckwheat, 214,898 bushels. The several yields compared with those returned in the census of 1840 give the following results:

Crops.	1840	1850	Movement.		
Wheat......	10,109,716 bus.	11,232,616 bus.	*incr.* 1,122,900 bus.	or 11.1	per. cent.
Rye........	1,482,799 "	458,930 "	*decr.* 1,023,869 "	or 69.7	"
Indian corn.	34,577,591 "	35,254,319 "	*incr.* 676,728 "	or 1.9	"
Oats........	13,451,062 "	10,179,045 "	*decr.* 3,272,017 "	or 24.3	"
Barley......	87,430 "	25,437 "	*decr.* 61,993 "	or 70.9	"
Buckwheat..	243,822 "	214,898 "	*decr.* 28,924 "	or 11.8	"

NEW IRON ESTABLISHMENT.

UNION WORKS,

Corner of Canal and Seventh Streets,

RICHMOND.

TURNER, STEELE, HAGAN & Co.

MACHINISTS AND FOUNDERS,

Are prepared to execute all descriptions of Work in their line of business with promptness and fidelity.

J. HUNTER & CO.

MANUFACTURERS OF

BAR, BAND, HOOP AND ROD IRON,

RAIL ROAD FROG STEEL, &c. &c.

NEAR THE PETERSBURG RAIL ROAD BRIDGE,

RICHMOND.

JAMES WALSH,

No. 60 MAIN STREET,

RICHMOND,

IMPORTER AND MANUFACTURER OF

GUNS,

PISTOLS AND RIFLES.

Keeps constantly on hand a very large stock of DOUBLE and SINGLE BARREL GUNS of every variety of length, calibre and style of MOUNTING and FINISH of his own Importation and Manufacture.

PISTOLS.

Colt's celebrated Five Shooter; Allen's Six Barrel Revolving Pistol. Single Self-Cocking Pistol. Pocket and Belt Pistols. Dueling Pistols.

Percussion Caps, Powder Flasks and Shot Belts, Bird Bags, Dog Cauls, Dog Collars and Chains, Fishing Poles in joints, Silk, Grass, Flax and Cotton Fishing Lines, Floats, Reels and Silk Gut, Limerick, Kirbey, Hemmings, and Virginia Fish Hooks, Gold and Silver Mounted Canes, with and without Swords, Pen, Pocket and Desk Knives, Spy Glasses, Travelers' Compasses, Pocket Books and Wallets, Money Purses and Belts, Superb Razors and Strops, &c.

Other Food Crops.—Rice, 17,154 (in 1840, 2,596) pounds; peas and beans, 521,581 bus.; potatoes—Irish, 1,316,933 bus., and sweet, 1,813,671 bushels. The potato crop of the census of 1840 amounted to 2,944,660 bushels, and hence the increase in 1850 is 185,944 bushels, or at the rate of 6.3 per centum.

Miscellaneous Crops.—Tobacco, 56,803,218 pounds; cotton, 3,947 bales of 400 pounds; hay, 369,098 tons; clover-seed, 29,-727 bushels; other grass seed, 23,428 bushels; hops, 11,506 pounds; hemp—dew-rotted 90 tons, and water-rotted 51 tons; flax, 999,450 pounds; flax-seed, 52,318 bushels; silk cocoons, 517 pounds; maple-sugar, 1,227,665 pounds; molasses, 40;322 gallons; beeswax and honey, 880,767 pounds; wine, 5,408 gallons, etc. The value of orchard products $177,137, and of market-garden products $183,047. The principal crops exhibited in the censuses of 1840 and 1850 are comparatively as follows:

Crops.	1840.	1850.	Movement.			
Tobacco...........	75,347,106 lbs.	56,803,218 lbs.	*dec.*	18,533,888 lbs.	or 24.6	per ct.
Cotton...........	3,494,483 "	1,578,800 "	*dec.*	1,915,683 "	or 54.8	"
Hay...............	364,708½ tons	369,098 tons	*inc.*	4,390½ t's	or 1.2	"
Hops..............	10,597 lbs.	11,506 lbs.	*inc.*	909 lbs.	or 8.6	"
Hemp—dew rotted		90 t's				
" water "	25,594½ t's	57 "	*dec.*	56,015,720 "	or 97.7	"
Flax..............		999,450 lbs				
Silk cocoons......	3,191 lbs.	517 "	*dec.*	2,674 "	or 83.9	"
Maple sugar......	1,541,833 "	1,227,665 "	*dec.*	314,168 "	or 20.3	"
Wine.............	13,911 gals.	5,408 gals.	*dec.*	8,503 gals	or 61.1	"

"The correctness of the returns as to hemp, in the seventh census, has not yet been perfectly verified. There has been some doubt whether, in a number of instances, the marshals have not written *tons* where they meant *pounds*. (Has not the reporter in this instance written *tons* where he meant *pounds*, and *vice versa?*—Ed. of Gaz.) If, however, the returns are allowed to stand without reduction, it would appear that the cultivation of hemp or flax has materially changed since 1840. In the returns of that year, as stated above, both of these articles were included under the same head. In 1840 those of Virginia gave 25,594 tons of hemp and flax together. In 1850 only 141 tons of hemp, and 500 tons of flax were returned. Such a falling off would amount to almost an abandonment of the culture of hemp in that State, which there is no reason to suppose has taken place."—*Report of Superintendent of the Census, Dec. 1st,* 1852.

Home-made Manufactures were produced in the year ending

THOMAS SAMSON, JAMES PAE.

RICHMOND FOUNDRY,

CORNER BYRD AND FIFTH STREETS,

RICHMOND.

SAMSON & PAE,

SUCCESSORS TO AND PARTNERS OF THE FORMER FIRM OF

ARE PREPARED TO FURNISH ALL KINDS OF

IRON AND BRASS CASTINGS,

MILL MACHINERY,

STATIONARY AND PORTABLE STEAM ENGINES,

Saw Mills, Pumps, Etc.

FROM THE EXTENSIVE ASSORTMENT OF

PATTERNS

which they have accumulated, and the experience they have acquired in their business, during the last twenty years, they trust they can accommodate those who may favor them with a call, as to quality of materials and workmanship, and on the most reasonable terms.

1st June, 1850, to the value of $2,156,312. The same description of manufactures returned in the census of 1840 were valued at $2,441,672.

Manufactures.—Total capital invested, $18,108,793; value of all raw material, fuel, etc., consumed in the year, $18,103,433; average number of hands employed —males and females ; monthly cost of labor $ —male $ and female $; value of manufactures produced in the year, $29,592,019. The whole number of manufacturing establishments in operation on the 1st June, 1850, and producing to the value of $500 and upwards annually, was 4,433—in the Eastern District 2,293, and in the Western District 2,140, and these were distributed to the several counties as exhibited in the general table. Of the whole number 27 were cotton factories; 121 woolen factories; 122 iron manufactories—29 making pig iron, 54 making castings, and 39 making wrought iron; 341 tanneries, etc. Total capital invested in manufactures, in the year represented in the census of 1840, $11,360,861.

In the manufacture of *cotton goods*, the capital employed is $1,908,900; cotton consumed 17,785 bales, and coal 4,805 tons; value of all raw material, fuel, etc., $828,375; hands employed 2,963—males 1,275, and females 1,688; monthly cost of labor, $24,774—male, $12,983, and female, $11,791; products of the year—sheeting, 15,640,107 yards, and yarn 1,755,915 pounds, valued at $1,486,384. In 1840 there were in the State 22 cotton mills, and 1 dyeing and printing establishment, together employing 1,816 hands, and a capital of 1,299,020, and producing in the year, goods to the value of $446,063

In the manufacture of *woolen goods*, capital to the amount of $392,640 is invested; wool consumed in the year, 1,554,110 pounds, and coal 357 tons, valued together at $488,899; hands employed 658—males 478, and females 190; monthly cost of labor $10,571—to males $8,688 and to females $1,883; products of the year—cloth 2,037,025 yards, and yarn 398,705 pounds, valued at $841,013. The capital invested in the woolen manufacture in 1840, was 112,350, hands employed 222; value of yearly manufactures $147,792; which statements include also the statistics of fulling-mills.

The condition of the iron manufacture is exhibited in the following statistical aggregates:

Specifications.	Pig Iron.	Cast Iron.	Wrought Iron.	Total.
Capital invested..........*dollars*	513,800	471,160	791,211	1,776,171
Ore used..................*tons*...	67,319	—	—	67,319
Pig Iron used............. " ...	—	7,114	17,296	24,410
Blooms used............. " ...	—	—	2,500	2,500
Old metal used........... " ...	—	205	—	205
Mineral Coal consumed.... " ...	39,982	7,878	66,515	114,375
Coke & Charcoal consumed. *bush.*	1,311,000	71,600	103,000	1,485,600
Value of all raw material, etc. *doll.*	158,307	297,014	591,448	1,046,769
Hands employed—male.... *number*	1,115	810	1,295	3,220
" " female.. "	14	9	—	23
Monthly cost of labor... . *dollars*	14,328	16,312	30,469	61,109
Iron produced............ *tons*...	22,163	5,577	15,328	43,068
Value of year's products... *dollars*	521,924	674,416	1,254,995	2,451,335

In 1840, Virginia had in operation 42 furnaces, that in the preceding year had produced 18,810½ tons of cast iron, and 52 bloomeries, forges, and rolling-mills, which had produced 5,886 tons of bar iron.

The *tanneries* employ a capital of $676,983; hands employed 906—males 900, and females 6; monthly cost of labor $13,705 —male $13,643, and female $62; sides of leather tanned 378,400, and skins tanned 74,573, together valued at $894,876. In 1840 there were in the State 660 tanneries, employing 1,422 hands, and a capital amounting to $838,141; and which had produced during the preceding year, 135,782 sides of sole leather, and 206,216 sides of upper leather.

The capital invested in the manufacture of *malt and spirituous liquors* amounts to $100,915. Quantities and kinds of grain, etc., consumed—barley 20,000 bushels, corn 250,700 bushels, rye 62,680 bushels, oats 450 bushels, and hops 14 tons; hands employed 123; qualities of liquor produced—ale, etc., 5,500 barrels, and whiskey, etc., 879,440 gallons. In the census year 1840, Virginia had 1,454 distilleries, producing in the year 865,725 gallons; and 5 breweries, producing 32,960 gallons; hands employed 1,631, and capital invested $187,212.

The manufactures, others than the above specified, consist of a great variety of important productions, as machinery of all kinds, carriages, harness, etc.; and Virginia has also a large number of merchant and other mills. As a flour-producing State, it stands first in its brands, and is only behind one or two other States in the extent of production. It has also large and valuable tobacco manufactories.

Foreign Commerce.—Virginia, in respect of foreign commerce,

PREMIUM AWARDED TO

TALBOTT & BROTHER,

FOR THE BEST

Portable Steam Engine & Saw-Mill

EXHIBITED AT THE FAIR OF THE

VIRGINIA STATE AGRICULTURAL SOCIETY,

Richmond, Nov. 4th, 1853.

TALBOTT & BROTHER,

SUCCESSORS TO THE

SHOCKOE MANUFACTURING COMPANY,

MANUFACTURE

Locomotive Engines and Tenders,

AND

RAIL ROAD WORK OF ALL KINDS.

Portable and Stationary Steam Engines; Circular Saw Mills, complete; Vertical Saw and Grist Mill Irons; Tobacco Manufacturers' Fixtures; and Brass and Iron Castings, and Wrought Iron Work of every description.

holds a seventh or eighth rank among the States of the Union. According to the official returns for the year ending 30th June, 1850, the value of its exports to foreign countries amounted to $3,415,646, and of its imports to $426,599. This would indicate that the great bulk of its commercial material is carried to the ports of other States for exportation, and the foreign merchandise consumed within the State is brought through the same channels. That such is the case is well known, and hence we find that the coasting trade is unusually extensive, chiefly carried on by the shipping of northern ports. This was not always so, for at one time Virginia stood at the head of the commercial States, and its shipping held the same rank in foreign ports as that now occupied by the mercantile marine of New York. Of the total exports in 1850, $3,413,158 was the value of domestic products, and of these to the value of $2,365,241 was shipped in American and $1,047,917 in foreign vessels—the remainder of the aggregate value ($2,488) was foreign produce re-shipped in American vessels. Of the imports $172,878 was the value of merchandise landed from American and $253,721 from foreign vessels. The shipping employed in the carrying trade consisted as follows:

Nationality of shipping.	Entered.			Cleared.			Total.		
	Vessels.	Tons.	Crews.	Vessels.	Tons.	Crews.	Vessels.	Tons.	Crews.
American	69	12,190	564	187	42,091	1,710	256	54,281	2,274
Foreign	88	18,775	828	98	23,367	956	186	42,142	1,784
Total	157	30,965	1,392	285	65,458	2,664	442	96,423	4,058
Alexandria	59	10,638	442	64	11,534	474	123	22,172	916
Norfolk	74	14,281	684	140	26,765	1,163	214	41,046	1,847
Petersburg	9	3,517	131	5	1,946	63	14	5,463	194
Richmond	8	1,811	76	69	24,321	908	77	26,132	984
Tappahannock	7	718	42	7	892	44	14	1,610	86

The shipping owned in the several districts of the State in 1850, amounted to 74,071 tons; of this 18,043 tons was "registered" shipping—7,092 permanent, and 10,591 temporary: 52,535 tons was "enrolled and licensed"—51,514 tons permanent, and 1,021 temporary; and 3,493 tons was "licensed under 20 tons." The tonnage of the districts was as follows—Alexandria, 8,738 tons; Norfolk, 24,135 tons; Petersburg, 2,708 tons; Richmond, 8,458 tons; Yorktown, 4,807 tons; Tappahannock, 5,824 tons; Accomac, 4,083 tons; East River, 4,869 tons; Yeocomico, 3,284 tons; Cherrystone, 1,232 tons, and

Wheeling, 5,934 tons. Of the enrolled and licensed tonnage, all of which is employed in the coasting and river trade, 8,726 tons are navigated by steam power—in the Atlantic districts, 2,792 tons, and in Wheeling district, on Ohio River, 5,934 tons. Within the year specified there were built in the State—1 ship, 1 brig, 27 schooners, and 5 steamers—total, 34 vessels, of an aggregate burden of 3,584 tons. The serial statistics of the foreign commerce from 1791 to 1850, are comprised in the following table:

Year.	Exports.	Imports.	Year.	Exports.	Imports.	Year.	Exports.	Imports.
1791..	$3,130,865..	$——	1811	$4,822,307	$——	1831	$4,151,475	$488,522
1792..	3,552,825..	——	1812	3,091,112	——	1832	4,510,650	553,639
1793..	2,987,098..	——	1813	1,819,722	——	1833	4,467,587	690,391
1794..	3,321,636..	——	1814	17,581	——	1834	5,469,240	837,325
1795..	3,490,041..	——	1815	6,676,976	——	1835	6,064,063	691,255
1796..	5,268,655..	——	1816	8,212,860	——	1836	6,192,040	1,106,814
1797..	4,908,713..	——	1817	5,628,442	——	1837	3,702,714	813,862
1798..	6,113,451..	——	1818	7,016,246	——	1838	3,986,228	577,142
1799..	6,292,986..	——	1819	4,392,321	——	1839	—	—
1800..	4,430,689..	——	1820	4,557,957	——	1840	4,778,220	545,685
1801..	5,655,574..	——	1821	3,079,209	1,078,490	1841	5,630,286	377,237
1802	3,978,363..	——	1822	3,217,389	864,162	1842	3,750,386	316,705
1803..	6,100,708..	——	1823	4,006,788	681,810	1843	1,957,165	187,062
1804..	5,790,001..	——	1824	3,277,564	639,787	1844	2,942,279	267,654
1805..	5,606,620..	——	1825	4,129,520	553,562	1845	2,104,581	267,658
1806..	5,055,396..	——	1826	4,596,732	635,438	1846	3,529,299	209,004
1807..	4,761,234..	——	1827	4,657,938	431,765	1847	5,658,374	386,127
1808..	526,473..	——	1828	3,340,185	375,238	1848	3,681,412	215,081
1809..	2,894,125..	——	1829	3,787,431	395,352	1849	3,373,738	241,935
1810..	4,822,611..	——	1830	4,791,644	405,739	1850	3,415,646	426,599

Internal Communication, etc.—The railroads and canals of Virginia, which are among the most magnificent works of the kind in the Union, extend generally from the Atlantic ports to the West, and are continued through Ohio, Kentucky, and Tennessee, to all the chief places in the north-west, west and south-west. Alexandria, Richmond, and Norfolk, are the initial points on the Atlantic; from Alexandria diverge the Orange and Alexandria Railroad and the Manassas Gap R. R.—the one directed toward Gordonsville, where it joins the Central road, and the other crossing the first mountains, and passing down the valley to Harrisburg and Staunton, there unites with the same line; the Central Railroad, starting at Richmond,

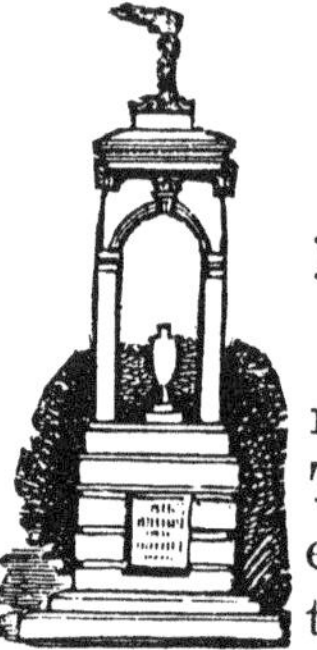

MILLER & VINCENT,

RICHMOND MARBLE WORKS,

Main st., nearly opposite 2d Baptist Church.

Monuments, Tombs, Fonts, &c., executed in a manner not to be surpassed here or elsewhere. The public are respectfully invited to call and examine specimens of work executed by them as the best test of their merit.

WILSON WILLIAMS,

GROCER,

WHOLESALE AND RETAIL,

CORNER MAIN and 18th STREETS,

RICHMOND.

GREAT REDUCTION IN THE PRICE OF HATS AND BOOTS.

From Fifteen to Twenty per cent. saved by buying from

J. H. ANTHONY,

COLUMBIAN HOTEL BUILDING,

RICHMOND.

Moleskin Hats, of best quality, $3 50; second best quality, $3 00; Fashionable SILK HATS, $2 50; Fine Calfskin Sewed BOOTS, $3 50; Fine Calfskin Sewed SHOES, $2 25.

J. H. ANTHONY has made arrangements with one of the best makers in the city of Philadelphia to supply him with a handsome and substantial calfskin sewed BOOT, which he will sell at the unprecedented low price of $3 50.

HENRY BULL & CO.

Manufacturers of every description and style of

MARBLE MANTLES,

Monuments, Tombs, &c. &c.

All work done at this establishment warranted to give satisfaction. Orders from the country solicited. Work can be forwarded to all parts of the State without delay.

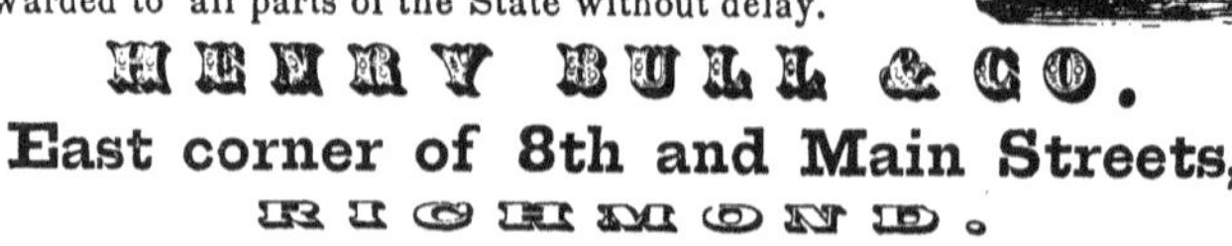

East corner of 8th and Main Streets,

RICHMOND.

passes through Gordonsville, Staunton, etc., to Covington, and there unites with the Covington and Ohio railroad, extending westward to Point Pleasant, on the Ohio, there uniting with the Ohio system, and to the mouth of Big Sandy River, where it joins the Kentucky lines to Maysville, Lexington and Louisville, and through them connects with the lines stretching to the north and toward Nashville and New Orleans, and from Norfolk and Petersburg a line extends through the southern counties to the Tennessee line, whence it is continued to Knoxville, connecting at that point with numerous lines directed to every important central station in the south-west, etc. These railroads furnish to the State ample means of transportation, and will carry to and from the seaboard an immense commercial material. They will also be the means of reviving the general commerce of the State, and of furnishing an outlet at Virginian ports for much of the produce of Ohio, Kentucky, and Tennessee, which now finds its way to more northern markets. In the north-west several lines are being built to connect the systems of Pennsylvania and Maryland with those of Ohio and the West, and of these the North-western railroad is perhaps the most important, as it will furnish the shortest route from Cincinnati to Baltimore. In the south-east the Seaboard and Roanoke Railroad furnishes an important route from the seaboard into North Carolina. The great southern line of railroads also passes through Virginia, having Fredericksburg, Richmond and Petersburg in its route, and being continued south and south-west to Wilmington, Columbia, etc. This is the route of the great southern mail. There are, besides these numerous short lines, branches, etc., diverging from the main lines to several important points. The whole extent of completed railroad in the State on the 1st January, 1853, was 624 miles, and about 800 miles more were in course of construction.

The canals of Virginia are—the James river and Kanawha Canal, the Dismal Swamp Canal, and the Alexandria Canal. The Baltimore and Ohio Canal, though in Maryland, is to all intents and purposes, as much a canal of Virginia as of that State, being only separated from it by the channel of the Potomac river. The Alexandria Canal, which is a continuation of the Baltimore and Ohio Canal, from Georgetown to Alexandria, is seven and a half miles long, and is carried over the Po-

EXCHANGE

RICHMOND.

JOHN P. BALLARD, Proprietor,

Located in the centre of the Business portion of the City and within a few minutes' walk of the State House, Governor's Mansion, Public Buildings, Capital Square, &c.

Omnibuses will be in waiting at the Cars and Steamers, to convey passengers to this Hotel.

The above is one of the largest and most elegantly furnished Establishments in the United States, and kept in a superior manner, by a Gentleman of known reputation and popularity.—EDITOR.

tomac on a splendid aqueduct. The James River and Kanawha Canal, second only in extent and importance to the Erie Canal of New York, is carried through the valley of James River, and is now complete to Balcony Falls, from which point it will be continued along the valley of the Kanawha River to the Ohio. This great work has been of vast advantage to the interior of Virginia, and on an average transports about $12,000,000 valuation of merchandise. "Without the Erie Canal," says Governor Floyd, "the city of New York would have been second still to Philadelphia." Great as the advantages of this work unquestionably are, those of the James River and Kanawha Canal are undoubtedly superior. It possesses the striking advantage of lying five degrees south of the great northern work, and is therefore free from the ice which obstructs the navigation there for so large a portion of the year. It touches the Ohio River far south of any water communication from the Atlantic whatever, and at a point south of which there can be across the country no other water connection. It will command all the trade of a great part of Ohio, Kentucky, Indiana, Illinois, and Missouri, and most probably those regions lying still higher up toward the sources of the Missouri after that period it is unsafe to send produce north. "We will see," says the Governor, "canal boats laden at the falls of St. Anthony or Council Bluff discharging their cargoes at Lynchburg, Richmond and Norfolk," etc. This work is now rapidly progressing to completion. The Dismal Swamp Canal connects Chesapeake Bay with Albemarle Sound, extending from Deep Creek to Joyce's Creek, 23 miles. At present it is chiefly valuable as an avenue for the transportation of the lumber, naval, stores, etc., of the region through which it passes. With such works as the above, who cannot but foresee that Virginia will, at no distant day, be one of the most successful commercial States of the Union, and its ports, so long forsaken, the marts of a trade not surpassed by that of the present great emporia of the country.

Banks.—In October, 1850, Virginia had 6 Banks and 31 branch banks. The condition of these establishments at that date was as follows: *liabilities*—capital $9,814,545; circulation $10,256,967; deposits $4,717,732; due other banks $338,841; and *assets*—loans and discounts $19,646,777; stocks $269,914;

HUGH W. FRY & SONS,

WHOLESALE

GROCERS,

AND AGENTS FOR THE SALE OF

PERUVIAN AND MEXICAN GUANO,

Corner of Pearl and Cary streets,

RICHMOND.

H. W. TYLER,

Grocer and Commission Merchant,

WHOLESALE AND RETAIL DEALER IN

ALE, CIDER, FISH, &c.

AND PROVISIONS OF EVERY KIND,

Seventeenth Street, corner of Main st.

RICHMOND.

RAWLINGS & MILLER,

AND GENERAL

COMMISSION MERCHANTS,

IMPORTERS AND DEALERS IN

OLD WINES AND LIQUORS,

CORNER 14TH (OR PEARL) AND CARY STREETS,

RICHMOND.

real estate $764,282; other investments $210,498; due by other banks, $1,925,652; notes of other banks, $552,153; and specie, $2,928,174. Since the date of these returns several banks have been established in accordance with the new banking law, depositing security for the redemption of their notes. The returns above given are those of the old chartered banks, which enjoy a high credit at home and abroad. These are—The Bank of the Valley, at Winchester, with branches at Charlestown, Leesburg, Romney, Staunton, and Christianburg; the Bank of the Virginia at Richmond, with branches at Buchanan, Charlestown, Danville, Fredericksburg, Lynchburg, Norfolk, Petersburg and Portsmouth; the Exchange Bank of Virginia, at Norfolk, with branches at Abington, Alexandria, Clarkesville, Petersburg, Richmond, Salem and Weston; the Farmers' Bank of Virginia, at Richmond, with branches at Alexandria, Charlottesville, Danville, Farmville, Fredericksburg, Lynchburg, Norfolk, Petersburg, Winchester, and Wythesville; the Merchants' and Mechanics' Bank, at Wheeling, with branch at Morgantown; and the North-western bank of Virginia, at Wheeling, with branches at Jeffersonville, Parkersburg, and Wellsburg.

Government, etc.—The present constitution of Virginia was adopted in convention on the 1st of August, and ratified by the people on the 25th of October, 1851. It superseded the constitution of 1776 and the amendments of 1831.

The *right to vote* is given to every white male citizen 21 years old, resident of the State two years, and of the county, city, or town one year next preceding an election. The exceptions are those common to other States. Votes are given *viva voce*, and not by ballot; but dumb persons may so vote. The general election is held on the fourth Thursday of October bienially.

The *Legislature* is styled the General Assembly, and consists of a House of Delegates and a Senate. The house consists of 152 members, chosen biennially, apportioned on the basis of the white population. The Senate is based on population and taxation combined, and consists of 50 members, elected in districts by the voters therein for the term of four years, one-half of the number being chosen biennially. Delegates must have attained the age of 21, and senators that of 25 years, and none but qualified voters are eligible for election. Persons

holding lucrative offices, ministers of the Gospel, salaried officers of banks, and attorneys of the Commonwealth are ineligible. Any elective officer removing from his district vacates his office. In 1865, and decennially thereafter, there shall be a re-apportionment. The sessions of the Legislature commence on the second Monday of January biennially, and continue not more than 90 days, unless a prolongation be concurred in by three-fifths of all the members, nor in any case shall a session be extended beyond the ordinary term for more than 30 days. Bills may originate or be amended in either house.

The *executive power* is vested in a Governor, elected by the people for four years, commencing from the 1st January succeeding election. The governor is ineligible for any other office during his term, and can be elected for two successive terms. He must be 30 years of age, a native citizen of the United States, and for 5 years a citizen of the State. He must reside at the seat of Government. A Lieutenant-governor, with like qualifications, etc., is elected for a like term, and is the constitutional successor of the governor in case of death or disability; he is also *ex-officio* president of the Senate.

The principal administrative officers are—a Secretary of the Commonwealth, a Treasurer, and an Auditor of Public Accounts. These are elected by joint vote of the General Assembly for two years. For the purpose of electing the Board of Public Works, the State is divided into three districts, each of which shall elect one commissioner. Their term is six years, and they are so classified that one of their number shall retire every two years. The General Assembly, by a three-fifths vote, may abolish the board.

The *judiciary* is vested in a Supreme Court of Appeals, District Courts, and Circuit Courts. In each circuit, (21 in number,) a judge is elected by the voters for the term of eight years, and who holds two circuit courts in the counties of his circuit annually. In each district, (10 in number,) a district court is held by the judges of the circuits constituting the District, and the Judge of the Supreme Court for the Section, any three of whom may hold a court. Judges of the Supreme Court of Appeals are also elected by the voters for 12 years, each section (5 in number) electing 1 Judge. The 5 judges so elected constitute the Supreme Court, any three of whom

may hold a circuit. It has jurisdiction only where the matter in controversy is not less in value than $500, except in certain specified cases. Special Courts of Appeal may be organized. Circuit Judges must not be less than 30, nor Supreme Court Judges less than 35 years of age, and no election for judges shall be held within 30 days of the time of holding the election for President, for Congressmen, or for members of the State Legislature. Officers of the Supreme and District Courts are appointed by the Judges thereof; but Clerks of Circuits are elected by the voters for six years. When a Governor is elected, an Attorney-General is also elected for the term of four years.

County Courts are held monthly by not less than three, nor more than five Justices. Each county is divided into districts, and each district elects 4 Justices for the term of 4 years. The Justices so elected choose one of their own body to attend each term of the Court, and classify the rest for the performance of their duties. The voters of each county elect also a Clerk of the County Court, and a Surveyor, for 6 years, an Attorney of the Commonwealth for 4 years, and a Sheriff, and Commissioner of the Revenue, for 2 years. Constables and overseers of the poor are elected by the voters.

Among the *miscellaneous provisions* of the constitution are the following: the writ of *habeas corpus* shall not be suspended, nor shall any bill of attainder be passed, nor any *ex-post facto* law, nor any law impairing the obligation of contracts, or taking private property without just compensation, or abridging the freedom of speech, or of the press, or establishing any religion, or prescribing any religious test, or conferring any privileges or advantages on any one sect or denomination; no law shall embrace more than one object, and when amended, shall be re-enacted at length; provision may be made, rendering ineligible for office those who fight or are engaged in a duel; the Senate shall try impeachments made by the House, and may sit for this purpose during recess; slaves hereafter emancipated shall forfeit their freedom by remaining in the Commonwealth more than 12 months; restrictions may be imposed upon emancipation, but the General Assembly shall not emancipate; it may relieve the State from the free negroes by removal or otherwise; yeas and nays shall be taken on all tax

and appropriation bills; no incorporated company shall be released from its liability to the State; nor shall the faith of the State be pledged for the debts of any company; *seven per cent.* of the State debt existing, 1st January, 1852, shall be annually set apart as a sinking fund to redeem said debt; no loans shall be contracted for a longer period than 34 years; whenever a debt is contracted, there shall be set apart annually, for 34 years, a sum exceeding by one per cent. the aggregate amount of the annual interest agreed to be paid thereon at the time of its contraction, which sum shall be a part of the sinking fund; stocks held by the Commonwealth may be sold, but the proceeds must be applied to the payment of the public debt; no charter shall be granted to any church, but title to church property may be granted to a limited extent; no lottery shall be authorized, and the buying and selling of tickets shall be prohibited; no new county shall be formed with an area less than 600 square miles; powers shall be conferred on the Courts exclusively to grant divorces, to change the names of persons, and direct the sale of infants' estates; there shall be a periodical registration of voters, and of births, marriages, and deaths, annually; a census shall be taken every five years after the national census.

Federal Representation.—In accordance with the act of 23d May, 1853, Virginia elects *thirteen* representatives to the Congress of the United States.

The *militia force* of the State, in 1851, consisted of 125,128 men of all arms, of which number 6,494 were commissioned officers, and 118,634 non-commissioned officers, musicians, artificers, and privates. Of the commissioned officers 32 were general officers, 66 general staff-officers, 1,423 field-officers, etc., and 4,973 company officers. All white persons between the ages of 18 and 45 years are subject to military duty.

The *principal benevolent* institutions of the State are the Lunatic Asylum, at Staunton, and the Institution for the Deaf and Dumb and the Blind, at the same place. These institutions are liberally supported by annual legislative appropriations.

Public Finances, etc.—The aggregate debt of Virginia, on the 1st April, 1851, was as follows: Revolutionary War debt (6 p. c.,) $24,039 17; war debt of 1812 (7 p. c.,) $319,000; in-

R. & G. WHITFIELD,

WHOLESALE AND RETAIL

LUMBER DEALERS,

Corner of Cary and 10th streets,

RICHMOND.

WILLIAM TAYLOR,

GROCER AND COMMISSION MERCHANT,

AND DEALER IN

ALE, CIDER, &C.

Nos. 9 and 11 East Main streets,

RICHMOND.

E. H. SKINKER,

GROCER

AND

COMMISSION MERCHANT,

NO. 59 CARY STREET,

RICHMOND.

On hand a full stock of Groceries, Iron, Steel, Tin Plates, &c.
Particular attention given to the sale of FLOUR, WHEAT, CORN, and other Coutry Produce.

JAMES W. VERSER. JAMES BOISSEAU.

VERSER & BOISSEAU,

SUCCESSORS TO WM. EGGLESTON;

Grocers and Commission Merchants,

No. 27 Pearl Street,

RICHMOND.

Personal attention given to the sale of Country Produce, &c.

ternal improvement debt (6 p. c.,) $9,364,916 04; internal improvement debt (5 p. c.,) $1,065,600; internal improvement debt (5½ p. c.,) $25,300; debt for subscription to banks, $450,107—total debt, $11,248,962 21; but of this there was held by State agents, under the control of the Legislature—by Literary Fund $1,125,606 50, and by Board of Public Works $375,-912 41, or in all $1,501,518 91, leaving an actual outstanding debt of $9,747,443 30. The State is also liable conditionally for guaranteed bonds for internal improvements $3,947,894. The State holds assets, consisting of stocks and debts due—productive of $7,060,565 48, and—not now productive, $6,052,-266 53: total $13,112,832 11. The valuation of property, real and personal, assessed for taxation, in 1850, amounted to $381,376,660. The valuation of the same, according to the U. S. census of that year, was $430,701,082. The valuation for taxes in May, 1852, amounted to $415,542,189 70, being an increase of over $34,000,000 in two years, and it was estimated that there was other property not taxed to the value of $50,-000,000.

The chief sources of *income* for the year were as follow: ordinary revenue and taxation, $676,256 09; dividends on bank stock, $286.542 94; bonus on bank dividends, $46,093 36; internal improvements, $64,029; interest on loans to internal improvement companies, $90,771 61; militia fines, $13,509 76; annuity from Old James River Company, $21,000; loans obtained to pay subscriptions to joint-stock companies, etc., $1,-238,395 19; temporary loans, $100,000; Washington Monument Fund, $22,115 69; and sales of articles made at the Penitentiary, $11,000. The *expenditures* were as follows: expenses of General Assembly, $103,867 25; officers of government, $93,647 45; criminal charges, $39,554 82; contingent expenses of Courts, $32,931 65; militia, $19,344 55; Virginia Military Institute, $20,710; public Guard at Richmond, $21,-340 18; comm. of revenue, $32,106 90; lunatics and lunatic asylums, $100,390 71; deaf and dumb and blind asylums, $18,901 29; interest on public debt, $559,634 47; contingent fund, $16,672 40; public roads, $5,601 50; general appropriations, $27,162 02; revision of laws, $28,801; penitentiary, $27,502 84; redemption of public debt, $239,500; advance to Board of Public Works, $197,000; Washington monument,

$29,860 25; dividends to stockholders of Old James River Company, $20,895; surveys, $3,500; subscriptions to internal improvement companies out of loans received, $1,185,527 28; primary schools, $45,674 03; and annuity to University of Virginia, $150,000.

Educational Statistics.—The number of schools reported in 126 counties and towns, for the year 1850-51, was 3,904, and the number of poor children 72,876, of which 31,655 had attended schools during the year. Amount expended for tuition, including books, compensation of officers, and all other expenses, $68,135 93. Average actual attendance of each child at common schools, 52¾ days. Average cost per annum of each scholar $2 15. The permanent capital of the Literary Fund amounted on the 1st October, 1850, to $1,533,710 82; and the revenue derived therefrom, for the year, amounted to $97,883 66. Academies, seminaries, and private schools, are numerous in all the cities and towns, and many of these are institutions of favorable reputation. The statistics of the collegiate establishments and professional schools, in 1851, are as follow:

Collegiate Institutions.	Location.	Founded.	Prof's.	Alum.	Stud's.	Vols.
William & Mary Col. (Epis.)	Williamsburg	1692	7	—	36	5,000
Hampden Sidney Col	Prince Edwards co.	1783	6	1,500	25	8,000
Washington Col.	Lexington	1789	6	600	50	4,950
University of Virginia	Charlottesville	1819	10	3,500	383	16,000
Randolph-Macon Col. (Meth)	Boydton	1832	7	147	80	8,000
Richmond Col. (Baptist)	Richmond	1832	5	5	50	1,200
Emory & Henry Col. (Meth.)	Emory	1838	5	65	100	7,807
Rector College (Baptist)	Pruntytown	1839	3	—	50	2,500
Virginia Military Institute	Lexington	1839	6	107	120	2,000
Bethany College	Bethany	1841	6	80	141	3,500
Professional Schools.						
Episco. Theol. School of Va.	Fairfax county	1822	4	229	38	5,000
Union Theol. Sem. (Presb)	Prince Edwards co.	1824	3	175	20	4,000
Virginia Baptist Seminary	Richmond	1832	3	—	67	1,000
Law Depart., Univ. of Va.	Charlottesville	—	1	—	70	—
Law Dept. Wm. & Mary Col.	Williamsburg	—	1	—	32	—
Med. School, Univ. of Va.	Charlottesville	1825	3	—	95	—
Med. Dept. Hamp. Sid. Col.	Richmond	1838	7	40	90	—
Winchester Medical College	Winchester	—	5	—	—	—

William and Mary College is, with the exception of Harvard University, the oldest literary institution in the country, and is distinguished for its large proportion of graduates who have risen to eminence, some of whom have held the highest stations in the nation. Thomas Jefferson was a graduate of this college. It was founded on a donation of land, 20,000 acres, granted in the reign of William and Mary. The buildings are of brick, and sufficient to accommodate 100 students. It was

formerly allowed a representative in the General Assembly. Hampden-Sidney College was established in 1774, and named after those martyrs who perished in the good old cause—John Hampden, and Algernon Sidney. It was chartered in 1783. More instructors have emanated from this college than from any other southern institution. Connected with the college is a Literary and Philosophic Society, and an Institute of Education. There are also several societies among the students. The University owes its origin and peculiar organization to Mr. Jefferson. It possesses philosophical and chemical apparatus, together with a fine cabinet of minerals and fossils, and an anatomical and miscellaneous museum. The observatory, a short distance from the university, is furnished with the requisite astronomical instruments. The organization of the university differs materially from that of any other institution in the Union. The students are not divided into four classes, with a course of studies embracing four years, but the different branches are styled "schools," and the student is at liberty to attend which he pleases, and graduate in each when prepared. In order to attain the degree of M. A., the student must graduate in the several schools of mathematics, ancient languages, moral philosophy, natural philosophy, chemistry, and in some two of the modern languages. This institution is in every respect organized and justly regarded as a university of the first class. The Virginia Military Institute is conducted on the plan of instruction observed at West Point, and is a highly valued institution, and has been liberally encouraged by State appropriations.

Religious Denominations.—The statistics of the several religious denominations in the State in 1850 were as follow:

Denominations.	No. of Churches.	Church accom.	Value of Property.	Denominations.	No. of Churches.	Church accom.	Value of Property.
Baptist	639	241,689	$687,918	Methodist	1,002	315,763	$721,008
Christian	16	4,900	7,595	Moravian	8	1,500	2,550
Congregatio'l	—	—	—	Presbyterian	236	101,625	567,165
Dutch Reform	—	—	—	R. Catholic	17	7,930	126,100
Episcopal	167	73,884	527,150	Swedenbourg	—	—	—
Free	107	35,025	61,900	Tunker	8	4,400	8,200
Friends	14	6,300	18,825	Union	47	13,250	24,025
German Ref'd	9	3,800	16,200	Unitarian	—	—	—
Jewish	1	600	4,000	Universalist	1	200	500
Lutheran	50	18,750	52,445	Minor Sects	8	2,825	18,050
Mennonite	6	2,250	5,550				

—making a total of 2,336 churches, with accommodation for 834,691 persons, and valued at $2,849,176.

AMERICAN SALOON

AND

EATING HOUSE,

THOMAS GRIFFIN,

PROPRIETOR,

No. 84 MAIN STREET,

RICHMOND.

This new and well known Established RESTAURANT is kept constantly supplied with every Delicacy of the season, from the Northern and Southern Markets.

HAVING SUPERIOR COOKS,

EXTENSIVE AND WELL FURNISHED ROOMS,

And every facility for the purpose, he feels authorized to say that he can furnish

Suppers, Dinners, &c.

In a style not surpassed by any similar Establishment in this City.

FAMILIES, PARTIES OR CLUBS,

Attended to at all times with promptness and dispatch.

Virginia forms a diocess of the Protestant Episcopal Church, and comprises the Roman Catholic Diocesses of Richmond and Wheeling, and also a portion of the Archdiocess of Baltimore, the last being that portion of the District of Columbia retroceded in 1846.

Public Libraries.—The Report of the Librarian of the Smithsonian Institution, made in 1851, states the public libraries of Virginia as follows: one State Library—14,000 volumes; four social—3,313 volumes; nine college—45,790 volumes; eight students'—10,466 volumes; five academic and professional—12,951 volumes; one scientific and historical—1,200 volumes; two public—1,460 volumes. Total—thirty libraries, and 89,180 volumes.

Periodical Press.—Virginia, on the 1st June, 1850, had 100 periodical issues—in politics 31 were whig, 22 democrat, and 47 neutral, the latter including those devoted to literature, science, religion, and all the character of which had not been ascertained. Of the whole number, 20 were published daily, 6 tri-weekly, 7 semi-weekly, 60 weekly, 4 monthly, and 1 quarterly; and the circulation of the dailies was 32,750 copies at each issue; of the tri-weeklies, 700 copies; of the semi-weeklies, 6,500 copies; of the weeklies 41,936 copies; of the monthlies, 13,150 copies; and of the quarterly, 1,000 copies. There were published in Augusta County, (Staunton,) 3 weekly; Albemarle, (3 in Charlottesville,) 3 weeklies and 1 monthly; in Alexandria, one daily, one tri-weekly, and one weekly; in Botetourt, Berkley and Brooke, each two weeklies; in Campbell, (Lynchburg,) three semi-weeklies; in Dinwiddie, (Petersburg,) two dailies and one tri-weekly; in Fauquier, two weeklies; in Fairfax, one weekly; in Frederick, (Winchester,) two weeklies; in Greenbrier, one weekly; in Harrison, two weeklies; in Hardy, one weekly; in Hampshire, two weeklies; in Henrico, (Richmond,) six dailies, one semi-weekly, two weeklies, five monthlies, and one quarterly; in Jefferson, three weeklies; in Kanawha, one weekly; in Loudoun, two weeklies; in Lewis, Marshall, and Munroe, each one weekly; in Monongalia, three weeklies; in Marion and Nansemond, each one weekly; in Norfolk, (Portsmouth 6, and Norfolk 7,) seven dailies, four tri-weeklies, and two weeklies; in Ohio, (Wheeling,) three dailies and two weeklies; in Preston, Prince Edward, and Pittsylva-

R. P. RICHARDSON. B. W. RICHARDSON.

RICHARDSON & CO.

95 MAIN STREET,

RICHMOND,

IMPORTERS AND JOBBERS IN ENGLISH, FRENCH, GERMAN AND AMERICAN

FANCY GOODS,

STAPLE DRY GOODS,

EMBROIDERIES, LACES, GLOVES, CRAVATS,

Ribbons, Percussion Caps, Hooks and Eyes, Buttons, Threads, Pins, Needles, Combs, &c. A large and splendid assortment of

CARPETINGS OF ALL DESCRIPTIONS,

Constantly on hand, consisting of Tapestry Velvet, Tapestry Brussels, Common Brussels, Three Ply, Superfine, Fine and Common;

Bigelow's Power-loom Brussels Carpets,

PERSIAN, HEAVY WILTON, CHENNILLE, BRUSSELS AND TUFTED

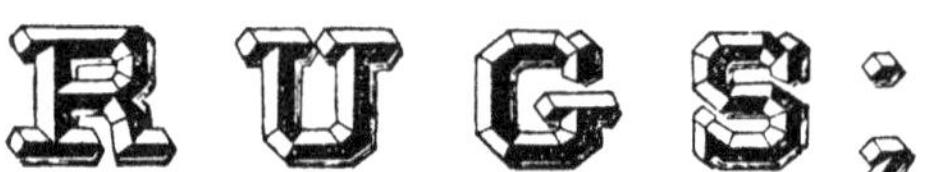

ENGLISH AND AMERICAN

PAINTED FLOOR CLOTHS,

ALL WIDTHS;

4-4, 5-4 and 6-4 White and Check

CANTON MATTING,

Bockings, Mats, Stair Rods, &c.

nia, each one weekly; in Rockbridge, Rockingham, and Shenandoah, each two weeklies; in Spottsylvania, (Fredericksburg,) one daily, two semi-weeklies, and three weeklies; in Tazewell, one weekly; in Washington, two weeklies; and in Wood and Wythe, each one weekly.

Pauperism.—The whole number of paupers relieved and supported within the year ending 1st June, 1850, was 5,118, of whom 4,933 were native born and 185 foreigners; and the whole number of paupers at the date specified was 4,458; of whom 4,356 were natives and 102 foreigners. Cost of support, etc., during the year, $151,722.

The name of Sebastian Cabbot stands at the head of the early navigators to the Western World, which he discovered in 1496, and afterwards made many visits to it.

Historical Sketch.—The name of Virginia, though now belonging only to the present State of that name, was originally given to the whole extent of country afterward divided into the thirteen colonies. It was bestowed upon the country which he attempted to colonize, by Sir Walter Raleigh, in honor of Elizabeth, England's *virgin* queen. The settlement within the limits of the present State were not, however, effected until April, 1607, and this was the first permanent settlement by the English

in America. Previous to this many ineffectual efforts had been made to plant colonies on the Atlantic coast. At length the matter was undertaken by a company, to which a patent was granted by James I, and which was called the London Company, to distinguish it from the Plymouth Company, which subsequently settled New England. Three ships with 105 persons, sailed from London in December, 1606, and after a tedious and circuitous passage entered the Bay of Chesapeake in April, 1607. On a peninsula a little distance up James River, a settlement called Jamestown was begun. The colonists soon experienced the difficulties of their new position, and to the great exertions of Capt. John Smith, distinguished among the adventurers of the age, the colony was indebted to its preservation. An incident which occurred at this period has lent to its history the attractions of romance. While on a foraging expedition he was taken prisoner by the Indians, who determined to put him to death; his head was placed on a stone, and the savages were about to dispatch him with clubs, when Pocahontas, the daughter of the principal chief, Powhatan, after vainly imploring mercy for him, rushed forward, and resting her head upon that of the captive, appeared determined to share his fate. Powhatan relented, and soon after permitted Smith to return home. Two years after, when the Indians had plotted the destruction of the colony, Pocahontas, faithful to the attachment she had formed, disclosed the plot to the English, and the Indians finding them on their guard abandoned the project. Such was the distress of the colonists in 1610, that the survivors had actually embarked to return to England, when Lord Delaware, who had been appointed Governor, arrived with supplies and 150 men, and persuaded the colonists to remain. Under this governor and his successor the settlement prospered; useful industry succeeded to their previous habits, and aided by a fertile soil, they were enabled to raise large stocks of provisions. In 1619, the first legislature was convened, and about this period 1,200 additional emigrants arrived, among whom were 150 young women, who were sold to the planters for wives. Negro slaves were first brought into the country at this time. In 1622 the Indians surprised the settlements and massacred some 347 of the colonists; and the whole colony would have shared the same fate, but that timely information had been

SOUTHERN

JOHN DOOLEY,

No. 81 MAIN STREET,

RICHMOND,

Manufacturer and Dealer in every variety and style of

HATS AND CAPS,

LADIES' FANCY FURS.

Country Merchants and others are requested to call and examine his extensive assortment before purchasing elsewhere, as his Stock is one of the most extensive in the country.

given the inhabitants of Jamestown of the conspiracy. To this famine succeeded, which was, however, alleviated by the arrival of provisions from England. A reinforcement arriving at the same time, war was levied against the Indians, and in a short time most of the neighboring tribes were subdued or slain. Two years afterward the company was dissolved and the charter resumed by the king. All power was vested in commissioners, and under their rule the colony suffered grievously. Sir John Hervey, the royal governor, appointed in 1629, was seized by the people and sent home a prisoner. He was succeeded by Sir William Berkley, who called an assembly of burgesses, and governed the province with mildness and prudence.

On the revolution in England, the Virginians adhered to the cause of the monarch, and even after the death of Charles I refused to acknowledge the commonwealth. Submission was forced by sending against them an armament; but the sentiments of the colonists were again declared, for even before the restoration in England the authority of Charles II had been acknowledged in Virginia. In 1661, an assembly was called by the governor, and in the succeeding year the Church of England was established by law. Notwithstanding this remarkable loyalty of the Virginians, they were made to suffer grievously from the arbitrary and monopolizing system of the home government. The navigation act, and other measures of a similar nature adopted to this time, weighed heavily on the people, and in addition to these grievances, the king, regardless of the rights of the landed proprietors, granted to his courtiers large tracts of land, to which the settlers were legally entitled. From these causes arose an insurrection, memorable in the history of Virginia, and known as Bacon's Rebellion. Colonel Bacon, an eloquent and ambitious man, put himself at the head of the people, who had assembled with the ostensible object of a foray against the Indians. The governor, by advice of the legislature, issued a proclamation of rebellion against them, and so exasperated the leaders of the expedition as to direct its object from hostilities against the Indians to war against the government. They marched to Jamestown, and after dispersing the assembly, Bacon called a convention, and assumed the reins of government. Civil war with all its horrors now

ensued. Jamestown was burnt, and the colony given up to pillage. After several months' bloodshed and confusion, Bacon died suddenly, and for want of a leader his party dispersed. It was long, however, before prosperity revived in the colony. Soon after these events, Berkeley returned to England, and was succeeded by Lord Culpepper, who brought with him several bills drawn up by the ministry of England, to which he required the assent of the legislature, on pain of being treated as rebels. The objects of these acts was the increase of his emoluments. During the reigns of Charles II. and James, the colony suffered much, and rejoiced greatly in the change of government that drove the Stuarts from the throne. The Revolution, indeed, brought to Virginia internal tranquillity, and a long succession of prosperous years. Nothing occurred to interrupt its growth in wealth and power. In 1732, she gave birth to the most illustrious of her sons, the great statesman and warrior, who was destined afterward to achieve and consolidate the independence of all the colonies. During the war between France and England, prior to 1754, her local situation exempted her from hostilities. From 1754 to 1758, when the French began to put in operation their scheme to unite Canada and Louisiana, the frontiers of Virginia were harassed by incursions of French and Indian parties; to repel which a regiment was raised, in which Washington first distinguished himself. On the conclusion of peace, when the British attempted to raise a revenue within the colonies, the statesmen of Virginia were among the first to raise the voice of opposition. The eloquence and talents of her orators contributed greatly to excite public feeling on this occasion. The services and sufferings of Virginia in the war of the Revolution were at least as great as those of any other State, and in Virginia the last important measure of the war took place, in the surrender of Cornwallis. Since the peace of 1783, Virginia has retained an elevated rank in the family of States. Fruitful of illustrious men, that State has given seven Presidents to the Union. During the war of 1812, her citizens displayed great patriotism in opposing the common enemy, and her maritime frontier suffered severely from predatory incursions. Within the last few years the progress of the State in population and material greatness has been wonderfully rapid; and her territory be-

LEWIS GINTER. JOHN F. ALVEY.

FANCY DRY GOODS.

GINTER & ALVEY,

NO. 16 PEARL STREET,

RICHMOND,

Importers and Dealers in

HOSIERY, GLOVES, HANDKERCHIEFS, CRAVATS, EMBROIDERIES,

Trimmings, Sewing Silk, Buttons, Combs, Thread and Fancy Goods.

P. HORTON KEACH,

No. 91 Main Street,

RICHMOND,

WHOLESALE AND RETAIL

Manufacturer and Dealer in

LADIES' DRESS TRIMMINGS,

Odd-Fellows' & Masonic

REGALIA,

Banners, Flags, Jewels, &c.

Also Dealer in Hosiery, Gloves, Yarn, Worsted, Fancy and Staple Goods. Every variety of Trimmings made to order.

AGENT FOR HUNT'S CELEBRATED SEWING MACHINE.

JAMES J. BINFORD. JOHN D. BLAIR. WM. P. MAYO.

BINFORD, MAYO & BLAIR,

WHOLESALE AND RETAIL DEALERS IN

FOREIGN AND DOMESTIC

DRY GOODS,

CARPETING, &c.

NO. 93 MAIN STREET,

RICHMOND.

yond the mountains—a wilderness to the last generation, has become equal to the old settlements in all that constitutes national wealth. In 1850 the constitution of the State was adjusted to its present condition and circumstances.*

Succession of Governors.—PRESIDENTS OF COUNCIL: Edward M. Wingfield, 1607; Jno. Radcliffe, 1607; Jno. Smith, 1607; George Percy, 1608;—COMPANY'S GOVERNORS: Lord de la War, 1610; Sir Thos. Dale, 1611; Sir Thos. Gates, 1611; Sir Thos. Dale, 1614; Captain George Yeardly, 1616; Samuel Argal, 1617; (*to the year* 1618, *Sir Thomas Smith presided over the council and company in England, while the above-named actually governed in Virginia;*) Sir George Yeardley, 1618; Sir Francis Wyatt, 1621; Sir George Yeardley (acting,) 1626; Sir George Yeardley, 1626; Francis West, 1627; John Pott, 1628; Sir John Harvey, 1629; John West, 1635; Sir John Harvey, 1636; Sir Francis Wyatt, 1639; Sir William Berkeley, 1641; Richard Kempe, 1644; Sir William Berkeley, 1645; Richard Bennet, (elected), 1652; Edward Digges, 1655; Sam'l Mathews, 1656; Sir Wm. Berkeley, 1659; Francis Morrison (appointed;) Sir William Berkeley 1662; Herbert Jeffreys, (Lieuten't Gov.) 1677; Sir Henry Chichely, (Dep. Gov.) 1678; Lord Culpepper, 1680; Nicholas Spencer, (Pres. of Council,) 1680; Lord Howard, (Gov.) 1684; Nathaniel Bacon (Pres. Council,) 1688; Francis Nicholson (Lt. Gov.), 1690; Sir Edmund Andros (Gov.,) 1692; Francis Nicholson, 1698; Edward Nott, 1705; Edmund Jennings, 1706; Alexander Spotswood, 1710; Hugh Drysdale, 1722; Robert Carter (Pres. of Council,) 1726; Wm. Gouch (Gov.,) 1727; Thomas Lee, (Pres. of Council,) 1749; Lewis Burwell, 1749; Robert Dinwiddie (Gov.,) 1752; Francis Fauquier, 1758; John Blair (Pres. of Council,) 1767; Lord Botetourt (Gov.,) 1768; Wm. Nelson (Pres. of Council,) 1770; Lord Dunmore, 1772; PRESIDENTS OF CONVENTION (Provisional Gov.,)

* If it be not beneath the dignity of history, it may be interesting to our readers to state how Virginia came to acquire the soubriquet of the "Old Dominion." After the death of Charles I, and the usurpation of Cromwell, the British colonies in America were required to swear allegiance to the Protector. But Virginia persisted in retaining her loyalty to the *Old Dominion*—that is, to the dynasty of the Stuarts, which was represented in the person of Charles II, who had taken refuge in Holland. After the death of Cromwell, Charles was recalled, and proclaimed King of England, Scotland, Ireland and *Virginia*, and ordered her arms to be quartered with those of Great Britain as an independent member of the Empire. This was done in compliment to Virginia, who had invited him to reign over her, but the death of Cromwell restored him to the throne of his ancestors. We think that Virginia was fortunate; for surely a more worthless tyrant never held the reins of empire.

CLOTHING!

KEEN, BALDWIN & CO.

Manufacturers of and Dealers in

SUPERIOR CLOTHING

AND

FANCY DRESS ARTICLES,

102 Main St. Richmond.

Keep constantly on hand a full assortment of

Dress Coats,
Frock Coats,
Over Coats,
Cloth Cloaks,
Cass. Pants,
***Silk* Vests,**
Satin Vests,
Velvet Vests,
Marseilles Vests,
Shirts and Collars,
Cravats & Scarfs,
Gloves & Hosiery,
Buck Underwear,
Silk "
Merino "
Cotton "
Rubber Goods,
Umbrellas.

And a full assortment of all other Goods usually kept in a Gentlemen's

Furnishing Store

All of which they pledge themselves to furnish those who favor them with a call, on as good terms as any other house in the Union.

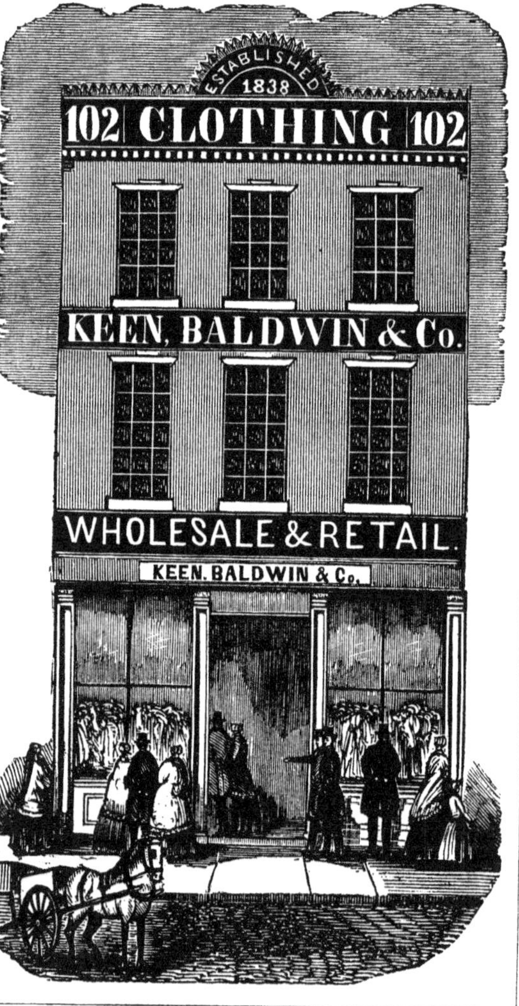

Peyton Randolph, 1775, and Edmund Pendleton, 1775;—CONSTITUTIONAL GOVERNORS; Patrick Henry, 1776; Thos. Jefferson, 1779; Thomas Nelson, 1781; Benjamin Harrison, 1781; Patrick Henry, 1784; Edmund Randolph, 1786; Beverley Randolph, 1788; Henry Lee, 1791; Robert Brooke, 1794; James Wood, 1796; James Monroe, 1799; John Page, 1802; William H. Cabell, 1805; John Tyler, 1808; James Monroe, 1811; George W. Smith, 1811; James Barbour, 1812; Wilson C. Nicholas, 1814; James P. Preston, 1816; Thomas M. Randolph, 1819; James Pleasants, 1822; John Tyler, 1825; William B. Giles, 1826; John Floyd, 1829; Littleton U. Tazewell, 1833; Windham Robertson (acting,) 1836; David Campbell, 1836; Thomas W. Gilmer, 1839; John Rutherford (acting,) 1841; John M. Gregory (acting,) 1842; James McDowell, 1842; William Smith, 1845; William Smith, 1847; John B. Floyd, 1849; Joseph Johnson, 1852.

RICHMOND, on the bank of James River, 130 miles above its entrance into Chesapeake Bay, is the political capital of the State.

PROCEEDINGS OF THE

VIRGINIA COMMERCIAL CONVENTION.

RESOURCES, INDUSTRY AND IMPROVEMENTS OF VIRGINIA—HER CONTEST FOR THE TRADE OF THE WEST, AND PROPOSED FOREIGN TRADE.—The committee appointed to report to the convention the most efficient means of achieving its important objects, have performed that duty, so far as the materials existed for a proper statistical exposition of the value of the trade of Virginia, as well as the facilities completed, or in progress, for its transportation to the exporting cities of the state.

The commercial prosperity of Virginia is based upon the

J. E. WADSWORTH. D. B. TURNER. G. S. PALMER.

WADSWORTH, TURNER & CO.

IMPORTERS AND WHOLESALE DEALERS IN

STAPLE AND FANCY

DRY GOODS,

No. 18 PEARL STREET,

RICHMOND.

THOS. R. PRICE & CO.

No. 89 Main Street,

RICHMOND,

Keep always on hand an Assortment of the very best

 G O O  ,

DRY GOODS,

Selected expressly for Retail.

☞ Their experience and advantages in business enable them to sell at the very lowest prices for good articles.

THOMAS U. DUDLEY. WM. F. JOHNSTON.

DUDLEY & JOHNSTON,

Wholesale and Retail Dealers in

STAPLE & FANCY DRY GOODS,

No. 145 MAIN STREET,

RICHMOND,

Keep always on hand a supply of Carpetings, Rugs, Baizes, Irish Linen, Table Damasks, Huckabacks, Linen Sheetings, &c.

JOHN C. SHAFER,

TAILOR & DRAPER,

EXCHANGE BUILDING,

Fourteenth Street,

RICHMOND.

employment of the Chesapeake ports; and no project for acquiring the materials or the means of exportation, can be successful, which does not contemplate their employment.

The country tributary to the Chesapeake, possesses advantages not surpassed by any other on the Atlantic. Nature has been so bounteous, that the difficulty has been, not so much to discover a good site for a city, but to discriminate between the numerous excellent locations presented. Norfolk, Richmond, Petersburg, Fredericksburg, and Alexandria, have all been established to receive and conduct the trade of Virginia.

From the individuality of these local interests, it has been heretofore impossible to adopt any system of improvement calculated to promote the exclusive advantage of any one of the cities referred to. Apprehensive that the limited trade legitimate to each might be diverted to some rival, impediments have been thrown in the way of great lines of communication with the interior of our own and other States, calculated perhaps, to vary the local direction of some particular trade, but destined, in the end, to compensate each of these cities, by its dividend of a trade far surpassing in magnitude and value any particular loss. The evils of rivalry will, however, be no longer felt, each of these cities having received a line of internal communication, many of which are now converging to a common point of union; interests heretofore supposed antagonistic are now harmonized in the completion of a plan common to them all, and weapons brightened by the conflict of a generous rivalry are now wielded in the achievement of a common triumph. It is thus that the construction of the Southside rail road, and the James River canal, makes the prosecution of the Virginia and Tennessee railroad alike important to Lynchburg —to whose public spirit is so largely due the conception and execution of that great project—to Richmond and to Petersburg. The extension of the great central-railroad to the Ohio, no longer a subject of exclusive interest to Richmond, appeals to the support of Alexandria. The completion of the Dock connections will connect Norfolk with the James River and Kanawha Canal, and interest that city in its extension to the Ohio. The Richmond and Danville railroad is, upon the same principle, a work from which Petersburg and Richmond may derive common benefits.

Convinced, therefore, that their interest and duty alike demand a cordial alliance, the cities of Virginia will hereafter bestow upon the extension of the great lines of improvement here indicated, their earnest and combined co-operation.

Since, however, the partial completion of these great improvements has already bestowed upon the cities of Virginia a large accumulation of trade, it becomes necessary to encourage the establishment of a commercial marine, of sail-ships and steamers, to convey abroad our own trade, and exchange for it the productions of other nations. The export and import trade of Virginia is now taxed with transport coastwise for exportation from northern cities: it is burthened with the charges of northern merchants; whilst the whole commercial profits resulting from freights, exchanges, as well as from the importation and supply of the goods received on exchange, result exclusively to northern capital and to northern enterprise.

We state this fact in no spirit of sectional prejudice, but as a consequence of our own supineness. We think it time that a trade so circuitous, and a tribute so unworthy, should cease. We should export from and import into the Chesapeake cities of Virginia, by vessels owned and manned by Southern men. No State can expect to preserve its prosperity which does not provide for its citizens the varied pursuits in which industry and enterprise shall receive an adequate reward.

In estimating the present value of the Chesapeake trade, so far as materials are at hand for a correct estimate, we will find that the James River and Kanawha Canal, its principal tributary, contributed during the last year $6,123,865 49, the products of the interior; whilst it carried into the interior, merchandise and other articles, valued at $7,727,224 29.*

The business of the central railroad has doubled within the past year; its downward tonnage amounting to 25,000 tons, and its upward transportation is perhaps one-half that amount. The Richmond and Danville, the Richmond and Petersburg, and Richmond and Fredericksburg railroads, contribute considerable additions to the aggregate of trade upon the James River.

Amongst other important items of an export trade, we may mention that the total inspections of Virginia tobacco amount to 50,000 hogsheads, of which the larger portion is shipped to

*An. Report of J. R. and K. Co., Nov. 1850.

Europe; whilst the remainder, with a large amount not inspected, is manufactured in the interior for consumption at home and abroad.

The flouring mills in Richmond manufactured, last year, 1,723,100 bushels of wheat, and are expected this year to manufacture 1,587,100 bushels. This flour is shipped to Rio, through northern houses, in vessels whose return cargoes consist chiefly of coffee. This coffee is, in turn sent back in Northern vessels to Virginia for consumption—the freights, commissions, and commercial profits of both the export and import trade, being a direct loss to the State of Virginia, to which this trade rightfully belonged.

During the present year, however, some of the most enterprising merchants of Richmond have shipped nine cargoes of flour, directly to Rio, the vessels to return to this port with hides, coffee, and other products of South America. We are moreover informed that a larger amount of goods will be imported this year to Richmond than has been imported in any one year for a series of years; and that the direct import would have been far larger but for the want of ships in this trade, which compelled our merchants to ship through northern ports.

During the year ending July 1st, 1851, the foreign trade of James River gave employment to a number of foreign and American vessels. From a statement furnished from the Custom House, in Richmond, it will be seen that the tonnage employed in the direct foreign trade between Europe and the waters of the James River amounts to nearly 30,000 tons. This amount is itself amply sufficient to give employment to two steamers of 2,500 tons burthen.

If it were in our power to present the commercial statistics of the cities of Norfolk, derived from the Roanoke River, the Dismal Swamp Canal, and other sources; the rapidly increasing trade of Alexandria, derived from the Chesapeake and Ohio Canal, and from the country adjacent to her; of Petersburg and Fredericksburg; we do not doubt but that an amount of Chesapeake trade could be demonstrated adequate to sustain at once, by the energetic and united patronage of our merchants, a direct trade with Europe and South America. The materials for this trade already exist. Any doubt, however, which may be entertained of the present amount of Virginia

commerce becomes unimportant, in view of the immense accessions to follow the completion of the improvements referred to. Whilst we pause to make the figures, the fact is upon us. A succinct statement of the works of artificial improvement now in progress and actually completed will serve to embody the facilities upon which we may rely, and to develop the capacity of transportation upon which the future trade of Virginia must principally depend. We think, therefore, it sufficiently appears that, looking alone at the present trade of our cities, we have ample encouragement to commence at once upon this undertaking, with the fair prospects of trade enough to insure handsome profits to capitalists who may embark therein.

But when we glance upon the future trade which these cities must enjoy, we are still more encouraged. We will first inquire in regard to the number of miles of railroads and canals now constructed. Your committee have been furnished with the following very valuable statistics by the second auditor:

Statement of the Railroads in Virginia, Completed and in Progress.

	Length.	Completed.
Baltimore and Ohio Railroad	251	90
Richmond and Danville Railroad	147	35
Richmond and Petersburg Railroad	22	22
Clover Hill Railroad	15	15
Southside Railroad	122	10
Manasses Gap Railroad	60	—
Petersburg and Roanoke Railroad	60	60
Seaboard and Roanoke Railroad	77	77
Appomattox Railroad	9	9
Winchester and Potomac Railroad	32	32
Virginia Central Railroad, including the Blue Ridge Railroad	138	98
Virginia and Tennessee Railroad	208	10
Orange & Alex'a RR. including branch to Warrenton, 10 ml's	100	10
Richmond, Fredericksburg and Potomac Railroad	76	76
Greensville and Roanoke Railroad	21	21
Northwestern Railroad	120	—
Miles	1,455	565
Chesapeake and Ohio Canal	185	185
James River and Kanawha Canal	—	200
Dismal Swamp Canal	—	23
Fredericksburg Valley Plank Road	40	1
Staunton to James River	40	—
Boydton to Petersburg	75	—
Junction Valley	65	—

It thus appears that there are now completed in Virginia 565 miles of railroad, and 418 miles of canals; and that there are

CARTER'S SPANISH MIXTURE.

THE GREAT PURIFIER OF THE BLOOD!

NOT A PARTICLE OF MERCURY IN IT.

LET THE AFFLICTED READ AND PONDER!

An Infallible Remedy for Scrofula, King's Evil, Rheumatism, Obstinate Cutaneous Eruptions, Pimples or Pustules on the Face, Blotches, Boils, Ague and Fever, Chronic Sore Eyes, Ring Worm or Tetter, Scald Head, Enlargement and Pain of the Bones and Joints, Stubborn Ulcers, Syphilitic Disorders, Lumbago, Spinal Complaints, and all Diseases arising from an Injudicious Use of Mercury, Imprudence in Life, or Impurity of the Blood.

☞ This great alterative medicine and Purifier of Blood is now used by thousands of grateful patients from all parts of the United States, who testify daily to the remarkable cures performed by the greatest of all medicines,

"CARTER'S SPANISH MIXTURE."

Neuralgia, Rheumatism, Scrofula, Eruptions on the Skin, Liver Disease, Fevers, Ulcers, Old Sores, Affections of the Kidneys, Diseases of the Throat, Female complaints, Pains and Aching of the Bones and Joints, are speedily put to flight by using this great and inestimable remedy.

For all diseases of the Blood, nothing has yet been found to compare with it. It cleanses the system from all impurities, acts gently and efficiently on the Liver and Kidneys, strengthens the Digestion, gives tone to the Stomach, makes the Skin clear and healthy, and restores the Constitution, enfeebled by disease or broken down by the exceeses of youth, to its pristine vigor and strength.

For the Ladies, it is incomparably better than all the cosmetics ever used. A few doses of CARTER'S SPANISH MIXTURE will remove all sallowness of complexion, bring the roses mantling to the cheek, give elasticity to the step, and improve the general health in a remarkable degree, beyond all the medicines ever heard of.

The large number of certificates which we have received from persons from all parts of the United States, is the best evidence that there is no Humbug about it. The press, hotel keepers, magistrates, physicians and public men, well known to the community, all add their testimony to the wonderful effects of this GREAT BLOOD PURIFIER.

Call on the AGENT and get a Circular and Almanac, and read the wonderful cures his truly greatest of all Medicines has performed.

None genuine unless signed BENNETT & BEERS, Proprietors, No 3 Pearl street, Richmond, Va., to whom all orders for supplies and agencies must be addressed.

For sale by Druggists and Country Merchants every where.

now in the course of construction 890 miles of railroad, and 220 miles of plank roads. We have, then, the gratifying result, that there are nearly 2,000 miles of rail-roads and canals constructed, or in progress of construction, in our State. The appropriations for these works are already made, and the money has been almost entirely raised at home, without the necessity of incurring a foreign debt. The State of Pennsylvania, to make her improvements, has incurred a debt of near $40,000,000, to pay the interest on which requires a semi-annual export of over a million of dollars, to be paid the foreign bondholders. On the other hand, our State debt is comparatively small, and owned chiefly at home by our citizens.

But this view becomes still more encouraging, when we recollect that these improvements will be finished at the farthest within the next four years. As each mile is finished, an increase will be given to the trade of our cities; and when the Virginia and Tennessee Railroad, the Richmond and Danville Railroad, and the Seaboard and Roanoke Railroad are finished, they will be at once connected with a net-work of railroads through North Carolina, South Carolina and Georgia, on the one hand—and Tennessee, Ohio, Kentucky, Alabama, Mississippi and Louisiana on the other. It is certainly a source of pride to know that we have quietly effected so much. Speculation would be at fault in estimating the trade that must follow the completion of these works. The rapid increase of our cities will be one certain effect, while the appreciation of real estate, and the profits of every industrial pursuit, will be increased. At the same time the heart of the patriot will rejoice that this acquisition of strength, wealth, population and power must result in restoring the South to her former position in the Union, and may render that Union, as bequeathed us by our forefathers, more stable and firm—its obligations every where observed, and every where sustained and beloved for the benefits conferred upon its citizens.

Georgia has now 1,000 miles of rail-road—South Carolina is extending her iron arms in every direction, and in two or three years every part of the State will be provided with railroad facilities. North Carolina has giant schemes on foot, which she is prosecuting with a giant's strength. Tennessee will soon extend the Virginia railroad, and the railroad extending

from Charleston and Savannah to Chattanooga, to Memphis, on the Mississippi. Alabama, Mississippi and Louisiana are seeking connections with these roads, and soon we shall see the South more highly improved by railroad facilities than the North, owing to the level nature of the country and the cheapness of labor and materials in the South. Charleston alone is moving, with far-seeing sagacity for this increased trade. We feel pride and pleasure in her means, and we heartily hope she may prosper in her former enterprise to establish direct trade by means of ships and steamers, owned by Southerners. We believe there is space enough, and a back country sufficiently ample, if we are true to ourselves, to secure the prosperity of all our Southern towns; and their prosperity, so far from causing us to fall, will but add to our own prosperity. But how can the people of Virginia hope to contend with Charleston in the generous competition for this trade, unless equal facilities are provided in our harbors for shipping directly to Europe? If we pause in the contest, the trade will have been fixed in the direction of Charleston, and we may strive in vain to regain what is strictly our own.

To illustrate the advantages to be anticipated, we may refer to the enlightened and enterprising commonwealth of Massachusetts. The large expenditures made for the construction of railroads, and the results of that system, have there vindicated the wisdom which dictated it.

In that State the length of railroads in 1840 was 433 miles; it is now 1,033. The value of property in the several counties of the State has increased from $299,878,329 in 1840, to $590,531,881 in 1850—an increase in the value of property during ten years, of $290,653,552, or about one hundred per cent.

In Boston, which is the centre of the whole system of Massachusetts railroads, the following result is obtained:

	Population.	Wealth.
1840	171,992	$120,114,574
1850	269,874	266,646,844

Showing an increase of 60 per cent. in population, and 140 in wealth.

Looking at the commercial returns of our own ports, the seaports of Virginia do not appear to have increased with that ra-

CHARLES STEBBINS. BENJAMIN K. PULLEN.

STEBBINS & PULLEN,

IMPORTERS AND DEALERS IN

EARTHENWARE, CHINA AND GLASS,

Pier, Mantle and Toilet Looking Glasses, Britannia and Plated Ware, Gas Fixtures, Lamps, Casters, Table Cutlery, &c.

IRON FRONT BUILDING,

No. 101 Broad Street, Corner of 9th Street,

RICHMOND.

Particular attention paid to Packing.

GENNETT & JAMES,

WATCH MAKERS & JEWELERS,

14 Main Street, Eagle Square,

RICHMOND,

Have on hand a large assortment of all articles embraced in our line of business.

OF SUPERIOR MANUFACTURE,

SILVER TEA SETS, in whole Sets, or single Pieces, SILVER PITCHERS, GOBLETS, CUPS, SPOONS and FORKS, SOUP LADLES, BUTTER KNIVES, DESSERT KNIVES, FISH and PASTRY KNIVES, PLATED FORKS, SPOONS, &c.

WATCHES repaired by experienced workmen.

Old Gold and Silver exchanged for new.

pidity which the general prosperity of the State would indicate: indeed, our direct imports appear to have diminished. These unfavorable indications are, however, contradicted by the positive gain in the assessed value of real estate, and by the increased value of subjects of taxation within the State. The stagnation of our commerce is to be attributed to physical obstacles which separate the productive interior from our seaboard, whilst the enterprise of other States and cities has actually constructed improvements for the mere factorage of our produce, which we would not undertake for the positive increase of the fee simple value of the property, and the exclusive commerce of its enhanced products.

It is thus that towns in Western Virginia have sprung up, manufactures have been established, minerals have been made available, agricultural produce has been created, all of which seeks a market in the cities of Cincinnati, New Orleans, Philadelphia and Baltimore; whilst even Savannah, in Georgia, has participated in those productions of Virginia, which could not have paid the cost of exportation eastward to the Chesapeake cities of Virginia. The cities enumerated have supplied the Valley and Western Virginia with merchandise in exchange for its productions. The commerce of Virginia, like some fountains choked up and neglected, cheers with its shattered streamlet every region except that to which its free and fertilizing current would naturally and gladly have directed itself.

We cannot make this valuable, though dispersed trade, the subject of exact estimate. It is reflected in the increased population and taxable resources of the State, so lately the subject of elaborate exposition in the constitutional convention.

We select, however, for illustration of its value, and of the obstacles which impede its exportation, the trade on the Monongahela. This river has been improved by lock and dam, so that steamers can ascend probably within the limits of Virginia. Its trade will compare favorably with that of many rivers in Eastern Virginia; yet the natural line of exportation of its products, is by the Ohio and Mississippi rivers, the Gulf of Mexico, and coast of the Atlantic, to the markets of the East, or to Europe. The aggregate line of water transportation from Clarksburg, in Harrison county, to New York, is not less than 4,000 miles. The time employed is not less than 90 days;

yet the direct line of transit to the Chesapeake, would not exceed 400 miles, whilst the time in reaching market might be reduced to a few days. Baltimore is providing a means of direct transit to accommodate this region of country, much of which has heretofore traded with Philadelphia; but after Baltimore shall have loaded her vessels with this product of Virginia, and supplied in return the merchandise for its consumption, she will be compelled to send it within the territory of Virginia for exportation to the outlet of the Chesapeake.

A similar difference between the natural and artificial communication of that part of Western Virginia bordering on the Ohio river, and of the valley of the Kanawha with the Atlantic cities, will be found to exist, whilst a small portion of southwestern Virginia sends produce to Alabama and Georgia, purchases groceries in New Orleans, and imports its merchandise through Charleston, South Carolina. Let it be remembered that this is a trade to be developed. The land is not a wilderness, requiring the life and labor of generations to reduce it to efficient production. The trade already exists; it has grown up under obstacles. It has been driven from its natural outlets, to enrich a distant and foreign interest in other States. But the fact of its development under such disadvantages, proves that it may readily be secured, whilst the anxious interest of the whole West proves the alacrity with which it would cooperate in the regeneration of the commercial interest of the Virginia cities.

There may be persons, however, incredulous that the trade of Virginia, now exported from northern, western and southern cities, can be directed to the ports of the Chesapeake. It will not be doubted that the greater portion of the products of the valley and western Virginia are destined for consumption in the northern States or in Europe. These products would adopt the most direct line of transit between production and consumption, but for the natural obstacles which intervene and condemn them to the tedious, tortuous and perilous navigation of the rivers and coast. The direct line of transit would pass through the Chesapeake ports of Eastern Virginia.

So long as the route of the water-borne produce of Western Virginia was cheaper than any artificial line of direct transit, any attempt to divert that trade might have been hopeless.

HARTWELL & CO.

DEALERS IN

J. W. WATSON,

ONE OF THE OLDEST AND MOST SUCCESSFUL

DAGUERREIAN ARTISTS

IN THIS COUNTRY,

Takes pleasure in calling the attention of the Public to his Large and extensive

DAGUERREIAN GALLERY,

110 MAIN STREET,

RICHMOND.

MAMMOTH SKY-LIGHT.

With this advantage and the best assistants, besides his personal attention at all times, he flatters himself that he is prepared to execute Pictures in a manner that cannot be surpassed in the United States.

GOLD LOCKETS, PINS, FANCY FRAMES, CASES, &c., always on hand, in which he will place pictures on very moderate terms. Persons are respectfully invited to call and examine a fine collection of specimens, whether they may wish pictures or not.

J. W. WATSON,

First door above Mitchel & Tyler's Jewelry Store.

The opinion that no railroad could succeed, unless it connected populous points by a short line, has been reversed by experience. Considering the railroad and locomotive almost as a revelation for the South, we may be pardoned for referring to the causes which are now producing through their agency such important social, commercial, and political results. Time has become an essential element in the value of merchandise and staple productions. No producing region, and no mercantile community can adopt a slow and circuitous delivery in competition with others producing or vending the same articles with greater facilities of transportation than themselves. Travel and postal communication now tolerate no delay or impediment. It is impossible to present any formula to show how far shortening the time of transit is equivalent to a positive reduction of freight. The telegraphic and express lines, every where well sustained, prove the estimated value of time to be very great; though it varies of course, with the fear of competition, with the value of the commercial subjects, and with the relative importance of individual transactions. But we see from the opening of the artificial lines of Boston, New York and Philadelphia, that the commercial patronage of the interior is immediately transferred to the most rapid and direct lines of outlet and intercommunication. It is thus that the great cities of the North have severally penetrated the interior with artificial lines, until they have taken from the open and untaxed current of the Mississippi the commerce produced upon its borders. These great artificial outlets have been competing among themselves for the commerce of the interior, until they now offer not only superior certainty, and reduced time of delivery, but they offer upon many articles cheaper freights than the river and coast routes referred to. We copy from the New Orleans Crescent a notice of the reversing of the natural current of trade, resulting from the construction of the great artificial lines referred to:

"For years past cotton has gone up the Ohio River from Tennessee, through the Pennsylvania and New York canals, to all the factories in the interior of these States, and often the cities of Philadelphia and New York. We recollect, last September, of one shipment of upwards of seven hundred bales, shipped from Louisville, via the Ohio and New York canals, to New York city. The freights were less than by the way of New Or-

AMERICAN

MAIN STREET,

OPPOSITE CAPITOL SQUARE,

RICHMOND.

J. MILDEBERGER SMITH,

(FORMERLY AT JONES'S HOTEL, PHILADELPHIA,)

PROPRIETOR.

This Hotel is the best located in Richmond, being on *Main street, near the Banks, opposite Capitol Square*, and commanding a fine view of the city.

Thankful for past favors, the proprietor respectfully asks a continuation of public patronage—assuring his friends that no exertions shall be spared to conduce to their comfort while at the

AMERICAN,

And to make it all that a First Class Hotel should be.

BOARD, PER DAY, $2.00.

leans, and the difference in exchange and insurance was near two per cent. in favor of the northern route.

"The amount of cotton that passed up the Ohio last year is estimated, by one familiar with the trade, at sixty thousand bales. This season, nearly all the boats from the Tennessee and Cumberland rivers, bound up the Ohio River, are freighted more or less with cotton. The packets between Memphis and Louisville and Cincinnati, of which there are several lines, take cotton up the rivers nearly every trip.

"The quantity of tobacco that takes its course up the River from the lower Ohio, for the Eastern markets by northern routes, is rapidly increasing. That raised in Ohio and Kentucky, above Cincinnati—and among the latter, the celebrated Mason county tobacco—nearly all goes by the way of the canals to the Eastern markets. By a statement recently published, the difference in the cost of transportation from Louisville to New York is four to five dollars per hogshead in favor of the northern route, while the article escapes the sweat which it undergoes on shipboard while passing through our latitudes.

"Grain is now carried from the Wabash to New York by the canals, at the same cost of freight as is charged by the way of New Orleans; but by the northern route they incur no waste, no risk of damage by heating, and save the whole cost of sacking, for it is carried in the bulk, and the same number of measured bushels are delivered in New York as are received on board the canal boat from the shipper. The lard, pork and flour from the same region are taking the same direction. Last autumn the rich regions of Ohio, Indiana, and Illinois were flooded with the local bank-notes of the eastern States advanced by the New York houses on produce to be shipped by them by the way of the canals in the spring.

"These moneyed facilities enable the packer, miller and speculator to hold on to their produce, with the opening of navigation in the spring; and they are no longer obliged as formerly to hurry off their shipments during the winter by the way of New Orleans, in order to realize funds by drafts on their shipments. The banking facilities at the East are doing as much to draw trade from us as the canals and railways which eastern capital is constructing.

"All the lead from the upper Mississippi now goes East by

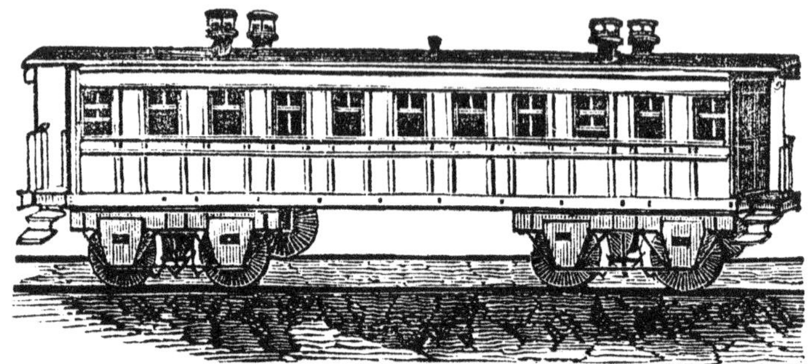

UNION
RAIL ROAD CAR WORKS,
PORTSMOUTH.

FREIGHT, PASSENGER, BAGGAGE,
AND
EXPRESS CARS,
Market, Coal, Lumber & Hand Cars,
Manufactured at this Establishment,

Of the best material, and in the most approved manner, with either Plate or Spoke Wheels and Axles, of Salisbury or other Iron.

TRUCKS FITTED UP,
OR
AXLES AND WHEELS SEPARATELY,

Will be furnished at the shortest notice and shipped to any part of the United States.

Having extensive arrangements and superior facilities for Manufacturing at this establishment, orders will be received and Contracts made for Equipping Entire Roads at short notice.

JOHN A. GREEN, *Proprietor.*

the way of Milwaukie. But the most recent and astonishing change in the course of the northwestern trade, is to behold, as a friend tells us, the number of steamers that now descend the Upper Mississippi, loaded to the guards with produce, as far as the mouth of the Illinois River, and then turn up that stream with their cargoes to be shipped to New York via Chicago.

"The Illinois canal has not only swept the whole produce along the line of the Illinois River to the East, but it is drawing the products from the upper Mississippi through the same channel; thus depriving not only New Orleans, but St. Louis, of a rich portion of their former trade."

To this we may add the fact, that cargoes of corn have been recently shipped from Iowa, down the Mississippi, along the Illinois canal, by way of the lakes, to the city of New York.

The cause of this astonishing result may be thus explained.

Artificial lines afford not only the most speedy means of transportation, but the unity and system of their administration gives them great advantage over the efforts of individual enterprise. They have a basis of travel and mail monopoly, which enables them to discriminate in favor of any specific article of commerce, the factorage and financial results of which may be sufficient to generally indemnify them for the abatement of freight, whilst the revenue of the improvement is sustained by an increased charge upon business not subject to competition, or by the large amount of trade which they command. These exclusive resources, rapidity, certainty and safety of transportation, with the power of discrimination, has enabled, these great lines to wrest from the Mississippi so much of its produce.

To establish the capacity of artificial to compete with natural lines, we publish the following tabular statement, showing the contest between New York and New Orleans for the trade of the Mississippi:

New York and New Orleans in Western Trade.

	Population.	Coal Trade.
1840	2,429,721	66,303,892
1850	3,093,813	156,397,929

An increase of 25 per cent. in population, and 150 per cent. in trade, by canals, in ten years.

Produce of West received by New York Canals.

1842	$22,751,013
1850	55,474,937

An increase of 145 per cent.

Produce of West received at New Orleans.

1842	$43,716,045
1850	96,897,873

Or an increase of 120 per cent.; or a comparative increase by New York, of 25 per cent. over New Orleans in Western produce in five years! In the three years, 1848, 1849 and 1850, the receipts at New Orleans by river were 2,312,121 bbls. flour; at New York, 8,636,207 bbls. Pork:—New Orleans, 1,536,817; New York, 211,018 bbls. Beef:—200,901 bbls. New Orleans; New York, 264,072 bbls. Wheat:—New Orleans, 852,497 bushels; New York, 8,798,759. Corn:—New Orleans, 9,758,-750 bushels; New York, 11,178,228 bushels. Bacon:—New Orleans, 135 millions pounds; New York, 26 millions. Lard:—New Orleans, 293 millions pounds; New York, 21 millions. Butter:—New Orleans, eight millions pounds; New York, 97 millions, &c.

We have adverted to these well-established facts, and explained the rationale of their operations to show that the trade of northern cities is derived by artificial ways from the great producing valley of the West. If this be the case—if productions prefer the lakes, railways and the canals of the North to the river and gulf outlet—why should not the products of Western Virginia, which almost circumnavigate their own State, which pursue a distant, indirect and unsafe line of transit, replete with every danger of river, cape and coast, prefer the direct communications *through* Virginia, and the more congenial destiny of encouraging our own ports? There is no reason. Their anxiety to complete these artificial outlets proves its practicability. All the vast aggregate of trade, now existing in Western Virginia, destined for Atlantic exportation, may be safely added to that which we have already demonstrated as subject to be employed in this great enterprise. We may safely say, that if all the existing commerce of Virginia, for exportation, could be collected in her own Atlantic ports, it would not fall short of twenty millions of dollars, nor would her consumption of merchandise be less. Besides this, the very organization of commercial facilities would guarantee an immense accession of mineral and agricultural productions.

In this connection, we must press upon all interested the indispensable importance of providing for the improvement of the James River, the common outlet of much of the Chesa-

peake trade. Its obstructions affect the trade of Norfolk, Richmond, Lynchburg and Kanawha; and each of them is alike interested in securing the perfect navigation of this noble stream. Your committee have not chosen to awaken controversy by designating any particular mode by which this shall be done; they are aware that if the interests now appealed to, shall be convinced of its paramount importance, the means will be readily devised for its accomplishment. The able and comprehensive report of Lieutenant Stansbury will prove the entire practicability of this work, and the moderate means to be employed in its completion.

We may properly add to these resources, which are directly derived from Virginia alone, the products of the States connected with her, by the lines of improvement now under construction. Tennessee, and Kentucky, and North Carolina, will naturally find their most direct outlet through the Virginia and Tennessee, the Southside and Seaboard rail-roads, now under continuous and connected construction to the interior of the State referred to. The prosecution of the Canal or Central railroads, or the construction of a branch road into the Ohio Valley, will add much from those quarters; and but a few years will elapse before the perfected facilities will bring this great commerce to the legitimate ports of exportation. We will not enlarge upon the commercial results of extending these lines into the interior of the southwestern States, and the national and international intercourse which will pour through Virginia, invigorating her local improvements, freighting her vessels, and filling her ocean steamers. It will be plain, upon investigation, that no cities South of Virginia have the commercial advantages of her own—none have the varied products, the local patronage, the rapid communication with transatlantic cities. Enterprise is now doing all it can to shorten the line of ocean transit. In this the cities of Virginia cannot compete with Boston or New York for the transatlantic intercourse of the northwestern States; but the mail and merchandise transportation, with the travel between the great southwest and the cities of Europe, belong legitimately to the Virginia ports of the Chesapeake, and will be certainly secured.

In embarking in this contest her citizens and commercial cities have a high duty to perform; they must shake them-

JOHN T. TOMPKINS,

AND

UNDERTAKER,

CHURCH STREET, NORFOLK.

Always on hand Mahogany, Walnut, Metallic and Stained Wood Coffins, &c.

Orders from the Country promptly attended to.

MILES P. BUTCHER,

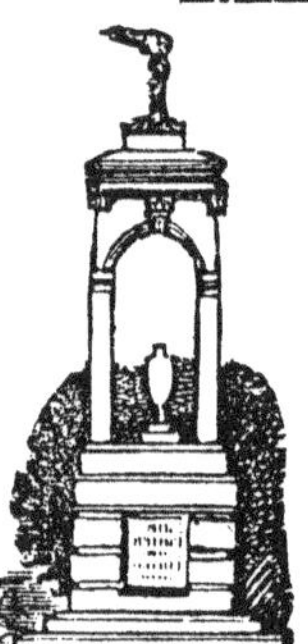

SUCCESSOR TO ROBERT DALRYMPLE,

Keeps on hand and executes to order every description of

Monuments,
Tomb Stones,
Grave Stones, &c.

MARBLE AND GRANITE WORK

Of every description executed to order.

East of Old Custom House,

WIDE WATER STREET, NORFOLK.

W. E. FOSTER.

GUNS, RIFLES OR PISTOLS

Made to order, Stocked, Repaired, or altered to Percussion. BELLS put up; LOCKS repaired; KEYS fitted; BRANDS and PUNCHES cut; CANES and UMBRELLAS repaired, and all kinds of light Jobbing attended to by faithful and experienced workmen.

selves of every sin of selfishness or of jealousy. They must co-operate with a rivalry of devotion to the common cause. There should be no greater jealousy between Richmond and Norfolk than between Philadelphia and New York—yet, though separated from each other by a greater distance, the joint population of the two former cities is scarcely equal to a suburb of either of the two latter. There can be no incompatibility of interest in the harmony of these and other Virginia cities. Let them unite their patronage upon the great designs of internal improvement, and upon the organization of a foreign commerce, and their destinies are established.

Yet the competition will be intense. It will require energy, union and perseverance. The North has enterprise, capital, experience; the South possesses the world staples of cotton, sugar, tobacco, with an immense mercantile consumption. The prize is worthy the efforts of the most gifted intellect, or the most matured experience. It is a strife to be fought with weapons congenial to the enlightened humanity of the present age. It is a contest fraught with consequences scarce inferior to those which hung upon our first great struggle. Virginia has the deepest veneration for the Union, a cordial admiration of those sister States with whom she contends for her heritage; but she cannot break the bread of dependence, or sink into the position of an inferior to those who were her equals.

If the commerce to which we have adverted be not utterly fabulous—if its capacities be not perverted by a mere introduction into our own cities—if the sons and brothers of those who subjected a wilderness to civilization, and gave an empire to freedom, who, braving a deadly climate and a desperate strife, planted the flag of Yorktown upon the Sierras of Mexico, be not utterly recreant to the instincts of their race, then must the glorious and peaceful triumph of commercial independence reward their patriotism and enterprise. The rewards of industry and of enterprise will be reserved to our own citizens, and the shameful tribute be abolished for ever.

The committee respectfully recommends the adoption of the following resolutions:

Resolved, As the opinion of this committee, that lines of mail or other steamers, or other vessels, from Hampton Roads to some port or ports of Europe, ought to be established; and

GRIFFIN BARNES'

SASH, BLIND AND DOOR

MANUFACTORY.

Nos. 122 and 37,

CORNER OF

Church and Union Sts.

NORFOLK.

WOOD TURNING IN ALL ITS BRANCHES

CARPENTERS AND BUILDERS

From the Country and neighboring Towns will find it to their interest to call before purchasing elsewhere, as all orders received by me will be

PROMPTLY ATTENDED TO AND NEATLY EXECUTED.

JOHN D. COUPER,

CORNER OF

MAIN AND GRANBY STS.

OPPOSITE NEW CUSTOM HOUSE,

NORFOLK.

STONE WORK

FOR VARIOUS PURPOSES,

Executed with faithfulness, and on accommodating terms.

Tombs, Monuments, Head Pieces, &c.

ALWAYS ON HAND AND MADE TO ORDER.

Orders from the Country promptly attended to.

G. F. ANDERSON. W. D. REYNOLDS.

ANDERSON & REYNOLDS,

GROCERS

AND

COMMISSION MERCHANTS,

No. 10 ROANOKE SQUARE,

NORFOLK.

Special attention given to the sale of Flour, Grain and all other kinds of produce.

Virginia, North Carolina, Tennessee, Kentucky, and such other States as are disposed to aid in the enterprise, should be appealed to; and an appeal should also be made to Congress to bestow upon such line the same mail facilities which are extended to the northern lines; and the bars which now obstruct the navigation of James River should be removed.

Resolved, That committees be appointed to memorialize Congress and the Legislature of Virginia, and to prepare an address to the public, upon the subject aforesaid, and the great importance to the people of Virginia, and the South generally, that they should conduct their own trade directly on their own bottoms, and with their own men and means.

Resolved, that lines of packet-ships, screw-propellors, or mail steamers, ought to be established between the exporting cities of Virginia, and the West Indies and South America.

Resolved, also, That the people of Virginia be requested to hold meetings in their several counties, cities and towns, to effect the object of the foregoing resolution; and that to this end it be recommended to them to adopt some organization by the appointment of standing and corresponding committees, or otherwise as to them shall seem best.

Resolved, That the merchants of our Atlantic cities ought to import directly to our Virginia ports the productions of foreign countries used and consumed in this and the adjoining States; and that it be recommended to the merchants of the interior, and the people at large, to aid them in this noble enterprise.

GAZETTEER.

ADD'S VALLEY, a post office of Tazewell county, Virginia.

ABINGDON, a handsome town, capitol of Washington county, Virginia, is pleasantly situated in a valley between the main forks of Holston river, about 7 miles from each, 304 miles W. by S. from Richmond, and nearly 8 miles from the boundary of Tennessee. It is the most considerable and flourishing town in the S. W. part of Virginia. The situation is elevated, the town is well built, and the principal street is macadamized. It contains 6 churches, 2 academies, 2 printing offices, and manu-

STOVES

AND

HOT-AIR FURNACES,

Of all kinds, for all purposes.

METALLIC ROOFING,

GUTTERS & PIPES

FOR BUILDINGS.

Block Tin, Tin Plate, Sheet Copper, Bar and Sheet Lead, Sheet Iron, &c.

ETHEREAL OIL,

AND LAMPS FOR USING IT.

In store a large and varied assortment of all kinds of Copper and Tin Wares, at wholesale and retail, lower than any other establishment in Va. Copper Work for Steamers, Mills, Distilleries, &c., &c., executed in the best manner, with due regard to the steam pressure.

Shower Baths and Bathing Apparatus, of all the Newest and most approved Patterns.

North Carolina

AND

VIRGINIA HOTEL,

Commerce Street, near Main, Norfolk,

FRESH PICKLED AND SPICED OYSTERS,

Of the best quality, put up to order at the shortest notice.

MRS. FRANCES HARMANSON,

Late MRS. WILSON.

Board, per Week,	$5 00	Dinner,	50
" " Day,	1 00	Supper,	25
Breakfast,	25	Lodging,	25

J. M. FREEMAN & SONS,

IMPORTERS AND DEALERS IN

FINE LEVER WATCHES,

SHIP CHRONOMETERS,

DIAMONDS AND GOLD JEWELRY,

SILVER AND PLATED WARE, FANCY GOODS, &c.

factories of leather, saddles and harness. Abingdon is on the route of the great railroad which is in progress of construction between Lynchburg on one hand, and Knoxville, Tennessee, on the other, which, when finished, will form part of the most direct route from New York to New Orleans. Population about 1,800.

ACADEMY, a post-office of Pocahontas county, Virginia.

ACCOMACK, a county in the E. part of Virginia, bordering on Maryland, has an area of about 480 square miles. It forms part of a peninsula which is washed by Chesapeake bay on the W., and by the Atlantic on the E. The county is about 48 miles long, and 10 miles wide. It comprises numerous low, sandy islands extending along the seacoast, one of which is 8 miles in length. The county was formed from Northampton in 1672, and the name was derived from a tribe of Indians who once frequented this region. The surface is level, the soil light and moderately fertile. Wheat, Indian corn, and oats are the staples. Capital, Accomack Court-House, or Drummond Town. Population 18,790, of whom 12,903 are free, and 4,987 slaves.

ACCOMACK COURT-HOUSE, (DRUMMOND TOWN,) a small post-village, situated nearly in the centre of the above county, of which it is the capital, 193 miles E. by N. from Richmond. Population about 500.

ACQUINTON, a post-office of King William county, Virginia.

ADALINE, a post-office of Marshall county, Virginia.

THOMAS JEFFERSON,
Born April 2d, 1743.

ALBEMARLE, a county in the E. central part of Virginia, has an area of about 700 square miles. The James River forms its southern boundary, and it is drained by the Rivanna and Hardware rivers, affluents of the James river, which rise by several small branches in the W. part of the country. The Blue Ridge forms its N. W. boundary, and a ridge called South-west Mountain, or Carter's Mountain, extends across the county in a N. E. and S. W. direction. The surface is beautifully diversified, and the scenery in all parts of the

SAMUEL R. BROWN, WILLIAM McCLEAN.

BROWN & McCLEAN,

FARMERS' HEAD QUARTERS,

No. 11 WATER STREET, NORFOLK,

DEALERS IN

ENGLISH, SWEDE, AMERICAN AND RUSSIAN

IRON OF ALL SIZES,

Anvils, Bellows, Vices, &c., manufacturers of Farming Implements, Horse Power Machinery, &c. Every article connected with the Iron and Agricultural Implement business, is kept by us and for sale at Manufacturers' prices. Our Catalogues may be had by mail or otherwise, by applying at the Depot.

WATCHES & JEWELRY.

C. F. GREENWOOD,

No. 2. West Wide Water Street,

NORFOLK,

Has on hand an extensive and well selected stock of

WATCHES, CLOCKS, JEWELRY,

SILVER WARE AND FANCY GOODS,

To which he is constantly adding by fresh selections of the latest styles of goods from the first importing houses at the North. His present stock embraces, in part, gold and silver hunting and open faced patent lever watches, duplex, anchor lever and cylinder watches, gold breast pins, finger rings, ear rings, bracelets, lockets, chains, slides, studs, &c.

Strict personal attention paid to the repairing of fine watches, clocks, jewelry, &c , at moderate charges.

county is exceedingly picturesque. The soil of the valleys and river bottoms is remarkably fertile, and a large portion of the highlands is susceptible of cultivation. Indian corn, wheat, oats, hay, tobacco, wool, and butter are the staples. In 1850 it produced 798,354 bushels of corn; 278,575 of wheat, 191,549 of oats; 4,328 tons of hay; 1,456,300 pounds of tobacco, and 164,882 pounds of butter. The produce of corn was greater than that of any other county in the State. It contained in that year 44 churches, and 4 newspaper establishments. There were 550 pupils attending public schools, and 465 attending academies and other schools. The Rivanna river is navigable in the eastern part of the county, which is intersected by the Central railroad of Virginia, lately constructed, while the James River Canal passes along the South border. Albemarle is among the most populous and highly cultivated counties of Virginia, and is distinguished as the native place of Thomas Jefferson, third President of the United States, whose residence, Monticello, is beautifully situated 3 miles S. E. from Charlottesville, commanding a magnificent view of the distant mountains, and of the Rivanna river, which flows in the immediate vicinity. Capital, Charlottesville. Population, 25,800, of whom 12,462 were free, and 13,338 slaves.

ALDIE, a small post-village of Loudoun county, Virginia, on Little river, 149 miles N. from Richmond. A slackwater navigation is in progress of construction, which will extend from this village to the Potomac, a distance of 17 miles.

ALEXANDRIA, a county in the N. E. part of Virginia, bordering on the Potomac river, opposite Washington City, has an area of about 36 square miles. The surface is hilly; the soil thin. Indian corn, wheat, oats, and hay are the staples. In 1850 the county produced 28,380 bushels of corn; 6,238 of wheat; 6,312 of oats; and 412 tons of hay. There were 1 cotton factory, 1 grist mill, 2 iron foundries, 1 tannery, 2 chandleries, and 2 agricultural implement manufactories. It contained 12 churches, and 3 newspaper establishments. There were 619 pupils attending public schools, and 304 attending academies or other schools. The Potomac is navigable for large ships on the border of the county. The Orange and Alexandria railroad terminates at Alexandria, the capital of the county; and a canal has been made from that city to George-

town, District of Columbia. Population, 10,008, of whom 8,626, were free, and 1,382 slaves. This county formerly constituted a part of the District of Columbia. It was retroceded to Virginia during the Congress of 1845–6.

ALEXANDRIA, a city port of entry and capital of Alexandria county, Virginia, on the right bank of the Potomac, 7 miles below Washington. Lat. 38° 49′ N., Lon. 77° 4′ W. The river, here one mile wide, forms a commodious harbor, sufficiently deep for the largest ships. The city is pleasantly situated on undulating ground, with a fine view of the capitol at Washington and of the broad Potomac. The streets cross each other at right angles, and are generally well paved and lighted with gas. The public buildings are a court-house and about 12 churches. There are 3 banks, 2 newspaper offices, and several excellent schools. The water of the river has recently been introduced into the city by means of machinery. A considerable amount of shipping is owned here, in which corn, tobacco, and stone coal are exported. A canal has been opened to Georgetown intersecting the Chesapeake and Ohio canal, and a railroad 90 miles long extends from this city to Gordonsville on the Central railroad. These improvements were finished in 1852, and have attracted considerable trade to this port. The manufacture of cotton cloths has recently been introduced here, and is carried on quite extensively, a number of mills being in successful operation. Population about 5,000.

ALLBRIGHT, a post-office of Preston county, Virginia.

ALLEGHANY, a county situated a little S. W. from the centre of Virginia, has an area of about 500 square miles. It is intersected by Jackson's river, which unites with the Cow Pasture river on the E. border, to form the James river; and it is also drained by Potts and Dunlap creeks. The main Alleghany chain forms its boundary on the N. W.; a ridge called Middle Mountain extends along the S. E. border, and the Warm Springs and Peter's mountains extend across the middle of the county. The scenery of this county is remarkably fine, particularly at the passage of Jackson's river, through one of the mountains. The soil of the valleys is fertile.. Indian corn, wheat, oats, hay, and butter are the staples. In 1850 the county produced 88,426 bushels of corn; 16,937 of wheat; 42,210 of oats; 1,211 tons of hay, and 29,712 pounds of butter.

M. A. SANTOS & SON,

WHOLESALE DRUGGISTS,

NORFOLK,

Have Constantly on Hand an Extensive Supply of

DRUGS, PAINTS, OILS, VARNISHES, DYE STUFFS,

Perfumery, Looking Glass Plates, Window, Coach, and Hollow Glass, Glue, Sand Paper, Chewing Tobacco, Snuff, Garden, Flower and Grass Seeds, Surgeons' Instruments, &c.

SEGARS.

PRINCIPE, HAVANA, PLANTATION AND HALF SPANISH.

MANUFACTURERS OF

Genuine Blistering Plaster, Myrtle Tooth Wash, Persian Hair Oil, Improved Indelible Ink, Permanent Blue Ink, Superior Cologne Water, Whooping Cough Syrup, Syrup of Sarsaparilla, U. S. B., Fluid Extract of Buchu, &c.

Agents for Sarsaparilla Preparations and nearly all Patent Medicines. Dealers in Garden and Grass Seeds, Exotic Plants, Evergreens, Trees, &c.

☞ Country Storekeepers, Druggists, and Physicians supplied at low rates.

W. P. STEWART & CO.

IMPORTERS,

Wholesale and Retail Dealers in

FOREIGN AND DOMESTIC

DRY GOODS,

No. 25 MAIN, AND No. 17 HILL STREET,

NORFOLK.

Orders punctually attended to.

THOMAS LEWIS,

FASHIONABLE READY MADE

CLOTHING STORE,

NEXT DOOR TO WALTER'S HOTEL,

MAIN STREET, NORFOLK.

We have on hand a large and well selected stock of Coats, Pants, Vests, Linen Bosom Shirts, Netted Shirts and Draws, Gloves, Suspenders, Stocks Handkerchiefs, Umbrellas, Canton Draws, Collars, Bosoms, Socks, &c., &c., all of which

WILL BE SOLD LOW FOR CASH.

N. B. Clothing made to order at the shortest notice.

It contained in that year 2 iron furnaces, 2 forges, 2 flour mills. There were 10 churches, 153 pupils attending public schools, and 30 attending an academy. Iron ore is found in the county. The James River canal is designed to terminate at Covington, the county seat. A railroad is projected from this point to the Ohio river at Guyandotte. The Red Sweet Springs of this county have some celebrity, and have been finely improved. Capital, Covington. Population, 3,515, of whom 2,821 were free, and 694 slaves.

ALLEN'S CREEK, a post-office of Amherst county, Virginia.

ALPINE DEPOT, a post-office of Morgan county, Virginia.

ALTO, a post-office of Louisa county, Virginia.

ALUM ROCK, a post-office of Alleghany county, Virginia.

ALUM SPRINGS, a post-office of Rockbridge county, Virginia.

AMACETTA, a post-office of Wayne county, Virginia.

AMBLER'S MILLS, a post-office of Louisa county, Virginia.

AMELIA, a county toward the S. E. part of Virginia, has an area of 300 square miles. The Appomattox river forms about half of the boundary, inclosing it on nearly all sides excepting the south: it is also drained by Namazine Flat and Deep creeks. The surface is somewhat diversified; the soil of the valleys is naturally fertile, but impoverished by long cultivation. A portion of the land has been "turned out," and can be bought at a merely nominal rate. Indian corn, wheat, oats, tobacco, and butter are the staples. In 1850 the county produced 250,251 bushels of corn; 109,960 of wheat; 70,075 of oats; 1,786,788 pounds of tobacco, and 56,790 pounds of butter. It contained in that year 3 grist mills and 2 coach factories. There were 14 churches, 145 pupils attending public schools, and 61 attending academies or other schools. The county is intersected by the Richmond and Danville Railroad. Organized in 1734. Capital, Amelia Court House. Population, 9770, of whom 2951 were free, and 6819 slaves.

AMELIA COURT HOUSE, a post-village, capital of Amelia county, Virginia, 47 miles S. W. from Richmond; contains very few dwellings.

AMHERST, a county in the S. central part of Virginia, has an area of 418 square miles. The James river flows along its S. W. and S. E. borders, forming in its course almost a right angle, and constituting about half of the entire boundary. The Blue

Norfolk Furniture Depot,

No. 34 Mechanics' Hall, Main Street,

NORFOLK.

O'BRIEN & QUICK

Respectfully solicit the attention of strangers visiting the city to their stock of

CABINET FURNITURE,

Consisting of a well selected assortment of all articles suitable for the Parlor, Dining Room, Chamber and Kitchen, of good quality and city make, such as

Sofas,
Chairs,
Bureaus,
Wardrobes,
Safes,
Lounges,

Sideboards,
Sofa & Extension Tables,
Looking Glasses,

Of all sizes and prices; Cottages, French and high-post Bedsteads, Children's Chairs,—all kinds—Washstands, with and without marble, and other articles too tedious to enumerate.

☞ We pledge ourselves to sell (articles being equal,) 5 per cent. less than any other establishment.

Ridge forms the boundary of the county on the N. W., and the surface is beautifully diversified by mountains and valleys. The passage of James river through the Blue Ridge is a sublime feature in the scenery of this region. The soil is naturally fertile. Indian corn, wheat, oats, hay, tobacco, and butter are the staples. In 1850 the county produced 358,183 bushels of corn; 122,088 of wheat; 94,262 of oats; 948,261 pounds of tobacco, and 84,968 of butter. It contained 24 churches; 250 pupils attending public schools, and 130 attending academies and other schools. A canal has been opened along James river, on the border of the county. The county was formed from Albemarle in 1761. Capital, Amherst Court House. Population, 12,699, of whom 6746 were free, and 5953 slaves.

AMHERST COURT HOUSE, a small post village, capital of Amherst county, Virginia, about 15 miles N. by E. from Lynchburg.

AMISSVILLE, a small post-village of Rappahannock county, Virginia, 121 miles N. W. from Richmond, has about 75 inhabitants.

AMSTERDAM, a post-village of Botetourt county, Virginia, 181 miles W. from Richmond, contains 1 brick church and several tradesmen's shops.

ANANDALE, a post-office of Fairfax county, Virginia.

ANDERSON, a post-office of Walker county, Georgia.

ANDREWS, a post-office of Spottsylvania, Virginia.

ANGERONA, a post-office of Jackson county, Virginia.

ANNSVILLE, a small village of Dinwiddie county, Virginia, about 75 miles N. W. by W. from Norfolk.

ANTHONY'S CREEK, a post-office of Greenbrier county, Virginia.

APPERSONS, a post-office of Charles City county, Virginia.

APPOMATTOX, a river in the S. E. part of Virginia, rises in Appomattox county, and flowing in a general eastward direction forms the boundary between several counties on each side, passes by the city of Petersburg and enters the James river at City Point. It is a valuable stream for navigation, having a narrow and deep channel. Large vessels ascend to Petersburg, about 20 miles from its mouth, and batteaus to Farmville, perhaps 100 miles farther. The whole length is estimated at 150 miles. The navigation is good at all seasons for boats of 5 or 6 tons to Farmville.

APPOMATTOX, a county in the S. E. central part of Virginia, has an area of 260 square miles. It is bounded on the N. W.

NORFOLK
SEMINARY FOR YOUNG LADIES.

This Institution has been recently established in this City, and is now in successful operation, and offers peculiar advantages to those young Ladies wishing to obtain a finished

CLASSICAL, ENGLISH, AND ORNAMENTAL EDUCATION,

being provided with accomplished Teachers in every department, and every suitable facility, viz: A COMMODIOUS SCHOOL HOUSE, *Recitation Rooms, Maps, Globes and Reference Books*, that every branch may be illustrated and fully understood. The Course of Study is as extensive as in any Female College.

FACULTY.

Mrs. M. A. Southgate,
Rhetoric, Botany, &c.

Miss Susan F. Smith,
English Literature.

Miss Delia H. Wynne,
English Literature and Music.

Mr. James Southgate, jr.,
Latin, Greek and Mathematics.

Professor Geay,
Modern Languages

Professor W. F. Grabau,
Music—Piano and Guitar.

TERMS.

Board and Tuition, per session of 5 months,........	$100 00
Washing,........	7 50
Tuition in Literary Department,........	25 00
" " Academic "	20 00
" " Preparatory, "	15 00
French, Spanish, German and Italian, each,........	10 00
Music on Piano,........	25 00
Music on Guitar........	20 00
Painting in Oil Colors,........	15 00
Painting in Water Colors,........	10 00
Grecian Embroidery and Worsted Work,........	5 00
Use of Instrument,........	2 50

by the James river and canal, and drained by the sources of the Appomattox river, from which the name is derived. The surface is diversified by several small ranges of mountains, and covered with extensive forests. The soil is generally fertile. Indian corn, wheat, oats, tobacco, hay, and butter are the staples. In 1850 the county produced 186,855 bushels of corn; 76,345 of wheat; 92,116 of oats; 964,100 pounds of tobacco, and 83,299 of butter. It contained in that year 1 iron furnace, 5 flour mills, and 2 tanneries. There were 22 churches, 361 pupils attending academies and other schools. It is intersected by the South Side railroad, extending from Petersburg to Lynchburg, which is a source of much improvement. A plank road has lately been laid in the county. Capital, Clover Hill. Population, 9193, of whom 4394 were free, and 4799 slaves.

Appomattox Depot, a post-office of Amelia county, Virginia.

Aquia creek, in the E. part of Virginia, flows through Stafford county into the Potomac river, and is navigable for schooners several miles from its mouth.

Aquia, a post-office of Stafford county, Virginia.

Ararat, a post-office of Patrick county, Virginia.

Arbuckle, a post-office of Mason county, Virginia.

Arcola, or Gum Springs, a post-village of Loudoun county, Virginia, 146 miles N. from Richmond, contains a few stores.

Arnolton, a small village in the S. W. part of Campbell county, Virginia, about 110 miles W. S. W. from Richmond.

Ashland, a post-office of Cabell county, Virginia.

Ashton's Mills, a post-office of Frederick county, Virginia.

Aspengrove, a post-office of Pittsylvania county, Virginia.

Assamoonic, a post-office of Southampton county, Virginia.

Athens, a post-office of Caroline county, Virginia.

Auburn, a post-office of Fauquier county, Virginia.

Augusta, a county in the central part of Virginia, forming part of the Great Valley which extends along the N. W. base of the Blue Ridge. The area is about 900 square miles. The Shenandoah and Calf Pasture rivers arise in the county. The S. E. boundary is formed by the Blue Ridge; the surface of the valley is elevated and hilly; the soil is calcareous, and very productive of grain and grass. In 1850 there were raised 419,006 bushels of wheat; 505,800 of Indian corn; 250,026 of oats; 15,225 tons of hay, and 275,483 pounds of butter. The

quantity of hay was greater than was produced in any other county of the State, except Rockingham county; and that of butter greater than in any except Loudoun county. There were 41 flour and grist mills, 20 saw mills, 2 iron furnaces, 2 iron forges, 13 tanneries. It contained 41 churches; 745 pupils attending public schools, and 226 attending academies or other schools. Fine limestone underlies a great part of the valley, and extensive beds of anthracite coal have been opened. A description of the celebrated Weyer's cave of this county will be found under the head of VIRGINIA. The Central railroad of Virginia passes through this county and connects it with Richmond. Augusta county was formed from Orange in 1738. Capital, Staunton. Population, 24,610, of whom 10,557 were free, and 5053 slaves.

AUSTINVILLE, a post-office of Wythe county, Virginia.

AVO, a post-office of Patrick county, Virginia.

AYLETT'S, a post-office of King William county, Virginia, 28 miles N. E. from Richmond.

BATCHELOR'S HALL, a post-office of Pittsylvania county, Va.

BACK CREEK, in the N. E. part of Virginia, rises in Frederick county, flows northeastward through Berkely, and enters the Potomac about 10 miles N. from Martinsburg.

BACK CREEK VALLEY, a post-office of Frederick county, Va.

BACON'S CASTLE, a post-office of Surry county, Virginia.

BAILEYSBURG, a small post village near the S. extremity of Surry county, Virginia, about 50 miles S. S. E. from Richmond.

BAKER'S RUN, a post-office of Hardy county, Virginia.

BALCONY FALLS, a post-office of Rockbridge county, Virginia, on James river, 153 miles, W. from Richmond.

BALLARDSVILLE, a small post village in the N. part of Boone county, Virginia, about 250 miles W. by N. from Richmond.

BALLSVILLE, a post-office of Powhatan county, Virginia.

BANISTER, a river in the S. part of Virginia, rises in Pittsylvania county, and flowing in a south-easterly course, enters the Dan river in Halifax county, about 10 miles below the village of Banister. It is navigable by batteaus from its mouth to Meadsville.

BANISTER, or HALIFAX COURT-HOUSE, a flourishing post-village, capital of Halifax county, Virginia, on Banister river, 10 miles above its entrance into the Dan river, and on the Richmond

and Danville railroad, 120 miles S. W. from Richmond. The situation is elevated and pleasant. Banister has a very active mercantile business, in which a capital of $200,000 is invested. It is the terminus of three lines of stages. The Banister river is navigable for batteaus from its mouth to Meadsville, about 10 miles above the court-house. A rich mine of plumbago has recently been opened, 6 miles from this place. Population in 1853, about 1,600.

BAPTIST VALLEY, a post-office of Tazewell county, Virginia.

BARBER'S CROSS ROADS, a post-office of Isle of Wight county, Virginia.

BARBOUR, a county in the N. W. part of Virginia, has an area of 330 square miles. It is intersected by Tygart's Valley river, a branch of the Monongahela, and also drained by Buchanan river and Elk creek. The western part is hilly and the eastern mountainous: a ridge called Laurel Mount, forms the E. boundary. The soil in many parts is good, and particularly adapted to pasturage. Indian corn, wheat, and grass are the staples. In 1850 this county produced 209,673 bushels of corn; 38,110 of wheat, 9916 tons of hay, and 147,649 pounds of butter. It contained 19 churches, and 546 pupils attending public schools. Stone coal and iron are abundant. It was formed in 1843, from Harrison, Lewis, and Randolph, and derived its name from a distinguished family of Virginia. Capital, Philippi. Population, 9005, of whom 8892 were free, and 113 slaves.

BARBOURSVILLE, a small post-village, capital of Cabell county, Virginia, on the Guyandotte river, 7 miles from its entrance into the Ohio, and 352 miles W. N. W. from Richmond. The main road leading from the Virginia Springs to the Ohio river passes through this village. Population, about 250.

BARBOURSVILLE, a small post-village of Greene county, Virginia, 76 miles N. W. from Richmond, has a pleasant situation, and contains several stores and mechanic shops.

BARBOURVILLE, a post-office of Orange county, Virginia.

BARHAMSVILLE, a post-office of New Kent county, Virginia.

BARKSDALE, a post-village of Halifax county, Virginia, 132 miles S. W. from Richmond.

BARNETT'S MILLS, a small post-village of Fauquier county, Virginia, on the Rappahannock river, 93 miles N. by W. from Richmond.

BARRACKSVILLE, a village of Marion county, Virginia, on the Baltimore and Ohio railroad.

BARRY'S BRIDGE, a post-office of Lunenburg county, Virginia.

BARTER BROOK, a post-office of Augusta county, Virginia.

BASNETTSVILLE, a post-office of Marion county, Virginia.

BATH, a county in the central part of Virginia, contains 725 square miles. It is intersected by the Cowpasture and Jackson's rivers, branches of James river. The surface is traversed by valleys and mountain ridges of the Alleghany chain, and displays a profusion of magnificent scenery. The highlands produce valuable timber and excellent pasture. The productions are corn, wheat, oats, hay, fruits, wool, butter, &c. Cattle and horses are exported. In 1850 there were raised 73,671 bushels of Indian corn; 17,502 of wheat; 42,676 of oats; 3853 tons of hay; 12,271 pounds of wool, and 36,120 of butter. There were 9 saw mills, 8 grist mills, 4 wool-carding mills, 2 agricultural implement manufactories, and 2 tanneries. It contained 6 churches; 70 pupils attending public schools, and 85 attending academies or other schools. Limestone and iron ore are abundant. Bath county derives its name from the numerous medicinal springs which occur in it. Capital, Warm Springs. The county was organized in 1791. Population, 3426, of whom 2479 were free, and 947 slaves.

BATH COURT HOUSE, Bath county, Virginia. See WARM SPRINGS.

BATH or BERKELEY SPRINGS, Capital of Morgan county, Virginia, is situated about 3 miles from the Potomac river and Baltimore and Ohio railroad, and 186 miles N. N. W. from Richmond. The Berkeley springs, which arise in the midst of this town, are esteemed very efficacious in dyspepsia, neuralgia, chronic rheumatism, &c., and are frequented by large numbers of invalids. The temperature is 74°. The accommodations are elegant, and sufficiently extensive for 700 persons.

BATH ALUM, a post-office of Bath county, Virginia.

BATH ALUM SPRINGS, a fashionable watering place of Bath county, Virginia, situated at the eastern base of the "Warm Springs Mountain," 164 miles W. N. W. from Richmond, and 6 miles S. E. from the Warm Springs. The proprietor has expended above thirty thousand dollars in the erection of buildings and other improvements.

BAY VIEW, a post-office of Northampton county, Virginia.

BEALETON, a post-office of Fauquier county, Virginia.

BEATY'S MILLS, a post-office of Marion county, Virginia.

BEAVER CREEK, a post-office of Campbell county, Virginia.

BEAVER DAM, a post-office of Goochland county, Virginia.

BEAVER DAM DEPOT, a post-office of Hanover county, Virginia.

BECKLEY, a post-village, capital of Raleigh county, Virginia, 210 miles in a direct line W. from Richmond. The county has a mountainous surface, and is very thinly inhabited.

BEDFORD, a county in the S. central part of Virginia, has an area of 504 square miles. The James river forms its N. E., the Staunton its S. W. boundary, and Otter creek flows through the middle. The county has an elevated surface, and the scenery is delightful, the N. W. boundary passing along the summit of the Blue Ridge, which here attains in the Peaks of Otter the height of 5,307 feet above the sea. The soil is highly productive. Indian corn, wheat, oats, tobacco, and butter are the staples. In 1850 there were raised 602,362 bushels of corn; 178,990 of wheat; 294,852 of oats, the greatest quantity produced in any one county of the State, except Halifax county; 1,955,436 pounds of tobacco, and 238,233 of butter. There were 5 tanneries, 14 flour, grist and saw mills, and 4 tobacco factories. It contained 40 churches; 638 pupils attending public schools, and 72 attending academies or other schools. The James River canal passes along the border, and the Virginia and Tennessee railroad passes through the county. Bedford county was formed from Lunenburg in 1763. Capital, Liberty. Population, 24,080, of whom 14,019 are free, and 10,061 slaves.

BEELER'S STATION, a post-office of Marshall county, Virginia.

BELLE HAVEN, a post-office of Accomac county, Virginia.

BELLEVILLE, a post-office of Wood county, Virginia.

BELLFAIR MILLS, a post-office of Stafford county, Virginia.

BELL POINT, a post-office of Giles county, Virginia.

BELL ROI, a post-office of Gloucester county, Virginia.

BELL'S CROSS ROADS, a post-office of Louisa county, Virginia.

BELL'S VALLEY, a post-office of Rockbridge county, Virginia, 147 miles W. from Richmond.

BELMONT, a post-office of Loudoun county, Virginia.

BENNETT'S MILLS, a post-office of Lewis county, Virginia.

BENTEVOGLIO, a post-office of Albemarle county, Virginia.

SPENCER SCOTT. A. L. SCOTT. P. H. PORTER. G. A. KEEN.

S. & A. L. SCOTT & CO.

FASHIONABLE

MERCHANT TAILORS

AND MANUFACTURERS OF

GENTLEMEN'S CLOTHING,

OF THE BEST QUALITY,

SYCAMORE STREET,

PETERSBURG.

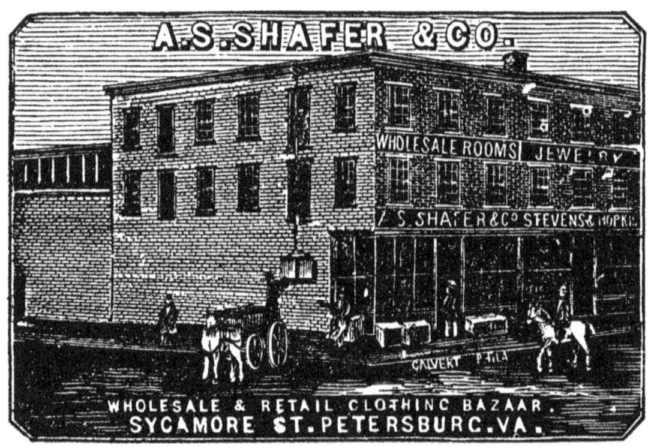

L. C. TAPPEY,

UPHOLSTERER & PAPER HANGER,

No. 58 SYCAMORE STREET,

PETERSBURG,

MANUFACTURES TO ORDER AND KEEPS ON HAND

BEDS,

SPRING, HAIR, COTTON & SHUCK

MATTRESSES,

PAPER HANGINGS, CURTAIN GOODS,

CARPETS AND RUGS,

WINDOW BLINDS, SHADES, OIL CLOTHS, &c.

☞ Orders for any article in his line, from town or country customers, executed with dispatch.

Bentleyville, a post-village of Halifax county, Virginia, on Staunton river, 115 miles S. W. from Richmond.

Bentonville, a post-office of Warren county, Virginia.

Bergen's Store, a post-office of Pittsylvania county, Virginia.

Berkeley, a county in the N. E. part of Virginia, bordering on the Potomac river, which separates it from Maryland, has an area of about 250 square miles. It is bounded on the S. E. by Opequan creek, and intersected by Back creek. It occupies the most northern part of the Valley of Virginia. The surface is hilly and mountainous, the soil of the valleys and river bottoms is mostly fertile. Wheat, Indian corn, oats, hay, and butter are the staples. In 1850 the county produced 356,234 bushels of wheat; 171,686 of corn; 50,531 of oats; 6,667 tons of hay, and 157,850 pounds of butter. There were 24 flour mills, 11 grist mills, 14 saw mills, 1 paper mill, 1 railroad machine shop, and 4 tanneries. It contained 30 churches, 550 pupils attending public schools, and 102 attending academies or other schools. Limestone underlies a large part of the county; anthracite coal and iron are abundant. The streams furnish considerable water-power. The county is intersected by the Baltimore and Ohio Railroad. Organized in 1772, and named probably from Sir William Berkeley, formerly Governor of Virginia. Capital, Martinsburg. Population, 11,771, of whom 9,815 were free, and 1,956 slaves.

Berkley Springs, Virginia. See Bath.

Berlin, a post-office of Southampton county, Virginia.

Berryville, a small town, capital of Clarke county, Virginia, on Opequan creek, and on the turnpike from Winchester to Washington, 12 miles E. from the former, and 158 miles N. by W. from Richmond. It has some trade, and contains an academy and 1 or 2 churches.

Bestland, a post-office of Essex county, Virginia.

Bethany, a post-village of Brooke county, Virginia, on Buffalo creek, 7 miles from the Ohio river, and 16 miles N. E. from Wheeling. The surrounding country is fertile and beautiful. The village is the seat of Bethany College, which was established in 1841, by Alexander Campbell, a Baptist minister.

Bethel, a post-office of Mercer county, Virginia.

Beverly, a post-village, capital of Randolph county, Virginia, on the Tygart's Valley river, 210 miles N. W. from Richmond, is pleasantly situated in a valley among the Alleghany mountains. It has a few stores and shops.

Bickley's Mills, a post-office of Russel county, Virginia.

Big Bend, a post-office of Gilmer county, Virginia.

Big Cedar Creek, a post-office of Green Brier county, Virginia.

Big Cole, a post-office of Boone county, Virginia.

Big Glades, a post-office of Russel county, Virginia.

Big Island, a post-office of Bedford county, Virginia.

Big Lick, or Gainsboro, a small post-village of Roanoke county, Virginia, 170 miles W. by S. from Richmond. The Virginia and Tennessee railroad passes through it.

Big Meadow, a post-office of Grayson county, Virginia.

Big Otter, a post-office of Braxton county, Virginia.

Big Skin Creek, a post office of Lewis county, Virginia.

Big Springs, a post-office of Pocahontas county, Virginia.

Birch River, a post-office of Nicholas county, Virginia, 284 miles W. by N. from Richmond.

Birchton, a post-office of Braxton county, Virginia.

Black Face, a post-office of Nottoway county, Virginia.

Black Heth, a post-office of Chesterfield county, Virginia.

Black Rock, a post-office of Rappahannock county, Virginia.

Blacks and Whites, a post-office of Nottoway county, Virginia.

Blacksburg, a post-village of Montgomery county, Virginia, about 200 miles W. by S. from Richmond. Population, about 250.

Blackshire's, a post-office of Marion county, Virginia.

Blacksville, a post-village of Monongalia county, Virginia, 20 miles N. W. from Morgantown. The line between Virginia and Pennsylvania passes through the village. It has a few stores, and about 100 inhabitants.

Black Walnut, a small post-village of Halifax county, Virginia, 138 miles S. W. from Richmond.

Black Water, a post-office of Sussex county, Virginia.

Blackwater River, in the S. part of Virginia, rises at the foot of the Blue Ridge, and flows eastward through Franklin county into the Staunton river.

A. G. McILWAINE. R. D. McILWAINE. R. A. MARTIN. J. B. DUNN.

McILWAINE, SON & CO.

GROCERS

AND

COMMISSION MERCHANTS,

PETERSBURG.

CITY GUN, RIFLE & PISTOL

Manufacturing and Importing Warehouse.

CHARLES LEONARD,

No. 15 OLD STREET,

PETERSBURG,

SIGN OF THE RIFLE.

Merchants and Sportsmen can always find the largest assortment in the State of Double and Single Guns, Rifles, Pistols, Bowie Knives, Sporting Apparatus, Fishing Tackle, Walking Canes, Diamond Grain Powder, Cutlery and Fancy Articles of every description.

N. B. All kinds of fire arms manufactured and repaired.

BOOTH & SOMMERS,

SYCAMORE STREET,

PETERSBURG,

MANUFACTURERS OF AND DEALERS IN

PLAIN JAPANNED AND PLANISHED TIN WARE,

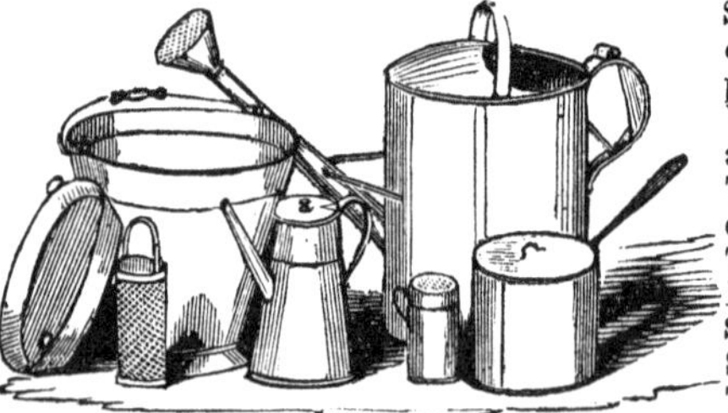

Stoves, Ranges and Hot air Furnaces of the latest and most approved patterns; Sheet Iron and Copper Ware, Force and Suction Pumps of any capacity. Always on hand, Tea and Coffee Urns, Chafing Dishes, Oyster Dishes, Dish Covers, Tea and Coffee Biggins, Nursery Lamps with China Cup and Kettle. Sheet Lead, Zinc and Iron Coal Scuttles, Scales and Weights, Bath Tubs, Water Rams, Water Closets, Stationary Washstands, Lead Pipe—all sizes—Copper, Iron, &c.

Also, Roofing, Guttering and Jobbing.

Blackwater River, in the S. E. part of Virginia, rises in Prince George county, and flowing in a general S. E. course, falls into Nottoway river, near the boundary between Virginia and North Carolina, after forming the boundary between Southampton on the right, and Isle of Wight and Nansemond on the left.

Block House, a post-office of Scott county, Virginia.

Bloomery, a post-office of Hampshire county, Virginia.

Bloomfield, a post-village of Loudoun county, Virginia, 168 miles N. by W. from Richmond, has a church and a few stores.

Bloomsburg, a post-village in Halifax county, Virginia, about 116 miles W. S. W. from Norfolk.

Blue Ridge, a post-office of Botetourt county, Virginia.

Blue Spring, a post-office of Smythe county, Virginia.

Bluestone, a small river in the S. W. part of Virginia, rises in Tazewell county, flows north-eastward through Mercer county, and falls into the New river, 5 miles above the mouth of the Greenbrier.

Blue Stone, a post-office of Tazewell county, Virginia.

Body Camp, a post-office of Bedford county, Virginia.

Bolington, a post-office of Loudoun county, Virginia.

Bonbrook, a post-office of Franklin county, Virginia.

Bone Creek, a post-office of Ritchie county, Virginia.

Boone, a new county in the W. S. W. part of Virginia, has an area of 525 square miles. It is bounded on the N. E. by Coal river, an affluent of the Kanawha, and also drained by Little Coal river and Laurel creek. The surface is hilly and mountainous, and mostly covered with forests. The soil in some parts is fertile. Indian corn, wheat, oats, grass, and ginseng are the staples. In 1850 this county produced 134,040 bushels of corn; 3,215 of wheat; 19,185 of oats, and 33,996 pounds of butter. There were 2 saw mills, and 1 coal-mining establishment. It contained 6 churches, and 171 pupils attending public schools. Boone county was formed out of portions of Logan and Kanawha counties, and named in honor of Daniel Boone, the renowned pioneer of the West. Capital, Boone Court-House. Population, 3,237, of whom 3,054 were free, and 183 slaves.

Boone Court-House, a small post-village, capital of Boone county, Virginia, on the Little Coal river, 245 miles in a direct

HALSEY, TUPMAN & CO.

LATE B. F. HALSEY & Co.

MANUFACTURERS AND DEALERS IN

FURNISHING GOODS,

CUSTOM WORK,

East side of Sycamore Street,

PETERSBURG.

R. W. HARRISON & CO.

WHOLESALE AND RETAIL DEALERS IN

HATS, CAPS, FURS,

UMBRELLAS,

Walking Canes, &c. &c.

SYCAMORE STREET,

PETERSBURG.

W. AUGUSTUS MUIR. SAMUEL STEVENS.

MUIR & STEVENS,

IMPORTERS AND DEALERS IN

CHINA, EARTHENWARE AND GLASS,

Pier, Mantle, and Toilet Looking Glasses,

BRITANNIA AND PLATED WARE,

Cornell's Solar and Lard Lamps,

REFRIGERATORS,

SHOWER BATHS & WATER COOLERS,

Girandoles, Casters, &c.

WHOLESALE AND RETAIL,

Corner of Sycamore and Bollingbrook Streets,

PETERSBURG.

☞ **Particular attention paid to Packing.**

line W. from Richmond. The surrounding country is very thinly settled.

Boon's Mills, a post-office of Franklin county, Virginia, 184 miles W. by S. from Richmond.

Boothsville, a village of Marion county, Virginia, with about 150 inhabitants.

Booton's Tan-Yard, a post-office of Madison county, Virginia.

Boston, a post-office of Culpepper county, Virginia.

Botetourt, a county in the S. W. central part of Virginia, has an area of 550 square miles. It is intersected by James river, and also drained by Craig's and Catawba creeks. The Blue Ridge forms the S. E. boundary, and the surface is broken by other high ridges. The famous Peaks of Otter rise near the boundary between this and Bedford county. The soil in some parts is good. Indian corn, wheat, oats, hay, and butter are the staples. In 1850 this county produced 368,141 bushels of corn; 121,694 of wheat; 154,063 of oats; 5,531 tons hay, and 140,885 pounds of butter. There were 6 flour mills, 5 saw mills, 3 iron furnaces, 2 iron foundries, 1 iron forge, and 1 woolen factory. It contained 21 churches, 428 pupils attending public schools, and 62 attending academies or other schools. The James River canal has been opened from Richmond to Buchanan, in this county, which is intersected by the Virginia and Tennessee railroad. Organized in 1769, and named in honor of Governor Botetourt. Capital, Fincastle. Population, 14,908, of whom 11,172 were free, and 3,736 slaves.

Botetourt Springs, a post-village in Roanoke county, Virginia.

Bower's, a post-office of Southampton county, Virginia.

Bowlesville, a post-office of Fluvanna county, Virginia.

Bowling Green, a post-village, capital of Caroline county, Virginia, on the road from Richmond to Fredericksburg, 45 miles N. from the former, is situated in a fertile and healthy region. It contained 2 churches, 3 stores, 2 mills, and about 300 inhabitants.

Bowman, a post-office of Marshall county, Virginia.

Bowman's Mills, a post-office of Rockingham county, Virginia.

Bowyer's Knob, a post-office of Fayette county, Virginia.

NOAH WALKER & CO.

WHOLESALE AND RETAIL

CLOTHIERS,

SYCAMORE STREET;

PETERSBURG,

Keep constantly on hand a very large and splendid assortment of superior ready made clothing of their own manufacture, embracing every variety of style and fashion which for make, quality of material or price, defy competition. They also have an endless variety of gent's furnishing goods of their own importation and manufacture, such as handkerchiefs, cravats, neck ties, shirts, undershirts, gloves, hosiery, umbrellas, &c., all of which will be sold at as low a figure as can be purchased in any of the Northern or Eastern markets.

T. W. BRADBURY,

DEALER IN

FOREIGN AND DOMESTIC

DRY GOODS,

PETERSBURG.

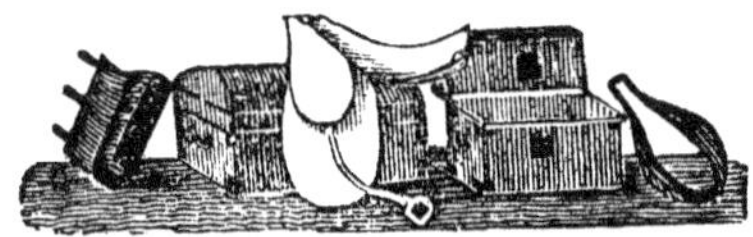

DANIEL PERKINSON,

SADDLE AND HARNESS

MANUFACTURER,

AND DEALER IN

CARRIAGES, BUGGIES, &c.

BANK STREET,

PETERSBURG.

Boydtown, a post-village, capital of Mecklenburg county, Virginia, 6 miles N. from the Roanoke river, and 90 miles S. W. from Richmond. A plank-road, 76 miles long, connects it with Petersburg. It contains 3 churches and a number of stores. About a mile from Boydtown is the Randolph Macon College, under the direction of the Methodists.

Brake's Run, a post-office of Hardy county, Virginia.

Branchville, a post-office of Southampton county, Virginia.

Brandonville, a thriving post-village of Preston county, Virginia, 280 miles N. W. from Richmond. A turnpike road extends from this village to Fishing creek.

Brandy Station, a post-office of Culpepper county, Virginia.

Braxton, a county in the N. W. central part of Virginia, has an area of 646 square miles. It is intersected by the Elk and Little Kanawha rivers, and also drained by Holly river and Birch creek. The surface is hilly and rough, extensively covered with forests, the soil is well watered and generally fertile. Indian corn and grass are the staples. In 1850 this county produced 137,120 bushels of corn, and 72,409 pounds of butter. There were 6 grist mills, 4 saw mills, 2 wool-carding mills, 1 salt-boiling establishment, and 1 tannery. It contained 2 churches. Stone coal is found in several places, and salt springs in the North part of the county. This county was formed in 1836, and named in honor of Carter Braxton, one of the signers of the Declaration of Independence. Capital, Sutton. Population, 4,212, of whom 4,123 were free, and 89 slaves.

Braxton Court-House, Virginia. See Sutton.

Brentsville, a small post-village, capital of Prince William county, Virginia, on the Occoquan creek, 104 miles N. from Richmond, contains 1 church, and a few stores.

Brickland, a post-office of Lunenburg county, Virginia.

Bridgeport, a small post village in Harrison county, Virginia, about 200 miles N. W. from Richmond.

Bridge Water, a small post-village of Rockingham county, Virginia, on the North river, a branch of the Shenandoah, about 125 miles N. W. from Richmond, has an active trade, and contains several mills propelled by water-power.

Bridle Creek, a post-office of Grayson county, Virginia.

Briscoe Run, a post-office of Wood county, Virginia.

Bristersburgh, a post-office of Fauquier county, Virginia.

JOHN STEVENSON. JAMES WEDDELL.

STEVENSON & WEDDELL,

Importers and Wholesale Dealers in

STAPLE AND FANCY

DRY GOODS,

SYCAMORE STREET,

PETERSBURG.

JAMES KERR. LEONARD A. MARBURY.

KERR & MARBURY,

IMPORTERS AND DEALERS IN

China, Glass, Earthen & Stone Ware,

Britannia and Silver Plated Ware,

LAMPS, LOOKING GLASSES,

Shower Baths,

REFRIGERATORS, &c.

SYCAMORE, OPPOSITE TABB STREET,

PETERSBURG.

☞ Particular attention paid to packing goods for transportation.

THOMAS W. RIZSTON,

PREMIUM CLOTHING STORE,

PETERSBURG.

Having all my stock made to order, I am always prepared to give the very best made garments at the lowest prices. Call and examine my superior stock of

CLOTHING AND FURNISHING GOODS.

Always on hand a large assortment at fair prices. My Motto is "Quick Sales and Small Profits, for Cash."

Bristol Station, a post-office of Prince William county, Va.

Brixton, a post-office of Alexandria county, Virginia.

Broadford, a post-office of Smythe county, Virginia.

Broad Run, of Loudoun county, Virginia, flows northward, and falls into the Potomac about 10 miles S. E. from Leesburg.

Broad Run, a small stream in the N. E. part of Virginia, rises in Fauquier county, flows south-eastward, and unites with Cedar run to form the Occoquan river, about 1 mile below Brentsville. It is a valuable mill stream.

Brock's Gap, a post-office of Rockingham county, Virginia.

Brooke county, Virginia, is part of the narrow strip which forms the N. N. W. extremity of the State, bordering on Pennsylvania and Ohio, containing 75 square miles. The Ohio river bounds it on the W. The surface is hilly; the soil highly productive. Indian corn, wheat, hay, wool, pork, and beef are the staples. In 1850 there were raised 150,571 bushels of corn; 65,516 of wheat; 4,755 tons of hay, and 123,572 pounds of wool, (being the greatest quantity produced in any one county of the State.) There were 5 flour mills, 4 saw mills, 1 cotton factory, 1 iron foundry, 1 glass manufactory, and 2 earthenware manufactories. It contained 11 churches, and 103 pupils attending academies or other schools. The county contains coal and iron ore. Population, 5,054, of whom 5,023 were free, and 31 slaves.

Brooklynn, a post-village of Halifax county, Virginia, about 140 miles S. W. from Richmond.

Brooklynn, a thriving post-village of Halifax county, Virginia, 145 miles S. W. from Richmond.

Brookneal, a small post-village in Campbell county, Virginia, 120 miles W. S. W. from Richmond.

Brooksville, a post-office of Albemarle county, Virginia, 100 miles W. by N. from Richmond.

Brownsburg, a post-village of Rockbridge county, Virginia, 143 miles W. from Richmond, contains a few stores and mills. Population, about 200.

Brown's Cove, a post-office of Albemarle county, Virginia, 109 miles W. N. W. from Richmond.

Brownsville, a post-office of Greenbrier county, Virginia.

Brucetown, a small post-village of Frederick county, Va.

Bruington, a post-office of King and Queen county, Virginia.

Q. & W. L. MORTON,

IMPORTERS AND DEALERS IN

HARDWARE, CUTLERY, GUNS,

AND

BOLTING CLOTHS,

SYCAMORE STREET.

PETERSBURGH.

N. B.—Agents for the sale of all kinds of Coal and Wrought Mill Irons, and French Burr and Esopas Mill Stones.

JOHN A. MUIR. CHARLES S. BRYAN.

MUIR & BRYAN,

IMPORTERS AND WHOLESALE DEALERS IN

FOREIGN & AMERICAN

HARDWARE, CUTLERY, GUNS, &c.

SIGN OF THE 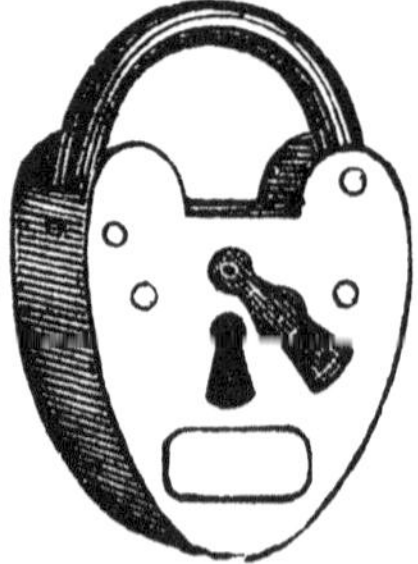 SYCAMORE ST.

PETERSBURG.

BRUNSWICK, a county in the S. S. E. part of Virginia, bordering on North Carolina, has an area of 600 square miles. The Nottaway river forms its N. E. boundary, the Roanoke touches its S. W. extremity, and the Meherrin river flows through the middle of the county from W. to E. The surface is somewhat undulating; the soil of medium quality. The exhausted lands have recently been improved by the use of guano and other manures. Tobacco, Indian corn, wheat, oats, sweet potatoes, hay, and cotton are the staples. In 1850 this county produced 2,155,017 pounds of tobacco; 394,200 bushels of corn; 79,287 of wheat; 98,782 of oats; 34,959 of sweet potatoes; 2,889 tons of hay, and 108 bales of cotton. There were 3 tanneries, and 1 agricultural implement manufactory. It contained 11 churches, 108 pupils attending public schools, and 164 attending academies or other schools. It is intersected by a plank-road leading to Petersburg. Organized in 1720. Capital, Lawrenceville. Population, 13,894, of whom 5,438 were free, and 8,456 slaves.

BUCHANAN, a village of Botetourt county, Virginia, on James river, 181 miles W. from Richmond, and opposite the village of Pattonsburg, with which it is connected by a fine bridge. It is situated in a beautiful valley, at the head of navigation, and has an active trade. Both villages together contain 3 or 4 churches, 1 bank, 1 printing office, and several tobacco factories and mills. Incorporated in 1832. This place is connected with Richmond by the James River canal, and has a turnpike extending to Salem.

BUCHANAN RIVER, in the N. W. part of Virginia, rises in Randolph county, and flowing in a N. N. E. course, enters the Tygart's Valley river a little above Philippi, in Barbour county.

BUCKHANNON, a post-office of Upshur county, Virginia.

BUCKINGHAM, a county in the S. E. central part of Virginia, has an area of 680 square miles. The James river forms its boundary on the N. and N. W., the Appomattox washes the Southern border; it is also drained by Willis and Slate rivers. The surface varies from level to hilly: Willis mountain, in the S. E. part, is the principal elevation. The soil is not naturally rich, excepting in the vicinity of the rivers. Tobacco, Indian corn, wheat, oats, and live stock are the staples. In 1850 this county produced 304,711 bushels of corn; 133,819 of wheat;

DUNN & SPENCER,

PETERSBURG,

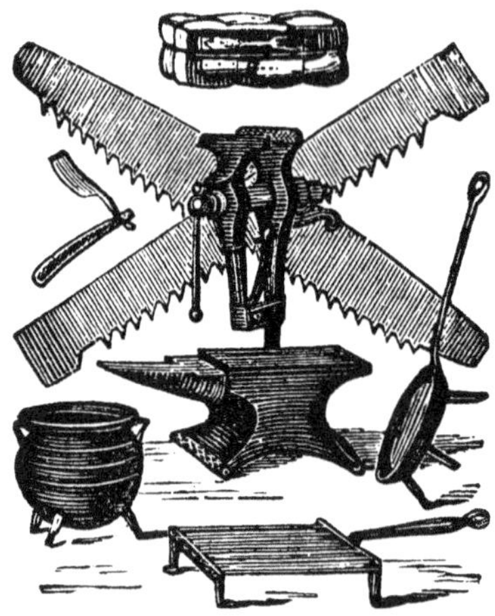

IMPORTERS AND DEALERS IN

ENGLISH, GERMAN AND AMERICAN

HARDWARE,

CUTELRY, GUNS,

AND

EDGE TOOLS,

Mill Stones, Mill Irons,

BOLTING CLOTH,

Leather and India Rubber

MACHINE BELTING,

Railroad Shovels, Picks, &c.

AT LOWEST PRICES.

JULIUS ROBINSON,

(SUCCESSOR TO NEWMAN & GREENTREE,)

WHOLESALE AND RETAIL DEALER IN

Ready-Made Clothing,

Of every Description,

West side of Sycamore street,

Next to the Confectionery Store of S. H. Marks & Son,

PETERSBURG,

Is prepared to furnish all kinds of Goods pertaining to his line of business with dispatch, and at the very lowest prices.

☞ COUNTRY MERCHANTS who purchase goods from me, and do not sell in the season in which they are bought, can return them and receive new goods for the next season.

JULIUS ROBINSON.

117,091 of oats; 2,342,987 pounds of tobacco, and 83,480 of butter. There were 2 flour and grist mills, 3 saw mills, and 1 tannery. It contained 19 churches, 194 pupils attending public schools, and 96 attending academies or other schools. Gold mines are worked in the vicinity of Willis mountain, and yield large profits. Valuable slate quarries have been opened on the bank of Slate river, and iron is found in the county. The Buckingham White Sulphur springs were once more frequented than at present. The James River canal passes along the border of the county. Organized in 1761, and named from Buckingham, a county of England. Capital, Maysville. Population, 13,837, of whom 5,676 were free, and 8,161 slaves.

Buckingham Court-House, a post-office of Buckingham county, Virginia.

Buckingham Mine, a post-office of Buckingham county, Va.

Buckland, a small post-village of Prince William county, Virginia, 116 miles N. from Richmond, contains 1 church and a few shops.

Buena Vista Furnace, a post-office of Rockbridge county, Virginia.

Buffalo, a thriving post-village of Putnam county, Virginia, is pleasantly situated on the Great Kanawha river, 21 miles from its mouth, and 340 miles W. by N. from Richmond. It has excellent facilities for trade and manufactures, and is the most important place in the county. The hills in the vicinity contain large bodies of bituminous coal and iron ore. Population, about 400.

Buffalo Ford, a post-office of Wythe county, Virginia.

Buffalo Forge, a post-office of Rockbridge county, Virginia, 156 miles W. from Richmond.

Buffalo Gap, a post-office of Augusta county, Virginia.

Buffalo Springs, a post-office of Amherst county, Virginia.

Buford's, a post-office of Bedford county, Virginia.

Bull Creek, a post-office of Wood county, Virginia.

Bulltown, a post-office of Braxton county, Virginia.

Bunger's Mill, a post-office of Greenbrier county, Virginia.

Bunker Hill, a post-office of Bedford county, Virginia.

Burgess's Store, a post-office of Northumberland county, Va.

Burke's Garden, a post-office of Tazewell county, Virginia.

Burke's Station, a post-office of Fairfax county, Virginia.

MITCHELL & TYLER,

No. 108 MAIN STREET,

RICHMOND,

DEALERS IN

CLOCKS, WATCHES AND JEWELRY,

SILVER

AND

PLATED WARE,

MILITARY

AND

FANCY GOODS,

GOLD, SILVER,

STEEL,

AND

TORTOISE SHELL

SPECTACLES

AND

EYE GLASSES,

Of best quality and in great variety. Glasses fitted to same.

☞ Particular attention paid to WATCH WORK in all its branches.

Burkesville, a post-village of Prince Edward county, Virginia, on the Richmond and Danville railroad, at its junction with the South Side railroad, 52 miles W. from Petersburg.

Burlington, a small village of Roanoke county, Virginia.

Burlington, a small village of Hampshire county, Virginia, on Patterson's creek, 205 miles N. W. from Richmond.

Burnersville, a post-office of Barbour county, Virginia.

Burning Spring, a post-office of Wirt county, Virginia.

Burnt Ordinary, a post-office of James City county, Va.

Burntville, a post-office of Brunswick county, Virginia.

Burwell's Bay, a post-office of Isle of Wight county, Va.

Bush's Mills, a post-office of Lewis county, Virginia.

Butcher's Store, a post-office of Randolph county, Virginia.

Cabell, a county in the W. part of Virginia, bordering on the Ohio river, which separates it from the State of Ohio, has an area of 448 square miles. The Guyandotte river flows through the county into the Ohio. The surface is uneven; the soil partly fertile. Indian corn and oats are the staples. In 1850 this county produced 281,826 bushels of corn, and 44,912 of oats. There were 9 flour and grist mills, 9 saw mills, 4 wool-carding mills, and 4 tanneries. It contained 14 churches, 274 pupils attending public schools, and 20 attending an academy. The main thoroughfare from Richmond to the Ohio river passes through the county. Formed in 1809, and named in honor of William H. Cabell, governor of Virginia in 1808. Capital, Barboursville. Population 6299, of whom 5910 were free, and 389 slaves.

Cabell Court House, a post-office of Cabell county, Virginia.

Cabin Point, a small post-village in Surry county, Virginia.

Cacapon, pronounced cap'on, or Great Cacapon, a river in the north part of Virginia, rises among the Allegany mountains in Hardy county; flows through Hampshire and Morgan counties, and falls into the Potomac about 4 miles west from Bath or Berkeley springs. Its general course is N. N. E., and its whole length is estimated at near 140 miles. It flows through a mountainous region, abounding in iron and stone coal, and affords a copious supply of water-power. The Little Cacapon traverses Hampshire county, a few miles west from the river just described, and enters the Potomac 5 miles below the junction of the main branches of that river.

SILVER MEDAL

Awarded by the First Virginia Mechanics' Institute,

November 16, 1854,

TO

M. P. SIMONS,

DAGUERREOTYPIST,

151 MAIN STREET, EAGLE SQUARE,

RICHMOND.

Likenesses taken equally well in all weather, and from the smallest size to the size of life. Call and see the extensive collection of specimens,—among them are doubtless many of your own friends.

OSBORNE'S GREAT NATIONAL

OPPOSITE THE EXCHANGE BANK.

Every department connected with this establishment has been fitted up in superb order. GILT CORNICES, with our NATION'S STARS AND STRIPES, ornament the many windows. The ladies' dressing room will be found lacking in nothing that will add to the comfort of the visiters. The floors are covered with beautiful carpet—the walls with rich satin paper. Portraits of all our eminent Statesmen adorn the walls—large Chandeliers ornament the place.

The SKY-LIGHT is the very best that can be built. The work-room is furnished with one of W. H. Lewis' Patent Buffing Machines.

None can form an idea of this establishment without paying it a visit. All the proprietor asks is a call, to satisfy one and all that he has no need of self-praise, or need of humbugging the people with *flesh-tints*,—neither does he need to advertise to work for nothing. His motto is, *fair prices and good work.*

A. J. OSBORNE.

☞ One of NUNNS & CLARK'S PIANOS kept for the use of the ladies.

CACAPON DEPOT, a post-office of Morgan county, Virginia.

CACAPONVILLE, a post-office of Hampshire county, Virginia.

CA IRA, a post-village of Cumberland county, Virginia, on Willis river, 60 miles west from Richmond, has a church, a flour mill, and a few shops.

CALFPASTURE RIVER, Virginia. See NORTH RIVER.

CALLAGHANS, a post-office of Allegany county, Virginia.

CALLANDS, a post-office of Pittsylvania county, Virginia.

CAMPBELL, a county in the south part of Virginia, has an area of 576 square miles. James river forms its boundary on the North, and Staunton river on the South; it is also drained by Otter and Falling rivers. The surface is hilly and broken, the soil generally productive. Tobacco, Indian corn, wheat, oats, and hay are the staples. The uplands are partly covered with forests of the oak and pine. In 1850 the county produced 2,534,730 pounds of tobacco; 339,267 bushels of corn; 100,500 of wheat; 167,254 of oats, and 2168 tons of hay. There were 36 tobacco factories, 1 cotton and woolen factory, 5 flour mills, and 4 iron foundries. It contained 42 churches, 3 newspaper offices; 344 pupils attending public schools, and 650 attending academies and other schools. Iron ore is found, and granite is abundant in the county. The James River canal passes along the northern border. The Virginia and Tennessee railroad, and the South side railroad, connect with each other at Lynchburg, the chief town of the county. Organized in 1784, and named in honor of General William Campbell, an officer in the war of the Revolution. Capital, Campbell Court House. Population, 23,245, of whom 12,379 were free, and 10,866 slaves.

CAMPBELL COURT HOUSE, a small village, capital of Campbell county, Virginia, 130 miles W. S. W. from Richmond, and 12 miles S. from Lynchburg.

CANICELLO, a post-office of Rockbridge county, Virginia.

CANNADAY GAP, a post-office of Floyd county, Virginia.

CAPE CHARLES, the southern point of Northampton county Va., at the entrance of Chesapeake bay, 25 miles N. N. E. from Norfolk. The lighthouse is N. E. from Cape Charles, on the North end of Smith's Island, and shows a revolving light, about 65 feet above the level of the sea. Lat. 37° 3′ N., lon. 76° 2′ W.

CAPE HENRY, on the N. E. coast of Virginia, at the entrance of Chesapeake bay, on the S. side 12 miles S. by W. from Cape

RICHMOND
BOOK AND STATIONERY WAREHOUSE.
A. MORRIS,
BOOKSELLER,
STATIONER & PUBLISHER,

DEALER IN

PIANOS,

MELODEONS,

And other Musical Instruments, as well as

FANCY GOODS,

WRITING DESKS,

PAINTINGS,

ENGRAVINGS, &c.

97 MAIN STREET,

RICHMOMD,

Has constantly on hand, and for sale at moderate prices, a general assortment of

SCHOOL BOOKS,

LAW, MEDICAL, RELIGIOUS AND

MISCELLANEOUS BOOKS,

In every department of Literature, Science and Art.

PUBLISHER OF

CALL'S VIRGINIA REPORTS, [6 vols.] WASHINGTON'S REPORTS, [2 Vols.] TATE'S INDEX TO THE VIRGINIA REPORTS, TATE'S AMERICAN FORM BOOK,—TUCKER'S COMMENTARIES ON THE LAWS OF VIRGINIA,—ROBINSON'S PRACTICE, and other Law Books.

Charles. Lat. 36° 56′ N., lon. 76° 4′ W. On it is a fixed light, 120 feet above the level of the sea.

CAPEVILLE, a post-village of Northampton county, Virgihia, on the E. side of Chesapeake bay.

CAPON BRIDGE, a post-office of Hampshire county, Virginia.

CAPON SPRINGS, a post office of Hampshire county, Virginia.

CARLTON'S STORE, a post-office of King and Queen county, Virginia.

CAROLINE, a county in the E. part of Virginia, has an area of about 480 square miles. The Rappahannock forms its boundary on the N., and the Mattapony flows through the county. The surface is uneven; the soil near the rivers is fertile. Indian corn, wheat, and tobacco are the staples. In 1850 this county produced 629,994 bushels of corn; 173,353 of wheat, and 663,155 pounds of tobacco. There were 42 flour, grist, and saw mills, 2 manufactories of coaches, 2 of agricultural implements, and three tanneries. It contained 28 churches; 616 pupils attending public schools, and 115 attending academies or other schools. The Federicksburg and Richmond railroad passes through the county. Organized in 1727. Capital, Bowling Green. Population, 18,456, of whom 7795 were free, 10,661 slaves.

CARROLL, a county in the S. S. W. part of Virginia, bordering on North Carolina, has an area of 440 square miles. The New river, or Kanawha, flows along the western border of the county, which is also drained by Reedy Island river and Chestnut creek. The Blue Ridge forms its boundary on the S. E. Much of the land is rough and hilly; the greater part, however, is well adapted to grazing. Indian corn, wheat, oats, hay, horses, cattle, and swine are the staples. In 1850 this county produced 132,189 bushels of corn; 11,578 of wheat; 82,847 of oats; 2,715 tons of hay, and 56,178 pounds of butter. There were 2 grist mills, 3 iron forges, and 3 tanneries. It contained 12 churches, and 900 pupils attending public schools. Copper, iron ore, and lead are found in the county. The Grayson Sulphur Springs, on the bank of New river, have some reputation as a place of summer resort. It is intersected by two new turnpike-roads. Organized 1842, having been previously included in Floyd county. Capital, Hillsville. Population, 5909, of whom 5755 were free, and 154 slaves.

AUG. ANDERSON. ALEXIUS GREENE. J. A. HAWES.

AUG. ANDERSON & CO.

MANUFACTURERS & JOBBERS OF

STRAW & SILK GOODS,

AND

MILLINERY ARTICLES,

RICHMOND.

E. D. KEELING,

MERCHANT TAILOR,

AND DEALER IN

GENTLEMEN'S

FURNISHING GOODS,

136 Main Street,

2d Door below 12th,

RICHMOND.

**Shirts, Collars,
Bosoms, Stocks,
Cravats,
Dressing Robes,
Ties, Scarfs,
Hosiery, Gloves,
Suspenders,
Drawers,
Under Shirts,
Handkerchiefs, &c.**

Strangers and citizens generally are invited to call and examine my extensive stock of fashionably made

CLOTHING,

Consisting of every variety of

GARMENTS,

Made from goods of the best importation and in the best and neatest style. Also on hand

CLOTHS,

DOESKIN CASSIMERES

AND

VESTINGS

Of every description.

CARRSVILLE, a post-office of I. of Wight county, Virginia.

CARTER'S BRIDGE, a post-office of Albemarle county, Virginia, 91 miles W. by N. from Richmond.

CARTERSVILLE, a village of Cumberland county, Virginia, on the James river and canal, 47 miles W. from Richmond. It has 1 church, several stores, and about 50 dwellings.

CASCADE, a post-office of Pittsylvania county, Virginia.

CASSVILLE, a post-office of Monongalia county, Virginia.

CASTLE CRAIG, a post-office of Campbell county, Virginia.

CASTLEMAN'S FERRY, a post-office of Clark county, Virginia.

CASTLETON, a post-office of Culpepper county, Virginia.

CATAWBA CREEK, in the S. W. central part of Virginia, flows north-eastward through Roanoke county, and enters the James river in Botetourt county.

CATAWBA, a post-office of Botetourt county, Virginia.

CAVE SPRING, a post-office of Roanoke county, Virginia.

CEDAR BLUFF, a post-office of Tazewell county, Virginia.

CEDAR CREEK, a post-office of Frederick county, Virginia.

CEDAR FIELDS, a post-office of Isle of Wight county, Virginia.

CEDAR GROVE MILLS, a post-office of Rockbridge county, Virginia, 145 miles W. from Richmond.

CEDAR HILL, a post-office of Augusta county, Virginia.

CEDAR MOUNT, a post-office of Wythe county, Virginia.

CEDAR POINT, a post-office of Page county, Virginia.

CEDAR RUN, a creek in the N. E. part of Virginia, rises in Fauquier county, flows E., and unites with Broad run, near Brentsville, in Prince William county, forming the Occoquan.

CEDAR SPRING, a post-office of Wythe county, Virginia.

CEDARVILLE, a post-office of Washington county, Virginia.

CENTRAL PLAINS, a post-office of Fluvanna county, Virginia.

CENTRAL POINT, a post-office of Caroline county, Virginia.

CENTRE CROSS, a post-office of Essex county, Virginia.

CENTREVILLE, a post-village of Fairfax county, Virginia, 27 miles W. from Washington, contains 1 church, and a few stores. Population, about 250.

CENTREVILLE, a small village of Monroe county, Virginia, on Indian creek, about 240 miles W. from Richmond.

CENTREVILLE, a small village of Tyler county, Virginia, on Middle Island creek, 16 miles from the Ohio river, and 7 miles

from Middlebourn, the county seat. It has turnpikes leading in several directions, and contains a number of stores.

CHALK LEVEL, a post-office of Pittsylvania county, Virginia.

CHAMBERS' MILLS, a post-office of Buckingham county, Va.

CHAMBLISSBURG, a post-village of Bedford county, Virginia, 150 miles W. by S. from Richmond.

CHANCELLORSVILLE, a post-village of Spottsylvania county, Virginia, 76 miles N. by W. from Richmond.

CHANTILLY, a post-office of Fairfax county, Virginia.

CHAPMANVILLE, a post-office of Logan county, Virginia.

CHARLEMONT, a post-office of Bedford county, Virginia.

CHARLES CITY, a county in the S. E. part of Virginia, has an

W. H. HARRISON,
Born in this county, February 9, 1773.

JOHN TYLER,
Born in this county, March 29, 1790.

area of 184 square miles. James river forms its entire boundary on the S. and the Chickahominy on the N. and E. The surface is rolling. Indian corn and wheat are the staples. In 1850 this county produced 178,940 bushels of corn, and 81,229 of wheat. There were six saw mills. It contain 13 churches, 92 pupils attending academies or other schools. James river is navigable by steamboats on the border of the county. Charles City was one of the eight original shires into which Virginia was divided in 1634. It has given birth to two Presidents of the United States, Harrison and Tyler. Capital, Charles City Court House. Population, 5,200, of whom 2,436 were free, and 2764 slaves.

CHARLES CITY COURT HOUSE, a post-village, capital of Charles City county, Virginia, 30 miles S. S. E. from Richmond.

CHARLESTON, a handsome post-town, capital of Kanawha county, Virginia, is situated on the North bank of the Great Kanawha river, at the junction of Elk, 60 miles from the Ohio, 308 miles from Richmond. The river at this place is about 300 yards wide, and is navigable for steamboats 16 miles above. The principal thoroughfare from the S. W. to the Virginia Springs and Richmond passes through it; the great Railroad from Covington to the Ohio river, when completed, will doubtless bring large accessions to its rapidly increasing trade and importance. Its principal street extends about two miles on the bank of the Kanawha. It contains a court house, a jail, a large number of stores, of all kinds, several steam mills, saw and flour mills, tan-yards, cooper shops, &c.; 4 or 5 churches, schools, a branch bank, 4 hotels, a printing office, from which is issued the old and well established weekly paper, Kanawha Republican, and about 250 dwelling houses. Population, about 2000. The county courts are held on the second Monday in every month; quarterly, in March, June, August, and November. The district court of the United States is held here twice each year. The county around contains abundance of iron, coal, and salt springs.

CHARLESTOWN, a flourishing post-village, capital of Jefferson county, Virginia, on the Winchester and Potomac railroad, 168 miles N. from Richmond, 60 miles N. W. from Washington, and 8 miles S. W. from Harper's Ferry. It is surrounded by a fertile and beautiful region, which forms part of the Valley of Virginia. Colonel Charles Washington, a brother of General Washington, resided at this place, and was the proprietor of the land on which the town is built. Charlestown contains 3 or 4 churches, 1 academy, 1 bank, and about a dozen stores. Population estimated at 1500.

CHARLOTTE county, in the S. S. E. part of Virginia, has an area of 550 square miles. Stauton river washes its entire S. W. border. The surface is uneven; the soil is partly fertile and partly poor. Tobacco, Indian corn, wheat, and oats are the staples. In 1850 this county produced 3,868,040 pounds of tobacco; 372,867 bushels of corn; 85,653 of wheat; and 171,872 of oats. There was one tannery, besides some other establishments. It contained 25 churches, and 436 pupils attending public schools. The Richmond and Danville railroad passes through the county.

Formed from Lunenburg in 1794. Capital, Marysville. Population, 13,955, of whom 4967 were free, and 8988 slaves.

CHARLOTTESVILLE, a flourishing town, capital of Albemarle county, Virginia, on the right bank of the Rivanna river, and on the Central railroad, 81 miles W. by N. from Richmond, and 123 miles S. W. from Washington. It is beautifully situated in a fertile valley, and is connected by railroad with Richmond and other towns. One mile W. from the town is the University of Virginia, which was founded in 1819, under the auspices of Thomas Jefferson, and is endowed by the State. In 1852 it had 400 students, and a library of 18,000 volumes. An observatory is attached to this institution. Monticello, the residence of Jefferson, who was a native of Albemarle county, is 3 miles distant. Charlottesville contains churches of the Presbyterians, Episcopalians, Baptists, and Methodists, 2 banks, and 4 newspaper offices. Population in 1853, about 2600.

CHATHAM, a post-office of Smyth county, Virginia.

CHATHAM HILL, a post-office of Smyth county, Virginia.

CHEAT BRIDGE, a post-office of Preston county, Virginia.

CHEAT RIVER, of Virginia, the largest affluent of the Monongahela, is formed by the junction of the Laurel, Glade, Shavers, and Dry forks, which rise among the Allegany mountains, near the northern border of the Pocahontas county, and unite in the N. central part of Randolph county. Flowing thence N. and N. W. through Preston and Monongalia counties, it enters the Monongahela at the S. W. extremity of Fayette county, Pennsylvania. It traverses a hilly country, abounding in stone coal and iron, and well adapted to grazing. It is navigable 40 miles above Rowlesburg, (on the Baltimore and Ohio railroad,) though not in the lower part of its course, and furnishes fine water-power at several places.

CHERRY HILL, a post-office of Brooke county, Virginia.

CHERRY STONE, a post-office of Northampton county, Virginia.

CHESAPEAKE bay, the largest bay in the United States, enters Virginia between Cape Charles and Cape Henry, lat. about 37° N., lon. 76° W., and extends into Maryland as far as 39° 36′ N. lat., 76° 3′ W. lon. The length, following the curve, is about 200 miles; the breadth varies from 4 to 40 miles. The distance from Cape Charles to Cape Henry is about 12 miles. Probably no other bay on the globe is marked with so many arms or es-

CHAS. H. ROWLAND. THOS. B. ROWLAND. G. WM. ROWLAND.

ROWLAND & BROTHERS,

WHOLESALE GROCERS

AND

Commission Merchants,

NORFOLK.

GEORGE L. CROW'S

FURNACE, RANGE AND STOVE DEPOT,

WATER STREET, NORFOLK,

ROOFER, COPPERSMITH, PLUMBER, &c.

Copper, Tin, Japan, and Sheet Iron Ware, &c.

HOT AIR FURNACES,

A new and superior article possessing advantages over all others, in giving sufficient warmth, a full supply of unburnt air, producing in the apartments warmed a delightfully agreeable atmosphere of summer temperature, requiring little attention, easily regulated, consumes little fuel, very heavy and durable, and lower in price than any.

LATROBE HEATERS and other kinds put up at short notice on moderate terms

A NEW AND SUPERIOR COOKING RANGE,

Embracing all the modern improvements, embracing Beauty, Durability and Economy in the use of fuel, with perfect efficiency in operation. The simplicity of its construction, and the consequent facility with which it is managed, particularly commend it to the attention of those in want of a FIRST CLASS COOKING RANGE or STOVE.

tuaries as the Chesapeake. These are of various dimensions, and of the most fantastic forms. While many of them serve as outlets or reservoirs to the waters of the different rivers of Maryland and Virginia, others are scarcely fed by any permanent stream, being nothing more than mere arms or projections from the sea. The depth of the Chesapeake is sufficient for the largest ships to ascend the main bay nearly to the mouth of the Susquehanna. South-west from Cape Henry the rivers, harbors, and sounds are shallow; but with the Chesapeake commence deep bays which continue at no great distance from each other to the N. E. extemity of the Atlantic coast of the United States. The region drained by the Chesapeake bay, and the rivers flowing into it, embraces an area of about 70,000 square miles.

CHESTERFIELD, a county in the S. E. part of Virginia, has an area of 300 square miles. The Appomattox river forms its whole southern boundary, and the James river on the N. E. separates it from Henrico county and Richmond city. The surface is uneven, and the soil inferior, except the river bottoms. Indian corn, wheat, and oats are the staples. In 1850 this country produced 333,938 bushels of corn; 95,875 of wheat; 116,690 of oats, and 218,562 pounds of tobacco. It contains 5 cotton factories, 6 coal mines, and one iron foundry. There were 34 churches, and 567 pupils attending public schools. Coal is procured in considerable quantities from the mines of this county. The Richmond and Petersburg railroad passes through it. The county was formed from Henrico in 1748. Capital, Chesterfield Court House. Population, 17,489, of whom 8873 were free, and 8616 slaves.

CHESTERFIELD COURT HOUSE, a post-village, capital of Chesterfield county, Virginia, about 12 miles S. S. W. from Richmond.

CHESTNUT GROVE, a thriving post-village of Pittsylvania county, Virginia, near Sandy creek, 173 miles W. S. W. from Richmond, contains 3 stores, several tobacco factories, and about 100 inhabitants.

CHICKAHOMINY river, in the S. E. part of Virginia, rises in Hanover county and falls into York river about 8 miles above Jamestown. It divides Henrico and Charles City counties on the right from Hanover, New Kent, and James City counties on the left. It furnishes extensive water-power.

NORFOLK FEMALE INSTITUTE,

Rev. ARISTIDES S. SMITH, A. M.,

PRINCIPAL.

This Institution was designed to furnish to parents in the South a school in which they can secure for their daughters a thorough, practical, accomplished and Christian education; and it is believed that it offers advantages equal to any that can be obtained elsewhere.

The buildings are spacious and elegant, and are situated in a retired and pleasant part of the city.. The grounds attached to the Institute, embracing three-fourths of an entire square, are ornamented with a profusion of trees and shrubbery, and furnish ample room for both amusement and exercise.

The course of study is extensive, and is designed not only to aid the pupil in the acquisition of knowledge, but also to discipline the mind and train it to correct habits of thought and reflection.

The last Annual Catalogue shows a list of 126 pupils from six States, and nine instructors, all of them, with one exception, *gentlemen* of high attainments in their respective departments, and of much experience in the business of teaching. The Teacher of French, a native of France, and a lady of refined manners and finished education, resides in the Institute, and thus affords the boarding pupils peculiar facilities for learning to speak the language fluently and correctly.

TERMS, PER SESSION OF FIVE MONTHS.

Payable one half in advance, September 15th and the remainder in February 15.

Board, Washing, Bed, Bedding, Fuel and Lights	$175 00
Tuition in English Branches,	50 00
" " Modern Languages, each	20 00
" " Drawing and Painting,	20 00
" " Music on Piano or Guitar, with use of Instruments, $55,	75 00
" " Vocal Music,	10 00

REFERENCES:

Right Rev. Wm. Meade, D. D., and Rt. Rev. J. Johns, D. D., of Virginia. Rt. Rev. Thomas Atkinson, D. D., of N. C., Right Rev. N. H. Cobb, D. D., Ala., Rev. E. M. Forbes, Elizabeth City, N. C., Rev. L. L. Smith, Warrenton, N. C.

CHICKAHOMINY, a post-office of Hanover county, Virginia.

CHILDRESS'S STORE, a post-office of Montgomery county, Va.

CHINCOTEAGUE, a post-office of Accomack county, Virginia.

CHRISTIANSBURG a post-village, capitol of Montgomery county, Virginia, on the stage route from Richmond to Nashville, and on the Virginia and Tennessee railroad, 200 miles West by South from the former. It was laid out in 1792, and contains 2 churches and 1 bank, Population in 1853, about 500.

CHRISTIANSVILLE, a small post-village in Mecklenburg county, Virginia, about 77 miles South West from Richmond.

CHUCKATUCK, a post-village of Nansemond county, Virginia, 10 miles North from Suffolk, the county seat.

CHURCH HILL, a post-office of Halifax county, Virginia.

CHURCHVIEW, a post-office of Middlesex county, Virginia.

CHURCHVILLE, a post-village of Augusta county, Virginia, on the turnpike from Staunton to Parkersburg, 128 miles North West from Richmond, contains 2 churches, 2 stores, and 2 schools.

CIRCLEVILLE, a post-office of Loudoun county, Virginia.

CITY POINT, a post-village and port of entry of Prince George county, Virginia, on James river, at the mouth of the Appomattox, 34 miles South East from Richmond, and 10 miles E. N. E. from Petersburg. There is a good landing here, at which the large vessels engaged in the trade of Richmond and Petersburg receive and discharge their cargoes. The Appomattox railroad extends from this place to Petersburg.

CLARKE, a county in the North East part of Virginia, has an area of 208 square miles. It is traversed by the Shenandoah river, and also drained by Opequan creek. It occupies part of the Great Valley of Virginia, which extends along the North West base of the Blue Ridge. The surface is beautifully diversified; the soil is based on blue limestone, and is highly productive. Wheat, Indian corn, oats, hay, butter and live stock, are the staples. In 1850 there were raised 306,210 bushels of wheat; 166,897 of corn; 36,915 of oats; 2,236 tons of hay, and 75,314 pounds of butter. There were 7 flour mills, 2 grist mills, 4 tanneries, and 2 manufactories of cabinet ware. It contained 11 churches; 98 pupils attending public schools, and 77 attending academies or other schools. This county is intersected by the Winchester railroad and by several turnpike-roads. 'It

PHŒNIX FOUNDRY,

LYNCHBURG,

A. G. DABNEY,

PROPRIETOR.

The proprietor of this Foundry is Prepared to furnish all kinds of

IRON AND BRASS

CASTINGS,

MILL

MACHINERY,

STATIONARY

AND PORTABLE

STEAM ENGINES,

Saw Mills, &c.

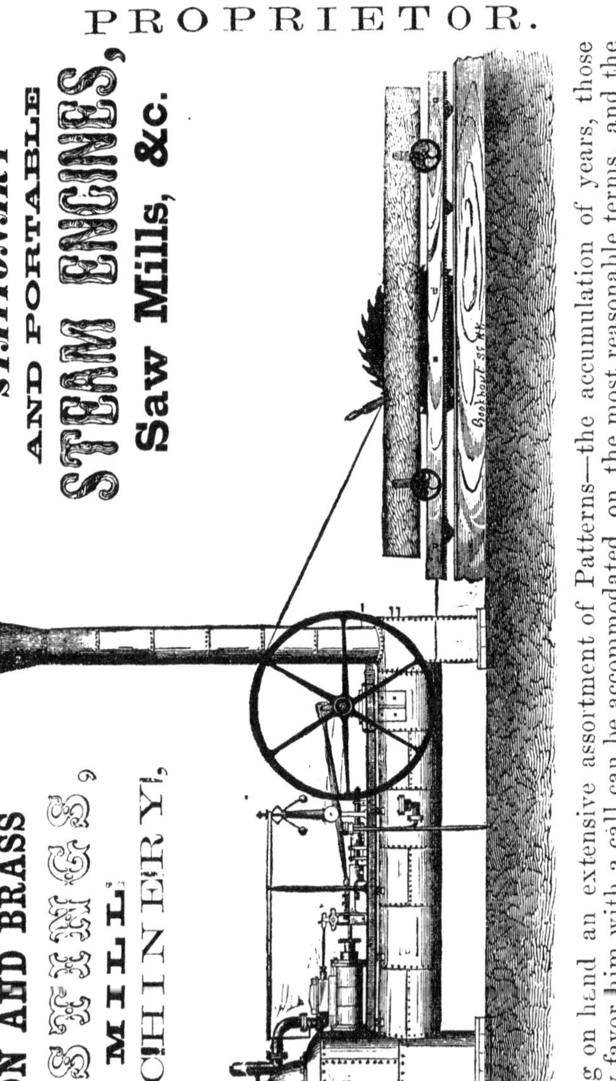

Having on hand an extensive assortment of Patterns—the accumulation of years, those who may favor him with a call can be accommodated on the most reasonable terms, and the quality of materials and workmanship are warranted unsurpassed by any establishment in the North or South.

was organized in 1836 out of part of Frederick county, and named in honor of General George Roger Clark, an officer in the war of the Revolution. Capital, Berryville. Population, 7352; of whom 3738 were free, and 3614 slaves.

CLARKSBURG, a post-village, capital of Harrison county, Virginia, on the W. fork of Monongahela river, at the mouth of Elk creek, 220 miles N. W. from Richmond. It is situated on a high table-land, environed by hills. It contains 2 or 3 churches, 2 academies, 2 printing offices, and numerous stores. Stone coal abounds in the vicinity. The North-Western railroad, a branch of the Baltimore and Ohio railroad, passes through the village. Population in 1853, about 1200.

CLARK'S MILLS, a post-office of Washington county, Virginia.

CLARKSVILLE, a thriving post-village of Mecklenburg county, Virginia, on the S. bank of the Roanoke river, a little below the confluence of the Dan and Staunton, 102 miles S. W. from Richmond. It has increased more rapidly perhaps during the last ten years than any other village in the state. It contains 3 or 4 churches, 1 bank, and over 1000 inhabitants. About 2000 hogsheads of tobacco are annually inspected here, and sent down the river in batteaux. A railroad is projected from this place to the Gaston and Raleigh railroad.

CLAY'S POINT, a post-office of Lewis county, Virginia.

CLAYSVILLE, a small village of Wood county, Virginia, on the Little Kanawha river, 7 miles above Parkersburg, has a fine water-power and several mills. Population about 100.

CLEAR BRANCH, a post-office of Washington county, Virginia.

CLEAR FORK, a post-office of Tazewell county, Virginia.

CLEEK'S MILLS, a post-office of Bath county, Virginia.

CLENDENIN, a post-office of Kanawha county, Virginia.

CLIFT MILLS, a post-office of Fauquier county, Virginia.

CLIFTON, a post-office of King George county, Virginia.

CLIFTON FORGE, a post-office of Allegany county, Virginia.

CLINCH RIVER, of Virginia and Tennessee, rises among the mountains in the S. W. part of the former State, and flowing S. W. into Tennessee, traverses the valley between Clinch and Powell mountains, and unites with the Holston and Kingston, to form the Tennessee river. Its whole length is estimated at above 200 miles. Small boats navigate it for more than half that distance.

Cline's Mill, a post-office of Augusta county, Virginia.

Clintonsville, a small post-village of Greenbrier county, Virginia, 231 miles W. from Richmond.

Clover Creek, a post-office of Highland county, Virginia.

Cloverdale, a post-office of Botetourt county, Virginia,

Cloverdale Hotel, a post-office of Bath county, Virginia.

Clover Green, a post-office of Spottsylvania county, Virginia.

Clover Hill, a pleasant post-village, capital of Appomatox county, Virginia, about 100 miles W. from Richmond, and 20 miles E. from Lynchburg. It is connected by a plank-road with James river, which is nearly 15 miles distant. The village has a handsome court house.

Club Creek, in the S. part Virginia, flows southward through Charlotte county, and enters the Staunton a few miles S. W. from Marysville.

Coal Hill, a post-office of Goochland county, Virginia.

Coal River, in the W. part of Virginia, rises in Fayette county, and flowing in a general N. W. direction, falls in the Great Kanawha river, in Kanawha county, after a course of probably not less than 60 miles.

Coal River Marshes, a post-office of Raleigh county, Virginia.

Coalsmouth, a post-office of Kanawha county, Virginia.

Cobham, a post-office of Albemarle county, Virginia.

Coldstream, a post-village of Hampshire county, Virginia, 20 miles N. W. from Winchester. It has 2 churches, and 1 flouring mill.

Collierstown, a post-village of Rockbridge county, Virginia, 154 miles W. from Richmond.

Collins Settlement, a post-office of Lewis county, Virginia.

Columbia, a post-village of Fluvanna county, Virginia, at the confluence of the Rivanna and James rivers, and on the James River canal, 52 miles W. by N. from Richmond, contains 1 church and a few stores.

Columbia Furnace, a small post-village in Shenandoah county, Virginia, about 160 miles N. N. W. from Richmond.

Columbian Grove, a post-office of Lunenburg county, Virginia, 10 miles E. from Lunenburg Court House.

Coman's Well, a post-office of Sussex county, Virginia.

Competition, a beautiful and thriving post-village, capital of Pittsylvania county, Virginia, on a small branch of Banister

river, 160 miles, S. W. from Richmond. It is situated in a rich farming district, and contains a number of handsome residences.

CONCORD, a post-office of Appomattox county, Virginia.

CONRAD'S STORE, a post-office of Rockingham county, Virginia.

CONWAY, or MIDDLE river, of Virginia, is a small stream flowing into the Rapidan, on the boundary between Greene and Madison counties.

COON'S MILL, a post-office of Boone county, Virginia.

COOPER'S, a post-office of Franklin county, Virginia, 172 miles W. S. W. from Richmond.

COOPER'S PLAINS, a post-office of Steuben county, Virginia.

COROWAUGH, a post-office of Isle of Wight county, Virginia.

COVE CREEK, a post-office of Tazewell county, Virginia.

COVESVILLE, a post-village of Albemarle county, Virginia, 103 miles W. N. W. from Richmond, has 1 church.

COVINGTON, a flourishing post-village, capital of Alleghany county, Virginia, on Jackson's river, a branch of James river, 196 miles W. by N. from Richmond. It is situated in a beautiful and healthful region among the Allegany mountains, and is to be the terminus of the James River canal, which is completed to Buchanan, in the adjoining county. Population in 1853, about 500.

COWPASTURE RIVER, of Central Virginia, unites with Jackson's river, near the E. extremity of Allegany county, forming the James river.

CRAB BOTTOM, a post-office of Highland county, Virginia.

CRAB ORCHARD, a post-office of Wythe county, Virginia.

CRAIG'S CREEK, in the S. W. central part of Virginia, rises in Giles and Montgomery counties, and falls into James river, in Botetourt county, after a course of about 50 miles.

CRAIG'S CREEK, a post-office of Botetourt county, Virginia.

CRAIG, a new county in the S. W. central part of Virginia. It is drained by the sources of Craig's creek, from which the name is derived. The surface is mountainous, the main Allegany extending along the N. W. border. The soil of the valleys is fertile. Indian corn, wheat, oats, and live stock are the staples. The census of 1850 furnishes no returns for this county, which was formed since that year out of parts of Giles, Botetourt, and Roanoke counties. Capital, Newcastle.

CRANBERRY PLAINS, a post-office of Carroll county, Virginia.

CRANBERRY SUMMIT, a thriving village of Preston county, Virginia, on the Baltimore and Ohio railroad, 243 miles West from Baltimore.

CRANESVILLE, a small post-village of Preston county, Virginia, about 250 miles N. W. from Richmond.

CRICHTON'S STORE, a post-office of Brunswick county, Virginia.

CRIGLERSVILLE, a post-office of Madison county, Virginia.

CROSS KEYS, a post-office of Rockingham county, Virginia.

CROSS ROADS, a post-office of Bedford county, Virginia.

CUB CREEK, a post-office of Charlotte county, Virginia.

CUCKOOVILLE, a post-office of Louisa county, Virginia, 46 miles N. W. from Richmond.

CULPEPPER, a county in the N. E. central part of Virginia, has an area of 673 square miles. The Southern and North-eastern borders are respectively washed by the Rapidan and by the North branch of the Rappahannock, which unite at the eastern extremity of the county. The N. part of the county is drained by Hazel river. The surface is finely diversified with hill and dale; the soil is of a deep red color, and highly productive. Wheat, Indian corn, oats, and wool are the staples. In 1850 there were raised 191,395 bushels of wheat; 359,670 of corn; 62,599 of oats; and 45,444 pounds of wool. There were 26 flour, grist, and saw mills; 2 woolen factories, and 1 agricultural implement manufactory. It contained 17 churches; 488 pupils attending public schools, and 105 attending academies or other schools. The Rappahannock river has been made navigable along the border of the county; small boats also navigate Hazel river. The county is intersected by the Orange and Alexandria Railroad, lately finished; and has a turnpike leading from the county seat to New Market. It contains several mineral springs, which are not yet much noted or improved. Organized in 1748, and named from Lord Culpepper, governor of Virginia in 1681. Population, 12,282, of whom 5599 were free, and 6683 slaves.

CULPEPPER COURT HOUSE, Virginia. See Fairfax.

CUMBERLAND, a county towards the S. E. part of Virginia, has an area of 310 square miles. The Appomattox bounds it on the S. E., the James river washes its N. border, and Willis river flows through the county. The surface is undulating;

the soil was originally fertile, but in some parts has been worn out. Wheat, Indian corn, and tobacco are the staples. In 1850 this county produced 118,616 bushels of wheat; 220,532 of corn; and 2,476,135 pounds of tobacco. There were 6 flour mills, 1 tobacco factory, and 1 iron foundry. It contained 16 churches; 275 pupils attending public schools, and 30 attending an academy. The county was formed from Goochland in 1748. Capital, Cumberland Court House. Population, 9751, of whom 3422 were free, and 6329 slaves.

CUMBERLAND COURT HOUSE, a post-village, capital of Cumberland county, Virginia, 55 miles W. from Richmond. It is situated on a ridge between the Appomattox and Willis rivers, about 5 miles from each.

CURDSVILLE, a small post-village of Buckingham county, Virginia, on Willis river, at the head of navigation. It has a large flouring mill.

DAGGER'S SPRINGS, a post-village of Botetourt county, Virginia, 18 miles N. from Fincastle. Extensive buildings have been erected for the entertainment of the public at this place.

DALLAS, a post-office of Marshall county, Virginia.

DANIELSVILLE, a post-village of Spottsylvania county, Virginia, 90 miles N. from Richmond.

DAN RIVER, of Virginia and North Carolina, rises in Patrick county, of the former state, at the S. E. base of the Blue Ridge, and flowing first S. E., it enters North Carolina, in Surrey county. It then pursues a general easterly direction, near the boundary between the two states, which it crosses no less than five times, and after a tortuous course of about 200 miles, it unites with the Staunton, or Roanoke, at Clarksville, in Mecklenburg county, Virginia. It is navigable by batteaus to Danville, Virginia, which is the principal town on its banks. The water-power at Danville is very abundant, but is not yet employed to any great extent. The area drained by this river is estimated at 4000 square miles.

DANVILLE, the principal village of Pittsylvania county, Virginia, on the Dan river, 5 miles from the North Carolina line, and 168 miles W. S. W. from Richmond. The town is pleasantly situated on high ground, near the head of navigation, and is a place of active business. It is surrounded by a fertile farming region, which abounds in stone coal, iron ore and lime-

stone. The canal which has been constructed around the falls at this place affords abundant water-power. A railroad is extending from Richmond to Danville. The village has 4 or 5 churches, 3 academies, 2 banks, and several iron foundries and mills. Population in 1850, 1514—in 1854, about 2500.

DARKSVILLE, a post-village of Berkley county, Virginia, on Sulphur Spring creek, 165 miles N. by W. from Richmond, contains 1 church and a few stores.

DARLINGTON HEIGHTS, a post-office of Prince Edward Co., Va.

DARVILLE, a post-office of Dinwiddie county, Virginia.

DAVIS' MILLS, a post-village of Bedford county, Virginia, 130 miles W. by S. from Richmond.

DAVIS' STORE, a post-office of Bedford county, Virginia.

DAWSONVILLE, a post-office of Greene county, Virginia.

DAYTON, a post-office of Rockingham county, Virginia.

DEATONSVILLE, a post-village of Amelia county, Virginia, 52 miles S. W. from Richmond.

DECKER'S CREEK, a post-office of Preston county, Virginia.

DEEP CREEK, a post-village of Norfolk county, Virginia, at the northern terminus of the Dismal Swamp canal, 10 miles S. from Norfolk. It has an active trade in shingles, which are procured from the Dismal Swamp, and shipped by schooners to the Northern cities.

DEERFIELD, a post-village of Augusta county, Virginia, 180 miles W. N. W. from Richmond.

DEER LICK, a post-office of Mason county, Virginia.

DE KALB, a post-office of Gilmer county, Virginia.

DENNISVILLE, a post-office of Amelia county, Virginia.

DENTONSVILLE, a village of Hanover county, Virginia, 22 miles N. from Richmond.

DIAMOND GROVE, a small post-village in Brunswick county, Virginia, 86 miles S. S. W. from Richmond.

DIANA MILLS, a post-village of Buckingham county, Virginia, on Slate river, 75 miles W. from Richmond.

DICKENSONVILLE, a post-office of Russell county, Virginia, 340 miles W. by S. from Richmond.

DICKINSON, a post-village of Franklin county, Virginia, 200 miles W. S. W. from Richmond.

DILLON'S RUN, a post-office of Hampshire county, Virginia, 16 miles E. from Romney, the county seat.

THE

ADAMS' EXPRESS COMPANY

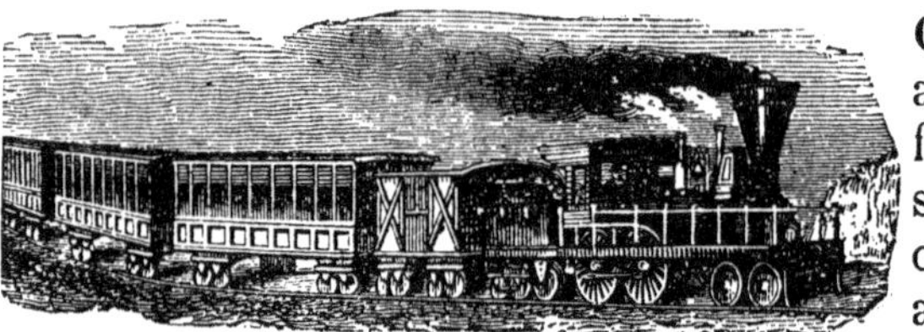

Offer unequaled advantages to all for the rapid and safe transmission of Boxes, Bales and Packages of

Goods and Articles of all descriptions,

To and from all places reached by

RAILROAD, STAGE OR STEAMBOAT.

RATES UNIFORM AND MODERATE!

No Commission charged for forwarding to places not reached by the Express.

Gold, Silver, Bank Notes, Jewelry,

And other valuable articles, always in charge of TRUSTY MESSENGERS!

FOR SALE

DRAFTS ON ENGLAND, IRELAND AND SCOTLAND,

FOR ANY AMOUNT FROM ONE POUND UP.

NOTES, BILLS, AND DRAFTS collected at any points where there are Express Agents, and prompt remittances guaranteed. We have Wagons to call for and deliver Goods (free of charge.

Office Corner of 14th & Main Streets, Richmond.

CHAS. RICHARDSON,

No. 4, UNDER EXCHANGE HOTEL, RICHMOND,

Importer of and Wholesale and Retail Dealer in

HAVANA & PRINCIPE

SEGARS,

SNUFF,

CHEWING AND SMOKING TOBACCO.

Has also for sale Segar Cases, Snuff Boxes, Pipes (of every description,) and other

FANCY ARTICLES.

DINWIDDIE, a county in the S. S. E. part of Virginia, contains 540 square miles. The Appomattox river bounds it on the N., and the Nottoway on the S. W.; it is also drained by Stony and Namazine creeks. The surface is undulating. Indian corn, wheat and tobacco are the staples. In 1850 this county produced 304,556 bushels of corn; 60,275 of wheat, and 1,782,521 pounds of tobacco. There were 3 cotton factories, 25 flour and grist mills, 7 saw mills, and 2 chandleries. It contained 36 churches, 3 newspaper offices; 223 pupils attending public schools, and 869 attending academies and other schools. The rocks which underlie this county are of the primitive formation. The railroad from Richmond to Weldon, North Carolina, passes through the county. Formed in 1752, and named in honor of Robert Dinwiddie, then governor of Virginia. Capital, Dinwiddie Court House. Population 25,118 of whom 14,238 were free, and 10,880 slaves.

DINWIDDIE COURT HOUSE, a post-village, capital of Dinwiddie county, Virginia, on Stony creek, 35 miles S. by W. from Richmond.

DINWIDDIE'S TAN YARD, a post-office of Campbell county, Virginia.

DISMAL SWAMP extends from near Norfolk, in Virginia, into North Carolina. Length from N. to S., about 30 miles; greatest breadth, 10 or 12 miles. It is in some parts covered with reeds, in others with a heavy growth of trees with a thick undergrowth. In the centre is Lake Drummond, covering about 6 square miles; when full, the surface is 21 feet above tidewater.

DODDRIDGE, a county in the N. W. part of Virginia, contains 300 square miles. It is drained by Hughes river and Middle Island creek. The surface is hilly, and the land adapted to pasturage. The principal staples are Indian corn, oats, and grass. In 1850 the county produced 59,423 bushels of corn; 13,398 of oats; 1860 tons of hay, and 35,200 pounds of butter. It contained 2 saw mills, 1 grist mill, and 1 wool-carding mill, 1 church, and 115 pupils attending public schools. The Middle Island creek is navigable by flat-boats, in which lumber is exported. Capital, West Union. Population, 2750, of whom 2719 were free, and 31 slaves.

DOE HILL, a post-office of Highland county, Virginia.

THE RICHMOND
FEMALE INSTITUTE

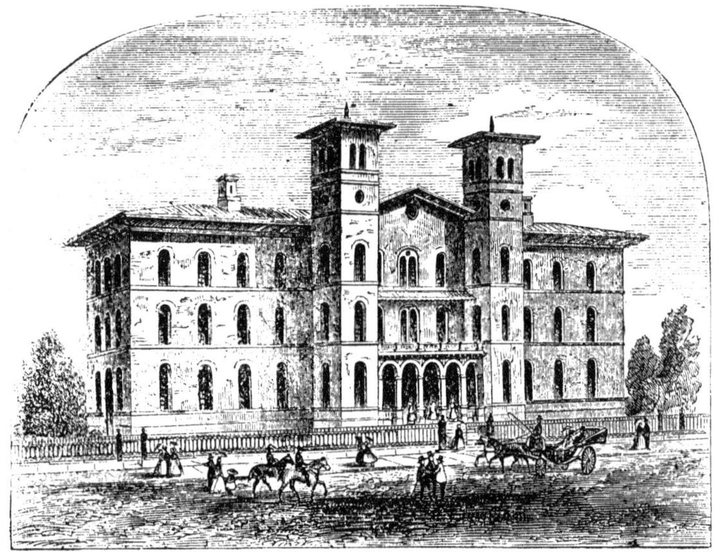

WAS INCORPORATED BY THE

Legislature of Virginia, March 2, 1853.

Its design is to elevate the grade of female education, and to afford young ladies all the facilities for learning which are offered to young men in our best colleges. Its buildings have been planned with great care and admirably adapted to the purpose. It is believed that nothing equal to them for convenience, is to be found in the whole South. The location, in one of the most desirable parts of Richmond, combines unusual advantages, being at once central and retired; and though so accessible and convenient, is almost as private and free from annoyance as the country itself. Every modern improvement which experience has sanctioned, was sought and adopted and provision is made, at an expense of *more than sixty thousand dollars*, to promote in every way the health, comfort and convenience of the pupils, as well as their advancement in learning.

The course of instruction is extensive and liberal. The great point aimed at, is thoroughness, especially in those fundamental parts of knowledge, which, it is too often thought, may be slighted with impunity. Those who have pursued successfully the regular course and passed an approved examination for a degree, will receive a diploma in accordance with the Charter, at the Annual commencement.

The session commences the first Monday in October, and closes the last Thursday in June. Thus the pupils give the golden season of labor to study, and spend the hot months in relaxation at home. Applications for admission may be addressed to the President,

REV. BASIL MANLY, Jr.

RICHMOND, Va.

DORNICKTOWN, a post-office of Monongalia county, Virginia.

DOUBLE BRIDGE, a post-office of Lunenburg county, Virginia, 87 miles S. W. from Richmond.

DOVER MILLS, a small post-village of Goochland county, Virginia, on Dover Creek and on the James River canal, 21 miles W. from Richmond. It has a valuable water-power and flouring mill.

DOVESVILLE, a post-office of Rockingham county, Virginia.

DRANESVILLE, a post-village of Fairfax county, Virginia, 17 miles W. from Washington.

DRAPER'S VALLEY, a post-office of Pulaski county, Virginia.

DRAPERSVILLE, a post-office of Mecklenburg county, Virginia.

DREWRYSVILLE, a small post-village in Southampton county, Virginia, 75 miles S. S. E. from Richmond.

DRYBURG, a post-office of Halifax county, Virginia, 129 miles S. W. from Richmond.

DUFFIELD'S, a post-office of Jefferson county, Virginia.

DUG SPUR, a post-office of Carroll county, Virginia.

DUMFRIES, a small post-village of Prince William county, Virginia, on Quantico creek, 90 miles N. from Richmond, was formerly a thriving place, containing 2 churches, and several mills, but it is now in decay.

DUNCAN, a post-office of Wood county, Virginia.

DUNLAP'S CREEK, in the S. W. Central part of Virginia, rises in Monroe county, flows north-eastward, and falls into Jackson's river, near Covington.

DUNMORE, a post-office of Pocahontas county, Virginia.

DUNNSVILLE, a post-office of Essex county, Virginia, 56 miles N. E. from Richmond.

DUPREE'S OLD STORE, a post-office of Charlotte county, Virginia.

DURRETTSVILLE, a post-office of Richmond county, Virginia.

EARLYSVILLE, a small post-village of Albemarle county, Virginia, 94 miles W. N. W. from Richmond.

EAST RIVER, a post-office of Mercer county, Virginia.

EASTVILLE, a post-village, capital of Northampton county, Virginia, 180 miles by water, E. by S. from Richmond, and a few miles E. from Chesapeake bay. It contains a court-house, 2 carriage shops, and several stores. Population, about 300.

EDENBURG, a thriving post-village of Shenandoah county, Vir-

JARRATT'S HOTEL,

THOMAS J. SOUTHALL,

PROPRIETOR,

Petersburg.

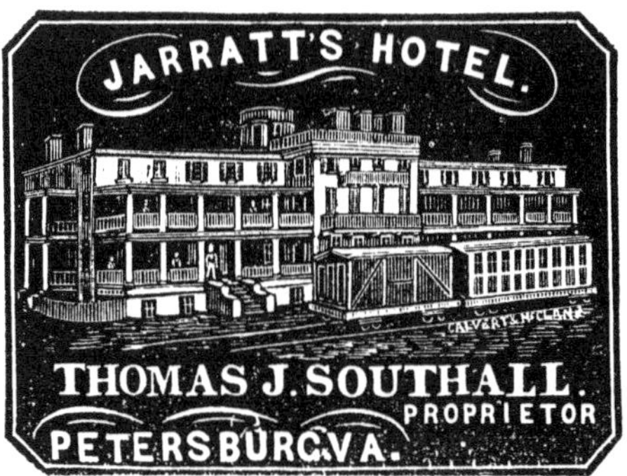

This large and popular Establishment, located at the Southern Depot, enjoys a large share of public patronage, and is capable of affording accommodation for 200 guests. It is favorably situated for those traveling North or South, who may wish to lay over, being in an elevated, airy, and healthy part of the city.

J. T. YOUNG,

DEALER IN

FINE WATCHES,

CLOCKS AND JEWELRY,

SILVER WARE AND FANCY GOODS,

SYCAMORE STREET, PETERSBURG.

☞ Watches and Jewelry repaired, and Engraving executed in the best manner, (copied and forwarded.)

Constantly on hand a full supply of

DRUGS, MEDICINES,

PAINTS, OILS,

Perfumery,

FANCY ARTICLES,

GARDEN, YARD & MEADOW SEEDS, &c.

Together with a good selection of

FRENCH, GERMAN, ENGLISH & AMERICAN

CHEMICALS,

All of which we warrant to be of the best quality.

LYON & RIVES
AND
WHOLESALE
RETAIL
DRUGS & MEDICINES.
PAINTS, OILS, SEEDS &c
No 3
APOTHECARIES & DRUGGISTS
No 3, POWELLS ROW,
PETERSBURG, VA

☞ Physicians', Merchants' and all other orders neatly and promptly executed.

ginia, on Stony creek, 6 miles from Woodstock. It is connected by a turnpike with Staunton.

EDGE HILL, a post-office of King George county, Virginia.

EDMONDS, a post-office of Brunswick county, Virginia.

EDOM, a post-office of Rockingham county, Virginia.

EDRAY, a post-office of Pocahontas county, Virginia.

EGYPT, a post-office of Monroe county, Virginia.

ELAMSVILLE, a post-village in Patrick county, Virginia, about 200 miles W. S. W. from Richmond.

EL DORADO, a post-office of Culpepper county, Virginia.

ELIZABETH, or ELIZABETHTOWN, a village in Wood county, Virginia, on the W. bank of Kanawha river, about 300 miles N. W. from Richmond.

ELIZABETH CITY, a county in the S. E. part of Virginia, bordering on Chesapeake Bay, at the mouth of James river, has an area of 50 square miles. Hampton Roads form its boundary on the south, and Back river washes its northern border. The soil is fertile. Indian corn, wheat, oats, and potatoes, are the staples. In 1850 this county produced 87,295 bushels of corn; 22,188 of wheat; 17,754 of oats, and 42,579 of potatoes. There were 3 flour and grist mills, 2 saw mills, and 2 brick yards. It contained 7 churches, 139 pupils attending public schools, and 110 attending an academy. This county occupies the extremity of the peninsula formed by James and York rivers. It was one of the eight original shires into which Virginia was divided in 1634. Capital, Hampton. Population, 4586, of whom 2438 were free, and 2148 slaves.

ELIZABETH RIVER, a small stream of Virginia, emptying itself into Hampton Roads. A light-ship is stationed on Craney Island flats, at its mouth.

ELIZABETHTOWN, Va. See GRAVE CREEK.

ELK CREEK, a post-office of Grayson county, Virginia.

ELK GARDEN, a post-office of Russell county, Virginia.

ELK HILL, a post-office of Amelia county, Virginia, 64 miles S. W. from Richmond.

ELK RIVER, in the W. part of Virginia, rises in Randolph and Pocahontas counties, interlocking sources with the Greenbrier and Monongahela rivers, and pursuing a general western course, falls into the Great Kanawha, at Charleston, in Kanawha county. The whole length is perhaps 200 miles. It is described as a

beautiful stream, and highly favorable to navigation. Boats can ascend in ordinary stages to Sutton, in Braxton county, more than 100 miles from its mouth.

Elk Run, a post-office of Fauquier county, Virginia, 90 miles N. by W. from Richmond.

Ellisville, a small post-village in Louisa county, Virginia.

Elon, a post-office of Amherst county, Virginia.

Emmaus, a post-office of Bedford county, Virginia.

Emory, a post-office of Washington county, Virginia.

Enfield, a post-village of King William county, Virginia, 36 miles N. E. from Richmond.

Erin Shades, a post-office of Henrico county, Virginia.

Essex, a county in the E. part of Virginia, has an area of about 300 square miles. The Rappahannock river forms the N. E. boundary. The surface in the W. part is uneven; the soil is generally sandy, and moderately fertile, having been improved by guano, lime, and marl. Indian corn and wheat are the staples. In 1850 this county produced 391,895 bushels of corn; 104,840 of wheat, and 57,747 pounds of butter. There were 16 flour and grist mills, and 1 tannery. It contained 11 churches, and 216 pupils attending academies and other schools. The river is navigable by small vessels along the border of the county. Formed in 1692. Capital, Tappahannock. Population, 10,206, of whom 3444 were free, and 6762 slaves.

Esteline Furnace, a post-office of Augusta county, Virginia.

Estillville, a post-village, capital of Scott county, Virginia, on Moccasin creek, 357 miles W. by S. from Richmond. Iron ore and coal are abundant at this place. It contains 1 or 2 churches, and about 60 dwellings.

Etna, a post-office of Hanover county, Virginia.

Evansham, Virginia. See Wytheville.

Evansville, a post-village in Preston county, Virginia, about 200 miles N. W. from Richmond.

Everettsville, a village in Albemarle county, Virginia, near the Virginia Central railroad, 70 miles N. W. from Richmond.

Faber's Mills, a post-village of Nelson county, Virginia, about 100 miles W. from Richmond.

Fabius, a post-office of Hardy county, Virginia.

Factory Hill, a post-office of Nansemond county, Virginia.

H. S. WHITTEMORE. C. A. WHITTEMORE.

H. S. WHITTEMORE & BROTHER,

Manufacturers of their GENUINE, PREMIUM, EAGLE, IMPROVED, LIVINGSTON, PEEKS-HILL, and SIDE HILL PLOWS; THRESHERS and HORSE POWERS, WHEAT FANS, HAY CUTTERS, CORN SHELLERS, CULTIVATORS, CAST IRON ROAD SCRAPERS, and other Agricultural Implements.

All kinds of WROUGHT and CAST IRON furnished to order; also the best FORCE PUMP, and ENGINE combined, for wells or springs.

FIRST PREMIUMS awarded to us at the Union Fair of Virginia and North Carolina, and at the State Fair of Virginia, at Richmond, in 1854, for the best SIDE HILL PLOW,—the special approbation of the Committee was given for the SUPERIOR STRENGTH and FINISH of our TOOLS.

All orders promptly attended to.

ON THE BASIN, LYNCHBURG.

S. G. MORGAN. W. H. CURLE. W. E. BURNHAM.

MORGAN, CURLE & BURNHAM'S

PLANING AND MOULDING MILL,

AND

SASH, BLIND & DOOR MANUFACTORY,

Canal Bank, Adjoining Gas Works,

LYNCHBURG.

The attention of Contractors and those intending to build, is respectfully invited to this Establishment, as we keep constantly on hand a general assortment of MOULDINGS, SASHES, BLINDS and DOORS, and also make to order, at short notice, on favorable terms.

All orders addressed to CURLE & BURNHAM will meet prompt attention, and work will be forwarded as directed.

FAIRFAX, a county in the N. E. part of Virginia, bordering on Maryland and the District of Columbia, has an area of 430 square miles. The Potomac river forms its boundary on the N. E. and S. E., and the Occoquan washes its S. W. border. The surface is hilly; the soil in some parts is sandy, and is not uniformly fertile. Much of the land has been worn out, and is no longer cultivated. Grain and cattle are the staples. In 1850 this county produced 207,531 bushels of Indian corn; 56,156 of wheat; 122,758 pounds of butter, and 4420 tons of hay. There were 5 flour and grist mills. It contained 16 churches, 1 newspaper office, 60 pupils attending public schools, and 295 attending academies and other schools. The county is intersected by two railroads leading to Alexandria. Mount Vernon, the residence of George Washington, is on the bank of the Potomac in Fairfax county, 15 miles below Washington. Formed in 1742, and named in honor of Lord Fairfax, the proprietor of a considerable district in the N. E. part of Virginia. Capital, Fairfax Court House. Population, 10,682, of whom 7432 were free, and 3250 slaves.

FAIRFAX, or CULPEPPER COURT HOUSE, a thriving post-village, capital of Culpepper county, Virginia, on the Orange and Alexandria railroad. It is surrounded by a finely diversified and fertile region, which is in a high state of cultivation. The business of the place has recently received a new impetus by the construction of the railroad. Fairfax contains 3 or 4 churches, and 2 newspaper offices. Founded in 1759. Population in 1853, estimated at 1000.

FAIRFAX COURT HOUSE, a small town, capital of Fairfax county, Virginia, 120 miles N. from Richmond, and 21 miles W. from Washington, contains the county buildings, and from 200 to 300 inhabitants.

FAIRFIELD, a post-village of Rockbridge county, Virginia, 144 miles W. from Richmond. Has 2 churches.

FAIR HILL, a post-office of Marshall county, Virginia.

FAIRMONT, a flourishing post-village, capital of Marion county, Virginia, on the W. bank of the Monongahela river, and on the Baltimore and Ohio railroad, 310 miles N. W. from Richmond. The river is navigable by steamboats from this point downward. A magnificent wire suspension bridge across the river connects the village with Palatine. A newspaper is pub-

lished here. The village contains one bank. Population in 1853, about 1200.

FALLING BRIDGE, a post office of Campbell county, Virginia.

FALLING RIVER, a small stream in the S. part of Virginia, rises in Campbell county, and flows into the Staunton or Roanoke river, near the S. E. extremity of the county.

FALLING SPRING, a post office of Greenbrier county, Virginia.

FALLING WATERS, a post village of Berkley county, Virginia, on the Potomac river, 188 miles N. by W. from Richmond.

FALLS CHURCH, a post office of Fairfax county, Virginia.

FALL'S MILLS, a post office of Cabell county, Virginia.

FALMOUTH, a post village of Stafford county, Virginia, on the Rappahannock river, 66 miles N. from Richmond, is the largest village in the county. The water power of the river is employed in two cotton factories and two flouring mills.

FANCY GROVE, a post office of Bedford county, Virginia.

FANCY HILL, a post office of Rockbridge county, Virginia, 164 miles W. from Richmond.

FARLEY, a post office of Culpepper county, Virginia.

FARMERS' GROVE, a post office of Southampton county, Va.

FARMINGTON, a post village of Marion county, Virginia, on the Baltimore and Ohio railroad.

FARMVILLE, a post village of Prince Edward county, Virginia, is finely situated on the Appomatox river, 68 miles W. S. W. from Richmond. The Southside railroad connects it with Petersburg and Richmond. The river is navigable for batteaus from this place to its mouth, and the village has an active trade. Farmville contains three churches, one bank, one newspaper office, and several tobacco factories. Population in 1853 about 1500.

FARNHAM, a thriving village of Richmond county, Virginia, five miles from the Rappahannock river.

FARROWSVILLE, a small post village of Fauquier county, Virginia, 130 miles N. by W. from Richmond.

FAUQUIER, a county in the north-eastern part of Virginia, has an area of about 680 square miles. It is bounded on the S. W. by the Rappahannock and its branch, the North river, and drained by Goose creek. The Blue Ridge extends along the N. W. border; the surface is finely diversified, and the soil is mostly very fertile. Wheat, Indian corn and grass are the

THOMAS S. JAMIESON,

MACHINIST

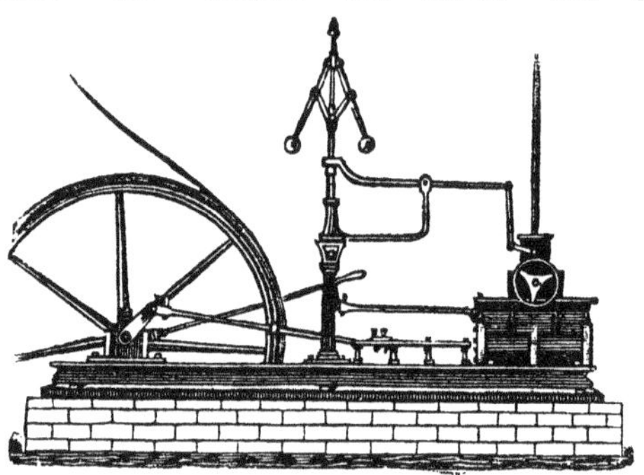

AND

IRON FOUNDER,

Corner Royal and Wilkes Streets,

ALEXANDRIA,

Is prepared to execute orders for

STATIONARY STEAM ENGINES,

MILL GEARING,

Shafting, Pulleys,

HANGERS, PUMPS, FANS,

Slide and Hand

DRILL PRESSES,

AND MACHINE WORK OF EVERY DESCRIPTION.

☞ Superior Castings made to order at short notice and on reasonable terms.

staples. In 1850 this county produced 386,324 bushels of wheat, 562,959 of Indian corn, 8523 tons of hay, 72,825 pounds of wool, and 210,711 pounds of butter. There were 17 flour mills, five grist and plaster mills, eight saw mills, seven tanneries, and one woolen factory. It contained 35 churches, two newspaper offices, 601 pupils attending public schools, and 322 attending academies and other schools. Several gold mines have been worked in the county. It also contains valuable beds of magnesia and soapstone. The Rappahannock is navigable by small boats. The county is traversed by the Orange and Alexandria railroad, and by the Manassas Gap railroad. The illustrious John Marshall, chief justice of the United States, was born in this county. Formed in 1759, and named in honor of Francis Fauquier, at that time Governor of Virginia. Capital, Warrenton. Population, 20,868, of whom 10,518 were free, and 10,350 slaves.

Fauquier White Sulphur Springs, a post village of Fauquier county, Virginia, on the Rappahannock river, 57 miles W. S. W. from Washington, is a beautiful and popular place of resort in summer.

Fayette, a county toward the W. part of Virginia, has an area of seven hundred and seventy square miles. It is traversed by the Kanawha or New river, bounded on the North by Gauley river, and on the N. E. by Meadow river. The county has a mountainous surface, abounding in wild and picturesque scenery. The principal elevations are Gauley and Sewell mountains. The famous cliff called Marshall's Pillar rises about 1000 feet above New River, a few miles from the county seat. Several fertile plateaus, or glades, destitute of timber, occur among the highlands of this county. The soil is generally good. Indian corn, wheat, oats, hay, cattle and butter are the staples. In 1850 this county produced 111,064 bushels of corn, 8414 of wheat, 56,037 of oats, 950 tons of hay, and 56,409 lbs. of butter. There were three boat yards, one wool-carding mill, and two tanneries. It contained six churches and 96 pupils attending public schools. Iron ore is found. The New river is a rapid stream, affording abundant water power in this part of its course. The county is intersected by the Covington and Ohio railroad, (not yet finished.) Capital, Fayetteville. Population, 3955, of whom 3799 were free, and 156 slaves.

FAYETTEVILLE, a small post village, capital of Fayette county, Virginia, 289 miles W. from Richmond, and about five miles from New river. A few miles from the village, New river flows along the base of a remarkable cliff or precipice of stupendous height, known by the name of "Hawk's Nest," or Marshall's Pillar. Chief justice Marshall measured it with a line, and found the height to be one thousand feet.

FELLOWSVILLE, a small village of Preston county, Virginia, on the turnpike from Winchester to Parkersburg.

FINCASTLE, a handsome post village, capital of Botetourt county, Virginia, 175 miles W. from Richmond. It is well built, and finely situated in a fertile and undulating valley, between the Blue Ridge and North mountain, about five miles E. from the latter. The Peaks of Otter, which rise on the border of the county, are among the highest points of the Blue Ridge. Fincastle contains four or five churches, two academies, and two printing offices. Laid out in 1772.

FLOYD, a county in the S. S. W. part of Virginia, has an area of 279 square miles. It is drained by Little river, an affluent of the New or Kanawha. The surface is high and mountainous, the county occupying the northwestern declivity of the Blue Ridge, which slopes gradually toward the valley of New river. The land is generally rough and in some parts unproductive, but a large portion is adapted to pasturage. Indian corn, wheat, oats hay, and live stock are the staples. In 1850 the county produced 104,630 bushels of corn, 23,992 of wheat,92,654 of oats, and 3226 tons of hay. There were seven grist mills, five flour mills, three wool-carding mills, and four tanneries. It contained nine churches, 832 pupils attending public schools, and 104 attending academies or other schools. The highlands contain copper, iron ore and other minerals. The county is plentifully supplied with water power. Organized in 1831, and named in honor of John Floyd, at that time governor of Virginia. Capital, Jacksonville. Population, 6458, of whom 6015 were free, and 443 slaves.

FLOYD COURT HOUSE, a post village, capital of Floyd county, Virginia, 180 miles W. S. W. from Richmond.

FLUKE'S, a post office of Botetourt county, Virginia, 163 miles W. from Richmond.

FLUVANNA, a county in the S. E. central part of Virginia, has

LEAVITT'S

IMPROVED

PORTABLE MILL.

The cut represents a valuable improvement in

Portable Mills,

Adapted to the various Crushing and Grinding purposes of a Farm, which are now required and found so profitable in the improved modes of feeding stock.

This Mill is peculiarly adapted to grinding corn and cob together, to shelling Corn and grinding Meal from Corn and other grains. This form of mill is so simple that a small boy can adjust it by turning a handle affixed to a screw, with perfect ease and certainty, either for shelling corn or grinding coarse or fine, and is by far the most convenient and portable article of the kind ever invented, weighing only about 250 pounds, worked by one, two, or four horses, and will grind from 4 to 10 bushels corn and cob meal per hour, from 3 to 5 bushels fine corn meal per hour, and will with one horse, shell from 10 to 15 bushels corn. The Mill requires no horse-power machinery, simply a lever attached to the outside grinder, the inside being stationary, and placed on a log either in the yard or barn. For simplicity and durability it will recommend itself to every Farmer, rich or poor, and can be put in operation in 6 hours.

The Subscriber is manufacturing the above Mills at Messrs. Smith & Perkins' Foundry, on Pitt street, Alexandria. All orders addressed to the undersigned will be promptly attended to, and Mills shipped to order, with full directions for putting them in operation.

Farmers are invited to call and examine the Mill at the above Foundry. It is confidently believed that this Mill will answer practically a better purpose than any that has been made at a cost of under four hundred dollars. It is the invention of Mr. CHARLES LEAVITT, of Quincy, Illinois, who obtained a patent in 1852, and has now been in operation 5 years, giving universal satisfaction.

R. McLAGAN.

an area of 170 square miles. The James river forms the S. boundary, and Rivanna river flows through the middle of the county. The surface is partly broken and partly level; the soil in some parts is fertile, in others almost barren. Tobacco is the staple product. In 1850 there were raised 1,054,974 lbs. of tobacco, 200,174 bushels of Indian corn, and 92,657 of wheat. There were nine flour and grist mills, ten saw mills, one gold mine which is worked, one cotton and one woolen factory. It contained 14 churches, 355 pupils attending public schools, and 63 attending academies or other schools. The James river canal passes along the border of the county. Gold has been found near Palmyra, the county seat. Formed from Albemarle county in 1777. Population, 9487, of whom 4750 were free and 4737 slaves.

FOWLER'S, a post office of Brooke county, Virginia.

FOXVILLE, a post village of Fauquier county, Virginia, on the Rappahannock river, 108 miles W. N. W. from Richmond.

FRANKFORD, a post village in Greenbrier county, Virginia, 180 miles W. by N. from Richmond.

FRANKFORT, a village of Greenbrier county, Virginia, 10 miles N. E. from Lewisburg, contains one or two churches.

FRANKFORT, a post village of Hampshire county, Virginia, on Patterson's creek, 203 miles N. W. from Richmond.

FRANKLIN, a county in the S. part of Virginia, has an area of 864 square miles. The Staunton river forms its N. E. boundary and the Blue Ridge extends along its N. W. border. The surface is hilly or rolling; the soil has a substratum of clay and is very productive. Tobacco, Indian corn and wheat are the staples. In 1850 there were raised 1,125,404 pounds of tobacco, 431,408 bushels of corn, 76,831 of wheat and 187,792 of oats. There were 14 flour, grist and saw mills, 2 iron forges, 1 iron furnace and fifteen tobacco factories. It contained 25 churches and 700 pupils attending public schools. Iron ore is found in several parts of the county. Formed in 1784. Capital, Rocky Mount. Population, 17,430, of whom 11,704 were free, and 5726 slaves.

FRANKLIN, a small village, capital of Pendleton county, Virginia, on the S. Branch of the Potomac, 20 miles from its source and 165 miles N. W. from Richmond.

FRANKLIN, a post village of Southampton county, Virginia,

FOWLE & CO.

ALEXANDRIA,

COMMISSON MERCHANTS,

AND SOLE AGENTS FOR THE SALE OF

MEXICAN GUANO,

Have always on hand a good supply of this Permanent Fertilizer.

They would call attention to the following analyses made by Drs. D. Stuart, of Baltimore, and Richard H. Stabler, of this city.

Proximate Analysis.

Organic Matter containing some azotized compounds capable of forming ammonia,	05.47
Water,	25.32
Ash, or proportion of mineral elements,	69.21
	100.00

Composition of the Ash.

Phosphoric Acid,	33.52
Lime,	26.35
Sand,	00.30
Magnesia and Soda with a trace of Potash,	09.04
	69.21

The Ash or mineral portion is very pure bone ash, in a state of minute division, containing a larger proportion of Phosphoric Acid than Bone Phosphate of Lime, say sixty-nine per cent.

ALEXANDRIA GAZETTE & VIRGINIA ADVERTISER,

PUBLISHED DAILY BY

EDGAR SNOWDEN,

At Eight Dollars per annum, payable half yearly.

ALEXANDRIA GAZETTE & VIRGINIA ADVERTIZER,

FOR THE COUNTRY,

IS PUBLISHED, REGULARLY, ON

Tuesdays, Thursdays and Saturdays,

At Five Dollars per annum, payable in advance.

THE VIRGINIA SENTINEL

IS PUBLISHED ON

TUESDAYS, THURSDAYS AND SATURDAYS,

BY

R. M. SMITH & J. W. FINKS,

At Five Dollars per annum.

A JOB OFFICE

IS CONNECTED WITH THE ESTABLISHMENT.

on the Blackwater river, and on the Portsmouth and Roanoke railroad, 88 miles S. S. E. from Richmond.

FRANKTOWN, a post office of Northampton county, Virginia.

FRAZIER'S BOTTOM, a post office of Putnam county, Virginia.

FREDERICK, a county in the N. N. E. part of Virginia, has an area of 378 square miles. The Opequan, Sleepy and Black creeks, affluents of the Potomac, rise within it and flow northeastward. The surface is beautifully diversified with mountain scenery; the principal elevation is the North mountain, extending along the western border. The county occupies part of the Great Valley of Virginia, and is one of the most wealthy and highly cultivated in the State. Wheat, Indian corn, oats, hay, butter, cattle and pork are the staples. In 1850 it produced 311,060 bushels of wheat, 199,242 of corn, 50,701 of oats, 6433 tons of hay and 193,394 pounds of butter. There were 35 flour mills, 38 saw mills, seven woolen factories, four tobacco factories, seven tanneries, one iron furnace, and one iron foundry. It contained 31 churches, 360 pupils attending public schools and 305 attending academies and other schools. Blue limestone underlies a large portion of the county. The streams furnish abundant motive power for mills and factories. A railroad extends from Harper's Ferry to Winchester, the capital of the county. Turnpike roads radiate in several directions from the latter town. Formed in 1738. Population 15,975, of whom 13,681 were free, and 2294 slaves.

FREDERICKSBURG, the chief town of Spottsylvania county, Virginia, on the right bank of the Rappahannock river, at the head of tide water, 65 miles N. of Richmond. It is pleasantly situated in a fertile valley, and has advantages for commerce and manufactures. The railroad from Washington to Richmond passes through the town, and a canal has been constructed from this place to a point on the river 40 miles above, by which large quantities of wheat, flour and tobacco are received for exportation. The river affords extensive water power, which, however, is not much used. Large quantities of fine granite and freestone are found in the vicinity. It contains five churches, one orphan asylum, two seminaries, three or four newspaper offices and two banks. Population in 1840, 3974, in 1850, 4062.

FRENCHTOWN, a post village in Lewis county, Virginia, 200 miles W. N. W. from Richmond.

CHARLES KOONES,

CABINET, CHAIR,

AND

SOFA MANUFACTURER,

No. 187 King St., Cor. of Columbus St.

ALEXANDRIA.

The subscriber has constantly on hand and will continue to manufacture the greatest variety of Rosewood, Walnut, Mahogany and Common Furniture, (Antique, French and Modern styles,) in the most fashionable and durable manner.

An examination of his Stock is invited.

A. L. GREGORY,

WHOLESALE AND RETAIL DEALER IN

STOVES,

TIN WARE,

HOT AIR FURNACES,

AND

PORTABLE FORGES.

Royal St., near the Market House,

ALEXANDRIA.

D. HAAS,

DAGUERREIAN ARTIST,

Exchange Block, Over Potomac Insurance Office,

KING STREET,

ALEXANDRIA.

All kinds of Morocco, Velvet, Papier Mache, Pearl Shell, Sontag and Fancy Cases constantly on hand.

Mr. HAAS offers to furnish Daguerreotypes at lower prices than they have ever been taken for in the State of Virginia, and at the same time guarantees faithful execution and perfect Likenesses which *will never fade!*

Friends' Grove, a small post village of Charlotte county, Virginia, 104 miles S. W. from Richmond.

Front Royal, a flourishing post village, capital of Warren county, Virginia, 140 miles N. N. W. from Richmond, and one mile E. from Shenandoah river. It is pleasantly situated in a valley between the river and the Blue Ridge. The railroad from Alexandria to Strasburg passes through this village, and a plank road 20 miles long connects it with Winchester. The water power of the river has been improved by the erection of numerous flouring mills. Population, about 500.

Gainesborough, Virginia. See Gainsborough.

Gaines Cross Roads, a small post village of Rappahannock county, Virginia, about 120 miles N. N. W. from Richmond.

Gainesville, a post office of Prince William county, Virginia.

Gainsborough, a post village of Frederick county, Virginia, 150 miles N. N. W. from Richmond, contains two churches, and about thirty houses.

Gainsborough, of Roanoke county, Virginia. See Big Lick.

Gap Mills, a post village of Monroe county, Virginia, 8 miles N. from the court house, has several mills and a woolen factory.

Garland's, or Garland's Store, a post office of Albemarle county, Virginia, 95 miles W. by N. from Richmond.

Gauley Bridge, a post village of Fayette county, Virginia, is situated just below the junction of the Gauley and New rivers, about 300 miles W. from Richmond. It is the head of navigation on the river, which presents here a beautiful fall of 22 feet.

Gauley River, in the W. central part of Virginia, rises in Pocahontas county, flows nearly westward through Nicholas county, and unites with the New river at Gauley Bridge, in Fayette county, 36 miles above Charleston. Below the junction, the river is called the Great Kanawha. The valley of Gauley river is about 60 miles long. This stream flows through a mountainous region. It affords little facilities for navigation.

Genito, a post village of Powhatan county, Virginia, on the left bank of the Appomattox river, twenty-nine miles W. from Richmond. It contains one store and one flouring mill.

Gerardstown, or Gerrardstown, a post village of Berkley county, Virginia, 166 miles N. by W. from Richmond, contains three churches.

JAMES A. ENGLISH. CHARLES M. CASTLEMAN. CHARLES A. BALDWIN.

ENGLISH, CASTLEMAN & CO.

KING STREET,

ALEXANDRIA,

IMPORTERS AND DEALERS IN

Hardware, Cutlery, Building Materials,

COACH AND SADLERY HARDWARE,

Bar Iron, Cast, Shear & Blister Steel,

HOLLOW WARE, NAILS, &c.

A large stock of the above goods kept constantly on hand and will be sold to Country Merchants as low as they can be procured in any Market.

ALSO A LARGE STOCK OF

ENGLISH & GERMAN

GUNS

AND

GUN FIXTURES.

An examination of their Stock is requested.

GERMAN SETTLEMENT, a post office of Preston county, Virginia, on the Baltimore and Ohio railroad, 270 miles N. W. from Richmond. The village is called Mt. Carmel.

GERMANTOWN, a village of Bath county, Virginia, half a mile from the Warm Springs. It has two stores, one hotel, and about 100 inhabitants.

GERMANTOWN, a post village of Fauquier county, Virginia, 95 miles N. by W. from Richmond.

GHOLSONVILLE, a small post village of Brunswick county, Va.

GILES, a county in the S. W. part of Virginia, has an area of about 550 square miles. It is intersected by the Kanawha or New river, and also drained by Walker's, Wolf, and Sinking creeks. Indian corn, wheat, oats, hay, butter and live stock are the staples. In 1850 this county produced 204,720 bushels of corn, 38,565 of wheat, 68,494 of oats, 1960 tons of hay and 83,120 pounds of butter. It contained 17 churches and 820 pupils attending public schools. Since the census of 1850 was taken the dimensions of the county have been reduced by the formation of Craig county out of the N. E. part. Capital, Parisburg. Population, 6570, of whom 5913 were free, and 657 slaves.

GILES COURT HOUSE, Va. See Parisburg.

GILMER, a county in the W. N. W. part of Virginia, has an area of 512 square miles. Indian corn, wheat, oats, hay and live stock are the staples. In 1850 this county produced 117,990 bushels of corn, 5652 of wheat, 22,085 of oats, 1023 tons of hay and 33,277 pounds of butter. It contained one saw mill, one tannery, five churches, and 159 pupils attending public schools. The county contains salt springs and iron ore. It is ntersected by the Parkersburg and Weston turnpike. Capital, Glenville. Population, 3475, of whom 3403 were free and 72 slaves.

GLADE SPRING, a post village of Washington county, Virginia, ten miles from Abingdon; is the seat of Emory and Henry college, founded by the Methodists in 1838.

GLENVILLE, a small post village, capital of Gilmer county, Virginia, on little Kanawha river, 210 miles in a direct line W. N. W. from Richmond.

GLOUCESTER county, Virginia, situated on Chesapeake bay, in the S. E. part of the State, contains 280 square miles. Large quantities of oysters and wood are exported to New York and

J. J. ROBERTS. E. S. PLUMMER.

MARSHALL HOUSE,

KING STREET,

ALEXANDRIA.

ROBERTS & PLUMMER, Proprietors.

Located in the centre of the business portion of the city, and within a few minutes' walk of all places of public Lectures and Amusement.

The Proprietors assure their friends that no pains will be spared to make their stay at the MARSHALL HOUSE an agreeable one.

Will be in waiting at the Cars and Steamboats to convey passengers to this Hotel.

BOARD PER DAY $1.75.

Philadelphia. In 1850 this county produced 336,063 bushels of corn, 65,551 of wheat, and 62 bales of cotton. There were 16 flour, grist and saw mills, and two tanneries. It contained 14 churches, 253 pupils attending public schools, and 95 attending academies or other schools. Formed in 1642. Capital, Gloucester Court House. Population, 10,527, of whom 4970 were free, and 5557 slaves.

GLOUCESTER COURT HOUSE, capital of Gloucester county, Virginia, 82 miles E. S. E. from Richmond.

GOLANDSVILLE, or GOLANSVILLE, a post village in Caroline co., Virginia.

GOOCHLAND, a county toward the S. E. part of Virginia, has an area of 260 square miles. James river forms the S. boundary through the whole length of the county. Tobacco, Indian corn, wheat and oats are the staples. Extensive mines of bituminous coal are worked here, and gold has been found in small quantities. In 1850 this county produced 624,208 pounds of tobacco, 276,338 bushels of corn, 141,999 of wheat and 104,018 of oats. There were 20 flour and saw mills, four coal mines, three tanneries and one nail factory. It contained 15 churches, and 320 pupils attending academies and other schools. Capital, Goochland Court House. Population, 10,352, of whom 4507 were free, and 5845 slaves.

GOOCHLAND COURT HOUSE, a post village, capital of Goochland county, Virginia, one mile N. from James river, and 28 W. from Richmond.

GOOSE CREEK, in the N. E. part of Virginia, rises in Fauquier county, flows north-eastward, crosses Loudoun county, and falls into the Potomac four miles E. from Leesburg, after a course of nearly 50 miles.

GORDONSVILLE, a post village of Orange county, Virginia, on the Central railroad, and at the terminus of the Orange and Alexandria railroad, 70 miles N. W. from Richmond.

GOSPORT.—See PORTSMOUTH.

GRANVILLE, a post village of Monongalia county, Virginia, on the Monongahela river, 295 miles N. W. from Richmond.

GRAPE ISLAND, a post office of Tyler county, Virginia.

GRAVE CREEK, a thriving post village, capital of Marshall county, Virginia, is pleasantly situated on the left bank of the Ohio, twelve miles below Wheeling. Big and Little Grave

TREDEGAR IRON & ENGINE WORKS
RICHMOND VA
ANDERSON DELANY & CO
MANUFACTURERS OF
SAW MILLS,
SUGAR MILLS,
LOCOMOTIVE & MARINE
ENGINES,
CRANKS, TOBACCO PRESSES,
CANNONS,
And heavy Machinery of every description.
N. B.—SHAFTS, ROLLS, and other important Castings made of Gun Iron.
ANDERSON, DELANY & CO.
RICHMOND.

creeks enter the river here, leaving an interval of a mile in width, on which the village is built. It is divided into two distinct villages, of nearly equal size, namely, Elizabethtown and Moundsville, the former of which is the seat of justice. The name of the post office is Grave creek. The town contains a classical academy, two steam flouring mills, and about 1200 inhabitants. Moundsville derives its name from the mammoth mound, in the vicinity, one of the largest in the United States.

Gravel Spring, a post office of Frederick county, Virginia.

Graves' Mills, a post office of Washington county, Virginia, 108 miles N. W. from Richmond.

Grayson, a county in the S. S. W. part of Virginia, bordering on North Carolina, contains 340 square miles. It is drained by the Kanawha river. The Iron Mountain extends along the N. W. border and the Blue Ridge along the S. E. The county contains iron ore, and is amply supplied with water power. Indian corn, oats, hay and live stock are the staples. In 1850 this county produced 177,266 bushels of corn, 110,770 of oats, 88,707 lbs. of butter and 3522 tons of hay. It contained 21 churches and 217 pupils attending public schools. Organized in 1793, and named in honor of a member of the Virginia convention which ratified the federal constitution. Capital, Independence. Population, 6677, of whom 6178 were free, and 499 slaves.

Grayson Court House, of Virginia. See Independence.

Grayson Sulphur Springs, of Carroll county, Virginia, on the bank of New river, 272 miles W. by S. from Richmond. These springs are surrounded by a hilly country remarkable for its salubrity. Buildings have been erected for the entertainment of visiters.

Greasy Creek, a post office of Floyd county, Virginia.

Great Bridge, a post village in Norfolk county, Virginia.

Great Kanawha, a river in North Carolina and Virginia, has its sources in Ashe county of the former State, between the Blue Ridge and the Iron Mountain. Flowing north-eastward it enters Virginia and breaks through the Iron mountain on the northern border of Grayson county. After crossing Pulaski county, it assumes a north-westerly course, and traverses several ridges of the Alleghany chain, known by the local names of Walker's, Peter's, and Greenbrier mountains. Below the passage of the latter ridge, the river flows through Fayette county to the mouth

FOR SCOTTSVILLE & COLUMBIA.

On and after Monday, January 8th, our Packet,

FARMER,

CAPT. G. WYTHE MUNFORD, Jr.

Will leave Richmond for Scottsville, every MONDAY, WEDNESDAY and FRIDAY, at 5 o'clock, P. M., and arrive at Scottsville at 11 o'clock, A. M., the next day. Returning, will leave Scottsville every TUESDAY and THURSDAY, at 2 o'clock, P. M., and arrive in Richmond at 8 o'clock, A. M., the next day,—and SUNDAYS at 10 o'clock, A. M., and arrive in Richmond at 4 o'clock, A. M., on MONDAYS.

THE PLOUGH-BOY

Will leave Richmond every TUESDAY, THURSDAY and SATURDAY, at 7 o'clock, A. M., and arrive at Columbia at 7½ o'clock, P. M. Returning, will leave Columbia at 7 o'clock, A. M., and arrive in Richmond at half past 7 o'clock, P. M.

Persons traveling on these Packets can get all their Meals on Board

FROM SCOTTSVILLE. TO	HOURS OF PASSING. Tuesdays and Thursdays.	HOURS OF PASSING. Sundays.
New Canton,	5 P. M.	1 P. M.
Columbia,	7¼ "	3¼ "
Elk Hill,	8¼ "	4¼ "
Pemberton,	9¼ "	5¼ "
Rock Castle,	10¾ "	6¾ "
Bowling Hall,	12 M.	8 "
Cedar Point,	12½ A. M.	8½ "

FROM SCOTTSVILLE. TO	HOURS FOR PASSING. Tuesdays and Thursdays.	HOURS FOR PASSING. Sundays.
Michaux Ferry,	1 P. M.	9 A. M.
Beaver Dam,	1½ "	9½ "
Dover Mills,	3¼ "	11¼ "
Manakin,	4 "	17 M.
Tuckahoe,	5 "	1 A. M,
Richmond,	8 "	4 "

CROUCH & HOOPER.

WOODWARD HOUSE,

MAIN STREET,

STAUNTON,

WOODWARD & COALTER, Proprietors.

of Gauley river, which enters it from the right hand. The Kanawha here attains a width of 500 yards, and takes the name of the Great Kanawha. The falls, which occur about two miles below the junction, are somewhat remarkable for picturesque beauty, and form the limit of navigation. The whole stream is precipitated over a ledge of rocks 22 feet in height. Continuing a north-western course, the river flows through a hilly region, abounding in salt springs and stone coal, passes by Charleston and enters the Ohio at Point Pleasant. Above the mouth of Gauley river it bears the local name of New river. The whole length is estimated at 400 miles, and the area drained, including its affluents, according to Darby, is 10,800 square miles. It is navigated by steamboats from its mouth about seventy-five miles.

Green Bank, a post office of Pocahontas county, Virginia.

Green Bay, a post office of Prince Edward county, Virginia.

Greenbottom, a post office of Cabell county, Virginia.

Greenbrier, a county in the West central part of Virginia. has an area of 880 square miles. It is intersected by the Greenbrier river, from which it derives its name. The surface is mostly occupied by mountain ridges of the Alleghany system and the intervening valleys. One of the former is called Greenbrier mountain. The mean height of the arable land is estimated at about 1500 feet above the sea. Grain and grass are the staples. In 1850 this county produced 182,119 bushels of Indian corn, 47,778 of wheat, 124,158 of oats and 6,359 tons of hay. It contained 22 churches, 900 pupils attending public schools, and 30 attending an academy. The main road from Richmond to the Ohio river passes through the county. The White Sulphur Spring of this county is the most celebrated watering place of Virginia. Formed in 1777. Capital, Lewisburg, Population 10,022, of whom 8,705 were free and 1,317 slaves.

Greenbrier Mountain, in Greenbrier and Pocahontas counties, in the West part of Virginia, has an elevation of more than 2,000 feet.

Greenbrier River, of Western Virginia, rises at the base of Greenbrier mountain in the North part of Pocahontas county, flows South-westward, crosses Greenbrier county, and enters the Kanawha or New river, on the border between Monroe and Mercer counties. The whole length is probably 150 miles. The mean

elevation of its valley is estimated at one thousand five hundred feet, as the mouth of the river has been found by measurement to be 1333 feet above the level of the sea.

GREENBRIER RUN, a post office of Doddridge county, Virginia.

GREENE, a county in the East central part of Virginia, has an area of 230 square miles. The Rapidan river forms the boundary on the North East. The surface is diversified by high ridges and valleys, a part of the county lying on the south-east declivity of the Blue Ridge. The soil of the valleys is fertile. Indian corn, wheat and tobacco are the staples. In 1850, this county produced 137,293 bushels of corn, 42,416 of wheat and 200,714 pounds of tobacco. There were six flour and grist mills, four saw mills, 2 tanneries and one wool-carding mill. It contained eight churches and 152 pupils actending public schools. A turnpike road has been commenced in the county. Organized in 1838. Capital, Stanardsville. Population 4400, of whom 2701 were free, and 1699 slaves.

GREENFIELD, a post village in Nelson county, Virginia, 90 miles W. N. W. from Richmond.

GREEN HILL, a post office of Campbell county, Virginia.

GREEN LEVEL, a post office of Southampton county, Virginia.

GREENSBURG, a post office of Preston county, Virginia.

GREEN SPRING RUN, a post office of Hampshire county, Va.

GREENSVILLE, a small village of Grayson county, Virginia, on the New river, 276 miles West by South from Richmond, was formerly the county seat.

GREEN VALLEY, a post office of Bath county, Virginia.

GREENVILLE, a county in the South East part of Virginia, bordering on North Carolina, contains about 300 square miles. The Nottoway river bounds it on the North, and it is intersected by the Meherrin river. The Staple productions are corn, wheat, tobacco and cotton. In 1850 there were raised 211,537 bushels of Indian corn; 17,619 of wheat; 138,000 pounds of tobacco; and 715 bales of cotton. It contained one iron foundry, 1 grist mill and one tannery, 12 churches and 125 pupils attending academies and other schools. The railroad from Richmond to Weldon, North Carolina, passes through the county. Organized in 1784. Capital, Hicksford. Population, 5,639, of whom 1,854 were free and 3,785 slaves.

GREENVILLE, a post village of Augusta county, Virginia, on

the South river, near its source, 120 miles W. N. W. from Richmond. It contains one academy, several stores, and one flouring mill. Population from 300 to 400.

GREENWOOD, a post office of Doddridge county, Virginia.

GREIGSVILLE, a thriving post village of Preston county, Virginia, on the Baltimore and Ohio railroad.

GRIFFINSBURG, a small post village of Culpepper county, Virginia, 103 miles N. N. W. from Richmond.

GRIFFITHSVILLE, a post office of Cabell county, Virginia.

GROVE HILL, a post office of Page county, Virginia.

GROVETON, a post office of Prince William county, Virginia.

GUEST STATION, a post office of Russell county, Virginia.

GUILFORD, a post office of Accomack county, Virginia.

GUINEY'S, a post office of Caroline county, Virginia.

GUYANDOTTE river, in the West part of Virginia, rises in the South East part of Logan county, and flowing in a general N. N. W. course, falls into the Ohio in Cabell county, about 10 miles above the mouth of the Sandy river.

GUYANDOTTE, a thriving post village of Cabell county, Virginia, on the Ohio river, at the mouth of the Guyandotte, 228 miles below Wheeling, and 360 miles West by North from Richmond. It is an important point of steamboat debarkation, and the terminus of a turnpike extending to the watering places, and to Richmond, with which it communicates by a daily line of stages. A railroad is projected between this place and Covington, to connect with the Central railroad. Guyandotte contains one or two churches and, perhaps, 1,000 inhabitants.

HADENSVILLE, a post office of Goochland county, Virginia.

HAGUE, a post village in Westmoreland county, Virginia.

HAINESVILLE, a post office of Berkley county, Virginia.

HALE'S FORD, a post office of Franklin county, Virginia.

HALEYSBURG, a post office of Lunenburg county, Virginia.

HALIFAX, a county in the South part of Virginia, bordering on North Carolina, has an area of 960 square miles. The Staunton or Roanoke river forms its entire boundary on the North and East. It is intersected by the Dan river, which unites with the former on the border of the county, and also drained by the Banister and Hycootee rivers. Tobacco, Indian corn, wheat, oats, cattle and swine are the staples. By the census of 1850 it produced more tobacco and oats than any other county in

C. C. BRADLEY,

MANUFACTURER AND DEALER IN

FURNITURE,

Corner of King and Alfred streets,

ALEXANDRIA.

JOHN H. PARROTT,

DEALER IN

PIANOS,

MELODEONS,

GUITARS,

ACCORDIONS VIOLINS, &c.

Music, Books, Stationery, &c.

KING STREET,

UNDER WASHINGTON HALL,

ALEXANDRIA.

STABLERS' DRUG WAREHOUSE,

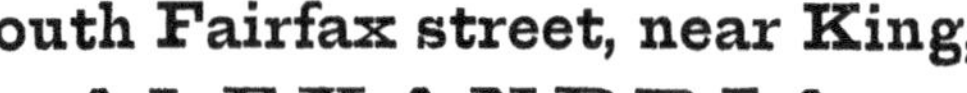

South Fairfax street, near King,

ALEXANDRIA,

ESTABLISHED 1792.

JOHN LEADBEATER,

(Surviving partner and successor of Wm. Stabler & Bro.)

WHOLESALE AND RETAIL

DRUGGIST,

Keeps constantly on hand a full stock of goods in his line, fresh and genuine, suitable for city or country trade.

Proprietor of Rice's Celebrated Worm Destroying Drops, &c.

Virginia: the quantity of the former was not exceeded by any county in the Union, excepting Prince George of Maryland. There were raised in that year 6,485,762 pounds of tobacco, 649,896 bushels of corn; 146,769 of wheat and 365,182 of oats. There were five flour mills, four grist mills, 2 manufactories of farming implements, and two tanneries. It contained 51 churches; 252 pupils attending public schools and 36 pupils attending an academy. A rich mine of plumbago has recently been discovered. The county is intersected by the Richmond and Danville railroad. Organized in 1752. Capital, Banister. Population, 25,962 of whom 11,510 were free, and 14,452 slaves.

Halifax Court House, Virginia. See Banister.

Hallsborough, a village of Chesterfield county, Virginia, 17 miles S. W. from Richmond.

Hallsborough, a post office of Powhatan county, Virginia.

Halltown, a post office in Jefferson county, Virginia.

Hambaugh's, a post office of Warren county, Virginia.

Hamburg, a post office of Shenandoah county, Virginia.

Hamilton, a post village of Loudoun county, Virginia, about 157 miles North from Richmond.

Hamlin, a post office of Cabell county, Virginia.

Hampden Sidney College, a post office of Prince Edward county, Virginia.

Hampshire, a county in the North part of Virginia, bordering on Maryland, contains 850 square miles. It is drained by the Cacapon river and by the North and South branches of the Potomac. The surface is occupied by the valleys and ridges of the Alleghany chain. The soil of the lowlands is mostly fertile. Indian corn, wheat, oats, hay, butter and wool are the staples. In 1850 it produced 292,252 bushels of corn, 177,343 of wheat, 84,118 of oats, 8996 tons of hay and 248,467 pounds of butter. There were 19 flour mills, one iron furnace, four woolen factories and 11 tanneries. It contained 33 churches, 1,500 pupils attending public schools, and 145 attending academies and other schools. The county contains extensive beds of coal and iron ore, which are easily accessible by the Baltimore and Ohio railroad. The streams afford excellent water-power. Capital, Romney. Population 14,036, of whom 12,603 were free and 1,433 slaves.

ISAAC ENTWISLE. WM. S. MOORE.

ENTWISLE & MOORE,

UNION STREET,

ALEXANDRIA,

MANUFACTURERS OF

STATIONARY

STEAM ENGINES

AND

BOILERS,

And every description of

MILL GEARING,

SHAFTINGS, PULLEYS,

HANGERS, PUMPS,

And Machine work generally.

Also, IRON FENCING, both Wrought and Cast, of superior quality, on shortest notice.

W. H. GARBER. JOHN B. BRECKINRIDGE. S. L. STEVENSON.

AMERICAN HOTEL,

STAUNTON,

WM. H. GARBER & CO., Proprietors.

SITUATED AT THE RAIL ROAD DEPOT.

☞ STAGES leave daily for all parts of the country.

HAMPSTEAD, a post village in King George county, Virginia, near the Potomac river, 56 miles N. N. E. from Richmond.

HAMPTON, a borough, capital of Elizabeth City county, Virginia, on the left bank of James river, about two miles from its entrance into the Chesapeake bay, and 96 miles S. E. from Richmond. The part of the estuary of James river, situated between this town and Norfolk, is called Hampton roads. Hampton is an old town, possessing much historic interest, and has been the birth place of several distinguished naval officers. Its present importance is derived principally from its proximity to forts Monroe and Calhoun. The former, in addition to its other sources of expenditure, has lately become one of the most fashionable places of resort in the South. The beach in the vicinity affords excellent bathing ground, and is thronged during the summer months with the wealthy and fashionable, and by some invalids, assembled there from Virginia, Maryland and the Southern States. Fort Monroe is two and a half miles from Hampton. The town contains four churches, several hotels and numerous stores. Settled in 1705. Population, about 1400.

HANCOCK, a new county, forming the N. N. W. extremity of Virginia, bordering on Pennsylvania and on the Ohio river, has an area of about 100 square miles. The Ohio river forms its boundary on the N. and W., separating it from the State of Ohio. The surface is hilly; the soil is fertile. Wheat, Indian corn, oats, wool, butter, and pork are the staples. In 1850 it produced 52,413 bushels of wheat, 52,392 of corn, 52,444 of oats, 63,666 pounds of wool, and 75,966 of butter. There were eight flour, grist and saw mills, twelve brick manufactories, and two potteries. It contained six churches, 360 pupils attending public schools, and 25 attending an academy. Stone coal and fireclay are among the most valuable minerals of the county. It was formed a few years ago, out of the Northern part of Brooke county. Capital, New Cumberland. Population, 4050, of whom 4047 were free, and three slaves.

HANOVER, a county in the E. part of Virginia, contains about 400 square miles. It is drained by the North Anna and South Anna rivers, which unite on the N. E. border of the county, and form the Pamunkey. The surface is hilly, and presents much diversity of soil. Wheat, maize, oats and tobacco are the

VIRGINIA HOTEL,

STAUNTON.

McCLUNG & PEYTON,

PROPRIETORS.

☞ The United States Mail Stage office is kept at this House.

ALEXANDRIA

BRASS FOUNDRY.

J. & L. CARR,

BRASS FINISHERS & BELL FOUNDERS,

PITT STREET,

Between Cameron and Green,

ALEXANDRIA.

ADDISON & HOWARD,

COMMISSION & FORWARDING MERCHANTS,

AND CASH DEALERS IN

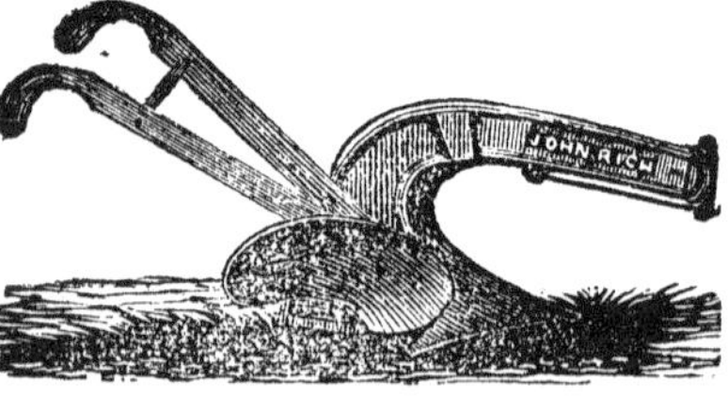

AGRICULTURAL IMPLEMENTS,

SEEDS, GUANO,

PLASTER, &c.

UNION STREET,

ALEXANDRIA.

☞ Particular attention paid to the sale of Wheat, Rye, Corn, &c. ☜

staples. In 1850 this county produced 377,616 bushels of Indian corn, 157,388 of wheat, 94,186 of oats, 404,550 pounds of tobacco, and 78,316 of butter. There were 24 flour and grist mills, three tanneries and two manufactories of farming implements. It contained 27 churches, 56 pupils attending public schools, and 352 attending academies or other schools. The dividing line between the primitive and tertiary formations passes through this county. It is intersected by the Central railroad, and by the Richmond and Potomac railroad. The streams afford extensive water power. Organized in 1720. Capital, Hanover Court House. Population 15,153, of whom 6,760 were free, and 8393 slaves.

HANOVER COURT HOUSE, capital of Hanover county, Virginia, is situated one mile from the Pamunkey river, and twenty miles N. from Richmond. The railroad from Richmond to the Potomac passes near it. This place is memorable as the scene of Patrick Henry's early triumphs, and in more recent times as the birth place of Henry Clay.

HANSONVILLE, a post office of Russell county, Virginia.

HARDIN'S TAVERN, a post office of Albemarle county, Virginia, 88 miles W. by N. from Richmond.

HARDWARE RIVER, rises in Albemarle county, near the centre of Virginia, and falls into the James river in Fluvanna county.

HARDWICKSVILLE, a post office of Nelson county, Virginia.

HARDY, a county in the N. part of Virginia, bordering on Maryland, has an area of about 1400 square miles. It is intersected by the S. branch of the Potomac, which, in its passage through the county, receives two affluents, called the North and South forks; the county is also drained by the N. branch of the Potomac, and by Cacapon and Lost rivers. The surface is very mountainous and rocky. The North mountain forms its E. boundary; the main Alleghany and Branch mountains extend across the county. The soil of the valleys is fertile. Indian corn, wheat, hay, cattle, pork and butter are the staples. In 1850 this county produced 327,846 bushels of corn, 85,225 of wheat, 6362 tons of hay, and 119,686 of butter. There were 21 flour, grist and saw mills, four wool carding mills, and five tanneries. It contained eighteen churches, 622 pupils attending public schools, and 57 attending academies or other schools. The county has valuable mines of iron ore. It was named in

CLOTHING,

WHOLESALE AND RETAIL.

J. D. GOODMAN,

No. 134 Main street, opposite Eagle Square,

RICHMOND,

Invites the attention of all in want of clothing and furnishing goods to his large and extensive stock, which he will guarantee to sell at prices as low, if not lower, than any other Establishment in the city. All articles warranted of the best make, from finest to lowest grades. It is needless, after the long trial which the Public has had with my goods, to say more. All I ask is a fair trial, and none will be dissatisfied.

A partial List of Clothing for Winter, Spring and Summer:

Double OVER SACKS,
Beaver OVER SACKS,
French Tiger COATS,
DRESS COATS,
Splendid SACKS,
FROCK COATS,
Heavy Business FROCKS,
French Beaver OVERCOATS,
OVERCOATS of all grades,
Mackinaw, Tweeds, &c.
French Business FROCKS,
Black and Fancy Cassimere PANTS,
CLOAKS, all grades,
VESTS of Silk, Satin, Merino, Wool, Velvets, Valencias, Cassimeres, &c.

In my stock of GENTLEMEN'S SUMMER WEAR, I am always prepared to show the **Newest Styles and Latest Patterns of Goods.** All kinds of *Linen Frocks and Sacks*—Merino, Camlet, Drap d'ete, Tweeds, and every other New Style which may present itself; Black, Fancy, White and other styles of *Pants*, and every kind of *Vests*, usually worn by Gentlemen, which I offer UNUSUALLY LOW.

I have paid particular attention to the articles of

SHIRTS AND DRAWERS.

I keep a large supply of Linen and Cotton Shirts, from $1 to $2 each; also, every variety of Under Shirts, Merino, Lambs' Wool, Shaker, Net, Flannel, heavy, knit do; also, Drawers of the celebrated patent, that fit equal to well cut pantaloons; also, Buckskin and Silk Under Shirts and Drawers; Collars, all styles and prices.

Every description of Umbrellas, Gloves, Stocks, Half Hose, Ties, Suspenders, Cravats, Money Belts, Scarfs, Suspender Ends, Pocket Handkerchiefs, &c.

BUCK, SILK, MERINO, &c.

INDIA RUBBER GOODS,

RUBBER OVERCOATS,

PANTS,

CLOAKS, LEGGINGS, GLOVES,

Also a large assortment of

TRUNKS, CARPET BAGS, &c.

honor of Samuel Hardy, a member of Congress from Virginia in 1784. Capital, Moorefield. Population, 9543, of whom 8283 were free, and 1260 slaves.

Hargrove's Tavern, a post office of Nansemond county, Va.

Harmony, a post village in Halifax county, Virginia, 110 miles S. W. from Richmond.

Harmony Grove, a post office of Taylor county, Virginia.

Harper's Ferry, a post village of Jefferson county, Virginia, is situated at the confluence of the Shenandoah with the Potomac river, where the united stream breaks through the Blue Ridge, 160 miles N. from Richmond, and 53 miles N. W. from Washington city. The scenery in the vicinity is in the highest degree beautiful and picturesque. Thomas Jefferson considered the "passage of the Potomac through the Blue Ridge one of the most stupendous scenes in nature, and well worth a voyage across the Atlantic to witness." The place was originally named Shenandoah Falls. Its present name is derived from a ferry long since established across the Potomac, which is also spanned by a fine bridge, about 800 feet in length. The village is compactly, though irregularly, built around the base of a hill, and is the centre of considerable trade. It contains four or five churches, several manufactories and flouring mills, a United States armory, in which about 250 hands are employed, producing, among other articles, some 10,000 muskets annually, and a national arsenal. In the latter are continually stored from 80,000 to 90,000 stand of arms. As these are subject to the orders of the executive department at Washington, the deficiencies occurring from time to time are supplied from the factories. Harper's Ferry is in the line of the Baltimore and Ohio railroad, and at the northern terminus of a railroad connecting it with Winchester. The Ohio and Chesapeake canal also passes along the opposite side of the Potomac.

Harper's Home, a post office of Brunswick county, Virginia.

Harper's Mills, a post office of Pendleton county, Virginia.

Harris, a post office of Louisa county, Virginia.

Harrisonburg, a neat and thriving post village, capital of Rockingham county, Virginia, 125 miles N. W. from Richmond. It is surrounded by a fertile and beautiful country, and has considerable business. There are three churches and two printing offices. Laid out in 1780. Population in 1853, estimated at 1300.

JOHN & GEORGE GIBSON,

HOUSE CARPENTERS

AND

BUILDERS,

North Corner of Cary and 6th Streets,

RICHMOND,

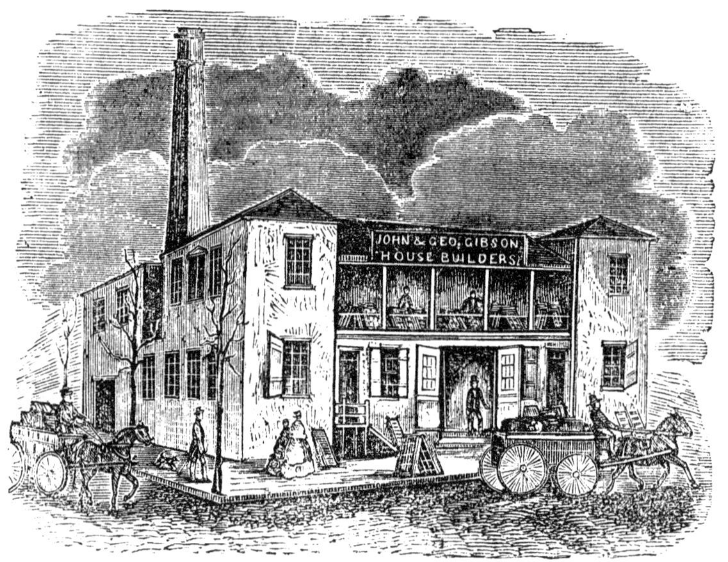

Execute all work in their line of business in a manner not to be surpassed. All kinds of

CARPENTER'S WORK

DONE IN A NEAT AND DURABLE MANNER.

All work executed by them is warranted, and their terms are reasonable and accommodating. Every description of

SASH AND BLINDS

Furnished in any quantity, at short notice, and on reasonable terms.

They solicit a share of public patronage.

HARRISVILLE, a small post-village, capital of Ritchie county, Virginia, 4 miles from the northwestern turnpike, and 37 miles E. from Parkersburg. It contains 2 churches.

HARTWOOD, a post-office of Stafford county, Virginia.

HAT CREEK, a post-office of Campbell county, Virginia.

HAWSBURG, a post-village in Rappahannock county, Virginia, 130 miles N. N. W. from Richmond.

HAYES' STORE, a post-office of Gloucester county, Virginia.

HAYLEYSBURG, a post-office of Lunenburg county, Virginia, 95 miles S. W. from Richmond.

HAY MARKET, a post-village in Prince William county, Virginia, 110 miles N. from Richmond.

HAYTER'S GAP, a post-office of Washington county, Virginia.

HAZARD FORGE, a post-office of Hardy county, Virginia.

HEAD OF CLINCH, a post-office of Tazewell county, Virginia.

HEAD WATERS, a post-office of Highland county, Virginia.

HEATHSVILLE, a handsome post-village, capital of Northumberland county, Virginia, is situated on the Northern Neck, 92 miles N. E. from Richmond, and 1 mile from the head of Coan river, a navigable inlet opening into the Potomac. It has a large church, an academy, and a mill.

HEBRON, a post-office of Tyler county, Virginia.

HEDGESVILLE, a thriving post-village of Berkley county, Virginia, 1 mile from the Baltimore and Ohio railroad, 187 miles N. by W. from Richmond. Population, about 300.

HEDGMAN'S RIVER, in the N. E. part of Virginia, flows along the S. W. border of Fauquier county, and unites with Thornton's river to form the North river, or Rappahannock.

HENDRICKS' MILLS, a post-office of Russell county, Virginia.

HENDRICKS' STORE, a post-office of Bedford county, Virginia.

HENRICO, hen-ri'co, a county towards the S. E. part of Virginia, has an area of 280 square miles. The James river forms its boundary on the S. W., and the Chickahominy on the N. E. The surface is diversified by hills of moderate height and declivity, presenting abrupt precipices along the banks of the rivers. The soil, with small exceptions, is light and inferior. Wheat, Indian corn, oats, hay, cotton, and butter are the staples. In 1850 this county produced 113,044 bushels of wheat; 266,011 of corn; 83,832 of oats; 2196 tons of hay; 338 bales of cotton, and 66,615 pounds of butter. There were 32 tobacco

factories, 10 flour and grist mills, 4 chandleries, 1 paper mill, 1 iron foundry, 4 coal mines, 5 saw mills, 1 iron forge, and 4 machine shops. It contained 44 churches, 15 newspaper offices, 859 pupils attending public schools, and 1123 attending academies and other schools. The dividing line between the tertiary and primary formations passes through the county. Large quantities of bituminous coal are procured in the western part. The falls of James river, at Richmond, afford extensive water-power. The James river and Kanawha canal has its eastern terminus in this county, and three lines of railways connect with each other at Richmond, namely, the Richmond and Danville, the Richmond and Petersburg, and the Richmond and Potomac. Henrico is the most populous county in the State. Richmond is the county seat and capital of Virginia. Named in honor of Prince Henry of England, son of James the first. Population about 60,000.

HENRIE'S FORK, a post-office of Gilmer county, Virginia.

HENRY, a county in the S. part of Virginia, bordering on North Carolina, has an area of about 325 square miles. Smith's river, an affluent of the Dan, flows through the county. The surface is hilly; the soil produces tobacco, Indian corn and wheat. In 1850 there were raised 1,013,079 pounds of tobacco; 232,311 bushels of corn, and 29,704 of wheat. There were 6 flour, grist, and saw mills, 2 tanneries, and 22 tobacco factories. It contained 13 churches, and 1391 pupils attending public schools. Formed in 1776, and named in honor of the celebrated orator, Patrick Henry. Capital, Martinsville. Population, 8872, of whom 5532 were free, and 3340 slaves.

HENRY, a post-office of Sussex county, Virginia.

HEREFORD'S, a post-office of Mason county, Virginia.

HERMITAGE, a post-office of Augusta county, Virginia.

HEVENER'S STORE, a post-office of Highland county, Virginia.

HICKORY FORK, a post-office of Gloucester county, Virginia.

HICKORY GROUND, a post-office of Norfolk county, Virginia.

HICKSFORD, a post-village, capital of Greenville county, Virginia, on the Meherrin river, and on the great Southern line of railroad, 62 miles S. from Richmond. The Greenville and Roanoke railroad extends from this point to Gaston.

HIGGINSVILLE, a post-office of Hampshire county, Virginia.

HIGHLAND, a county in the central part of Virginia, contains

JOHN & JOSEPH WALKER,

WHOLESALE DRUGGISTS,

DEALERS IN

PAINTS, OILS, WINDOW-GLASS,

DYE-STUFFS PERFUMERY, &c.

No. 41 SOUTH CHARLES STREET, NEAR LOMBARD STREET,

BALTIMORE.

WM. McGOWAN. JOHN C. McGOWAN.

JOHN McGOWAN & SONS,

GROCERS

AND

COMMISSION MERCHANTS,

No. 378 WEST MARKET STREET,

BALTIMORE.

C. C. O'NEIL,

COMMISSION MERCHANT

AND DEALER IN IMPORTED

BRANDIES, WINES, GIN,

Scotch & Irish Whiskey,

LONDON BROWN STOUT,

Scotch Ales, Domestic Liquors, Segars,

COUNTRY PRODUCE GENERALLY,

Choice Groceries, Teas, &c.

S. E. CORNER OF HOWARD AND PRATT STREETS,

(Near B. & O. R. R. Depot,)

BALTIMORE.

REFERS TO

DRAKELY & FENTON,
R. GARRETT & SONS,
C. C. JAMIESON, Prest. Bank of Balto.
MILLER & MAYHEW.

REYNOLDS, SMITH & CO.
G. R. GAITHER, Esq.
L. B. BANKS, Prest. U. M. Co. Md.

about 400 square miles. The head streams of the Potomac and James rivers rise within its limits, and flow in opposite directions. The surface is diversified by valleys and mountains, having the main Allegany on the N. W. border, and Jackson's River mountain in the middle. The highlands produce valuable timber and excellent pasture, and contain iron ore. Indian corn, wheat, oats, hay, and butter are the staples. In 1850 the county produced 54,241 bushels of corn; 22,456 of wheat; 34,644 of oats; 6354 tons of hay; and 83,067 pounds of butter. There were 3 grist mills and 4 tanneries. It contained 10 churches, and 135 pupils attending academies or other schools. Formed, in 1848, of parts of Bath and Pendleton counties. Capital, Monterey. Population, 4227; of whom 3863 were free, and 364 slaves.

HIGHLAND, a post-office of Ritchie county, Virginia.

HIGHVIEW, a post-office of Frederick county, Virginia.

HILL GROVE, a post-office of Pittsylvania county, Virginia.

HILLSBOROUGH, a post-village of Loudoun county, Virginia, 165 miles N. from Richmond. It contains 1 or 2 churches, 1 academy, and 2 flour mills. Population, about 300.

HILLSBOROUGH, a post-village of Tyler county, Virginia, on Middle Island creek, 6 miles from the Ohio river, has about 100 inhabitants.

HILLSVILLE, a post-village, capital of Carroll county, Virginia, 260 miles W. by S. from Richmond. It contains a court house, a church, and an academy. Population about 200.

HOLCOMB'S ROCK, a post-office of Bedford county, Virginia.

HOLLIDAY'S COVE, a post-office of Hancock county, Virginia.

HOLLY RIVER, a post-office of Braxton county, Virginia.

HOLSTON, a post-office of Washington county, Virginia.

HOLY NECK, a post-office of Nansemond county, Virginia.

HONEYVILLE, a post-village of Page county, Virginia, on Honey creek, 137 miles N. W. from Richmond. It contains 1 church and several mills.

HOODSVILLE, a post-office of Marion county, Virginia.

HOPE MILLS, a post-office of Page county, Virginia, 140 miles N. W. from Richmond.

HOREB, a post-office of Bedford county, Virginia.

HORN CREEK, a post-office of Gilmer county, Virginia.

HORNTOWN, a small post-village of Accomac county, Virginia,

is on a navigable creek which communicates with the Atlantic, 26 miles N. E. from Accomac Court House.

HORSE PASTURE, a post-office of Henry county, Virginia.

HOT SPRINGS, a post-village of Bath county, Virginia, 175 miles W. N. W. from Richmond. This place is situated in a narrow valley, and surrounded by a mountainous region which is remarkable for the salubrity of its climate and for the charming character of its scenery. There are several springs here, which vary in temperature from 98° to 106°, and are considered efficacious in the cure of dyspepsia, rheumatism, affections of the liver, etc. The water contains the sulphates of lime and of magnesia, the carbonates of lime and of magnesia, and sulphate of soda. A spring of extremely cold water rises in close proximity to one at 98°. Several bathing houses and other buildings have been erected here.

HOWARDSVILLE, a post-office of Albemarle county, Virginia.

HOYSVILLE, a post-village of Loudoun county, Virginia, 165 miles N. from Richmond.

HUGHES RIVER, of Western Virginia, rises in Lewis and Doddridge counties, flows Westward and enters the Little Kanawha river, near the northern border of Wirt county.

HUGHESVILLE, a post-village of Loudoun county, Virginia, 154 miles N. from Richmond.

HUMILITY, a post-office of Pulaski county, Virginia.

HUNTERSVILLE, a small post-village, capital of Pocahontas county, Virginia, 220 miles W. N. W. from Richmond, is situated between the Allegany and Greenbrier mountains.

HUNTING CREEK, a post-office of Accomac county, Virginia.

HURRICANE BRIDGE, a post-office of Putnam county, Virginia.

HUTTONSVILLE, a post-village of Randolph county, Virginia, 200 miles N. W. from Richmond.

HYCO, a post-office of Halifax county, Virginia.

HYCO FALLS, a post-office of Halifax county, Virginia.

HYDRAULIC MILLS, a post-village of Albemarle county, Virginia, 100 miles W. N. W. from Richmond.

ICE'S FERRY, a post-office of Monongalia county, Virginia.

INDEPENDENCE, a small post-village, capital of Grayson county, Virginia, 288 miles W. S. W. from Richmond. It is situated in a wild, mountainous region.

INDEPENDENCE, a small village of Preston county, Virginia, on the Baltimore and Ohio railroad.

INDEPENDENCE HILL, a post-office of Prince William county, Va.

INDIAN CREEK, a post-village of Monroe county, Virginia, 190 miles W. from Richmond.

INDIAN VALLEY, a post-office of Floyd county, Virginia.

IRELAND, a post-office of Lewis county, Virginia.

IRISBURG, a post-office of Henry county, Virginia.

IRON MOUNTAIN, in the S. W. part of Virginia, between Grayson and Smith counties, near the border of North Carolina. Its highest summit, termed Whitetop mountain, is said to be 4260 feet above the level of the sea.

ISLE OF WIGHT, a county in the S. E. part of Virginia, at the mouth of James river, which washes the N. E. border. It has an area of about 230 square miles. The Blackwater river forms the W. boundary. The surface is nearly level; the soil is generally thin and sandy. A portion of the land is occupied by swamps and pine forests. Indian corn is the staple product. Bacon of superior quality is exported. In 1850 there were raised 315,699 bushels of corn, and 89,713 of sweet potatoes. It contained 1 cotton factory, 1 saw mill, and 1 tannery; 19 churches, 149 pupils attending public schools, and 56 attending academies or other schools. The Isle of Wight was one of the eight original shires into which Virginia was divided in 1634. Capital, Smithfield. Population, 9353, of whom 5958 were free, and 3395 slaves.

IVES' STORE, a post-office of Princess Anne county, Virginia.

IVY CREEK MILLS, a post-office of Bedford county, Virginia.

JACKSON, a county in the W. N. W. part of Virginia, bordering on the Ohio river, which separates it from the State of Ohio, contains 405 square miles. The Ohio river washes its W. border, and it is drained by the Sandy and Big Mill Creeks. The surface is hilly; the soil is generally adapted to grazing, and there is good arable land near the streams. The chief productions are corn, wheat, oats, hemp, lumber, pork and cattle. In 1850 there were raised 257,242 bushels of Indian corn; 16,630 of wheat; 43,324 of oats, and 98,561 pounds of butter were made. There were 13 flour, grist, and saw mills, 1 wool-carding mill, and 2 tanneries; 3 churches, and 1350 pupils attending public schools. The county contains limetone of good quality. Capital, Ripley. Population, 6544, of whom 6491 were free, and 52 slaves.

JACKSON, a post-village of Louisa county, Virginia, 37 miles N. W. from Richmond.

JACKSON COURT HOUSE, Virginia. See RIPLEY.

JACKSON'S FERRY, a post-office of Wythe county, Virginia.

JACKSON'S RIVER of Virginia, the principal constituent of James river, is formed by two branches, the North and South forks, which rise in Highland county, in the N. central part of the State, and flowing south-westward, unite in Bath county. The river then pursues a southerly course to the mouth of Potts' creek, in Allegany county, where it turns toward the north-east, and flowing through rugged mountain passes, unites with the Cowpasture river, (the other branch of the James river,) near the boundary between Allegany and Botetourt counties, about 15 miles below Covington. The passage of this river through Waite's mountain is remarkable for its sublime scenery. The length of the main stream is estimated at above 50 miles, and each of the branches has about the same extent.

JACKSONVILLE, a small post-village, capital of Floyd county, Virginia, 230 miles W. by S. from Richmond. It contains the county buildings, a church, an academy, and about 250 inhabitants.

JACOB'S CHURCH, a post-office of Shenandoah county, Virginia.

JAKE'S RUN, a post-office of Monongalia Co., Virginia.

JAMAICA, a post-office of Middlesex Co., Virginia.

JAMES CITY, a county in the S. E. part of Virginia, contains 184 square miles. The York river bounds it on the N. E., the James river on the S., and the Chickahominy on the W. The surface is undulating. Corn, wheat, oats, and butter are cultivated. In 1850 this county produced 102,430 bushels of corn ; 25,476 of wheat ; 22,040 of oats ; and 17,785 pounds of butter. There were in that year 280 pupils attending academies and other schools. The exports consist of oak and pine wood for fuel, and oysters. This is one of the eight original shires into which Virginia was divided in 1634. Capital, Williamsburg. Population 4020, of whom 2152 were free, and 1868, slaves.

JAMES RIVER, the largest of the rivers which have their course wholly within the State of Virginia, is formed by the Jackson and Cowpasture rivers, which unite 15 miles below Covington, on the border between Allegany and Botetourt counties. Flowing first south-eastward through the mountains of Central Virginia, it is joined by the Calfpasture river from the left at the base of the Blue

Ridge, through which it forces a passage about 15 miles N. E. from the Peaks of Otter. It then flows south-eastward, passes by Lynchburg, and at the southern extremity of Amherst county changes its course to the north-east. Below Scottsville its general direction is east-south-east. After passing by Richmond, where the channel is divided by numerous islands, and the river descends over rocky rapids about 6 miles in extent, it gradually expands into an estuary of several miles in width, and flows into the southern extremity of Chesapeake bay, between Willoughby Point and Old Point Comfort. The whole length, exclusive of the branches, is about 450 miles. The tide ascends to Richmond, about 150 miles from the sea. It is navigable for vessels of 130 tons to the port of Richmond, from which point the James River and Kanawha canal has been constructed along the upper part of the river. This canal is completed to Buchanan, beyond the Blue Ridge, and is to be extended to Covington on Jackson's river. Here it will connect with the eastern terminus of the Covington and Ohio railroad, now in course of construction. James river passes through a fertile and populous country, and is an important channel of trade. The chief towns on its banks are Richmond, Lynchburg, Scottsville, Manchester, and Buchanan. That part of the estuary which lies between Hampton and Norfolk is called Hampton Roads.

JAMESTOWN, a village in James City county, Virginia, on the N. bank of Jamestown river, 50 miles E. S. E. from Richmond. The first English settlement in the United States was made at this place in 1608; nothing now remains but a few ruins.

JANATTS, a post-office of Sussex Co., Va.

JANELEW, a post-village of Lewis county, Virginia, about 280 miles N. W. from Richmond.

JARRETT'S, a post-office of Sussex county, Virginia.

JARRETT'S FORD, a post-office of Kanawha county, Virginia.

JEFFERSON, a county in the N. N. E. part of Virginia, bordering on the Potomac, which separates it from Maryland, has an area of 260 square miles. It is intersected by the Shenandoah, which enters the Potomac on the north-castern border, and bounded on the N. W. by Opequan creek. The county occupies part of the Great Valley of Virginia, having the Blue Ridge on its S. E. border. The surface is rolling, and the soil remarkably fertile. Wheat, Indian corn, hay, butter, cattle and swine are the staples. In 1850 this county produced 472,008 bushels of wheat; 287,395 of corn;

5558 tons of hay; 130,198 pounds of butter. There were 2 cotton factories, 23 flour mills, 5 cotton and woolen factories, 1 United States armory, and 2 iron foundries. It contained 20 churches, 1000 pupils attending public schools, and 165 attending acadamies or other schools. The rock which underlies the county is fine limestone. The passage of the Potomac through the Blue Ridge, at Harper's Ferry, so much admired for its picturesque effect, will be described under the head VIRGINIA. This county is intersected by the Baltimore and Ohio railroad, and by the Winchester and Potomac railroad. Organized in 1801. Capital, Charlestown. Population, 15,357, of whom 11,016 were free, and 4341, slaves.

JEFFERSON, a post-village of Powhatan county, Virginia, on the S. bank of James river, 35 miles above Richmond.

JEFFERSONTON, a post-village of Culpepper county, Virginia, on the Rappahannock river, 109 miles N. N. W. from Richmond. It contains 1 church and about 300 inhabitants.

JEFFERSONVILLE, a post-village, capital of Tazewell county, Virginia, one mile S. from Clinch river, and 300 miles W. by S. from Richmond. It is situated near the base of Rich mountain. It has 1 bank.

JEFFREY'S STORE, a post-office of Nottoway county, Vlrginia.

JENNING'S GAP, a post-village of Augusta county, Virginia, 133 miles W. N. W. from Richmond. There is a pass through North Mountain at this place.

JENNING'S ORDINARY, a post-office of Nottaway county, Va.,

JERUSALEM, a small post-village, capital of Southampton county, Virginia, on the Nottoway river, 75 miles S. S. E. from Richmond.

JETERSVILLE, a post-village of Amelia county, Virginia, 54 miles S. W. from Richmond.

JOHNSON'S SPRINGS, a post-village of Goochland county, Va., 28 miles W. from Richmond.

JOHNSONTOWN, a post-office of Northampton county, Virginia.

JONESBOROUGH, a post-village of Brunswick county, Virginia, about 90 miles S. by W. from Richmond.

JONES' MILLS, a post-office of Washington county, Virginia.

JONES' SPRING, a post-office of Berkeley county, Virginia.

JONESVILLE, a small post-village, capital of Lee county, Virginia, on Powell's river, 392 miles W. S. W. from Richmond. It is situated on a beautiful eminence, near the foot of Cumberland mountain. Population, about 300.

W. T. WALTERS & CO.

IMPORTERS AND DEALERS IN

LIQUORS,

No. 68 Exchange Place, Baltimore.

IN BONDED WAREHOUSES OF OUR OWN IMPORTATION:

Cognac Brandies—"Otard," "Hennessy," "Pinnet," "Martell," &c.
Rochelle Brandies—"Seignette," "Pellevoisin," "Durand & Co.," &c., &c.
Holland Gin " "Grape," "Crown," "Imperial Pear," &c. &c.
Wines—Including "Champagne," "Sherry," "Port," "Madeira," &c.

AMERICAN LIQUORS, included in which we guarantee the finest stock of OLD RYE WHISKEY in the United States, "BAKER," "JOHNSTON MARTIN," "PURE RYE," "EXTRA SUPERIOR," (STAR "SUPERIOR," and "MONONGAHELA."

Domestic Brandy, Gin, Pure Spirits, Tuscaloosa Extra, Rectified Whiskey, Bitters, Imitation Wine, &c. Ginger, Raspberry, Lavender and Wild Cherry Brandy. All guaranteed to be unsurpassed, and to give satisfaction or be taken back.

JUNCTION, a post office, of Hanover county, Virginia.

JUNCTION STORE, a post-office of Botetourt county, Virginia.

CANAWHA, a county in the W. part of Virginia, has an area of 1176 square miles. It is intersected by the Great Kanawha, from which the name is derived, and also drained by the Elk, Coal, and Pocatalico rivers. The surface is beautifully diversified by mountains, hills, and fertile valleys. The highlands are mostly covered with forests, and contain inexhaustible beds of stone coal. Indian corn, wheat, oats, hay, and butter are the staples of agriculture. Large quantities of salt are prepared from numerous springs on the banks of the Kanawha river, a few miles above Charleston. In 1850 this county produced 352,995 bushels of corn ; 25,074 of wheat ; 58,596 of oats, and 2014 tons of hay. There were 33 salt-boiling establishments, 9 grist mills, 14 saw mills, and 3 machine shops. It contained 25 churches ; 1300 pupils attending public schools, and 162 attending academies or other schools. The principal rock of the county is sandstone. Steamboats navigate the Kanawha river in this county, which is intersected by the Covington and Ohio railroad, unfurnished. Capital, Charleston. Population, 15,353, of whom 12,213 were free, and 3140 slaves.

KANAWHA SALINE, or MALDIN, a post-town in Kanawha county, Virginia, on Great Kanawha river, 260 miles W. N. W. from Richmond. Has a bank and numerous stores, 4 churches, 2 seminaries. Population about 1,000.

KASEY'S, a post-office of Bedford county, Virginia.

KEEZLETOWN, a post-office of Rockingham county, Virginia.

KELLYSVILLE, a post-office of Culpepper county, Virginia.

KEMPSVILLE, a post-village of Princess Anne county, Virginia, on the E. branch of Elizabeth river, at the head of tide-water, 124 miles S. E. from Richmond.

KENDRICK'S SPUR, a post-office of Patrick county, Virginia.

KENNEDY'S, a post-office of Brunswick county, Virginia, 66 miles S. S. W. from Richmond.

KERNEYSVILLE, a post-office of Jefferson county, Va.

KERR'S CREEK, a post-office of Rockbridge county, Virginia.

KESNICK DEPOT, a post-office of Albemarle county, Virginia.

KILMARNOCK, a post-village of Lancaster county, Virginia, on a small creek of Chesapeake bay, 90 miles E. by N. from Richmond. It contains 4 churches and several stores.

KIMBERLIN, a post-office of Giles county, Virginia.

KINDERHOOK, a post-office of Washington county, Virginia.

KING AND QUEEN, a county in the S. E. part of Virginia, has an area of 330 square miles. The Mattapony and York rivers form its boundary on the south-west, and the Piankatank on the N. E. The surface is undulating rather than hilly ; the soil is not very rich. Indian corn, wheat, wool, and butter are the staples. In 1850 this county produced 376,986 bushels of corn ; 68,755 of wheat ; 11,034 pounds of wool, and 48,883 of butter. It contained 2 saw mills and 1 tannery ; 18 churches, 281 pupils attending public schools, and 110 attending academies or other schools. The county contains large beds of marl, which is used in fertilizing the soil. Capital, King and Queen Court House. Population, 10,319, of whom 4555 were free, and 5764 slaves.

KING AND QUEEN COURT HOUSE, a small post-village, capital of the above county, on the Mattapony river, 49 miles E. by N. from Richmond.

KING GEORGE, a county in the E. part of Virginia, contains 176 square miles. The Potomac bounds it on the N. and E., and the Rappahannock on the S. The surface is hilly and the soil diversified. Corn, wheat, butter, and pork are the staples. In 1850, it produced 241,900 bushels of corn ; 76,707 of wheat, and 40,090 pounds of butter. There were 3 grist mills and 2 carpenter shops, besides other establishments. It contained 8 churches and 200 pupils attending public schools. Capital, King George Court House. Population, 5971 ; of whom 2563 were free, and 3403 slaves.

JAMES MONROE,
Born in Westmoreland County, April 2, 1759.

James Monroe was born in Westmoreland county, but first elected to a seat in the Legislature, by the county of King George,—in the 24th year of his age.

KING GEORGE COURT HOUSE, a small post-village, capital of the above county, 70 miles N. N. E. from Richmond.

KING WILLIAM, a county in the E. part of Virginia, has an area of 260 square miles. Its N. E. and S. W. borders are respectively washed by the Mattapony and Pamunky rivers, which unite at the

McINTOSH'S
HOWARD HOUSE,
HOWARD STREET,
BALTIMORE,
JOHN McINTOSH, Proprietor,

NATIONAL HOTEL,
CAMDEN STREET,
Opposite B. & O. R. R. Depot,
BALTIMORE,
G. W. LANE & CO.
PROPRIETORS.

☞ All Passengers and Baggage to and from the Baltimore and Ohio Depot, and Eastern and Western Shore Boats, will be carried without charge.

MURPHY'S
NEW
DEPOT RESTAURANT,
B. & O. R. R.
Corner of Camden and Howard Sts.
BALTIMORE.

TRAVELERS AND EPICURES CAN BE ACCOMMODATED.

BILL OF FARE
READY AT ALL HOURS.

Ladies' Refreshment & Oyster Saloon.

S. E. extremity of the county, and form the York river. The surface is undulating, the soil of the river bottoms is fertile. Indian corn, wheat, and butter are the staples. In 1850 this county produced 253,685 bushels of corn; 108,819 of wheat, and 32,580 lbs. of butter. There were 4 flour and grist mills, 1 tannery, and 2 manufactories of agricultural implements. It contained 9 churches, and 238 pupils attending academies and other schools. Pamunky river is navigable on the border of the county. Formed in 1701, and named in honor of William III, king of England. Capital, King William Court House. Population 8779; of whom 3048 were free, and 5731 slaves.

King William Court House, a small post-village, capital of the above county, is situated between the Mattapony and Pamunky rivers, two miles from the former, and 27 miles N. E. from Richmond.

Kingwood, a small post-village, capital of Preston county, Va., on the Cheat river, 280 miles N. W. from Richmond. The river affords excellent water-power.

Kinsale, a post-office of Westmoreland county, Virginia.

Kittoctan Creek, in the N. E. part of Virginia, flows through Loudoun county and falls into the Potomac above the Point of Rocks, after a course of about 30 miles.

Knob, a post-office of Tazewell county, Virginia.

Knob Fork, a post-office of Wetzel county, Virginia.

Lacey Spring, a post-office of Rockingham county, Virginia.

Lafayette, a post-village of Montgomery county, Virginia, on the Roanoke river, about 190 miles W. by S. from Richmond. Population from 200 to 300.

Lafayette Hill, a post-office of Fluvanna county, Virginia.

Lancaster, a county in the E. part of Virginia, bordering on Chesapeake bay, at the mouth of Rappahannock river, which forms its S. W. boundary. Area, 108 square miles. The surface is moderately uneven; the soil is sandy and light. Indian corn, wheat, and potatoes are the staples. In 1850 this county produced 120,530 bushels of corn; 24,424 of wheat; and 10,857 of sweet potatoes. There were 2 coach factories and 1 tannery. It contained 10 churches, 282 pupils attending public schools, and 46 attending an academy. Organized in 1652. Capital, Lancaster Court House. Population, 4708, of whom 2068 were free, and 2640 slaves.

Lancaster Court House, a post-village, capital of Lancaster

co., Virginia, 80 miles N. E. from Richmond, contains, besides the county buildings, several stores.

LAND OF PROMISE, a post office of Princess Anne county, Virginia.

LANDSDOWN, a post office of Prince William county, Virginia.

LANESVILLE, a small post village of King William county, Virginia, about 28 miles N. E. from Richmond.

LANGHORNE'S TAVERN, a post office of Cumberland county, Virginia, 61 miles west of Richmond.

LANGLEY, a post office of Fairfax county, Virginia.

LAUREL, a post-office of Washington county, Virginia.

LAUREL CREEK, a post-office of Floyd county, Virginia.

LAUREL FORK, a post-office of Carroll county, Virginia.

LAUREL GROVE, a post-office of Pittsylvania county, Virginia.

LAUREL HILL, a post-office of Lunenburg county, Virginia, 94 miles S. W. from Richmond.

LAUREL MILLS, a post office in Rappahannock county, Virginia.

LAUREL POINT, a post office of Monongalia county, Virginia.

LAWRENCEVILLE, a pleasant post village, capital of Brunswick county, Virginia, on Great creek, about 70 miles S. S. W. from Richmond. It contains a court house and two handsome churches. Population from 300 to 400.

LEADING CREEK, a post village of Lewis county, Virginia, 18 miles W. from Weston.

LEADSVILLE, a post office of Randolph county, Virginia.

LEATHERWOOD'S STORE, a post office of Henry county, Virginia, 192 miles W. S. W. from Richmond.

LEBANON, a small post village, capital of Russell county, Virginia, is finely situated on an affluent of Clinch river, 325 miles W. by S. from Richmond.

LEBANON WHITE SULPHUR SPRINGS, a post office of Augusta county, Virginia.

LEE, a county forming the S. W. extremity of Virginia, bordering on Tennessee and Kentucky, has an area of 550 square miles. It is intersected by Powell's river, an affluent of the Clinch. Cumberland mountain forms the N. W. boundary, and Powell's mountain extends along or near the E. border; the soil of the valleys is fertile. Beef, pork and horses are the staples. Maple sugar is made for domestic consumption. In 1850 this county produced 485,725 bushels of Indian corn, and 107,030 of oats. There were

TO
PORK & BEEF BUTCHERS,
PRIVATE FAMILIES AND OTHERS.

F. B. DIDIER & BRO'S
IMPROVED
SAUSAGE OR PIE MEAT CUTTER
FOR 1854.
PATENT APPLIED FOR.

This celebrated Machine is warranted, with proper care and use, to cut or mince 4 lbs. of fine meat per minute; or 240 lbs. per hour,—not liable to get out of repair, and easily operated by a small boy. The simplicity of construction and the ease with which every part, subject to wear, may be replaced, serve to recommend this as the cheapest and most perfect machine ever invented. Being made entirely of Iron, (with one or two exceptions) renders it much more durable than those usually made of wood, and much easier kept sweet and clean, and no warping or swelling when necessarily used, as is the case with all others.

N. B. One great objection to Meat Cutters is that the knives are stationary. In our machine the objection is obviated, as the knives can be taken out, cleaned and put back in a minute. The machine is regulated for cutting fine or coarse meat by putting in more or less knives.

☞ It is warranted to cut Sausage or Pie meat equal to any Machine in the Country, both as regards quantity and quality. Also, warranted to cut five times the amount, and of a better quality than any cutter at the price,—Again, less complicated, more durable, requiring less power to operate it than any similar invention of the age.

☞ The Maryland State Agricultural Fair, and the Maryland Mechanics' Institute, awarded this Machine a first class Premium in the years 1851, 1852, and 1853; and encomiums of the like flattering character from discriminating Judges, have, on all occasions of competition, favored this useful article. Retail price $5.50.

A first rate article of Sausage Stuffer or Filler, retail from $4, $4.50, $5, $5.50.

N. B. Agricultural Implement Makers and Venders, Hardware Merchants and others, would do well to take this machine on sale, owing to its popularity and the liberal discounts made to the trade. The article is bound to be in the possession of every farmer and private family.

We have in store and ready for the season about 5000 Cutters, for which we solicit buyers. Wholesale and Retail.

F. B. DIDIER & BRO.

No. 37 North Paca Street,

BALTIMORE.

two iron forges and two tanneries. It contained 25 churches and 550 pupils attending public schools. Iron ore, saltpetre and limestone are abundant in the county. The streams furnish valuable water power. Organized in 1792, and named in honor of Henry Lee, at that time Governor of the State. Capital, Jonesville. Population 10,267; of whom 9480 were free, and 787 slaves.

LEED'S MANOR, a post office of Fauquier county, Virginia.

LEEDSVILLE, a village in Randolph county, Virginia, 175 miles N. W. from Richmond.

LEESBURG, a handsome post borough, capital of Loudoun county, Virginia, is situated near the Kittoctan mountain, three miles from the Potomac river, and 150 miles N. from Richmond. The streets are well paved and the town is built in a neat and substantial manner. It contains a court house, three churches, a bank, an academy and two newspaper offices. It is surrounded by a fertile, well cultivated country, which presents a variety of landscapes. Population in 1850, 1,691; in 1853 about 2,000.

LEESVILLE, a post village in Campbell county, Virginia, 110 miles W. S. W. from Richmond.

LEETOWN, a small post village of Jefferson county, Virginia, 165 miles N. from Richmond.

LEON, a post village in Madison county, Virginia, 160 miles N. W. of Richmond.

LEVEL GREEN, a post office of Giles county, Virginia.

LEWIS, a county in the N. W. part of Virginia, has an area of 530 square miles. It is intersected by the W. fork of Monongahela river. The surface is rocky, hilly, and in some parts mountainous. The soil of the valleys produces pasture and Indian corn. In 1850 there were raised 235,675 bushels of corn, and 9190 tons of hay. There were seven flour, grist and saw mills, and four tanneries. It contained 15 churches, and 1602 pupils attending public schools. Stone coal is found in the county. A turnpike has been constructed from Weston to Fairmont, on the Baltimore and Ohio railroad. Formed in 1816 and named in honor of Colonel Charles Lewis. Capital, Weston. Population 10,031, of whom 9663 were free and 368 slaves.

LEWISBURG, a thriving post village, capital of Greenbrier county, Virginia, 214 miles west from Richmond, and nine miles west from the White Sulphur Springs. It is surrounded by a beautiful and healthy region among the mountains, and is a place of active

FRENCH BURR MILLSTONES AND BURR BLOCKS,

WARRANTED.

Bolting Cloth.
Calcined Plaster.

Esopus Millstones,
Cologne, Cocalico,
AND

MORRIS & TRIMBLE,

WEST FALLS AVENUE, NEAR PRATT STREET BRIDGE,

BALTIMORE,

Manufacturers of French BURR MILLSTONES, *warranted* of superior quality and workmanship, being made from Burr Blocks of their own importation and selected from the best quarries in France.

Orders, with reference in any of the Eastern Cities, promptly executed.

From the Baltimore American.

NEW BRICK MACHINE.

Among the many astonishing evidences of the power of machinery, and the perfection to which it has attained, none seem more worthy of examination and commendable notice than the Steam Brick Works of Mr. Francis H. Smith. The proprietor has in constant operation one of his first class machines, for which a gold medal was awarded him by the Maryland Institute. Since that time, however, he has introduced such improvements as, in the opinion of scientific men, warrant the merit of a new invention. The *modus operandi*, nevertheless, is quite simple. The clay is wheeled along on a plank scaffolding to the pulverizer at the top of the machine, which converts it into dust immediately, and incorporates it with the water thrown thereupon. In this state it is thrown into the machine, which revolves steadily, pressing the clay down into sets of moulds, five in each frame, which move on a railway beneath. The moulds are then transferred to a light barrow, moved to the yard and discharged in the usual way. The clay is worked much stiffer than it can be done with the hand, and gives a solidity to the brick and correctness of form rarely equaled. We timed the operation by the watch, and found it producing 30 bricks per minute—the average speed, however, is 25 per minute. It will easily produce 15,000 per day.

We next saw in operation a similar machine, worked by a horse, with the same result—the bricks being equal in every respect, and fifteen made per minute. Machinery has hitherto been directed to work either the dry clay or soft mud. The present invention is intended for a medium between these extremes, and to mould the bricks from clay, tempered to a consistence fit for the potters' wheel, or suitable for front brick, and, consequently, in quality, they must nearly resemble the latch brick.

The work is performed by ordinary laborers, chiefly boys. Each person must be promptly at his post, for the machine will not allow laziness nor indulgence—it waits for no one.

THE NEW

BRICK MACHINE

Is now in constant operation at my Yard on LOCUST POINT. If driven by steam, the clay is taken from the bank, passed through a pulverizer (which removes the stone,) into the soak pit, where it receives the water, thence to the machine, which is geared to make 6½ revolutions per minute, turning out five bricks each time, or 1750 bricks an hour, including contingencies. Ten men and six boys, all common laborers, take the clay from the pit and place the bricks on the floor. If there be no stone the pulverizer is not required; the clay is then thrown into the pit, mixed with water, and after remaining all night is ready for use. Machine $425; Pulverizer $75, with right to work it.

If driven by a horse, the clay is thrown into heaps, and each successive layer saturated; after remaining in soak all night it is shoveled into the machine. They were formerly built of two sizes, four and five mould. By a recent improvement the speed of the shaft is increased without changing the gait of the horse, and thus the smaller size can make 1000 bricks per hour, worked by four men and four boys. It is liable to no accident except from stone, which is apt to break a mould. Price $275.

For further particulars, in a pamphlet containing full instructions on Brick Burning, address

FRANCIS H. SMITH, Baltimore.

business. The court of appeals for the western counties is held at Lewisburg. It contains three churches, one academy and one printing office.

LEWIS' STORE, a post office at Spottsylvania county, Virginia.

LEWISVILLE, a post village of Brunswick county, Virginia, 78 miles S. S. W. from Richmond.

LEXINGTON, a handsome post village, capital of Rockbridge county, Virginia, on the North river, an affluent of James river, 146 miles W. from Richmond, and 35 miles N. W. from Lynchburg. It is situated in a valley, and surrounded by beautiful mountain scenery. Washington College founded at this place in 1798, and endowed by General Washington, has a library of 4950 volumes. The Virginia Military Institute was established here by the Legislature of Virginia, in 1838–9. Lexington contains four or five churches, two seminaries, two printing offices, and several fine brick residences. It was laid out in 1778. Population, 1733.

LIBERIA, a small village of Prince William county, Virginia.

LIBERTY, a beautiful post village, capital of Bedford county, Virginia, on the Virginia and Tenn. railroad, 25 miles W. from Lynchburg. It has a sublime view of the peaks of Otter, which are not less than seven miles distant, though they appear to be in the immediate vicinity. Liberty has a handsome court house, four churches and about 700 inhabitants.

LIBERTY HALL, a post office of Washington county, Virginia.

LIBERTY MILLS, a post village in Orange county, Virginia, 79 miles N. W. from Richmond.

LIGONS, a post office of Charlotte county, Virginia.

LISBON, a post village in Bedford county, Virginia, 150 miles W. by S. from Richmond.

LITTLE COAL river, in the W. part of Virginia, rises in Logan county by two branches, called the Pond and Spruce forks, and falls into Coal river in Kanawha county.

LITTLE GUYANDOTTE river, in the W. part of Virginia, falls into the Ohio, after forming a part of the boundary between Mason and Cabell counties.

LITTLE KANAWHA river, of Western Virginia, rises in Braxton county, passes through Gilmer, Wirt and Wood counties, and enters the Ohio at Parkersburg. Its general direction is W. N. W. its length perhaps 150 miles. The country through which it flows

is hilly and contains extensive beds of stone coal, and a number of salt springs. This river is navigable only a few miles.

Little Level, a post office of Pocahontas county, Virginia.

Little Plymouth, a small post village of King and Queen county, Virginia, 57 miles E. from Richmond.

Little River, in the N. E. part of Virginia, is a small affluent of Goose creek, in Loudoun county. It has been rendered navigable from its mouth to Aldie, by means of dams.

Little River, a post office of Floyd county, Virginia.

Little Skin Creek, a post office of Lewis county, Virginia.

Littleton, a post office of Sussex county, Virginia.

Litwalton, a post office of Lancaster county, Virginia.

Lively Oak, a post office of Lancaster county, Virginia.

Lloyd's, a post office of Essex county, Virginia, 62 miles N. E. from Richmond.

Loch Leven, a post office of Lunenburg county, Virginia.

Loch Lomond, a post office of Goochland county, Virginia.

Locust Creek, a post office of Louisa county, Virginia, 33 miles N. W. from Richmond.

Locust Dale, a post office of Madison county, Virginia.

Locust Grove, a post office of Orange county, Virginia, 86 miles N. W. from Richmond.

Locust Hill, a post office of Middlesex county, Virginia.

Locust Lane, a post office of Fayette county, Virginia.

Locust Mount, a post office of Accomack county, Virginia.

Locustville, a post office of Accomack county, Virginia.

Lodore, a post office of Amelia county, Virginia.

Logan, a county in the W. S. W. part of Virginia, bordering on Kentucky, has an area of 825 square miles. It is intersected by the Guyandotte river, and bounded on the S. W. by the Tug fork of Sandy river. The county slopes toward the north west. The surface is mountainous and overspread with extensive forests; the soil is generally good. Indian corn, oats and butter are the staples. In 1850 it produced 154,943 bushels of corn; 20,014 of oats, and 31,374 pounds of butter. It contained six churches, and 175 pupils attending public schools. The highlands of this county abound in stone coal and iron, which are not much used at present. Formed in 1824 and named in honor of a distinguished chief of the Mingo tribe. Capital, Lawnsville, or Logan Court House. Population, 3620; of whom 3533 were free, and 87 slaves.

J. H. HASKELL,

MACHINE CARD MANUFACTURER,

MANUFACTURERS' ARTICLES,

Belt and Hose Maker,

33 South Eutaw Street,

BALTIMORE.

Also Agent for the sale of Pearl and other Starch.

DIXON, BALBIRNIE & DIXON,

ARCHITECTS,

117 Baltimore Street, Cor. of South Street,

BALTIMORE.

All Professional Business confided to them promptly attended to.

Artificers' Works Measured, &c.

Designs, Plans and Specifications prepared and sent by Mail.

RESIDENCES.

THOMAS DIXON,	THOMAS BALBIRNIE,	JAMES M. DIXON,
610 W. Fayette St., Franklin Place.	54 Saratoga Street.	893 W. Fayette St.

MAYNARD & ROSE,

DEALERS IN

LEATHER, TRIMMINGS AND FINDINGS,

N. E. Corner Cheapside and Lombard Street,

BALTIMORE.

We name in part such as

SHOE FINDINGS

Patent Leather,
French Calf Skins,
German " "
Country Calf Skins,
City " "
Oak Sole Leather,
Hemlock "
Harness Leather,
Skirting "
Buff Upper "
Buff Horse "
Lining Skins,
Muslin and Linen Lasting,
Satin Francois,
Italian Cloths,
Moroccos of all kinds,
Bindings " " "
Silk Laces, " "
Cotton " " "
And Findings generally.

Also WATER PROOF CORK SOLES, which will be sold to dealers at Factory Prices.

Merchants and others visiting the city would do well to call on us before purchasing elsewhere. Our stock is fresh and has been selected with considerable pains in order to procure the most suitable articles for the trade generally. Orders from the country will be filled promptly, and be as well selected as if buyers visited the city themselves.

JAMES A. MAYNARD,
CURRIER.

PETER ROSE,
OF THE LATE FIRM OF DARRAUGH & ROSE.

LOGAN COURT HOUSE, or LAWNSVILLE, a small post village, capital of Logan county, Virginia, on the Guyandotte river, 350 miles W. from Richmond.

LOMBARDY GROVE, a post village of Mecklenburg county, Va.

LONDON BRIDGE, a post village in Princess Anne county, Virginia, 100 miles S. E. from Richmond.

LONG BOTTOM, a post office of Marshall county, Virginia.

LONG BRANCH, a post office of Franklin county, Virginia.

LONG CREEK, a post office of Louisa county, Virginia.

LONG MEADOW, a post office of Page county, Virginia.

LONG PINE, a post office of Bedford county, Virginia.

LORENTZ'S STORE, a post office of Lewis county, Virginia.

LORENZOVILLE FOUNDRY, a post office of Shenandoah county, Virginia.

LORETTO, a small post village of Essex county, Virginia, 69 miles N. E. from Richmond.

LOST CREEK, a post office of Harrison county, Virginia.

LOST RIVER, a post office of Hardy county, Virginia.

LOUDOUN, a county in the N. E. part of Virginia, bordering on Maryland, contains 486 square miles. The Potomac river forms its N. E. boundary, and it is drained by Goose creek. The surface is hilly, having the Blue Ridge on the N. W. border, and the Kittoctan mountain near the middle of the county. The soil varies from a rich alluvion to an unproductive clay, but a large portion of it is fertile. Wheat, Indian corn, oats, grass, pork, and beef are the staples. In 1850 this county produced 563,930 bushels of wheat; 749,428 of corn; 117,055 of oats; 11,990 tons of hay, and 422,021 pounds of butter. The quantity of butter was the greatest produced by any one county of the State, and that of wheat greater than in any except Rockingham county. There were 54 flour, grist and saw mills, one iron furnace, three woolen factories, and nine tanneries. It contained 33 churches, two newspaper offices, 1703 pupils attending public schools, and 85 attending academies or other schools. The county contains limestone, marble, granite, gneiss, and other primitive rocks. It was formed from Fairfax county in 1757, and named in honor of the Earl of Loudoun. Capital, Leesburg. Population, 22,079, of whom 16,438 were free, and 5641 slaves.

LOUISA, a county in the E. central part of Virginia, has an area of about 500 square miles. The North Anna river forms its north-

NUT, BOLT & WASHER MANUFACTORY.

134 Thames Street, between Ann & Wolfe, F. P.

BALTIMORE.

FRAZIER & ATKINSON

Are extensively engaged in the manufacture of every description of

Nuts,
Burrs,
Washers,
Bucket, Coal Hod and Kettle Ears,
Bevel Rings,
Flyer Bottoms,
Plow Points,
Chain Links,
Clinch Rings.

The attention of Machinists, Car Builders, Agricultural Implement Makers, Ship Builders, Bucket Makers, Tin and Sheet-Iron Workers, and all others, is respectfully directed to the above articles, which are kept constantly on hand or made to order to suit the convenience of purchasers. RAIL ROAD and BRIDGE CONTRACTORS will find it to their advantage to call on us, as we are prepared to furnish TRACK and BRIDGE BOLTS, and Cold Punched NUTS of the largest dimensions. We are also prepared to do all kinds of JOB PUNCHING, viz: Railing, Window Bars, and Grating for Warehouses, Diagonal Braces, &c., &c. ☞ All Correspondence and Orders promptly attended to, and goods packed and forwarded to any portion of the United States.

Bolts of every description always on hand or made to order.

JOHN M. BRUCE,

COPPER SMITH,

32 Light Street, near Lombard,

BALTIMORE,

Is prepared to make to order or repair as follows:

Steam and Water Pipes for Steam Boats, Stationary Engines, Distilleries and other Purposes. Kettles of all dimensions, Mineral Water Founts and Pipes, Self-charging Mineral Water Apparatus and Pipes, all complete, on the most improved plans. Steam Drying Cylinder for Cotton and Woolen Mills. *All work done by me warranted.*

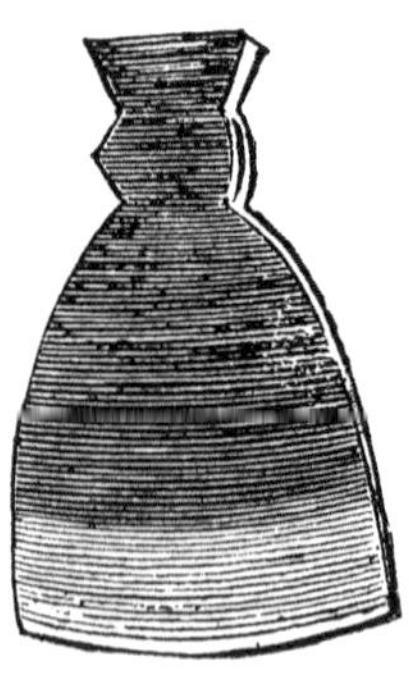

T. R. WISE,

Manufacturer of all kinds of

EDGE TOOLS,

And Sold, Wholesale and Retail,

No. 28 CONCORD ST.

FIRST DOOR NORTH OF PRATT STREET,

BALTIMORE.

Also Repairing of every description at moderate prices.

ern boundary; the county is also drained by the South Anna and Little rivers. The surface is hilly; the soil, originally fertile, has been partly worn out. Tobacco, Indian corn and wheat are the staples. In 1850 this county produced 1,584,285 lbs. of tobacco; 377,288 bushels of corn, and 199,521 of wheat. There were seven flour, grist and saw mills, one iron furnace and three tanneries. It contained 26 churches and 452 pupils attending public schools. Gold mines have been worked in this county, but are not very productive. It is intersected by the Central railroad of Virginia. Formed in 1742. Capital, Louisa Court House. Population 16,691, of whom 6827 were free, and 9864 slaves.

Louisa Court House, a small post village, capital of Louisa county, Virginia, on the Central railroad, 60 miles N. W. from Richmond.

Lovely Mount, a post-office of Montgomery county Virginia.

Love's Mills, a post-office of Washington county, Virginia.

Lovettsville, a post-village of Loudoun county, Virginia, 2 miles from the Potomac, and 166 miles north from Richmond. It contains 2 or 3 churches.

Lovingston, a post-village, capital of Nelson county, Virginia, 118 miles West from Richmond. It is beautifully situated on a branch of Tye river, and surrounded by hills, the summits of which afford a magnificent view of the Blue Ridge. The village has 3 churches and about 350 inhabitants.

Lumberport, a post-village in Harrison county, Virginia.

Lunenburg, a county in the S. S. E. part of Virginia, has an area of about 370 square miles. It is bounded on the North by Nottoway river, and on the South by the Meherrin river. The surface is uneven; the soil is moderately fertile. Indian corn and Tobacco are the staples. In 1850 this county produced 240,065 bushels of corn, and 2,274,668 pounds of tobacco. There were 7 flour and grist mills, 2 tanneries and 1 manufactory of farming implements. It contains 26 churches, and 450 pupils attending public schools. Formed in 1746. Capital, Lewistown. Population, 11,692; of whom 4505 were free and 7187 slaves.

Lunenburg Court House, or Lewistown, a small post-village capital of Lunenburg county, Virginia, 91 miles South West from Richmond. It has an elevated situation, and contains a handsome court house.

Luney's Creek, a post-village of Hardy co., Virginia.

TAYLOR,

FASHIONABLE

HATTER,

AND

Importer and Manufacturer of

FANCY FURS,

No. 5 CALVERT STREET,

(OPPOSITE BARNUM'S HOTEL,)

BALTIMORE.

Luray, a post-village, capital of Page county, Virginia, 136 miles North West from Richmond. It is pleasantly situated in a fertile limestone valley. Here is a quarry of fine marble. Luray contains several churches and about 500 inhabitants.

Lynchburg, a flourishing city of Campbell county, Virginia, is finely situated on a steep declivity on the right (S.) bank of James river, 120 miles W. S. W. from Richmond and 20 miles S. E. from the Blue Ridge. Lat. 37° 36′ N., lon. 79° 22′ W. The South Side railroad, leading to Petersburg and Richmond, connects here with the Virginia and Tennessee railroad, which is to form part of the most direct route from the Eastern States to those of the South-west, and to be one of the principal thoroughfares of the Union. The James River and Kanawha canal, the greatest public work in the State, following the course of the river from the falls at Richmond, is completed to Buchanan, about 50 miles above Lynchburg, and is to be continued to Covington. The distance between Richmond and Lynchburg by canal is 147 miles. The navigation of the canal renders this town the market of an extensive and fertile tract of country. The principal article is tobacco, of which about 15,000,000 pounds are inspected here annually. About 300,000 bushels of wheat are also received here every year. The city is supplied with river water from a reservoir which is elevated about 253 feet above the level of the river, and contains 400,000 gallons. This work was finished in 1829, at a cost of $50,000. The river is here about 200 yards wide, and is crossed by a fine bridge. It affords abundant water power, which is employed in the manufacture of cotton, wool, flour, &c. The city contains 9 churches, numerous schools, 3 printing offices, 3 banks, 3 savings banks, 1 cotton and woolen factory, 36 tobacco factories, 4 brass and iron foundries and 150 stores, in which the annual sales exceed $2,000,000. Capital employed in 1851 in manufactures, $725,000. The town was founded in 1786, and incorporated in 1805. In 1848 it contained 7678 inhabitants. Population in 1854, about 14,000.

McDonald's Mill, a post-office of Montgomery county, Va.

McDowell, a post-office of Highland county, Virginia

McElroy, a post office of Doddridge county, Virginia.

McFarland's, a post-office of Lunenburg county, Virginia, 79 miles South West from Richmond.

McGalvysville, a post-office of Rockingham county, Virginia.

McKinney's, a post-office of Ritchie county, Virginia.

Macksburg, a post-office of Giles county, Virginia.

Maddox, a post-office of Hanover county, Virginia.

Madison, a county in the North East central part of Virginia, has an area of 280 square miles. The Rapidan river forms its boundary on the S. S. E. and South West; it is also drained by Robertson's and Hazel rivers, which rise within its limits. The Blue Ridge forms the North West boundary of the county; the surface is diversified by other elevations, and is noted for the sublimity of its scenery. The soil of the valleys is fertile. The county is timbered with the oak, hickory, cherry and other trees. Indian corn, wheat, oats, hay, butter and live stock are the staples. In 1850 this county produced 343,443 bushels of corn, 136,684 of wheat, 21,890 of oats, 1,667 tons of hay, and 81,184 pounds of butter. There were 27 flour, grist and saw mills, 7 tanneries, and 1 woolen factory. It contained 15 churches, and 386 pupils attending academies and other schools. Extensive beds of copper ore are found in the Blue Ridge, but are not worked at present. The county is traversed by the Blue Ridge turnpike. Organized in 1792. Capital, Madisontown. Population, 9331; of whom 4607 were free, and 4724 slaves.

Madison Court House, capital of Madison county, Virginia, 70 miles North West from Richmond, 96 miles from Washington. It contains several churches, and there are 5 flouring mills in its vicinity. It has a healthy situation on high ground, and commands a beautiful view of the Blue Ridge. Population, about 800.

Madison Mills, a post-village of Madison county, Virginia, has a woolen factory.

Magnolia, a post-office of Washington county, Virginia.

Maiden Spring, a post-office of Tazewell county, Virginia.

Manassus Station, a post-office of Prince William county, Virginia.

Manchester, a post-village of Chesterfield county, Virginia, on the James river, opposite Richmond, with which it is connected by a bridge. It has a beautiful situation, and contains several elegant residences erected by peasons who do business in Richmond. It has 2 churches, and manufactories of tobacco, cotton and flour. Population in 1853 estimated at 1,800

MANGOHICK, a post-office of King William county, Virginia, 40 miles E. N. E. from Richmond.

MANNINGTON, a village of Marion county, Virginia, on the Baltimore and Ohio Railroad.

MANNSBOROUGH, a post-village in Amelia county, Virginia, 30 miles South West from Richmond.

MANSFIELD, a post-office of Louisa county, Virginia.

MARBLE HILL, a post office of Prince Edward county, Virginia, 83 miles W. S. W. from Richmond.

MARION, a county in the North West part of Virginia, has an area of about 300 square miles. It is drained by the Monongahela river and its branches, the West fork, and Tygart's Valley river, which unite within its limits. In 1850 the county produced 167,071 bushels of corn, 48,469 of wheat, 93,095 of oats, 6,125 tons of hay and 144,409 pounds of butter. There were 17 flour mills, 11 saw mills, 1 iron foundry and 3 tanneries. It contained 21 churches, and 720 pupils attending public schools. Mines of good stone coal are extensively worked, and iron ore is abundant. Steamboats ascend the river as far as the county seat; the Baltimore and Ohio railroad passes through the county. It is plentifully supplied with water-power. Organized in 1841–2, and named in honor of General Francis Marion, a prominent actor in the war of the Revolution. Capital, Fairmont. Population, 10,552, of whom 10,458 were free, and 94 slaves.

MARION, a small post-village, capital of Smythe county, Virginia, on the Middle fork of Holston river, 275 miles West by South from Richmond.

MARKSVILLE, a post-village of Page county, Virginia, 100 miles North West from Richmond.

MARLIN BOTTOM, a post-office of Pocahontas county, Virginia.

MARSHALL, a county in the North West part of Virginia, bordering on Pennsylvania and Ohio, has an area of about 230 square miles. The Ohio river washes its Western border, and Fishing and Grave creeks flow through the county. Indian corn, wheat, oats, apples and cattle are the chief products. In 1850 there were raised 302,130 bushels of corn, 74,976 of wheat, 114,345 of oats, and 132,100 pounds of butter were made. It contained 15 churches, 700 pupils attending public schools, and 60 attending an academy. Stone coal and water-power are abundant. Formed in 1835, and named in honor of John Marshall, late chief-justice of the United

States. Capital, Elizabethtown. Population, 10,138, of whom 10,089 were free and 49 slaves.

MARSHALLSVILLE, a post-office of Greenbrier county, Virginia.

MARTINSBURG, a flourishing post-village, capital of Berkley county, Virginia, on Tuscarora creek, and on the Baltimore and Ohio railroad, 180 miles North from Richmond. It is situated in a fertile and elevated region, a few miles West from the Blue Ridge. The town contains 4 or 5 churches, 2 academies, 2 newspaper offices, and 1 almshouse. Population in 1853, about 2,500.

MARTINSVILLE, a small post village, capital of Henry county, Virginia, on a branch of the Dan river, 207 miles W. S. W. from Richmond.

MARYSVILLE, a post village in Campbell county, Virginia, near Staunton river, 115 miles S. W. by W. from Richmond.

MARYSVILLE, a post village, capital of Charlotte county, Virginia, is situated near the railroad from Richmond to Danville, 100 miles S. W. from the former. It contains three churches, an academy, and about 600 inhabitants.

MASON, a county in the W. part of Virginia, bordering on the Ohio river, has an area of 3000 square miles. The Kanawha river flows through the middle of the county into the Ohio. Indian corn, wheat, cattle and swine are the staples. In 1850 it produced 399,-080 bushels of corn, and 20,545 of wheat. There were two flour mills, five grist mills, four saw mills, and two tanneries. It contained twelve churches, and 1150 pupils attending public schools. Timber and stone coal are abundant. Formed in 1804, and named in honor of George Mason, a distinguished statesman of Virginia. Capital, Point Pleasant. Population, 7539; of whom 6892 were free, and 647 slaves.

MASSANUTTEN, a post office of Page county, Virginia, 144 miles N. W. from Richmond

MASSIE'S MILLS, a post office of Nelson county, Virginia.

MATTAPONY RIVER, in the E. S. E. part of Virginia, rises in Spottsylvania county, and flowing in a general S. E. course after forming the boundary between King and Queen and King William counties, unites with the Pamunkey to form the York river.

MATTHEWS, a county in the E. part of Virginia, bordering on Chesapeake bay, near its southern extremity. It consists of a peninsula washed by Piankatank river on the N., by the Chesapeake on the E. and by Mobjack bay on the S. W., and joined to the main

land by an isthmus about one mile wide. Length 20 miles; greatest breadth eight miles. Area, about 90 square miles. The surface is extremely level; the soil is sandy and moderately fertile. Wheat, potatoes, oats, hay, and live stock are the staples. The forests consist of pine, chestnut, and a species of oak, valuable for ship building, which is an important branch of business in this county. In 1850 the county produced 7640 bushels of wheat; 13,292 of sweet potatoes; 19,405 of oats, and 1288 tons of hay. There were two saw mills, one tannery, nine churches, and 400 pupils attending public schools. Named in honor of General Matthews, an officer in the war of the Revolution and afterwards governor of Georgia. Capital, Westville. Population, 6714, of whom 3791 were free, and 2923 slaves.

MATTHEWS COURT HOUSE, a post village, capital of Matthews county, Virginia, 70 miles E. from Richmond, is situated near an arm of Chesapeake bay.

MATTHEWSVILLE, a village in Pocahontas county, Virginia, 170 miles N. W. by W. from Richmond.

MAYFIELD, a small post village of Isle of Wight county, Virginia, is pleasantly situated, 72 miles S. E. from Richmond.

MAYO, a small river of Virginia and North Carolina, rises by two branches, the North and South Mayo, in Patrick county, of the former State, and flowing south-eastward into North Carolina, enters the Dan river at Madison.

MAYO, a post office of Halifax county, Virginia.

MAYONING, a post village in Patrick county, Virginia.

MAYSVILLE, a post village, capital of Buckingham county, Virginia, is situated on Slate river, at the head of navigation, 27 miles from its mouth, and 87 miles W. from Richmond.

MEADOW BLUFF, a post office of Greenbrier county, Virginia.

MEADOW DALE, a post office of Highland county, Virginia.

MEADOW RIVER, a small stream in the W. central part of Virginia, rises in Greenbrier county, and flows along the boundary between Nicholas and Fayette counties into Gauley river.

MEADOW RIVER, a post office of Greenbrier county, Virginia.

MEADVILLE, a thriving post village of Halifax county, Virginia, on the Bannister river, at the head of navigation, about 136 miles S. W. from Richmond. Population in 1853, about 500.

MECHANICSBURG, a post office of Giles county, Virginia.

MECHANICS RIVER, a post office of Albemarle county, Virginia.

C. L. PORTER,

WHOLESALE MANUFACTURER OF

COAL HODS, ASH BUCKETS,

Fire Carriers, Ash Shovels, Coal Sifters, &c.

No. 18 CONCORD STREET,

BETWEEN LOMBARD AND PRATT,

BALTIMORE.

MOROCCO FACTORY.

G. H. LOCHER & CO.

MANUFACTURERS OF ALL KINDS OF

MOROCCO LEATHER,

No. 137 Front St., (Grubb's old Stand,)

Where they manufacture every variety of Morocco and Linings suitable for the trade. The proprietors are practical men, formerly of Pa., and are operating with Phila. hands. All who patronize them will find their stock as cheap and good as can be had in the East.

CHARLES FARINGER,

SOAP & CANDLE

MANUFACTURER,

CONSTITUTION STREET,

BALTIMORE.

Always on hand a large stock of articles in the line, of superior manufacture, and to be disposed of on reasonable terms.

MECHANICSVILLE, a post village of Louisa county, Virginia, 65 miles N. W. from Richmond. It has one church.

MECKLENBURG, a county in the S. S. E. part of Virginia, bordering on North Carolina, has an area of 500 square miles. It is intersected by the Roanoke river, bounded on the N. by the Meherrin, and also drained by Allen's, Bluestone, and many other creeks. Indian corn, wheat, oats, and tobacco are the staples. In 1850 the county produced 552,466 bushels of corn; 113,016 of wheat; 184,-695 of oats, and 4,863,184 pounds of tobacco. There were eight flour and grist mills, three tobacco factories, five tanneries, and two coach factories. It contained thirty churches, 284 pupils attending public schools, and 328 attending academies and other schools. Granite and other primary rocks underlie the surface. Organized in 1764. Capital, Boydtown. Population, 20,630, of whom 8168 were free, and 12,462 slaves.

MEHERRIN, a river of Virginia and North Carolina, rises in Lunenburg and Charlotte counties of the former State. It passes into North Carolina and flows along the boundary between Gates and Hertford counties, until it unites with the Nottoway river to form the Chowan. Its general direction is E. S. E., and its whole length is estimated at about 150 miles. It is navigable by sloops to Murfreesborough in North Carolina.

MEHERRIN DEPOT, a post office of Southampton county, Va.

MELON, a post office of Barbour county, Virginia.

MELROSE, a post office of Rockingham county, Virginia.

MERCER, a county in the S. W. part of Virginia, has an area of 440 square miles. It is intersected by the Blue Stone river, bounded on the E. by the Kanawha or New river, and also drained by Brush and other creeks. Indian corn, wheat, oats, hay, and live stock are the staples. In 1850 this county produced 105,946 bushels of corn; 12,284 of wheat; 35,280 of oats, and 1375 tons of hay. It contained four churches, and 400 pupils attending public schools. Organized in 1837. Capital, Princeton. Population, 4222; of whom 4045 were free, and 177 slaves.

MERCER SALT WORKS, a post office of Mercer county, Virginia.

MEREDITH'S TAVERN, a post office of Marion county, Virginia.

MERRIMAN'S SHOP, a post office of Prince Edward county, Virginia, 96 miles W. S. W. from Richmond.

MESSONGO, a post office of Accomack county, Virginia.

METOMPKIN, a post office of Accomack county, Virginia.

MIDDLEBOURNE, a thriving post village, capital of Tyler county, Virginia, on Middle Island creek, 45 miles S. by W. from Wheeling. It has a turnpike leading to the Ohio river, and contains a flouring mill.

MIDDLEBROOK, a post village of Augusta co., Va., ten miles S. W. from Staunton. It contains a church and about 60 dwellings.

MIDDLEBURG, a handsome post borough of Loudoun county, Virginia, on a small affluent of the Potomac, 143 miles N. from Richmond. It has three churches, a flourishing academy, seven stores and one tobacco factory. Population about 800.

MIDDLE FORK, a post office of Randolph county, Virginia.

MIDDLE ISLAND CREEK, in the N. W. part of Virginia, rises near the boundary between Lewis and Harrison counties. It furnishes ample water power.

MIDDLE MOUNTAIN, a post office of Botetourt county, Virginia.

MIDDLEPORT, a post office of Braxton county, Virginia.

MIDDLE RIVER, of Virginia, a branch of the Shenandoah, rises in Augusta county, flows eastward and unites with the North river near Port Republic, in Rockingham county.

MIDDLESEX, a county in the E. part of Virginia, bordering on Chesapeake bay, at the mouth of Rappahannock river. The latter forms the entire boundary on the N. E., and Piankatank river on the S. W. The length is 39 miles; mean breadth about 5 miles; area about 150 square miles. In 1850 there were raised 134,253 bushels of corn, and 30,762 of wheat. There were eight grist mills and five saw mills. It contained nine churches, 152 pupils attending public schools, and 74 attending other schools. Formed in 1675. Capital, Urbana. Population, 4394, of whom 2052 were free, and 2342 slaves.

MIDDLETOWN, a post village of Frederick county, Virginia, on the turnpike leading from Winchester to Staunton, 13 miles S. S. W. from the former. It contains two churches.

MIDDLEWAY, a post village of Jefferson county, Virginia, near Opequan creek, seven miles S. W. from Charlestown, contains two churches. Population, about 500.

MILFORD, a post village of Caroline county, Virginia, on the Richmond, Fredericksburg and Potomac railroad, 38 miles from Richmond.

MILFORD, a small village of Preston county, Virginia, on the turnpike from Branonville to Fishing creek.

E. M. BOSLEY,

IMPORTER OF

FOREIGN AND DOMESTIC

HARDWARE,

No. 4 LIGHT STREET WHARF,

FOUR DOORS SOUTH OF PRATT ST.

BALTIMORE.

J. P. EWALD,

Manufacturer of all kinds of

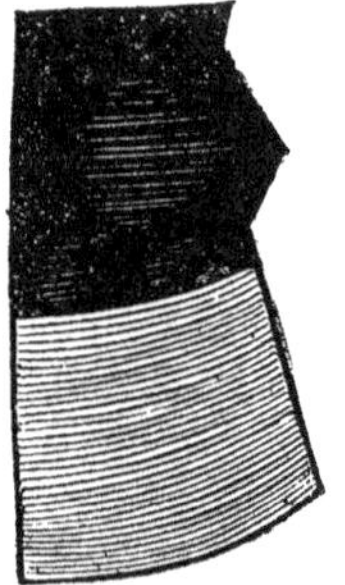

EDGE TOOLS,

And Sold, Wholesale and Retail,

NO. 25,

COR. E. PRATT & MILL STS.

NEAR MARKET SPACE,

BALTIMORE.

Also Repairing of every description at moderate prices.

JOHN D. HAMMOND,

SADDLE,  HARNESS,

AND

TRUNK MANUFACTURER,

WHOLESALE AND RETAIL,

No. 355 Baltimore Street,

(OPPOSITE THE EUTAW HOUSE,)

BALTIMORE,

Manufactures and keeps constantly on hand every description of

Harness, Trunks, Valises, Carpet Bags, Collars,

And every other article in his line. All orders executed with neatness and dispatch.

MILLBOROUGH SPRING, a post village of Bath county, Virginia, 157 miles W. N. W. from Richmond. Medicinal springs occur in the vicinity.

MILL CREEK, a post office of Berkley county, Virginia, abont 168 miles N. by W. from Richmond.

MILLDALE, a post office of Warren county, Virginia.

MILLER'S MILL, a post office of Bath county, Virginia.

MILLER'S TAVERN, a post office of Essex county, Virginia.

MILL FALLS, a post office of Marion county, Virginia.

MILLINGTON, a post office of Albemarle county Virginia.

MILL POINT, a post village in Pocahontas county, Virginia.

MILLVILLE, a post village of King George county, Virginia, about 70 miles N. N. E. from Richmond.

MILLWOOD, a post village of Clarke county, Virginia, 140 miles N. by W. from Richmond. It has one or two churches, and several flouring mills.

MINGO FLAT, a post office of Randolph county, Virginia.

MINT SPRING, a post office of Augusta county, Virginia.

MODEST TOWN, a small post village of Accomack county, Virginia, three miles from the Atlantic, and ten miles E. from Accomack Court House, contains two churches and a few shops.

MONONGALIA, a county in the N. W. part of Virginia, bordering on Pennsylvania, has an area of 630 square miles. It is intersected by the Monongahela and Cheat rivers. The surface is hilly. Laurel Hill, the most western ridge of the Alleghanies, passes through the E. part of the county. Much of the soil is fertile. Cattle, lumber, flour and iron are the chief exports. In 1850 this county produced 184,379 bushels of corn ; 52,370 of wheat ; 111,252 of oats ; 6013 tons of hay, and 145,178 pounds of butter. There were 25 flour and grist mills, 13 saw mills, one nail factory, one iron forge, two iron foundries, and three furnaces. It contained 31 churches, 548 pupils attending public schools, and 468 attending other schools. It is traversed by the Baltimore and Ohio Railroad. Stone coal is abundant. Formed in 1776. Capital, Morgantown. Population, 12,387 ; of whom 12,211 were free, and 176 slaves.

MONROE, a county in the S. W. central part of Virginia, contains 450 square miles. It is drained by the Greenbrier and New rivers, which unite on its N. W. border. In 1850 it produced 250,456 bushels of corn; 51,436 of wheat; 97,460 of oats; 6073 tons of hay, and 175,254 pounds of butter. There were four flour mills,

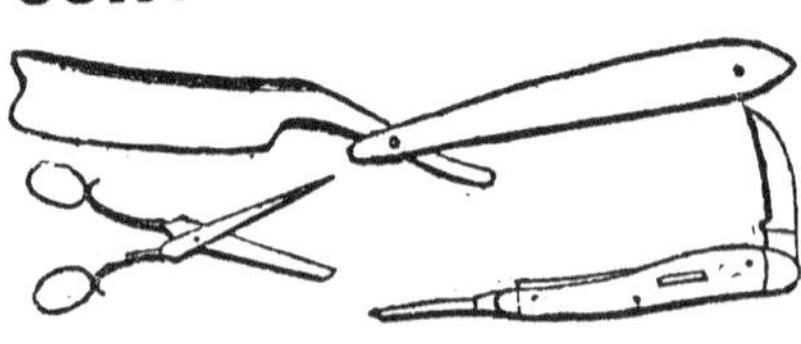

five saw mills, one woolen factory and five tanneries. It contained 27 churches, 498 pupils attending public schools, and 75 attending an academy. It abounds in mineral springs, some of which are frequented as watering places. Stone coal is found. The Covington and Ohio railroad is located through this county. Capital, Union. Population, 10,204, of whom 9143 were free, and 1061 slaves.

MONTAGUE, a post village of Essex county, Virginia, 54 miles E. N. E. from Richmond.

MONTEITHVILLE, a post office of Stafford county, Virginia.

MONTEREY, a post village, capital of Highland county, Virginia, on the Staunton and Parkersburg turnpike, 180 miles W. N. W. from Richmond. Population, over 100.

MONTGOMERY, a county in the S. S. W. part of Virginia, has an area of about 300 square miles. It is bounded on the W. by New river, and drained by the head streams of the Staunton, or Roanoke, and by Craig's creek. The county is situated at the north-western base of the Blue ridge, and has a mountainous surface. In 1850 it produced 266,616 bushels of corn; 51,827 of wheat; 106,120 of oats, and 4453 tons of hay. There were four saw mills and five tanneries. It contained twelve churches, 350 pupils attending public schools, and 20 attending another school. The county is intersected by the Virginia and Tennessee railroad. Formed in 1776. Capital, Christiansburg. Population, 8359, of whom 6888 were free, and 1471 slaves.

MONTPELIER, a post office of Hanover county, Virginia, 24 miles N. from Richmond.

MONTROSE, a post office of Westmoreland county, Virginia.

MOORFIELD, a post village, capital of Hardy county, Virginia, on the South branch of Potomac river, 178 miles N. W. from Richmond.

MORELAND, a post office of Fauquier county, Virginia.

MOREMAN'S RIVER, a post office of Albemarle county, Virginia, 104 miles W. by N. from Richmond.

MORGAN, a county forming the N. N. E. extremity of Virginia, bordering on the Potomac river, which separates it from Maryland, has an area of about 330 square miles. It is intersected by Cacapon river, and by Sleepy creek. In 1850 this county produced 46,247 bushels of corn; 40,584 of wheat, and 16,383 of oats. There were five flour and grist mills, two saw mills, and two tanneries;

J. M. OREM. W. S. HOPKINS.

OREM, HOPKINS & CO.

IMPORTERS OF

Cloths, Cassimeres, Vestings, Trimmings

AND

GOODS GENERALLY,

Adapted to Men's Wear,

No. 238 BALTIMORE STREET,

North Side, Four Doors West of Charles street,

BALTIMORE.

CHAS. J. LEREW. GEORGE SANDER. AUGUST MEYER.

LEREW, SANDER & CO.

SUCCESSORS TO CHARLES FISCHER & CO.

IMPORTERS OF

GERMAN, FRENCH & ENGLISH GOODS,

338 BALTIMORE STREET,

BALTIMORE.

CHAS. A. SMITH. GEORGE D. COCK. H. J. WERDEBAUGH.

SMITH & COCK.

NOTIONS.

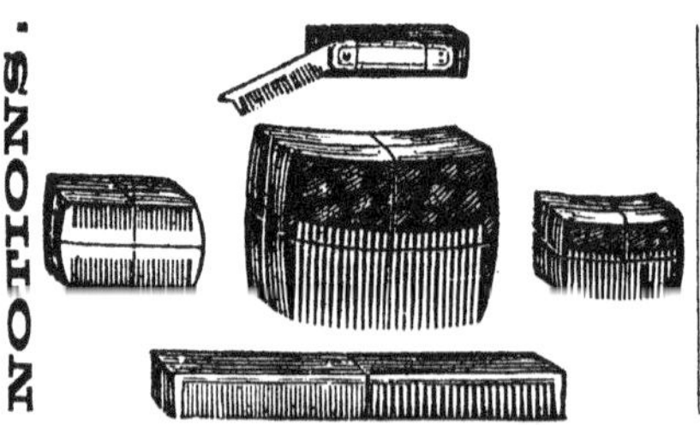

IMPORTERS OF

English, French & German

FANCY GOODS,

HOSIERY, GLOVES,

And Trimmings generally,

And Dealers in

COMBS, BUTTONS, BRUSHES, &c.

292 BALTIMORE STREET, CORNER OF SHARP,

BALTIMORE.

eleven churches, and 645 pupils attending public schools. The county contains large deposits of iron and stone coal. It is plentifully supplied with water power. The Berkley spring in this county is one of the oldest watering places in the United States. Organized in 1820, and named in honor of General Daniel Morgan, an officer in the war of the Revolution. Capital, Bath. Population, 3557; of whom 3434 were free, and 123 slaves.

Morgan's Ridge, a post office of Marion county, Virginia.

Morgantown, a thriving post village, capital of Monongalia county, Virginia, is finely situated on the Monongahela river, 295 miles N. W. from Richmond. It has facilities for trade by the steamboat navigation of the river. Morgantown contains a court house, a bank, three newspaper offices, and several mills. Population, about 1000.

Morrisville, a small post village of Fauquier county, Virginia, 95 miles N. by W. from Richmond.

Mossy Creek, a post office of Augusta county, Virginia.

Moundsville, Virginia. See Grave Creek.

Mountain Cove, a post village of Fayette co., Va., on the Kanawha river, 200 miles W. from Richmond. One paper is issued here.

Mountain Creek, of Culpepper county, Virginia, flows in an E. S. E. direction, and falls into the Rappahannock or North river.

Mountain Grove, a post office of Bath county, Virginia.

Mount Airy, a post village of Pittsylvania county, Virginia, 145 miles S. W. from Richmond. It has several churches and mills.

Mount Crawford, a post village in Rockingham county, Va.

Mount Gilead, a post village of Loudoun county, Virginia, 155 miles N. from Richmond.

Mount Horeb, a post office of Nelson county, Virginia, 111 miles W. from Richmond.

Mount Israel, a post office of Albemarle county, Virginia, 100 miles W. by E. from Richmond.

Mount Jackson, a post village of Shenandoah county, Virginia, on the Valley turnpike from Staunton to Winchester, 13 miles S W. from Woodstock.

Mount Level, a post village of Dinwiddie county, Virginia.

Mount Meridian, a small post village of Augusta county, Virginia, 118 miles N. W. from Richmond.

Mount Pleasant, a post village of Spottsylvania county, Virginia, five miles N. by W. from Richmond.

ROBERT POOLE. GERMAN H. HUNT.

UNION WORKS,

North Street, opposite Susquehanna Railroad Station.

POOLE & HUNT,

IRON FOUNDERS

AND

General Machinists and Car Builders,

Manufacturers of Steam Engines, Mill Gearing, Blowing Machinery, Hydraulic Presses, Sugar and Saw Mills, Portable Saw Mills and Engines, Machinists' Tools of all kinds, Shafting Pulleys and Hangers, Steam Boilers, Water Tanks, &c. Car Wheels and Axles filled to order. Wrought Iron Pipes arranged fo heating Buildings and other purposes. ☞ **CASTINGS made every day.**

MARYLAND

AGRICULTURAL WAREHOUSE,

AND

SEED STORE,

Wholesale and Retail, and Agency for the sale of all kinds of

COUNTRY PRODUCE,

As Received direct from the Producer.

☞ This is the only house of the kind South of New York.

F. P. DIDIER & BRO.

Successors to Hambleton & Didier,

No. 97 North Howard st., near Franklin st.

BALTIMORE.

Ploughs, Harrows, Wheat Fans, Grist Mills, Horse-powers, Threshers, Horse and Hand Rakes, Straw, Hay and Fodder Cutters, Vegetable Cutters, Corn and Cob Crushers, Shellers, Cultivators, Corn Planters, Ox Yokes and Bows, Grindstones, Cradles, &c., together with an endless variety of Field and Garden Tools, Fruit Trees, Fertilizers, &c. Agents for Dr. X. Bullenoe's invaluable Extract for Man and Horse. Cure guaranteed or no sale.

MOUNT SALEM, a post office of Kanawha county, Virginia.

MOUNT SIDNEY, a post village of Augusta county, Virginia, on the stage road from Winchester to Staunton, ten miles N. E. from the latter. It contains one church and one academy. Population estimated at 300.

MOUNT SOLON, a post village of Augusta county, Virginia, about 110 miles W. N. W. from Richmond.

MOUNTSVILLE, a post village of Loudoun county, Virginia, 150 miles N. from Richmond.

MOUNT VERNON, Virginia, the former residence of General Washington, on the W. side of the Potomac, six miles below Alexandria. It contains the mansion and tomb of the Father of his country.

MOUNT VINCO, a post office of Buckingham county, Virginia.

MOUNT ZION, a post office of Campbell county, Virginia.

MOUTH OF INDIAN, a post office of Monroe county, Virginia.

MOUTH OF POCAH, a post office of Putnam county, Virginia.

MOUTH OF SENECA, a post office of Pendleton county, Virginia.

MOUTH OF WILSON, a post office of Grayson county, Virginia.

MUD BRIDGE, a post office of Cabell county, Virginia.

MUDDY CREEK, a post office of Preston county, Virginia.

MURFEE'S DEPOT, a post office of Southampton county, Virginia.

MURRAYSVILLE, a post office of Jackson county, Virginia.

MURRELL'S SHOP, a post office of Nelson county, Virginia, 110 miles W. from Richmond.

NAMOZINE, a post office of Amelia county, Virginia.

NAMOZINE CREEK, in the S. E. part of Virginia, flows N. E. along the boundary between Amelia and Dinwiddie counties until it enters the Appomattox river.

NANSEMOND river, Virginia, in Nansemond county, enters Hampton Roads. It is navigable for small vessels 20 miles to Suffolk.

NANSEMOND, a county in the S. E. part of Virginia, bordering on North Carolina and the Dismal Swamp; the area is 400 square miles. Hampton Roads are situated on the N. border of the county, and it is partly traversed by Nansemond river, from which it derives its name. Lumber, tar and turpentine are the chief articles of export. In 1850 this county produced 252,842 bushels of Indian corn; 186,324 of sweet potatoes, (the greatest quantity of that article raised in any one county of the State, except Southampton,) and 3338 tons of hay. There were seven saw mills, four grist mills, eight shingle manufactories, one cotton mill, 19 churches, one news-

paper office, 298 pupils attending public schools, and 174 attending academies or other schools. The Portsmouth and Roanoke railroad passes through the county. Capital, Suffolk. Population, 12,283, of whom 7568 were free, and 4715 slaves.

NASH'S FORD, a post office of Russell county, Virginia.

NATURAL BRIDGE, a post office of Rockbridge county, Virginia.

NEABSCO MILLS, a post office of Prince William county, Va.

NEERSVILLE, a post office of Loudoun county, Virginia.

NEGRO FOOT, a post office of Hanover county, Virginia.

NELSON, a county a little S. E. from the centre of Virginia, has an area of 340 square miles. The James river washes the S. E. border, and it is drained by the Rockfish river. The Blue ridge forms the entire boundary on the N. W., and the surface is generally occupied by hills and valleys. The soil is fertile. Indian corn, wheat and tobacco are the staples. In 1850 there were raised 353,-432 bushels of corn; 122,230 of wheat, and 1,433,730 pounds of tobacco. There were 37 flour and grist mills, 12 saw mills, 6 tanneries, four wool-carding mills, and four distilleries; 21 churches, 347 pupils attending public schools, and 30 attending an academy. The canal, which extends along James river, connects the county with Richmond. Formed in 1807, and named in honor of Thomas Nelson, Governor of Virginia in 1781. County town, Lovingston. Population, 12,758; of whom 6616 were free, and 6142 slaves.

NESTORVILLE, a post office of Barbour county, Virginia.

NEWARK, a post office of Wirt county, Virginia.

NEW BALTIMORE, a post village of Fauquier county, Virginia, 105 miles N. by W. from Richmond, has 1 church and 1 academy.

NEWBERN, a post village, capital of Pulaski county, Virginia, on the Virginia and Tennessee railroad and the stage route from Baltimore to Nashville, 222 miles W. S. W. from Richmond. The situation is elevated and pleasant. The town has an active trade and cont ins two churches. Population from 300 to 400. The New river, near Newbern, passes along a vertical wall of rock, about 500 feet high and several miles in length, called the "Glass Windows."

NEW BRIGHTON, a post office of Fauquier county, Virginia.

NEW CALIFORNIA, a post office of Jackson county, Virginia.

NEW CANTON, a post village of Buckingham county, Virginia, on James river, at the mouth of Slate river, sixty-three miles W. from Richmond.

NEW CASTLE, a post village, capital of Craig county, Virginia,

ELEGANT PIANO FORTES!

BALTIMORE DEPOT FOR THE SALE OF

HALLET, DAVIS & CO'S

(BOSTON)

GRAND AND SQUARE PIANOS,

WITH ENTIRE IRON FRAME,

PATENT SUSPENSION BRIDGE,

ADMIRED ÆOLIAN ATTACHMENT,

AND OVER STRINGS.

GIVING GREAT VOLUME AND SWEETNESS OF TONE.

ALSO, HAINES, BROTHER & CUMMINGS' CELEBRATED NEW YORK PIANOS,

WITH OVER STRINGS.

A FINE ASSORTMENT OF

PRINCE & CO'S REPUTABLE MELODEONS,

FROM $45 TO $150,

Embracing those with ONE or Two SETS of REEDS and Two STOPS. Also the beautiful ORGAN MELODEON, (Goodman's Patent,) made by Messrs. Goodman and Baldwin. This Instrument has two *banks* of keys, which *couple* or may be used separately; and has *three sets of reeds*, giving great power, and being susceptible of producing many of the beautiful effects of the CHURCH ORGAN.

E. H. OSBORN,

No. 1 NORTH CHARLES STREET,

(One Door from Baltimore street,)

BALTIMORE.

☞ **Second-hand Pianos taken in Exchange for New.**

at the fork of Craig's creek, 193 miles W. from Richmond, contains one or two churches and an academy.

New Church, a post office of Accomack county, Virginia.

New Cumberland, a post village of Hancock county, Virginia, near the Ohio river.

New Glasgow, a small post village of Amherst county, Virginia, 119 miles W. from Richmond.

New Hope, a small post village of Augusta county, Virginia, 114 miles N. W. from Richmond, has one church.

New Kent, a county in the E. S. E. part of Virginia, has an area of 190 square miles. The Pamunkey river forms its boundary on the N. E., and the Chickahominy on the S. W. Indian corn, oats, potatoes, cattle and swine are the staples. In 1850 this county produced 178,813 bushels of corn; 37,346 of oats; 13,650 of sweet potatoes, and 38,031 pounds of butter. There were 12 flour and grist mills, 10 churches, and 300 pupils attending public schools. The Pamunkey or York river is navigable on the border of the county. Formed in 1654. Capital New Kent Court House. Population, 6064; of whom 2654 were free, and 3410 slaves.

New Kent Court House, capital of New Kent county, Virginia, 30 miles E. from Richmond.

New London, a post village of Campbell county, Virginia, 110 miles W. by S. from Richmond.

New Market, a small post village of Nelson county, Virginia, on James river, at the mouth of Tye river, 108 miles W. from Richmond.

New Market, a post village of Shenandoah county, Virginia, 150 miles N. W. from Richmond. There are several forges and factories in the vicinity which abounds in iron ore. It contains 3 or 4 churches.

New Martinsville, a post village, capital of Wetzel county, Virginia, on the Ohio river, at the mouth of Fishing creek, 40 miles below Wheeling.

New Milton, a post office of Doddridge county, Virginia.

Newport, a small village of Augusta county, Virginia, 18 miles W. from Staunton, the county seat, has two stores.

Newport News, a post office of Warwick county, Virginia.

New River, of Virginia. See Kanawha.

New Salem, a post office of Harrison county, Virginia.

Newsom's Depot, a post office of Southampton county, Virginia.

NEW STORE, a post office of Buckingham county, Virginia, 81 miles W. from Richmond.

NEWTON, a post office of Kanawha county, Virginia.

NEWTOWN, or STEPHENSBURG, a neat and thriving post village of Frederick county, Virginia, on the turnpike leading from Winchester to Staunton, eight miles S. by E. from the former. It contains two churches, a market house, and over 100 dwellings.

NEWTOWN, a small post village of King and Queen county, Virginia, 38 miles N. E. from Richmond.

NEW UPTON a post office of Gloucester county, Virginia.

NICHOLAS, a county in the W. central part of Virginia. The Kanawha river washes its S. W. border; it is traversed from E. to W. by the Gauley river, and also drained by Meadow river and Buffalo Creek. The surface is hilly and mountainous, and covered with extensive forests. A large part of the land is unproductive. Indian corn, oats, grass, and live stock are the staples. In 1850 there were raised 83,273 bushels of corn, 31,377 of oats, 2001 tons of hay, and 41,976 pounds of butter. It contained nine churches and 189 pupils attending public schools. A railroad is projected, which, when finished, will connect the county with the Ohio river. Formed in 1818. Capital Summerville. Population, 3963, of whom 3890 were free, and 73 slaves.

NICKLESVILLE, a post office of Scott county, Virginia.

NICKELL'S MILLS, a post office of Monroe county, Virginia.

NINEVEH, a post office of Warren county, Virginia.

NOLAND'S FERRY, a post office of Loudoun county, Virginia, 161 miles N. from Richmond.

NOMINY GROVE, a post office of Westmoreland county, Virginia.

NORFOLK, a county in the S. E. part of Virginia, bordering on North Carolina, has an area of 480 square miles. It is situated on the western shore of Chesapeake bay, on the estuary of James river, which is called Hampton Roads. Indian corn, oats and sweet potatoes are cultivated, and cypress lumber is one of the principal exports. In 1850 this county produced 307,245 bushels of corn, and 21,303 of sweet potatoes. There were three ship-yards, one cordage and three saw manufactories, two iron foundries, and one machine shop. It contained 36 churches, 13 newspaper offices, 1924 pupils attending public schools, and 363 attending academies or other schools. The county is intersected by the Dismal Swamp canal, which connects the Chesapeake with Albemarle sound, and

BOOKS, STATIONERY,

AND

DRAWING MATERIALS,

A large assortment of every thing in this line of business can always be obtained at *moderate prices and superior quality*, of

WILLIAM MINIFIE,

No. 114 BALTIMORE STREET,

BALTIMORE.

Who keeps the ONLY DEPOT where ALL the Drawing, requisites, used by the Architect, Engineer, Machinist, Water Color Artist, or Student of Drawing, can be obtained, such as Mathematical Instruments, in cases and in separate pieces, Scales of Ivory, paper and boxwood, in every variety; T. Squares, Triangles, Curves, Protractors, Tape Lines, Water Colors, in boxes and loose; India Ink; Camel's hair and Sable Pencils; Porcelain Cups, Pallets and Rests; Rubber; Pencils of all grades; black and colored Crayons; Porte-crayons; Stumps; Monochromatic Paper; French and English Crayon and Drawing Papers of all sizes; Tracing Linen; Tracing Paper, Bristol Boards; Graduated Boards; plain and colored Studies for Flowers, Fruits, Landscape, Ornament and the figures; blank Drawing Books; Elementary Studies, &c., &c., of the best qualities and at uniform prices, from which no abatement is made, except to Teachers and Wholesale Purchasers.

☞ *Orders per Mail will be promptly attended to, and filled on the same terms as if purchased in person.*

BOOKS ON SCIENCE and General Literature; COUNTING HOUSE and FANCY STATIONERY.

BLANK BOOKS

On hand or made to order in every style of Ruling and Binding.

GEORGE W. WEBB,

GOLDSMITH AND JEWELER,

Has removed to the OLD ESTABLISHED JEWELRY STAND on the

S. E. COR. BALTIMORE & CHARLES STS.

Where he intends keeping a well selected stock of

Fine Gold and Silver Watches,

SILVER & PLATED WARE,

RICH JEWELRY

AND

FINE FANCY ARTICLES.

In the MANUFACTURE and REPAIR OF JEWELRY, every attention will be paid to neatness and durability.

THE WATCH DEPARTMENT

Will be under the charge of Mr. JACOB BRADENBAUGH, who has had a long experience as a practical workman, and will give his personal attention to the REPAIRING of Fine Watches

Purchasers may rely upon getting articles of such quality as represented. Orders from the country attended to with fidelity and dispatch.

by the Portsmouth and Roanoke railroad. Capital, Portsmouth. Population, 33,036, of whom 22,636 were free, and 10,400 slaves.

Norfolk, a city and port of entry of Norfolk county, Virginia, is situated on the right or N. bank of Elizabeth river, eight miles from Hampton Roads, thirty two miles from the sea, 160 miles by water or 106 by land S. E. from Richmond. Lat. 36° 51′ N., lon. 76° 19′ W. The river, which is seven-eighths of a mile wide, separates it from Portsmouth. Next to Richmond, Norfolk is the most populous city of Virginia. It has more foreign commerce than any other place in the State, and together with Portsmouth is the most important naval station in the Union. The most conspicuous public buildings are the City Hall, which has a granite front, a cupola 110 feet high, and a portico of six Tuscan columns; its dimensions are eighty feet by sixty: the Norfolk Military Academy, a Doric structure, 91 feet by 47, with a portico of six columns at each end: the Mechanics' Hall, a Gothic building 90 feet by 60: Ashland Hall and a Baptist church with a steeple 200 feet high. It also contains 14 churches, one of which is Roman Catholic, nine seminaries, a hospital, an orphan asylum, three banks, and two reading rooms. Five newspapers are published here. The trade of Norfolk is facilitated by the Dismal Swamp canal, which opens a communication between Chesapeake bay and Albemarle sound, and by the Seaboard and Roanoke railroad, which connects it with the towns of North and South Carolina. The canal, constructed with great labor through the Dismal Swamp, is navigable by schooners, and brings to this place a very extensive trade in corn and lumber. A railroad is projected from this city to Petersburg. The entrance of the harbor is defended by forts Calhoun and Monroe. The capital invested in manufactures is about $570,000, and the value of the annual productions is estimated at $1,140,000. The reported value of real estate is $5,000,000. Norfolk was laid out in 1705, incorporated as a borough in 1736, and as a city in 1845. In 1776 it was burnt by the British. Population in 1850, 14,326; in 1854 about 20,000.

Northampton, a county in the S. E. part of Virginia, is situated on the eastern shore of Chesapeake bay, and forms the S. extremity

J. W. MIDDLETON & CO.

TIN PLATE & SHEET IRON WORKERS,

No. 30 South Calvert Street,

BALTIMORE.

Also a general assortment of BRITANNIA WARE, and all kinds of HOLLOW WARE, such as pots, Ovens and Tea Kettles, constantly on hand.

JOHN MALLON,

PUMP AND BLOCK MAKER,

Corner Pratt and South Streets,

BALTIMORE.

J. M. manufactures Oak and Pine WELL PUMPS, of any length; Patent plank Blocks, Patent solid Blocks, Iron bushed Blocks, Oars, Handspikes, Deck Plugs and all other articles in his line of business, on reasonable terms.

E. WHITMAN. E. W. ROBINSON.

E. WHITMAN & CO'S

New Agricultural Implement, Seed and Machine Warehouse,

No. 63 EXCHANGE PLACE, BALTIMORE.

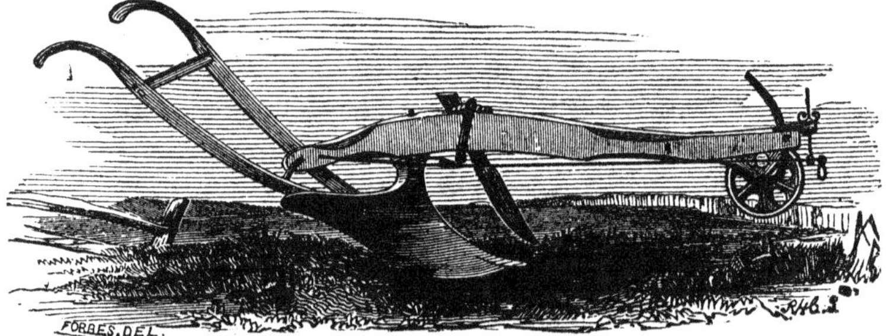

Farmers and Mechanics will find at our new Warehouse nearly every Implement, Machine or Tool used in their line of business.

Our arrangements with Northern manufacturers, together with our own facilities for manufacturing in Baltimore, enable us to avail ourselves of all new and valuable improvements, and to offer them to the public on the most favorable terms. Our stock probably embraces the greatest variety of any house of the kind in this country, among which may be found the following, viz:

AGRICULTURAL IMPLEMENTS AND MECHANICS' MACHINES.

Horsepowers,
Threshing Machines,
Wheat Fans,
Plows and Harrows,
Cultivators,
Wheat and Seed Drills,
Reaping Machines,
Cornshellers,
Straw Cutters,
Corn and Cob Crushers,
Plantation Mills,

Vegetable Cutters,
Hydraulic Rams,
Pumps of all kinds,
Shovels, Spades, Forks,
Rakes, Hoes, &c., &c.
Planing Machines for wood,
" " for iron,
Steam Engines,
Sash Moulding Machines,
Mortising and Tenoning Machines,

Circular and Upright Saws,
Engine and Hand Lathes,
Horizontal and Upright Drills,
Bolt Cutting Machines,
Portable and Smith's Forges,
Smith's Bellows,
Fan Blowers,
Stocks and Dies,
Smut Machines,
Belting, &c., &c.

Field and Garden Seeds, Fruit and Ornamental Trees, Peruvian and Mexican Guano, Poudrette, Bone Dust and Fertilizers of all descriptions.

of the peninsula which extends between that bay and the sea. The length is 36 miles, and the area 320 square miles. It is indented by numerous inlets on each side. The surface is level; the soil light and sandy. Indian corn and oats are the staples; fish and oysters are abundant. In 1850 there were raised 364,967 bushels of corn, 184,087 of oats, and 44,189 of sweet potatoes. There were three castor oil mills, and three coach manufactories; ten churches, and 622 pupils attending public schools. Northampton was one of the eight original shires formed in 1634. Capital, Eastville. Population, 7498, of whom 3850 were free, and 3648 slaves.

North Anna, a small river in the eastern part of Virginia, rises in Louisa and Orange counties, flows south east-ward, forming the boundary between Louisa and Hanover on the right, and Spottsylvania and Caroline on the left, and unites with S. Anna river, near the southern extremity of the latter counties, a few miles above Hanover Court House. The river formed by this confluence is the Pamunkey.

North Bend Mills, a post office of Tyler county, Virginia.

North River, in the central part of Virginia, rises in Augusta county, among the Alleghany mountains, flows southward through Rockbridge county, passes by Lexington and enters the James river immediately above its passage through the Blue Ridge, near the northern extremity of Bedford county. This stream in its upper part, is called the Calfpasture river. The whole length is about 100 miles.

North River, in the N. E. part of Virginia. This name is frequently applied to the Rappahannock above the mouth of the Rapidan. See Rappahannock.

North River, of Hampshire county, Virginia, is an affluent of the Great Cacapon river.

North River, of Rockingham county Virginia, one of the head streams of the Shenandoah proper, flows south-eastward and unites with the Middle and South rivers, near Port Republic, in the county just named.

North River Meeting House, a post office of Hampshire county Virginia.

Northumberland, a county in the E. part of Virginia, bordering on Chesapeake bay and on the estuary of the Potomac river, has an area of 150 square miles. Its eastern outline is indented by several inlets, two of which are called the Coan and Wicomico rivers. The surface is somewhat undulating, and the soil of me-

FRANKLIN L. BATES'S

LATEST IMPROVED

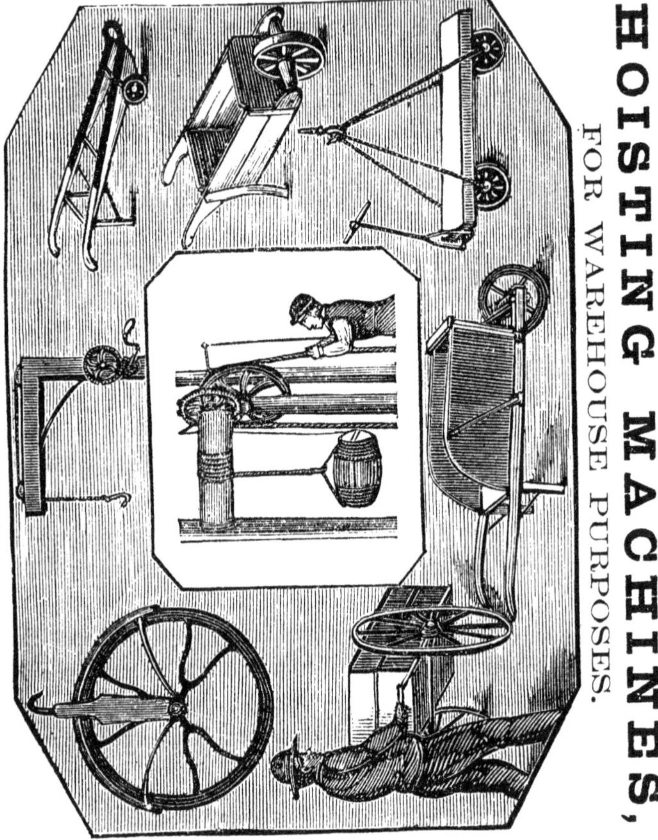

These Machines have now become in general use in Baltimore and many of the Southern and Western Cities, and have in every instance given the utmost satisfaction to those that have them in use. The subscriber now, with confidence, recommends them to every Merchant in the Union who has a Warehouse, as a safe and easy mode of transporting goods from one story to another. These Machines are warranted. Here are a few names of Merchants who have them in use in their Warehouses, to which I refer:

BALTIMORE:

JAMES PARKHURST, Bowly's Wharf,
J. HOOPER & SONS, Cheapside,
CHARLES E. JAY, Cheapside,
FREDERICK ROLISON, Paca street,
E. C. THOMAS, Baltimore street,
ROBERT M. HART, Baltimore street,
DUVALL, ROGERS & Co., Baltimore street,
J. R. MANN, McElderry's Wharf.

VIRGINIA:

E. H. SKINNER, Richmond,
SAMUEL H. HAYWOOD, Richmond,
CRENSHAW & BROTHER, "
WILLIAM BROWN, "
COL. W. W. WATTS, Portsmouth,
NIEMYER & WHITE, "
CAZENOR & CO., Alexandria,
HENRY DAINGERFIELD, Alexandria,
ROBERT H. HUNTON, "

DISTRICT OF COLUMBIA.

JACOB GIDEON, Washington,
W. M. SHUSTER & CO., Washington,
A. J. JOYCE, "
P. TYSON, Washington,
RICHARD J. RYAN, "

I could name many others, but deem these few references sufficient. I also make all kinds of TRUCKS and WHEELBARROWS and TRUCK WAGONS. In short, every kind of Machines for Hoisting or Removing goods in Warehouses, may be found at my Manufactory, being the only one of this kind in Baltimore. I am prepared to sell as cheap as any other manufacturer in the United States.

☞ Merchants and others will please give me a call and examine for themselves.

FRANKLIN L. BATES, East Falls Avenue,

Between Lombard and Pratt streets, adjoining the Bridge, Baltimore, Md.

dium quality. Indian corn, wheat, potatoes, cattle and swine are the staples. In 1850 this county produced 221,587 bushels of corn, 53,902 of wheat, 15,093 of sweet potatoes, and 29,773 pounds of butter. It contained three tanneries, eleven churches, and 279 pupils attending academies and other schools. Formed in 1648. Capital, Heathsville. Population, 7346, of whom 3591 were free, and 3755 slaves

North-West River Bridge, a post office of Norfolk county, Virginia.

Nortonsville, a post office of Albemarle county, Virginia.

Nottoway, or Nottaway river, in the S. E. part of Virginia, rises in Nottaway county, and flowing in a winding course along the border of Dinwiddie, and through Sussex and Southampton counties, unites with the Meherrin to form the Chawan river in Gates county, North Carolina, after a course of upwards of 110 miles.

Nottoway, a county in the S. S. E. part of Virginia, has an area of 330 square miles. The Nottaway forms its boundary on the S. Tobacco and Indian corn are the staples. In 1850 this county produced 2,109,314 pounds of tobacco, and 216,991 bushels of corn. There were 18 grist mills, and three tanneries. It contained 13 churches, 260 pupils attending public schools, and 16 attending an academy. The Richmond and Danville railroad passes through the county. Capital, Nottoway Court House. Population, 8437, of whom 2387 were free, and 6050 slaves.

Nottoway Court House, capital of Nottoway county, Virginia, on the Southside railroad, eight miles from its junction with the Richmond and Danville railroad, 60 miles S. W. from Richmond. Population about 200.

Oak Hill, a post office of Fauquier county, Virginia, 122 miles N. by W. from Richmond.

Oakland, a post office of Morgan county, Virginia.

Oakville, a small post-village of Appomattox county, Virginia, 103 miles W. from Richmond.

Oatland, a post village of Loudoun county, Virginia, on Goose creek, 150 miles N. from Richmond. It has several mills.

Occoquan river, in the N. E. part of Virginia, is formed by Broad run and Cedar run, which unite near Brentsville in Prince William county. It flows eastward to the boundary between that county and Fairfax, then runs south-eastward along the boundary until it enters the Potomac river 25 miles below Washington.

TO PRINTERS & PUBLISHERS.

10 PER CENT. SAVED AT THE

NEW TYPE FOUNDRY.

The undersigned has opened a TYPE FOUNDRY in the *City of Baltimore*, for the manufacture of

AND

PRINTERS' MATERIALS GENERALLY,

Newspaper Heads, Cuts, Brass Rule, Plain and Fancy Dashes of various patterns, Leads, Slugs, Single and Double Brass Galleys, Job Sticks, Brass Rule Cutters of an improved pattern, Lead Cutters, &c., &c.

We pledge ourselves to those who may patronize us, that every article furnished by us shall be of the best material and workmanship, as our long experience in the business (one of the Firm having superintended one of the largest Type Foundries in the country for several years,) will enable us to give satisfaction in all cases.

Newspaper Heads and Cuts Electrotyped.

Punctuality may be relied on in every case.

Place of business No. 9 Holliday street, near Baltimore street,

JOHN RYAN & BRO.

IRON FOUNDRY.

JOEL N. BLAKE,

IRON FOUNDRY AND MACHINE SHOP,

No. 40 EAST MONUMENT STREET,

BALTIMORE,

Makes to order all kinds of Wrought and Cast Iron Railings; Castings of all kinds, Steam Engines, Machinists' Tools, and all kinds of heavy and light Machinery, at the shortest notice, and on moderate terms. All orders promptly attended to.

OCCOQUAN, a post village of Prince William county, Virginia, on the Occoquan river, 99 miles N. from Richmond. It has extensive water power, with several mills and a cotton factory. Population from 300 to 400.

OHIO, a county in the N. W. part of Virginia, bordering on Pennsylvania, and on the Ohio river, contains about 140 square miles. The Ohio river separates it from the State of Ohio, and it is drained by Wheeling creek. Indian corn, wheat, oats, hay, butter and wool are the staples. The hills contain rich mines of bituminous coal, which is extensively used in manufactories. In 1850 the county produced 214,020 bushels of corn, 57,709 of wheat, 76,767 of oats, 4111 tons of hay, 104,722 pounds of butter, and 98,590 of wool. There were two cotton factories, three nail factories, five glass factories, one woolen factory, two wire manufactories, four iron foundries, three iron forges, 17 collieries, nine flour, three paper and two planing mills. It contained 15 churches, 3529 pupils attending public schools, and 400 attending academies or other schools. Capital, Wheeling. Population, 18,006, of whom 17,842 were free, and 164 slaves. Population in 1854 about 25,000.

OLD POINT COMFORT, a post village and watering place of Elizabeth City county, Virginia, 12 miles N. from Norfolk, situated at the entrance of Hampton roads, on the James river. The entrance is defended by fort Monroe. Here is a fixed light 50 feet above the sea. Lat. 37° N., lon. 76° 22′ W.

ONANCOCK, a post village of Accomack county, Virginia, 100 miles E. by N. from Richmond.

OPEQUAN CREEK, in the N. E. part of Virginia, rises in Frederick county, flows north-eastward, forming the boundary of Clarke and Jefferson counties on the right, and Frederick and Berkley on the left, until it falls into the Potomac.

ORANGE, a county in the E. part of Virginia, has an area of 230 square miles. It is bounded on the N. by the Rapidan, and drained by the head streams of North Anna river. Indian corn, wheat, oats, hay, tobacco and butter are the staples. In 1850 this county produced 267,140 bushels of corn, 121,825 of wheat, 30,750 of oats, 1881 tons of hay, 174,700 pounds of tobacco, and 54,814 of butter. There were 23 flour, grist, saw and plaster mills, one woolen factory, and five tanneries: nine churches, and 253 pupils attending public schools. The county contains limestone, iron ore, and small quantities of gold are found. It is intersected by the Orange and

IRA C. CANFIELD. WM. B. CANFIELD. JOS. H. MEREDITH.

CANFIELD, BROTHER & CO.

IMPORTERS, MANUFACTURERS AND DEALERS IN

WATCHES, FINE JEWELRY,

SILVER & PLATED WARE, MILITARY AND

WHOLESALE AND RETAIL,

No. 229 BALTIMORE STREET,

Cor. of Charles street,

BALTIMORE.

Their stock consists in part of Gold and Silver Watches, of the best makers, in Hunting, Magic and open Cases, some for ladies, set with Diamonds and Pearls and beautifully enameled; Gold Chains, Chatelaines, Seals, Keys, Charms, Gold Pens and Pencils; Rich Diamond, Pearl, Gold and Enameled Jewelry of the newest styles; Silver Coffee and Tea Sets, Silver Pitchers, Goblets, Cups, Waiters, Baskets, Casters, Silver Forks, Spoons, Dessert, Fish, Butter and Pastry Knives, Napkin Rings, Salt Cellars, &c., &c. Sheffiield and Birmingham Plated Ware, consisting of Epergnes, Waiters, Casters, Baskets, Candlesticks, Egg Stands, Butter Dishes, Forks, Spoons and Ladles. A very extensive variety of Fancy goods, consisting of Clocks, Bronzes, Candelabras, Glass and China Vases, Rich Dresden China and Parian Figures, Papier Mache Goods, Rosewood Dressing Cases and Writing Desks, Elegant Fans, Opera Glasses, Port Monnaies, Card Cases, Fine Paintings, Table Cutlery, &c.

They feel sure the advantage of personally selecting their goods at the different factories in Europe, and their own manufactories of Jewelry and Silver Ware here, enable them to offer inducements to purchasers equal to any other house in the United States.

JAMES MADISON,
Born in this county March 19, 1751.

ZACHARY TAYLOR,
Born in this county.

Alexandria railroad. Capital, Orange Court House. Population, 10,067, of whom 4146 were free, and 5921 slaves.

ORANGE COURT HOUSE, capital of Orange county, Virginia, 80 miles N. W. from Richmond, and 92 miles from Washington, contains two churches, and about 500 inhabitants.

ORANGE SPRINGS, a post village of Orange county, Virginia, 104 miles N. N. W. from Richmond.

OTTER BRIDGE, a post office of Bedford county, Virginia.

OTTER PEAKS, Virginia. See Peaks of Otter.

OTTER RIVER, a small stream in the S. part of Virginia, rises in Bedford county, at the base of the celebrated Peaks of Otter, and flowing south-eastward, falls into Staunton river in Cabell county.

OXFORD, a post office of Ritchie county, Virginia.

PACK'S FERRY, a post office of Monroe county, Virginia.

PADDYTOWN, a small village of Hampshire county, Virginia, on the N. branch of Potomac river, and about 210 miles N. W. from Richmond.

PAGE, a county toward the N. E. part of Virginia, contains about 300 square miles. The soil is of limestone formation and is highly productive. Wheat, Indian corn, hay and butter are the staples. In 1850 this county produced 128,430 bushels of wheat, 137,602 of corn, 2253 tons of hay, and 53,207 pounds of butter. There were 16 flour mills, three saw mills, one iron furnace, two iron forges, and five tanneries. It contained eleven churches, 463 pupils attending public schools, and 35 attending other schools. Iron ore and fine marble are abundant; copper and lead are also found. Capital, Luray. Population, 7600, of whom 6643 were free, and 957 slaves.

HOISTING WHEELS,

CASTINGS OF EVERY DESCRIPTION,

CORNER OF STILES AND PRESIDENT STREETS,

BALTIMORE.

JOHN G. MILLHOLLAND,

ENGINEER & MACHINIST,

East Falls Avenue, Near Pratt St. Bridge,

BALTIMORE,

Is prepared to execute all orders in his line for

MACHINERY,

Steam Engines, and other kinds of Machine work. Also, Planing and Turning of the largest descriptions. Orders by Mail promptly attended to.

N. B.—In connection with the above the Subscriber has just opened an

IRON FOUNDRY,

And is now prepared to furnish to order every description of Castings on the shortest notice and most reasonable terms.

Painsville, a post village of Amelia county, Virginia, forty-six miles W. S. W. from Richmond.

Palatine, a thriving post village of Marion county, Virginia, on the right bank of Monongahela river, opposite Fairmount. The Baltimore and Ohio railroad crosses the river at this place on a fine suspension bridge.

Palestine, a post village in Greenbrier county, Virginia.

Palmyra, a post village, capital of Fluvanna county, Virginia, on the Rivanna river, 60 miles W. by N. from Richmond.

Pamunkey river, in the S. E. part of Virginia, is formed by the union of North and South Anna rivers, on the border of Caroline and Hanover counties, and flowing in a general S. E. direction joins the Mattapony to form the York river. Its whole length is probably not less than 75 miles. This river separates King William county from Hanover and New Kent counties.

Parham's Store, a post office of Sussex county, Virginia.

Parisburg, a post village, capital of Giles county, Virginia, on the left bank of New river, 240 miles W. from Richmond.

Parkersburg, a thriving post village, capital of Wood county, Virginia, on the Ohio river, at the mouth of the Little Kanawha, 100 miles below Wheeling, and about 258 miles in a direct line W. N. W. from Richmond. It contains a court house, churches of four or five denominations, a bank, a printing office, and several steam mills. Population in 1853, about 3500.

Parnassus, a post village of Augusta co., Va., on the Warm Spring and Harrisonburg turnpike, 132 miles N. W. from Richmond.

Patrick, a county in the S. part of Virginia, bordering on North Carolina, has an area of 500 square miles. Indian corn, wheat, oats, tobacco, cattle, and swine are the staples. In 1850 there were raised 248,868 bushels of corn, 12,755 of wheat, 90,441 of oats, 429,699 pounds of tobacco, and 66,957 of butter. There were two flour and grist mills, 18 tobacco factories, two tanneries, one iron furnace, and one iron forge. It contained thirteen churches and 826 pupils attending public schools. Iron ore abounds in it. Formed out of a part of Henry county in 1791, and named in honor of the illustrious orator, Patrick Henry. Capital, Taylorsville. Population 9609, of whom 7285 were free, and 2324 slaves.

Patrick Court House, or Taylorsville, a post village, capital of Patrick county, Virginia, on the Mayo river, 226 miles S. W. from Richmond, and eight miles from the Tennessee line.

GEO. W. HARDESTY. FRANKLIN MILLS.

HARDESTY & MILLS,

BRASS FOUNDERS

AND MANUFACTURERS OF

BRASS FAUCETS

For Steam, Water, Gas & other purposes.

Also all the various articles used in the Plumbing Business,

Lovely Lane, between South and Calvert Streets,

(NEARLY OPPOSITE THE SUN IRON BUILDING,)

BALTIMORE.

H. & M. are now prepared to manufacture to order every variety of GAUGE and STEAM COCKS, (with or without Flanges,) used by Locomotive and Stationary Engine Builders, including Oil Cocks, Cups, Couplings, &c. Also Lager Beer Cocks. Every description of Brass Castings done daily. Turning and Finishing in all the various branches. Copper & Brass bought or exchanged for work.

SMITH & CURLETT,

MANUFACTURERS OF

FINE, FANCY & COMMON

SOAPS,

ADAMANTINE & TALLOW CANDLES,

LARD OIL,

Corner of Holliday and Pleasant Sts.

BALTIMORE.

CHARLES & JAMES WEBB,

SOAP & CANDLE

MANUFACTURERS,

N. W. Corner of Chew and Ensor Streets,

NORTH OF MADISON,

BALTIMORE,

Manufacture and have constantly on hand, MOULD and DIPPED CANDLES, and all kinds of SOAPS, which for quality cannot be excelled in this or any other city, which will be disposed of on reasonable terms.

PATTERSON'S CREEK, in the N. part of Virginia, rises in Hardy county, flows north eastward through Hampshire county, and enters the North branch of the Potomac, about eight miles S. E. from Cumberland, in Maryland.

PATTONSBURG, a thriving post-village of Botetourt county, Virginia, on the James river, 181 miles W. from Richmond, is connected by a handsome bridge with the village of Buchanan.

PATTONSVILLE, a post office of Scott county, Virginia.

PAWPAW, a post office of Morgan county, Virginia.

PEAKS OF OTTER, Virginia, between Bedford and Botetourt counties thirty miles W. by N. from Lynchburg. Their summits are about 4260 feet above the level of the sea.

PENDLETON, a county in the N. central part of Virginia, has an area of 620 square miles. It is intersected by the South or principal branch of Potomac river, and by two affluents of the same, called the North and South forks. The main Alleghany mountain forms its boundary on the N. W., the North mountain on the S. E., and Jackson's mountain extends across the county. Indian corn, wheat, oats, hay and cattle are the staples. In 1850 this county produced 109,838 bushels of corn, 44,137 of wheat, 29,930 of oats, 7664 tons of hay, and 69,306 pounds of butter. There were 20 flour and saw mills, seven wool carding mills, and seven tanneries. It contained twelve churches, and 225 pupils attending academies and other schools. Capital, Franklin. Population 5795, of whom 5473 were free, and 322 slaves.

PETERSBURG, a handsome and flourishing city and port of entry of Dinwiddie county, Virginia, on the right or S. bank of the Appomattox river, at the crossing of the Great Southern railroad, 22 miles S. from Richmond, and ten miles from the James river at city point. Lat. 37° 14′ N., lon. 77° 20′ W. It is the third town of Virginia in respect to population, and possesses extensive facilities for business. Vessels of 100 tons ascend the river to the town, and those of larger size to Waltham's landing, six miles below. The South Side railroad has its eastern terminus at this place, and the Appomatox railroad connects it with City Point, at the mouth of the river. Large quantities of flour and tobacco are exported from this place. Petersburg is well built, and

contains two churches of the Presbyterians, two of the Methodists, two of the Episcopalians, one of the Baptists, one of the Catholics, besides several places of worship for colored people. It has also three banks, several cotton factories, one woolen factory, two rope-walks, one iron furnace, six forges, and numerous mills of various kinds. Three newspapers are published here. The falls of the river, which arrest the ascent of the tide immediately above Petersburg, furnish extensive water power. Around these falls a canal has been constructed, by which means small boats ascend the river for the distance of about 100 miles. The shipping of this port, June 30, 1852, amounted to an aggregate of $484\frac{11}{59}$ tons registered, and $2109\frac{54}{95}$ tons enrolled and licensed. Of the latter, $2030\frac{80}{95}$ tons were employed in the coast trade, and $322\frac{59}{95}$ tons in steam navigation. The foreign arrivals for the year were 16, (tons, 10,147;) of which five (tons, 2773) were by American vessels. The clearances for foreign ports were 10, (tons, 5102;) of which 3906 were in foreign bottoms. Population in 1850, 14,010; in 1854, about 18,000.

PETERS' MOUNTAIN, Virginia, is situated on the boundary between Monroe and Giles counties.

PETERSTOWN, a post village of Monroe co., Va., on Rich creek, 247 miles W. from Richmond, has a water power and several mills.

PEYTONSBURG, a post village of Pittsylvania county, Virginia, 145 miles S. W. from Richmond.

PHILIPPI, a post village, capital of Barbour county, Virginia, on Tygart's Valley river, about 210 miles N. W. from Richmond.

PHILOMONT, a post village of Loudoun county, Virginia, 12 miles S. from Leesburg.

PIEDMONT, a village of Hampshire county, Virginia, on the North branch of the Potomac river, and on the Baltimore and Ohio railroad, 215 miles N. W. from Richmond. It contains machine shops of the railroad company.

PIEDMONT STATION, a post village of Fauquier county, Virginia.

PINEVIEW, a post office of Fauquier county, Virginia.

PITTSYLVANIA, a county in the S. part of Virginia, bordering on N. Carolina, has an area of about 1000 square miles. The Staunton river forms its N. boundary; the Banister river flows through the middle, and the S. border is crossed several times by the meanderings of the Dan. Tobacco, Indian corn and wheat are the staples. In 1850 this county produced 4,700,757 pounds of tobacco;

653,815 bushels of corn, and 123,934 of wheat. There were 25 flour, grist and saw mills, 43 tobacco factories, seven tanneries, and three distilleries. It contained 50 churches, one newspaper office, 697 pupils attending public schools, and 112 attending other schools. A railroad has been partly constructed from Richmond to Danville, the chief town of the county. Organized in 1767. Capital, Competition. Population 28,796, of whom 15,998 were free, and 12,798 slaves.

Pleasant Grove, a post office of Lunenburg county, Virginia, 89 miles S. W. from Richmond.

Pleasants, a new county in the N. W. part of Virginia, bordering on the Ohio river, which separates it from the State of Ohio. Indian corn, wheat, oats, hay, and cattle are the staples. Capital, St. Mary's.

Pocahontas, a county in the N. W. central part of Virginia, has an area of about 600 square miles. It is drained by the head streams of the Elk, Gauley, and Greenbrier rivers. The Greenbrier mountain extends across the county, while the main Alleghany forms its S. E. boundary. Indian corn, wheat, oats and live stock are the staples. In 1850 the county produced 51,949 bushels of corn, 11,806 of wheat, 52,998 of oats, 5911 tons of hay, and 76,080 pounds of butter. It contained one flour mill, one wool-carding mill, and one tannery; seven churches, 200 pupils attending public schools, and 40 attending another school. A cave has lately been discovered in the Elk mountain, which in the number and magnitude of its apartments, is said to be scarcely inferior to the celebrated Weir's cave. It is called Skeen's cave. Organized in 1821 and named in honor of the Indian princess, Pocahontas. Capital, Huntersville. Population, 3598, of whom 3331 were free, and 267 slaves.

Pocotalico, a river of Kanawha county, Virginia, falls into the Great Kanawha.

Poindexter's Store, a post village of Louisa county, Virginia, 68 miles N. W. from Richmond.

Point Pleasant, a post village, capital of Mason county, Virginia, on the Ohio river just above the mouth of the Kanawha river, 358 miles W. N. W. from Richmond.

Port Conway, a post village of King George co,. Va., on the left bank of the Rappahannock, 60 miles N. by E. from Richmond.

Port Republic, a post village in Rockingham county, Virginia, on the Shenandoah, about 100 miles W. N. W. from Richmond.

Port Royal, a post village of Caroline county, Virginia, on the right bank of Rappahannock river, 22 miles below Fredericksburg, Population about 600.

Portsmouth, a seaport and important naval depot of the United States, and capital of Norfolk county, Virginia, on the left bank of the Elizabeth river, opposite the city of Norfolk, eight miles from Hampton Roads, and 160 miles by water S. E. from Richmond. Lat. 36° 50′ N., lon. 76° 19′ W. The river, which is about half a mile wide, forms a safe and excellent harbor, accessible to vessels of the largest size, in which several ships of war are usually lying at anchor. The General Government has at Gosport, (a suburb of Portsmouth,) a large and costly dry-dock, which is capable of admitting the largest saips. Besides the United States naval hospital in the vicinity, a large and showy building of stuccoed brick, Portsmouth contains a court house, six churches, a branch of the Bank of Virginia, and the Virginia Literary, Scientific, and Military Academy. Portsmouth is the terminus of the Seaboard and Roanoke railroad, which with connecting lines, opens a communication with Charleston, South Carolina. Five newspapers are published here. Founded in 1752. Population, 8626.

Potomac, a large river of Virginia and Maryland, is formed by the North and South branches, which unite on the northern border of Virginia, about 20 miles S.E. from Cumberland. It flows first north-eastward to Hancock, passing through several ridges of mountains. It pursues a south-easterly direction, and receives from the right its largest affluent, the shenandoah, just before its passage through the Blue Ridge at Harper's Ferry. Flowing thence south-eastward nearly one hundred miles to Georgetown, it falls over the edge of the primitive formation, and changes its course to the south and south-west for a distance of about 50 miles. Again resuming its general direction, it expands in an estuary of six or eight miles in width, and flows into Chesapeake bay about 38° North lat., and 76° 10′ W. lon. The length, exclusive of the branches, is estimated at 350 miles. The principal towns on its banks are Cumberland, Georgetown, Washington and Alexandria. It is navigable for the largest vessels to Washington city. The Chesapeake and Ohio canal extends along this river from Cumberland to Georgetown. The Potomac forms the boundary between Maryland and Virginia.

Potomac Creek, in the East part of Virginia, flows through Stafford county into the Potomac river.

Pott's Creek, in the S. W. central part of Virginia, rises in Monroe county, flows north-eastward, and enters Jackson's river near Covington, in Alleghany county.

Powhatan county, situated in the S. E. central part of Virginia, contains 280 square miles. It is bounded on the North by the James river, and on the South by the Appomattox. Indian corn, wheat oats, and tobacco are the staples. In 1850 this county produced 215,155 bushels of corn, 115,437 of wheat, 89,189 of oats and 1,000,490 pounds of tobacco. It contained 19 churches and 305 pupils attending academies and other schools. The James River canal passes along the border. Organized in 1777. Capital, Scottsville. Population, 8,178, of whom 2,896 were free and 5,282 slaves.

Preston, a county in the N. W. part of Virginia, bordering on Pennsylvania and Maryland, contains nearly 800 square miles. It is drained by the Cheat river. The soil produces excellent pasture, and in some parts grain succeeds well. The principal exports are lumber, Indian corn, oats, pork and butter. In 1850 this county produced 144,276 bushels of corn, 153,496 of oats, 36,769 of wheat, 179,836 pounds of butter and 7,765 tons of hay. There were four tanneries, one woolen factory, 28 churches, 840 pupils attending public schools and 70 attending other schools. Limestone, sandstone and slate, alternate with beds of coal; iron ore is abundant. The streams afford a vast amount of water power. Named in honor of James B. Preston, at that time Governor of Virginia. Capital, Kingwood. Population, 11,708, of whom 11,621 were free and 87 slaves.

Pride's Church, a post office of Amelia county Virginia.

Prillaman's, a post office of Franklin county, Virginia.

Prince Edward, a county in the S. S. E. part of Virginia, has an area of about 300 square miles. It is bounded on the north by Appomattox river, and drained by Harris, Briery, Bush, and Sandy creeks. The surface is somewhat diversified; the soil is naturally good, but impoverished in some degree by a bad system of cultivation. Tobacco, Indian corn, wheat and oats are the staples. In 1850 this county produced 2,571,850 pounds of tobacco, 214,350 bushels of corn, 75,762 of wheat and 87,229 of oats. There were nine flour and grist mills, six tobacco factories, three tanneries and one iron foundry. It contained 24 churches, one newspaper office, 377 pupils attending public schools and 117 attending other schools. Copper, stone coal, and marl are found. The county is intersected by

CALVERT ST. CASH BROOM STORE,

No. 66 CALVERT STREET,

(Near Pratt Street Wharf.)

MANUFACTURER AND WHOLESALE DEALER IN ALL KINDS OF

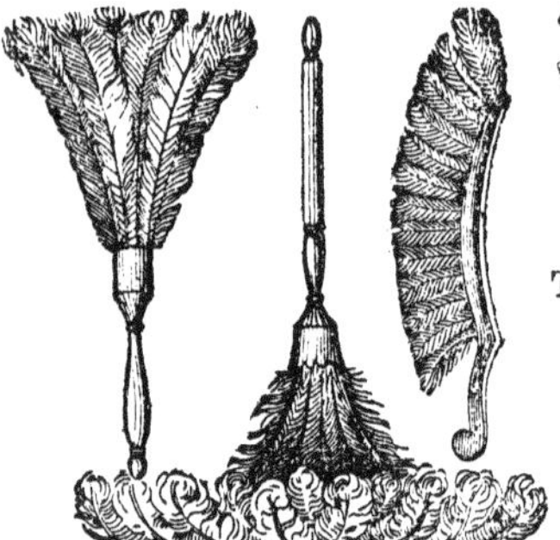

WOODEN, WILLOW

And Cedar Ware,

BRISTLE BRUSHES, MATS,

TWINE, CORDAGE, MATCHES,

BLACKING, CLOCKS,

WINDOW SHADES, &c. &c.

For the trade on the most reasonable terms.

SPENCER ROWE.

SUSQUEHANNA HOTEL,

OPPOSITE CALVERT STATION,

BALTIMORE.

The undersigned having leased the above hotel and put it in complete order, is prepared to accommodate his friends and the traveling public. The proprietor will be pleased to see his old friends, and promises to make their stay comfortable and satisfactory. Baggage taken to and from Calvert Station Free of Charge.

JOHN BARR, Proprietor,
(Formerly of Pennsylvania.)

DOUBLE SCREEN ROCKAWAY GRAIN FANS!

J. MONTGOMERY & BRO'S

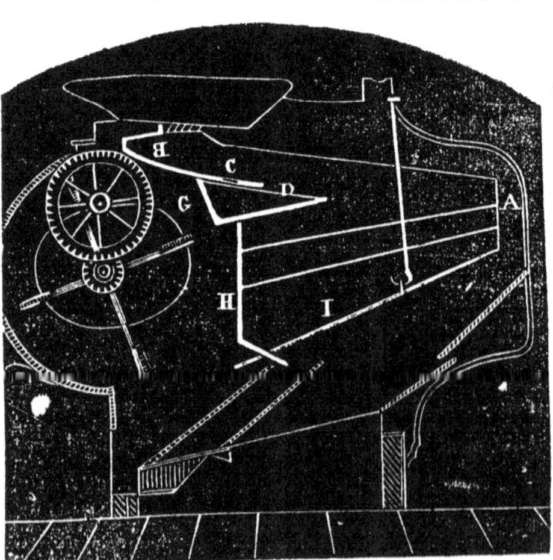

CELEBRATED DOUBLE SCREEN

ROCKAWAY

WHEAT FANS,

PATENTED

December 20th, 1853.

☞ These Fans have taken the First Premiums at eight of the principal Agricultural Fairs of Maryland, Virginia and North Carolina, in 1854. They are adapted to all kinds of grains. All orders will be thankfully received and promptly attended to. Address

J. MONTGOMERY & BRO.
No. 155 N. High Street,
BALTIMORE.

two lines of railway leading to Richmond, Danville and Lynchburg. Capital, Prince Edward Court House. Population 11,857, of whom 4,665 were free and 7,192 slaves.

PRINCE EDWARD COURT HOUSE, a small post village, capital of Prince Edward county, Virginia, 75 miles W. S. W. from Richmond. It contains, besides the county buildings, one or two churches and 2 academies.

PRINCE GEORGE, a county in the S. E. part of Virginia, has an area of about 300 square miles. James river forms its northern boundary, the Appomattox flows along its north-western border until it enters the former stream, and it is also drained by the sources of Blackwater river. Indian corn, wheat, oats and butter are the staples. In 1850 this county produced 261,510 bushels of corn, 81,042 of wheat, 23,600 of oats, and 32,988 pounds of butter. There were 19 manufactories of wooden ware, beside other establishments; 14 churches, and 198 pupils attending public schools. Capital, Prince George Court-house. Population, 7596, of whom 3,188 were free and 4,408 slaves.

PRINCE GEORGE COURT HOUSE, a post village, capital of Prince George county, Virginia, 24 miles S. S. E. from Richmond.

PRINCESS ANNE, a county in the S. E. extremity of Virginia, bordering on North Carolina and the Atlantic. The area is about 420 square miles. The Chesapeake bay washes its N. border; Cape Henry forms the N. E. extremity. Large quantities of firewood and lumber (pine and cypress) are procured from the forests for the Norfolk market. Indian corn is the staple product of the farms. In 1850 there were raised 347,141 bushels of corn, 60,024 of oats, and 1,593 tons of hay. There were four grist and saw mills and two farming implement manufactories; 17 churches and 819 pupils attending public schools. Formed from Norfolk in 1691. Capital Princess Anne Court House. Population, 7,669, of whom 4,539 were free, and 3,130 slaves,

PRINCESS ANNE COURT HOUSE, a post village, capital of Princess Anne county, Virginia, 137 miles S. E. from Richmond. It contains two churches.

PRINCETON, a post village, capital of Mercer county, Virginia, 270 miles West from Richmond. It has two churches.

PRINCE WILLIAM, a county in the N. E. part of Virginia, contains about 325 square miles. The Potomac river forms its boundary on the S. E., the Occoquan on the N. E., it is also drained by

Cedar Run, Broad Run, and Quantico creek. Indian corn, wheat, oats, hay and butter are the staples. In 1850 it produced 161,248 bushels of corn, 57,728 of wheat, 57,717 of oats, 2,309 tons of hay, and 79,079 pounds of butter. There were 19 flour, grist, plaster and saw mills, five wool-carding mills, one cotton factory and one woolen factory. It contained 13 churches and 316 pupils attending public schools. Formed in 1730. Capital, Brentsville. Population 8,129, of whom 5,631 were free and 2,498 slaves.

PULASKI, a county in the S. S. W. part of Virginia, contains about 250 square miles. It is intersected by New river, which also flows along the Eastern border; Little river, an affluent of the former, forms part of its eastern boundary. The county occupies a part of the great valley between Walker's mountain on the N. W. and the Blue Ridge on the S. E. Cattle are raised for exportation. In 1850 this county produced 175,510 bushels of Indian corn, 35,284 of wheat, 63,367 of oats, and 2,639 tons of hay. There were four grist mills, five saw mills, one flour mill, four wool-carding mills and five tanneries. It contained nine churches, and 292 pupils attending academies and other schools. The county contains abundance of iron and stone coal. It is intersected by the Virginia and Tennessee railroad. Organized in 1839, and named in honor of the Polish count, Pulaski. Capital, Newbern. Population, 5,118, of whom 3,647 were free and 1,471 slaves.

PUNGOTEAGUE, a post village of Accomack county, Virginia, 12 miles S. W. from Accomack Court House. It has two churches and a mill.

PUTNAM, a county in the West part of Virginia, touching the Ohio river, contains 350 square miles. It is intersected by the Great Kanawha river, navigable by steamboats. Indian corn, oats and butter are the staples. In 1850 the county produced 249,040 bushels of corn, 50,079 of oats and 59,862 pounds of butter. There were six grist mills, eight saw mills and 11 cooper shops. It contained 13 churches, 65 pupils attending public schools and 80 attending other schools. The hills contain immense beds of iron ore and bituminous coal. It was organized in 1848, including parts of Macon and Kanawha counties. Capital, Winfield. Population, 5,335, of whom 4,703 were free and 632 slaves.

QUILLINSVILLE, a post village in Scott county, Virginia, 320 miles West by North from Richmond.

RACOON, a post office of Preston county, Virginia.

M'LURE HOUSE,

WHEELING.

Dr. WATSON CARR, Proprietor.

This Magnificent Hotel, (the pride of Wheeling,) was built by the M'Lure House Company in 1851, and opened up January, 1853, simultaneously with the opening of the B. & O. R. R., at a cost of about $180,000, and furnished at a cost of $36,000, contains 150 finely ventilated rooms of capacious size, and is supplied with

HOT, COLD & SHOWER BATHS,

On different Floors, for the accommodation of Ladies and Gentlemen, and is kept in a style not surpassed by any House in the Union.

This House is most fortunately *not* situated on the River bank, and is therefore free from all the annoyances of wharf business, but is situated on the

Corner of Market and Monroe Streets,

In the most fashionable and business part of our thriving City and

Within three Minutes' Walk of the B. & O. R. R., C. O. R. R. and Steamboat Landing.

The Post Office and Court house are on the same square. **Express and Stage Offices in the Basement.**

All the appliances and attentions which have so eminently contributed to the comfort of the traveling community, and the boarders of the M'LURE HOUSE, will be continued with undeviating exactness, and at the unprecedeuted price of

$1.50 PER DAY!

And as the Proprietor is well acquainted with the wants of the traveling public, he is confident that he can meet their wishes in every particular.

This spacious Hotel contains thirty rooms more than the Eutaw House in Baltimore, and is more commodious than the Girard House of Philadelphia, and more than doubly as commodious as any Hotel in Wheeling.

OMNIBUSES and PORTERS always in attendance to convey passengers and baggage to and from this Hotel.

WATSON CARR, Proprietor.

RACOON FORD, a post village of Culpepper county, Virginia, on the Rapidan river, 90 miles N. N. W. from Richmond, contains several mills.

RALEIGH COURT HOUSE, Virginia. See BECKLEY.

RANDOLPH, a county in the North part of Virginia, bordering on Maryland, is about 80 miles in length, and 35 miles wide: area, about 2,800 square miles. It is drained by the head streams of the Buchanan, Cheat and Tygart's Valley rivers, branches of the Monongahela; it is traversed in the S. W. part by Elk river. Indian corn, wheat, oats, hay, butter and wool are the staples. In 1850 this county produced 87,468 bushels of corn, 11,740 of wheat, 44,789 of oats, 6,480 tons of hay and 56,339 pounds of butter. It contained 10 churches and 380 pupils attending public schools. Stone coal, iron, limestone, sandstone and slate are abundant. Salt is procured from some of its springs. Named in honor of John Randolph, of Roanoke. Capital, Beverly. Population, 5,243; of whom 5,042 were free and 201 slaves.

RAPIDAN river, of Virginia, rises on the S. E. base of the Blue Ridge. Flowing Southward and then Eastward, it forms the boundary between Green and Orange counties on the right and Madison and Culpepper on the left, and unites with the Rappahannock about 10 miles above Fredericksburg. Its length is estimated at 80 miles.

RAPID ANN, a post village of Madison county, Virginia, 102 miles N. W. from Richmond. It contains three churches and several stores.

RAPPAHANNOCK, a river in the East part of Virginia, is formed at the eastern extremity of Culpepper county, by the confluence of North and Rapidan rivers. Flowing in a south-easterly course, it falls over the primitive ledge, and meets the ocean tides at Fredericksburg, where it affords extensive water power. It now becomes a navigable stream, and after forming the boundary between several counties on each hand, enters the Chesapeake bay between Windmill and Stingray points.

RAVENSWOOD, a thriving post village of Jackson county, Virginia, on the Ohio river, at the mouth of Sand creek, 15 miles N. W. from Ripley. Population 200.

RECTORTOWN, a post village of Fauquier county, Virginia, 130 miles North by West from Richmond.

RED SULPHUR SPRINGS, a post village of Monroe county, Virginia, on Indian creek, 240 miles West from Richmond, and 38

miles S. W. from White Sulphur Springs. It is situated in a small valley among the Alleghany mountains, and is a place of fashionable resort, having been improved by the erection of expensive buildings. The temperature of the water is 54°

RED SWEET SPRINGS, a post office of Alleghany county, Virginia.

REEDY ISLAND RIVER, in the S. S. W. part of Virginia, rises in the Blue Ridge, flows north-westward through Carroll county, and enters the New river. Length about 70 miles; greatest width, 125 yards. It furnishes immense water-power.

REEDY RIPPLE, a post office of Wirt county, Virginia.

REHOBOTH, a post village in Lunenburg county, Virginia, 85 miles S. W. from Richmond.

RICEVILLE, a thriving post village of Pittsylvania county, Virginia, on Banister river, about 150 miles S. W. from Richmond. It has two stores.

RICHARDSVILLE, a post village of Culpepper county, Virginia, 95 miles N. N. W. from Richmond.

RICHMOND, a county in the East part of Virginia, has an area of 140 square miles, and a length of 30 miles. The Rappahannock river forms its entire boundary on the S. W. The surface is nearly level. The soil has lately been improved by the use of guano. Indian corn, wheat, potatoes and cotton are cultivated. Firewood is one of the chief articles of export, and large numbers of the inhabitants find lucrative employment in the oyster business. In 1850 this county produced 185,800 bushels of corn, 42,404 of wheat, 7,178 of sweet potatoes, 26,390 pounds of butter and 6,458 of wool. There were two coach manufactories and 1 saw mill. It contained nine churches and 220 pupils attending public schools. Organized in 1692. Capital, Warsaw. Population, 6448, of whom 4,171 were free and 2,277 slaves.

RICHMOND, p. city, port of entry, and cap. Henrico county, and capital of the State of Virginia; is situated on the N. E. bank of James river, at the lower falls at the head of tide water. Lat. (Capitol) 37° 32′ 17″ N.; long. from Greenwich 77° 27′ 28″ W., and from Washington 00° 25′ 58″ W. Distance by the most direct Railroad from Washington, 130 miles; from Baltimore, 168 miles; from Philadelphia, 266; from New York, 344 miles; from Boston, 580 miles; from Raleigh, 174 miles; from Wilmington, 248 miles.

The situation of Richmond is highly picturesque. The city is divided into two unequal parts by a valley, through which passes the

A. D. RICE. C. SWARTZ.

RICE & SWARTZ,

MANUFACTURERS OF

THRASHERS AND CLEANERS,

COMMON THRASHERS,

AND

REAPING AND MOWING MACHINES,

Martin's Ferry, Belmont County,

OHIO.

WHEELING STEEL WORKS.

STANTON, BELL, GOW & CO.

MANUFACTURERS OF

Springs, Axles, Steel Hoes,

PLOUGH STEEL, STEEL WINGS, &c.

NO. 187 MARKET STREET,

WHEELING.

S. M'CLALLEN. S. M'CLALLEN, Jr. C. D. KNOX.

M'CLALLENS & KNOX,

WHOLESALE DEALERS IN

ALSO,

WOOL & PALM HATS,

No. 113 MAIN STREET,

WHEELING.

JOHN L. NEWBY,

ATTORNEY & COUNSELLOR AT LAW,

WHEELING.

Shockoe creek to enter James river. It is chiefly built upon the hills and more elevated grounds on either side of this depression, which have a beautiful variety of surface, and afford in many parts highly picturesque situations for dwellings and for public edifices. Splendid views of the city and surrounding county are presented from different points, each varying the scene. The soil is red clay. The river flows over a bed of granite, of which there are inexhaustible quarries on its banks, extensively used for building and other purposes. The city is regularly laid out with streets crossing at right angles. Its entire area embraces about 3½ square miles, of which the built portion is about 3 miles long, and ¾ mile wide. The dwelling houses are generally neat and convenient, of brick and wood. Many private residences are very elegant and costly. The capitol occupies a very commanding situation on an elevated plain called Shockoe hill, in the Western division of the city. It stands in Capitol Square, a beautiful public ground containing about 8 acres, ornamented with trees, grass plats, walks, etc. It is a spacious and elegant building, surrounded on three sides by a lofty and imposing portico, in the Ionic order. It contains a statue of Washington, the only one ever taken from life, executed by Houdon, a celebrated French artist, and erected in 1788; a bust of Lafayette, etc. The City Hall, on Broad street, fronting Capitol Square, is an elegant edifice of Grecian architecture, with a portico at each end of four Doric columns. The Governor's House is at the east end of the square. The County Court-house is about one mile from the capitol. The State Penitentiary, in the Western suburbs, is 300 feet long and 110 broad, in the form of a hollow square, surrounded by extensive grounds. The Alms-house, a spacious building, is in the Northern suburbs. The Armory is a large edifice 320 feet long by 280 wide. The Female Orphan Asylum is supported partly by the corporation and partly by private munificence. There are about 25 churches, many of which are very handsome edifices. The Monumental Episcopal church stands upon the site of the Richmond Theatre, which was destroyed by fire, Dec. 26th, 1811, and whereby 66 white and 6 colored persons lost their lives. The congregation of the African church is one of the largest in the Union.

The Medical Department of Hampden Sidney College, founded 1838, in 1850 had 7 professors, 90 students, and 40 graduates. The Virginia Historical and Philosophical Society was founded in 1831. St. Vincent's and Richmond colleges, near the city, are flourishing

BANNER FACTORY

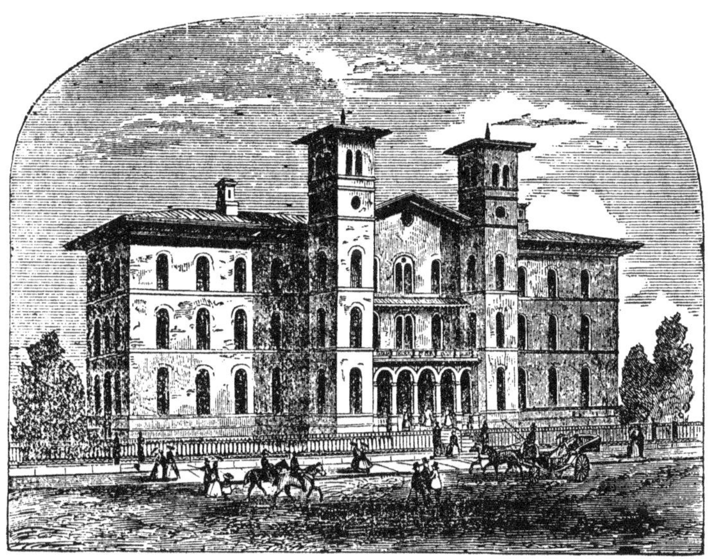

academies. The Richmond Female Institute is also a new and prosperous College,—the above is a view of this beautiful establishment. Among the numerous periodicals of Richmond, the following are celebrated for the ability and talent of their conductors viz: "Richmond Enquirer," "Richmond Whig," "Examiner," "Dispatch," "Post," "Literary Messenger." "Watchman and Observer," "Religious Herald."

The city government is vested in the Mayor, recorder, aldermen, and city council. The city is lighted with gas, and generally well paved; the markets are well supplied. The public water works were commenced in 1830, and cost about $120,000. By two forcing pumps, worked by water power, 800,000 gallons of water in 24 hours are lifted from James river, into three reservoirs, containing each 1,000,000 gallons, thence distributed over the city in pipes.

The principal manufactures are of tobacco, flour, iron, cotton, and woolens. Water power of unlimited extent is furnished by James river, which, within a few miles of the city descends eighty feet. Of tobacco there are 35 to 40 factories, among the most extensive is that of William H. Grant, (a view of the Banner factory we present on the opposite page,) and ten or twelve stemmeries, together employing about 2,500 blacks and manufacturing 12 to 15,000 hogsheads annually. Besides smaller mills, here are two of the most extensive flouring mills in the world, "Gallego" and "Hax-

FRANKLIN WORKS.

THEAKER, MITCHELL & CO.

MANUFACTURERS OF ALL KINDS OF

STEAM ENGINES, BOILERS, &c.

ALSO, EVERY DESCRIPTION OF

MILL MACHINERY,

RAIL ROAD CARS & R. R. MACHINERY GENERALLY,

On the most Approved Plans, and at Reduced Prices,

BRIDGEPORT, BELMONT COUNTY,

OHIO.

INGRAM & KNODE,

Washington Hall Restaurant,

Cor. Market & Monroe Streets,

WHEELING.

Coffee, Tea, Ham, Eggs, Beef Steak, Game in season.

BEYMER HOUSE,

No. 235 MAIN STREET,

WHEELING.

JAMES CALDWELL, Proprietor.

GEO. M. VARNEY,

MANUFACTURER OF

COMPOSITION ROOFS,

Keeps constantly on hand a good supply of *Roofing Paper*, and *Composition*, for which he can fill orders at the shortest notice. Also, manufacturer of

WAGONS, CARTS, DRAYS, &c.

Corner of Market and 1st Streets,

CENTRE WHEELING.

all," each running twenty or more pairs of stones, capable of producing 800 to 900 barrels of flour daily. There are three iron rolling mills, foundries of cannon, etc., and an extensive nail factory on Belle isle, producing 75,000 pounds of nails weekly. Four cotton mills work up nearly 3,000,000 pounds of cotton per annum, and a woolen mill 600,000 pounds of wool annually. Besides these, are large machine shops, a paper mill, etc.

There are three banks, having an aggregate capital of $2,143,000 three insurance companies, and three savings banks.

Four lines of railroad here connect, viz: Richmond, Frederick, and Potomac R. R., commencing at Aquia creek on the Potomac, 75 miles long; Richmond and Petersburg R. R., 22 miles long; the Central R. R. to Covington, and Danville R. R. completed to Keeseville, 73 miles. The James River Canal, completed in 1835 to Lynchburg, 146 miles, and in 1852 to Balcony Falls, is the principal channel of trade with the interior.

The following statement exhibits the amount of tonnage, and its estimated value, imported into Richmond on the James River and Kanawha Canal, during each of the 5 years, 1848–52, with its freight and tolls:

Year ending Oct. 31.	No. of Tons.	Estimated value.	Freights and tolls.
1848	125,054	$4,230,532 18	$192,750 38
1849	140,696	5,435,046 66	247,861 08
1850	137,589	6,123,865 49	213,741 47
1851	140,924	5,133,853 62	184,839 88
1852	153,377	7,145,837 43	220,947 84
Total (1848–52)	697,640	$28,069,135 38	$1,060,140 65

The following table exhibits the amount of tonnage, with its value and freightage, imported into Richmond, on the Richmond and Petersburg R. R., during each of the five years 1848–52.

Year ending Sept. 30.	Tonnage.	Estimated value.	Freight.
1848	20,301	$632,557 99	$18,301 62
1849	19,539	695,742 40	18,159 71
1850	22,861	1,377,665 45	21,560 83
1851	19,533	886,412 40	18,314 12
1852	27,932	1,262,248 85	24,752 89
Total (1848–52)	110,166	$4,854,627 09	$101,149 18

The following table exhibits the amount of tonnage, with its estimated value, and the freights and tolls on the same, imported into Richmond during 1852, by the various works of internal improvement leading into the city:

ROCK MILLS.

CUSHING & OSBUN,

MANUFACTURERS OF

GREEN WINDOW SHADES

AND

Enameled Carriage Oil Cloth,

BONNET AND BINDERS' BOARDS,

WHEELING.

JOHN BAYHA. DAVID BAYHA.

J. & D. BAYHA,

MANUFACTURERS OF

TIN AND SHEET IRON WARE,

WHOLESALE AND RETAIL. ALSO, DEALERS IN

Japanned & House Furnishing Hardware.

No. 137 Market Street,

WHEELING.

J. TURTON,

House, Sign, and Ornamental

PAINTER,

No. 128 Main, between Monroe and Union Streets,

WHEELING.

☞ Signs, Banners and Flags, transparent, plain and fancy; Graining, &c., executed with neatness and dispatch.

J. T. SCOTT,

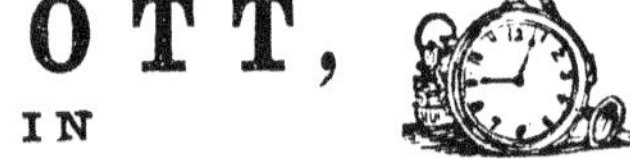

DEALER IN

WATCHES, CLOCKS, JEWELRY,

FANCY AND VARIETY GOODS,

No. 157 Main Street,

WHEELING.

All kinds of Watches, Clocks and Jewelry, carefully repaired and warranted.

Names of Companies.	No. of Tons.	Estimated value.	Freights and tolls.
James River, and Kanawha co.	153,377	$7,145,837 43	$220,947 84
R., Fredericksburg, and Potomac R. R.	4,807	285,000 00	19,252 03
Richmond and Petersburg R. R.	27,932	1,262,248 85	24,752 89
Richmond and Danville R R.	53,421	967,336 00	37,919 45
Virginia Central R. R.	17,450	1,000,000 00	55,989 20
Total	256,987	$10,660,422 28	$358,861 41

The foreign export trade is chiefly in tobacco to all parts of Europe, flour and grain occasionally, and in flour to Brazil. The import trade direct from Europe, or other countries, is now inconsiderable, having gradually diminished with the increased facilities of New York, by her regular packets and steamers to Europe. The channel of the river is winding, which, with the distance from the ocean, is a considerable impediment to navigation. Vessels drawing more than 10 or 11 feet water are prevented from coming up to the city by the bar, 7 miles below it, and such load at City Point, Bermuda Hundred, or Port Walthall. On June 30, 1850, the total tonnage of Richmond district was 8,458 tons. The registered tonnage was 3,161 tons, of which 1,588 tons were permanent and 1,573 tons temporary. The enrolled and licensed tonnage was 5,297 tons, consisting of 4,276 tons permanent, and 1,021 tons temporary, all of which were imployed in the coasting trade. During the year previous, the number of clearances for foreign countries was 69—24,321 tons; number of entrances do., 8—1,811 tons. Vessels built during the year, 8 (1 ship, 7 schooners)—1,479 tons.

The inspections of tobacco for several years are as follows:

Years.	Hhds.	Years.	Hhds.	Years.	Hhds.	Years.	Hhds.
1841	18,267	1844	19,147	1847	19,993	1850	17,986
1842	23,129	1845	21,902	1848	15,733	1851	15,678
1843	22,829	1846	19,572	1849	18,803	1852	24,119

In addition to which, from 10 to 16,000 hogsheads are here received from other inspections in the interior.

The following exhibits the inspections of flour of late years:

Years.	Bbls.	Years.	Bbls.	Years.	Bbls.
1846,	289,000	1848,	180,000	1850,	336.420
1847,	159,100	1849,	276,900	1851,	—

To which should be added 20 to 25 per cent. of inspections at Scottsville and Lynchburg, and brought to the Richmond market. The quantity of flour exported to Brazil for the year ending Sep-

A. T. GARDEN,

DEALER IN ALL KINDS OF

LEATHER, TANNERS' OIL,

SHOE FINDINGS, &c.

No. 19 UNION STREET,

WHEELING.

CASH PAID FOR HIDES AND LEATHER IN THE ROUGH.

WM. A. TURNER,

DEALER IN

CLOCKS, WATCHES,

JEWELRY, &c.

No. 178 MAIN STREET,

WHEELING.

Particular attention paid to repairing CLOCKS, WATCHES, &c.

J. K. DUNHAM & CO.

IMPORTERS AND DEALERS IN

CHINA, GLASS AND QUEENSWARE,

TABLE CUTLERY, BRITANNIA AND SILVER PLATED WARE,

Hall and Suspending Parlor Lamps, Lamp Wick, Tea Trays and House Furnishing Goods.

PLAIN, PRESSED AND CUT FLINT GLASSWARE,

FROM THE MANUFACTORY OF HOBBS, BARNES & Co.

No. 28 MONROE STREET,

WHEELING.

WM. J. ARMSTRONG,

DRUGGIST,

139 Market St., between Monroe & Union,

WHEELING.

tember, 30, 1848, was 74,425 barrels; 1849, 128,880 bbls.; 1850, 65,280 bbls.; 1851, 98,245 bbls.; 1852, 58,950. A considerable quantity of flour, destined for South America, is sent coastwise for re-shipment from New York, Baltimore, &c. The amount of other foreign shipments of flour in 1851, was 15,646 bbls., and increased in 1852 to 18,122 barrels.

The coal trade is considerable, and steadily increasing. The best bituminous coal is mined from 8 to 20 miles above the city, and iron ore abounds in the country beyond. Regular lines of steam packets run to Norfolk, Baltimore and New York.

The population has increased within the last ten or fifteen years more rapidly than at any previous period. Of the present population, about two-fifths are black. Population in 1800, 5,537; in 1810, 9,785; in 1820, 12,067; in 1830, 16,060; in 1840, 20,153; in 1850, 27,570; in 1854, including suburbs, about 45,000. The exceedingly healthy location of the city gives it a very low annual rate of mortality. The cemeteries are noted for their beauty and their monuments.

The site of Richmond was first visited by white men in 1609; the town was founded in 1742, and made the capital of the State in 1780. In 1787 it contained about 300 houses. In 1794 the canal around the falls was completed, which has added so much to its commercial advantages. In 1811, December 26th, occurred the fire by which seventy-two persons lost their lives in the destruction of the Richmond Theatre, among whom was the then governor of the State.

Directly opposite to Richmond are its suburbs of Manchester and Spring Hill, which are connected with the city by three bridges.

Ripley, a village, capital of Jackson county, Virginia, on Mill creek, 350 miles W. N. W. from Richmond. Population, about 200.

Ritchie, a county in the N. W. part of Virginia, has an area of 480 square miles. It is traversed by Hughes river and its North fork. The surface is hilly and broken, and mostly covered with forests. Indian corn, oats, hay, butter and livestock are the staples. In 1850 it produced 101,884 bushels of corn, 24,336 of oats, 2,503 tons of hay and 41,978 pounds of butter. There were two saw mills, 1 grist mill, one wool-carding mill and one tannery. It contained five churches, and 376 pupils attending public schools. The county is traversed by the north-western turnpike, and by the Parkersburg

G. A. FROBE,

CARRIAGE MANUFACTURER,

No. 103 Market street,

WHEELING.

C. ELIAS STIFEL,

MANUFACTURER OF

TIN AND SHEET IRON WARE,

WHOLESALE AND RETAIL,

ALSO IMPORTER OF

JAPANNED WARE,

AND DEALER IN

HOUSE FURNISHING HARDWARE,

No. 189 MAIN STREET,

WHEELING.

JAMES MELLOR,

DEALER IN

VARIETY GOODS AND MUSICAL INSTRUMENTS.

AGENT FOR

CHICKERING'S PIANO FORTES.

MARTIN'S GUITARS AND **PRINCE'S Melodeons.**

NO. 26 UNION STREET,

WHEELING.

JOHN KNOTE,

SADDLE MANUFACTURER,

AND DEALER IN

IMPORTED & DOMESTIC

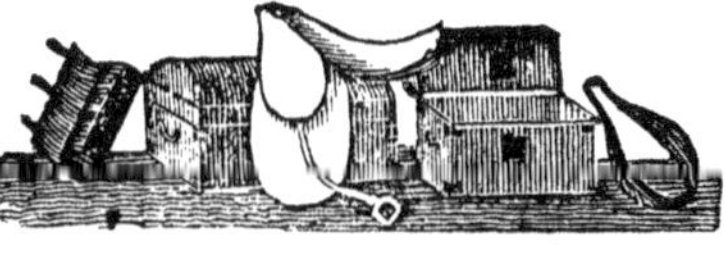

SADDLERS' HARDWARE,

Harness & Coach Trimmings,

Tacks, Webs, Hog, Sheep and Morocco Skins; Patent and Enameled Leather, Hames, Saddletrees, &c.

Old Stand, 153 Main street,

WHEELING.

branch of the Baltimore and Ohio railroad. Formed in 1843, and named in honor of Thomas Ritchie, Esq., editor of the Richmond Enquirer. Capital, Harrisville. Population 3,902, of whom 3,886 were free and 16 slaves.

RITCHIE COURT HOUSE, Virginia. See HARRISVILLE.

RITCHIEVILLE, a post village of Dinwiddie county, Virginia, 41 miles south from Richmond.

RIVANNA, a small river in the East central part of Virginia, rises at the foot of Blue Ridge, in Albemarle county, flows south-eastward through Fluvanna county, and enters the James river at Columbia. By means of dams and locks it is navigable to the Southwest mountain in Albemarle county, a distance of above 30 miles.

RIVESVILLE, a post-village of Marion county, Virginia, 282 miles N. W. from Richmond.

RIXEYVILLE, a small post village of Culpepper county, Virginia, 100 miles N. N. W. from Richmond.

ROANOKE, a river of Virginia and North Carolina, is formed by two principal branches, the Staunton and Dan, which rise in the southern part of Virginia, and unite at Clarksville, in Mecklenburg county, constituting the lower Roanoke. Flowing in an E. S. E. direction, it enters North Carolina and meets the tide water at Weldon, after passing over a series of rapids. Below this point, its general course is south-east, and it enters the western extremity of Albemarle sound at the mouth of Chowan river. It is a remarkably rapid stream, the fertile bottoms of which are subject to frequent inundations. The length of the main stream is estimated at 250 miles; but if we include the Staunton, which by some geographers is regarded as the Roanoke proper, it will probably exceed 450 miles. The lower falls of this river at Weldon, which form the limit of steamboat navigation, are about 150 miles from its mouth. By means of a canal around these falls, batteaux can ascend to Danville, on the Dan river.

ROANOKE, a county in the S. S. W. part of Virginia, has an area of 180 square miles. It is intersected by the Staunton river. The county forms part of the great valley of Virginia, situated between the Blue Ridge on the S. E. and another ridge of the Alleghanies on the N. W. The soil is highly productive. Indian corn, wheat, hemp and tobacco are the staples. In 1850 there were raised 235,760 bushels of corn, 104,134 of wheat, 103,643 of oats, and 362,682 pounds of tobacco. There were two flour mills, one tin-ware man-

ufactory and one tannery. It contained 12 churches, 185 pupils attending public schools and 137 attending other schools. The rock which underlies the surface is a fine limestone. The Virginia and Tennessee railroad (unfinished) passes through the county, and a turnpike connects it with the James River canal. Formed in 1838. Capital, Salem. Population, 8,477,—5,967 free, and 2,510 slaves.

Roanoke Bridge, a post village of Charlotte county, Virginia, 89 miles S. W. from Richmond.

Robinson's River, a small stream in the N. E. central part of Virginia, rises in Madison county, flows south-eastward, and enters Rapidan river on the boundary between that county and Orange.

Rockbridge, a county in the central part of Virginia, has an area of about 780 square miles. It is intersected by North river, which flows into James river, near the Southern extremity of the county, at the foot of the Blue Ridge. The county forms part of the great valley of Virginia, which is bounded on the S. E. by the Blue Ridge. The soil has a basis of fine limestone, and is highly productive. Grain and grass are the staples. In 1850 there were raised 372,705 bushels of Indian corn, 198,553 of wheat, 162,752 of oats and 7,626 tons of hay. There were three grist and saw mills, 13 flouring mills, four iron furnaces, three iron forges and one iron foundry; 18 churches, 239 pupils attending public schools and 314 attending academies and other schools. The James River canal passes through the Southern part of the county. Formed in 1778, and named from the *natural bridge of rock*, a description of which will be found under the head of Virginia. Population, 16,045, of whom 11,848 were free and 4,197 slaves.

Rockingham, a county in the N. E. central part of Virginia, has an area of 900 square miles. It is intersected in the S. E. part by the Shenandoah river proper, and also drained by the North fork of that river, and by Dry and North rivers, which rise within its limits. The county occupies part of the Great Valley, which is bounded on the S. E. by the Blue Ridge, and on the N. W. by the North mountain; the soil is generally very fertile. Wheat, Indian corn, oats, hay, cattle and butter are the staples. According to the census of 1850 this county produced more wheat and more hay than any other county in the State. In 1850 there were raised 608,350 bushels of wheat, 448,585 of corn, 164,976 of oats, 16,067 tons of hay, and 254,834 pounds of butter. It contained 41 flour mills, 22 saw mills, one iron furnace, one iron forge, four wool-carding mills,

and 16 tanneries; 30 churches, and 1,970 pupils attending public schools. A quarry of marble has been opened near the county seat, and limestone is abundant. The North river furnishes extensive water-power. Organized in 1788. Capital, Harrisonburg. Population, 20,294, of whom 17,963 were free and 2,331 slaves.

Rocky Mount, a post village, capital of Franklin county, Virginia, about 180 miles West by South from Richmond. It has several stores and an extensive iron furnace in the vicinity. Population, about 300.

Rocky Point, a thriving village of Monroe county, Virginia, 240 miles West from Richmond.

Rogersville, a post office of Halifax county, Virginia.

Romney, a post-village, capital of Hampshire county, Virginia, on the S. branch of the Potomac, 190 miles N. W. from Richmond, contains one bank.

Rose Hill, a post-office of Lee county, Virginia, near 400 miles W. S. W. from Richmond.

Rough Creek, a post-village of Charlotte county, Virginia, 105 miles S. W. from Richmond.

Rowlesburg, a village and station of Preston county, Virginia, is finely situated on the Cheat river, where it is crossed by the Baltimore and Ohio Railroad, 126 miles from Wheeling. The river is navigable 40 miles above this village, and it also affords abundant water-power.

Russell, a county in the S. W. part of Virginia, bordering on Kentucky, has an area of 1225 square miles. It is intersected by Clinch river, and also drained by the sources of the West fork of Sandy river. Guest's river forms part of the S. W. boundary. The Cumberland mountain forms its boundary on the N. W., and Clinch mountain extends along the S. E. border. A large portion of the county is mountainous and sterile, but the valleys contain some good land. Indian corn, oats and butter are the staples. In 1850 this county produced 378,919 bushels of corn; 154,305 of oats, and 162,478 pounds of butter. There were 2 flour, grist and saw mills, 5 tanneries, and 1 wool-carding mill. It contained 14 churches, 517 pupils attending public schools, and 80 attending other schools. Iron ore, stone coal and marble are found. Large quantities of maple sugar are made in the county. Named in honor of General William Russell, one of its principal citizens. Capital, Lebanon. Population 11,919,—10,937 free, and 982 slaves.

JOHN MOORE & CO.

MANUFACTURERS OF ALL KINDS OF

STEAM ENGINES, BOILERS, SHAFTING, MILL GEARING,

HEAVY AND LIGHT CASTINGS,

All of the newest patterns and most approved styles, and at low prices.

WHEELING.

DAVID MAASS,

BREWER,

SOUTH WHEELING.

David Maaß,

Besitzer einer

Deutschen Brauerei

in Süd-Wheeling, Va.

F. J. ROTHACKER,

MANUFACTURER OF

BEER, LAGER BEER, ALE,

MARKET STREET BREWERY,

WHEELING.

FREDERICK YAHRLING,

Corner of Main and Washington streets,

NORTH WHEELING.

SAGO, a post-office of Lewis county, Virginia.

SALEM, a post village of Fauquier county, Virginia, 114 miles N. N. W. from Richmond. The situation is high and pleasant. The village contains one church, an academy and several stores. The post-office is called Salem Fauquier.

SALEM, a neat post-village, capital of Roanoke county, Virginia, is situated on the Roanoke river, and on the Virginia and Tennessee railroad, 180 miles W. from Richmond. It stands in the great valley between the Blue Ridge and North mountain. It contains one bank, three churches and several mills.

SALT SULPHUR SPRINGS, a village of Monroe county, Virginia, 230 miles W. from Richmond, and 25 miles S. W. from the White Sulphur Springs. It is surrounded by beautiful mountain scenery, and is frequented by a large number of invalids and others. The water contains various salts of soda, magnesia and lime.

SALTVILLE, a post-village of Washington county, Virginia, on the N. fork of the Holston river, about 20 miles N. E. from Abingdon. It has two extensive salt-works.

SANDY BOTTOM, a post-office of Middlesex county, Virginia.

SANDY CREEK, in the S. part of Virginia, enters Banister river from the right hand, near Meadsville, in Halifax county.

SANGSTER'S STATION, a post-office of Fairfax county, Virginia.

SCOTT, a county situated in the S. W. part of Virginia, and bordering on Tennessee, containing 620 square miles. Is is drained by Clinch river and by the N. fork of Holston river. The surface is traversed by several parallel mountain ridges, one of which is called the Clinch mountain. The soil is mostly fertile and adapted to grazing. Wheat, Indian corn, and other kinds of grain also flourish. In 1850 this county produced 319,240 bushels of corn; 15,722 of wheat; 106,342 of oats, and 74,086 pounds of butter. There were 20 flour and grist mills, 7 wool-carding mills, and 2 tanneries It contained 20 churches, and 1,000 pupils attending public schools. Bituminous coal and iron ore are abundant. About three miles from Clinch river is one of the most remarkable natural objects of the State, known as the "Natural Tunnel." An affluent of the Clinch river, after flowing through a deep ravine inclosed by stupendous walls of stratified rocks, is confronted by a transverse ridge, about 300 feet in height, which has been perforated at its base by an arched tunnel to admit the passage of the stream. The spectator, standing by the margin of the stream, sees

W. & J. STEWART,

MANUFACTURERS OF ALL KINDS OF

STOVES, GRATES, PLOUGH IRONS, CASTINGS, &c.

LATEST STYLES OF PATTERNS,

North East Corner of Market Square, (Bridge Corner,)

WHEELING.

STEWARTS & CALDWELL,

MANUFACTURERS OF

COPPER, TIN & SHEET IRON WARE,

UPPER END MARKET SQUARE,

WHEELING.

JOHN H. HALL,

MANUFACTURER OF

SADDLES, HARNESS, BRIDLES

AND

SADDLE-BAGS,

VALISES, LADIES' AND GENTLEMEN'S

TRAVELING TRUNKS,

CARPET-BAGS, &c.

No. 105 Main Street,

WHEELING.

ISLAND TANNERY.

BERGER & HOFFMANN,

MANUFACTURERS OF EVERY DESCRIPTION OF

LEATHER,

AND DEALERS IN

TANNERS' OIL, WOOD, &c.

Store Room, No. 170, corner Market Alley and Main street,

WHEELING.

☞ Shoe Findings of all kinds on hand, and sold on moderate terms.

S. F. BLACK,

ATTORNEY AT LAW.

Office Hours, Wheeling, Va., ... 7 A. M. to 3 P. M.
" " Martinsville, Belmont county, Ohio, 3 to 7 P. M.

before him an enormous arch, rising 70 or 80 feet, surmounted by strata of limestone which measure more than 100 feet in a vertical direction, while the view on either side is bounded by gigantic ramparts of perpendicular rock. The county was formed in 1814, and named in honor of General Winfield Scott. Population, 9,829; of whom 9,356 were free, and 473 slaves.

SECOND CREEK, a post-office of Greenbrier county, Virginia.

SCOTTSBURG, a small post village of Halifax county, Virginia, 119 miles S. W. from Richmond.

SCOTTSVILLE, a thriving post village of Albemarle county, Virginia, is situated on the left bank of James river, 79 miles W. from Richmond. The navigation of the James river canal renders it a place of active and extensive trade, and an important depot for produce. The village, which is built chiefly of brick, contains 3 churches. Population in 1853, about 1200.

SCOTTSVILLE, a post village, capital of Powhatan county, Virginia, 32 miles W. from Richmond.

SEVEN ISLANDS, a post-office of Fluvanna county, Virginia.

SEVENMILE FORD, a post-office of Smyth county, Virginia.

SEVILLE, a post-office of Madison county, Virginia.

SEWELL MOUNTAIN, a post-office of Fayette county, Virginia.

SHACKELFORD'S, a post-office of King and Queen county, Virginia, 67 miles E. from Richmond.

SHADY SPRING, a post-office of Raleigh county, Virginia.

SHAKELFORD'S, a post-office of King and Queen county, Virginia.

SHANNONDALE SPRING, Jefferson county, Virginia, on the Shenandoah river, 5 miles from Charlestown, and 160 miles N. from Richmond. This beautiful and fashionable watering-place is more easily accessible from the Atlantic cities than any in Virginia. The water is impregnated with the salts of lime, magnesia and soda.

SHANNON HILL, a small post-village of Goochland county, Virginia, 25 miles W. from Richmond.

SHARON, a post-village in Wythe county, Virginia, 245 miles W. by S. from Richmond.

SHARONVILLE, a post-office of King William county, Virginia.

SHAWSVILLE, a post-office of Montgomery county, Virginia.

SHEETZ'S MILLS, a post-office of Hampshire county, Virginia.

SHENANDOAH RIVER, of Virginia, the largest affluent of the Potomac, is usually described as formed by the North and South forks which unite near Front Royal in Warren county. The South fork,

or Shenandoah proper, rises in Augusta and Rockingham counties, by three branches, called North, Middle and South rivers, which unite at Port Republic in the county last named. It pursues a north-easterly course, nearly parallel with the Blue Ridge, which is only a few miles distant, and falls into the Potomac at Harper's Ferry, just above its passage through the mountain. The distance by the windings of the river, from its mouth to Port Republic, is estimated at 170 miles. This river flows through the great valley of Virginia, an excellent tract for the growth of grain. It affords an ample supply of water-power at numerous points, and also extensive facilities for navigation. Small boats called gondolas ascend the main stream about 100 miles above Front Royal.

SHENANDOAH, a county in the N. E. central part of Virginia, forming part of the great limestone valley which extends along the W. base of the Blue Ridge. The area is about 500 square miles. It is drained by the N. fork of the Shenandoah river, from which the name is derived. The surface is diversified by valleys and ridges. The soil is generally productive. Wheat, corn, oats, hay, butter and live stock are the staples. In 1850 the county produced 196,338 bushels of wheat; 167,025 of Indian corn; 34,963 of oats; 4,641 tons of hay, and 79,196 pounds of butter. There were 19 flour mills, 3 saw mills, 1 wool-carding mill and 8 tanneries. It contained 10 churches, and 130 pupils attending public schools. The rocks which underlie the county are blue limestone, slate and sandstone. Iron ore is abundant, and affords an article of export; lead and copper also are found. There were in 1852, 4 iron furnaces and 4 forges in operation. A railroad extends from Strasburg in this county to Alexandria. Capital, Woodstock. Population, 13,768, of whom 12,857 were free and 911 slaves.

SHENANDOAH IRON WORKS, a post-office of Page county, Va.

SHEPHERD'S GROVE, a post-office of Culpepper county, Virginia.

SHEPHERDSTOWN, a post-town of Jefferson county, Virginia, on the Potomac river, near the Chesapeake and Ohio canal, 12 miles above Harper's Ferry. It is a place of considerable trade. A small stream which passes through the town affords motive-power for several flouring mills. Shepherdstown has 4 churches and 3 newspaper offices. Population estimated at 1,600.

SHILOH, a post-office of King George county, Virginia.

SHINNSTON, or SHINNSTOWN, a post-village in Harrison county, Virginia, 225 miles N. W. from Richmond.

H. W. PHILLIPS,

IRON AND BRASS FOUNDER,

MANUFACTURER OF

Steam Engines & General Machinist,

NORTH WHEELING,

ABOVE WATER WORKS.

Mill Engines,
Steamboat Engines,
Furnace Engines,
Rolling Mill Castings,
Grist and Saw Mill Work,
Threshing Machine Castings,
Engine Boilers,
Car wheels and R. Road Axles complete.

And all kinds of Machinery and Castings made to order on the most reasonable terms.

Peter Zimmer,
Besitzer einer

Deutschen Brauerei

in Süd-Wheeling, Va.

WM. MING NICOLL,

MANUFACTURER OF

BRIDLES,

HARNESS & TRUNKS,

OF ALL KINDS AND QUALITIES,

Old Stand, No. 109 Main Street,

WHEELING.

A. JAHN,

MANUFACTURER OF ALL KINDS OF

No. 98 MARKET STREET,

SECOND DOOR NORTH OF THE POST OFFICE,

WHEELING.

SHIRLEY, a post-office of Tyler county, Virginia.

SHREWSBURY, a post-office of Kanawha county, Virginia.

SIMPSON'S, a post-office of Floyd county, Virginia, 211 miles W. from Richmond.

SIMPSON'S CREEK, a post-office of Taylor county, Virginia.

SINCLAIR'S BOTTOM, a post-office of Smyth county, Virginia.

SINKING CREEK, a post-office of Botetourt county, Virginia.

SIR JOHN'S RUN, a post-office of Morgan county, Virginia.

SISSONVILLE, a post-village in Kanawha county, Virginia, 333 miles W. from Richmond.

SISTERVILLE, a thriving post-village of Tyler county, Virginia, is pleasantly situated on the Ohio river, about 35 miles below Wheeling and 9 miles W. from Middlebourn, the county seat. It has a good landing for steamboats, and it is the terminus of several turnpike-roads extending toward the interior. These advantages, together with the navigation of the Ohio, render this a place of active trade, which is rapidly increasing. Coal and iron ore are found in the vicinity. Population in 1853, 1,000

SKINQUARTER, a post office of Chesterfield county, Virginia.

SLASH COTTAGE, a small post village of Hanover county, Virginia, on the railroad from Richmond to Fredericksburg, about 20 miles North from the former. The railroad company have machine shops here. The great orator, Henry Clay, was born near this place, in the "Slashes of Hanover."

SLATE MILLS, a post-office of Rappahannock county, Virginia.

SLATE RIVER, a small stream rising in Buckingham county, Va., and flowing north-eastward, enters the James river on the N. E. border of that county. It is navigable for boats to Maysville, 27 miles from its mouth.

SLEEPY CREEK BRIDGE, a post office of Morgan county, Virginia.

SMITHFIELD, a handsome post village, capital of Isle of Wight county, Virginia, is finely situated on a navigable creek which opens into the James river a few miles from its mouth, 80 miles S. E. from Richmond. It contains three churches and several high schools. Population from 900 to 1,000.

SMITHFIELD, a small village of Monongalia county, Virginia, 10 miles N. W. from Morgantown.

SMITH'S CREEK, a post office of Washington county, Virginia.

SMITH'S CROSS ROADS, a post office of Morgan county, Va.

SMITH'S GAP, a post office of Hampshire county, Virginia.

FINE LIGHT, PLEASANT LOCATION.

FARIS' DAGUERREIAN GALLERY.

WE STUDY TO

PLEASE.

"The good is always beautiful,
The beautiful is good."

SATISFACTION

WARRANTED.

NEAR THE

SUSPENSION BRIDGE,

Wheeling.

Citizens and Strangers visiting this Gallery can have their portraits or miniatures, BAUTIFULLY CASED in Morocco, Velvet, Papier Mache, and other styles, or set in Medallions or Pins, Rings or Seals.

FIRE AND MARINE INSURANCE.

THE

"PROVINCIAL INSURANCE COMPANY."

CAPITAL 2,000,000,

BRANCH OFFICE AT WHEELING,

No. 99 MAIN STREET,

Where Fire and Marine Insurances are effected, and all claims for losses promptly adjusted by

N. C. ARTHUR, Agent.

J. W. HEISKELL,

DRY GOODS,

Market Street, Wheeling.

STEEN & BRO.

CLOTHING,

44 Water Street, Wheeling.

W. KELREY,

GROCER,

193 Market Street, Wheeling.

W. M. H. GREEAM,

SALESMAN at SEAMAN'S STORE,

WHEELING.

R. J. CAMPBELL,

SALESMAN at ELLICOTT'S STORE,

WHEELING.

JAMES W. WHEAT,

MEDICAL STUDENT,

WHEELING.

LEWIS BURGUER,

CLOTHING,

Main Street, Wheeling.

SMITH'S RIVER, a small stream which rises in Patrick county, in the South part of Virginia, and flowing south-eastward into North Carolina, falls into the Dan river near Leakesville.

SMITHSVILLE, a post village in Powhatan county, Virginia, 39 miles West from Richmond.

SMOKY ORDINARY, a post office of Brunswick county, Virginia.

SMYTH, a county in the S. S. W. part of Virginia, has an area of 625 square miles. The three branches of Holston river, named the North, Middle and South forks, rise near the N. E. border of the county, and flow through it in a S. W. direction. The Iron Mountain range forms the Southern boundary, and Walker's mountain extends along the N. W. border; the surface between these is an elevated valley. The river bottoms are very fertile. Indian corn, hay, oats and butter are the staples. In 1850 this county produced 301,222 bushels of corn, 34,742 of wheat, 139,580 of oats and 100,410 pounds of butter. There were seven saw mills, three iron furnaces, one iron foundry, one salt furnace and two tanneries. It contained 12 churches and 600 pupils attending public schools. Limestone and gypsum are abundant in the county; and the latter is used to fertilize the land. Extensive manufactories of salt are in operation on the S. W. border. Smyth county is intersected by the Virginia and Tennessee Railroad, not yet finished. Named in honor of General Alexander Smyth, member of Congress from Virginia. Capital, Marion. Population, 8,162, of whom 7,098 were free and 1,064 slaves.

SNICKERSVILLE, a thriving post village of Loudoun county, Virginia, on the turnpike from Winchester to Washington, 165 miles North by West from Richmond.

SNOW CREEK, a post office of Franklin county, Virginia.

SNOW HILL, a post office of Nicholas county, Virginia.

SOMERTON, a small post village of Nansemond county, Virginia, about 100 miles S. E. from Richmond.

SOMERVILLE, a post village of Fauquier county, Virginia, 85 miles North by West from Richmond.

SOUTHAMPTON, a county in the S. S. E. part of Virginia, bordering on North Carolina, has an area of about 600 square miles. It is intersected by the Nottaway river, bounded on the S. W. by the Meherrin, and on the East by the Blackwater river. The surface is nearly level, and extensively covered with forests of pine and cypress. The soil is alluvial, light and moderately fertile. Indian

T. SWEENEY & SON,

MANUFACTURERS OF EVERY VARIETY OF

FLINT GLASSWARE,

IMPORTERS AND DEALERS IN

CHINA, QUEENSWARE, LAMPS, GIRANDOLES,

TABLE CUTLERY, &c.

No. 65 Main Street,

WHEELING.

G. W. ECKHARDT,

MANUFACTURER AND WHOLESALE DEALER IN

North Wheeling.

J. ARNDT,

SMITH'S BELLOWS

MANUFACTURER,

Market street, North of Market Square,

WHEELING.

☞ He warrants his Bellows to be of superior quality. All orders promptly attended to.

CITY HOTEL,

No. 192 Market Square,

WHEELING.

J. ROBINSON, Proprietor.

Stage Passengers, Horses, Drivers, Wagoners, &c., will find the accommodations at this House equal to any in this city. The Stabling is large and commodious. Charges very low.

RED LION HOTEL,

No. 204 MARKET STREET,

WHEELING.

JACOB MERKLE, Proprietor.

corn, potatoes, hay, cotton and pork are the staples. Tar and turpentine are also exported. In 1850 the county produced 869 bales of cotton, 564,183 bushels of corn, 235,337 of sweet potatoes, and 3,321 tons of hay. The quantities of cotton and potatoes were the greatest produced in any one county of the State. There were two grist mills, two manufactories of coaches and one of saddles. It contained 23 churches, 288 pupils attending public schools and 68 attending academies or other schools. It is intersected by the Portsmouth and Roanoke railroad. Organized in 1748, and named from a town of England. Capital, Jerusalem. Population, 13,521, of whom 7,766 were free and 5,755 slaves.

South Anna, a small river in the eastern part of Virginia, rises near the north-western extremity of Louisa county, and flowing easterly unites with the North Anna, forming the Pamunky river. The whole length is probably 75 miles. It affords abundant water-power.

South Hill, a post office of Mecklenburg county, Virginia.

South Quay, a post office of Nansemond county, Virginia.

South River, of Virginia, a small branch of the Shenandoah, rises in Augusta county, flows in a north-easterly course, and unites with the other main branch at Port Republic, in Rockingham county.

Sparta, a post office of Caroline county, Virginia.

Spartapolis, a post village in Rockingham county, Virginia, 142 miles N. W. from Richmond.

Speedwell, a post office of Wythe county, Virginia.

Sperryville, a small post village of Rappahannock county, Virginia, about 120 miles N. W. from Richmond. A turnpike extends from this village to the Rappahannock river.

Spottedville, a post village of Stafford county, Virginia, 69 miles N. from Richmond.

Spottsylvania, a county in the E. part of Virginia, has an area of 400 square miles. The Rappahannock forms the boundary on the N. E., the North Anna river on the S. W., and the Mattapony rises within its limits. The surface is pleasantly diversified by hill and dale. The soil is generally fertile in the vicinity of the streams. Indian corn, wheat, oats, hay, butter and pork are the staples. In 1850 the county produced 265,753 bushels of corn; 102,953 of wheat; 47,347 of oats; 1,279 tons of hay, and 52,056 pounds of butter. It contained 2 flour mills and 2 tanneries, 20 churches, 6 newspaper offices, 300 pupils attending public schools and 461

attending academies and other schools. Two gold mines were worked in this county in 1850; granite and freestone are abundant. A canal about 45 miles long has been opened along the Rappahannock, above the falls, and the county is intersected by the Richmond and Potomac railroad. The Rappahannock affords valuable water-power at Fredericksburg. Organized in 1720, and named in honor of Alexander Spottswood, at that time governor of Virginia. Capital, Spottsylvania Court House. Population, 14,911, of whom 7,430 were free and 7,481 slaves.

SPOTTSYLVANIA COURT HOUSE, a post village, capital of Spottsylvania county, Virginia, on the Po river, 65 miles N. from Richmond.

SPOUT SPRING, a post office of Appomattox county, Virginia.

SPRINGFIELD, a post village of Hampshire county, Virginia. 197 miles N. W. from Richmond.

SPRINGFIELD, a village of Monroe county, Virginia, on Indian creek, about 245 miles W. from Richmond.

SPRING GARDEN, a post village in Pittsylvania county, Virginia, 135 miles S. W. by W. from Richmond.

SPRINGVALE, a post office of Fairfax county, Virginia.

SPRINGVILLE, a post office of Tazewell county, Virginia.

SPRUCE HILL, a post office of Highland county, Virginia.

STAFFORD, a county in the East part of Virginia, bordering on the Potomac river, which separates it from Maryland, has an area of 250 square miles. It is bounded on the south-west by the Rappahannock river, and also drained by the Aquia, Potomac and Accokeek creeks. The surface is hilly; the soil near the Potomac river is a light loam, moderately fertile; other parts are sandy and poor. Indian corn, wheat, oats, tobacco and hay are the staples. In 1850 it produced 178,651 bushels of corn, 58,923 of wheat, 38,750 of oats and 2,018 tons of hay. There were two flour mills, three grist mills, two saw mills and two cotton factories. It contained 12 churches, and 245 pupils attending public schools. Quarries of granite and freestone, suitable for building, have been opened, and gold has been found in small quantities. The Rappahannock affords excellent water-power at Falmouth. The county is intersected by the Richmond, Fredericksburg and Potomac railroad. Organized in 1675, and named from Stafford, a county of England. Capital, Stafford Court House. Population, 8,044, of whom 4,733 were free, and 3,311 slaves.

DOCTOR J. S. ROSE'S

CELEBRATED FAMILY MEDICINES.

Are free from Mercury, and can be taken without regard to Exposure.

They are recommended by Physicians at home and abroad, and thousands have been cured and benefited by using them.

Expectorant, or Cough Syrup, for Coughs, Colds, Consumption, Asthma, Bronchitis, and all Lung Diseases. It cures Consumption when taken in time, [In 50 cents and $1 bottles.

Alterative, or Blood Purifier, for Scrofula, Old Eruptions, and all Diseases arising from an impure state of the Blood, or a constitution impaired by the use of Mercury, ... Price $1

Carminative Balsam, for Cholera, Cholera Morbus, Bowel Complaints, and Dysentery, ... 25 cents.

Vermifuge, or Worm-Killer, a safe, sure, and reliable expeller of Worms, . 75 cts.

Alterative, or Family Pills, for Liver Complaints, Dyspepsia, Indigestion, Sour Stomach, and Costiveness, ... 25 cts.

Golden Pills, for falling of the Womb, Female Weakness, Debility and Relaxation, ... 50 cts.

Female Pills, a valuable remedy for Female Complaints, superior to Hooper's Pills, ... 25 cts.

Railroad, or Anti-Bilious Pills, so called because they go ahead of all other pills, for the Liver and bilious habits, ... 12½ and 25 cts.

Rheumatic Compound, an Internal Remedy for Rheumatism, either Acute or Chronic, ... 50 cts.

Dyspeptic Compound, a sure cure for Dyspepsia and Liver, ... 50 cts.

Magic Liniment, for Rheumatism, Sprains, Tooth-ache, and all pains of the body and Spinal and Liver Affections, ... 25 cts.

Tonic Mixture, for Chills, Fevers, and general Debility. A never failing remedy, ... 50 cts.

Compound Extract of Buchu, for all Diseases of the Kidneys and Bladder, and for Dropsy, ... 50 cts.

Croup Syrup. This remedy is never known to fail, and has saved thousands of children, ... 25 cts.

Hair Tonic, to prevent Baldness, and make the hair soft and lustrous. Highly recommended by the late Dr. Physick, ... 25 and 50 cts.

Astringent Compound, for Spitting Blood, Flooding, and all Bloody Discharges, 50 cts.

Nervous Cordial. For all Nervous conditions of the System, Neuralgia, Heart Disease, Palpitation, &c., ... 50 cts.

Pile Ointment. 50 cents. *Eye* and *Tetter Ointments*, ... 25 cts.

Eye Water and *Strengthening Plasters*. Superior to all others, . . . 25 cts.

Whooping-Cough Syrup. This preparation always gives relief and effects a cure, 50 cts.

Female Specific. A remedy for Painful Menstruation, Leucorrhœa or Whites, $1

Elixir of Opium. Superior to all other forms of Opium, ... 25 cts.

Pain-Curer. Cures all pain, external or internal; cures Chilblains, Corns, Bruises, Sprains, Tooth-ache, Ear-ache, Stiff Neck, Soar Throat, Pains in the Bowels and Stomach, Sudden Colds, &c., ... 12½, 25 and 50 cts.

Infant Cordial. Free from Opium, and producing easy sleep, ... 25 cts.

Acoustic Oil, for Deafness and Inflammation in the Ears, ... 50 cts,

Sarsaparilla Compound, for all Skin Diseases, and Purifying the blood, 50 cts. and $1

Sold by Druggists and all others in all cities and towns in Virginia and other States.

Stafford Court House, a small post-village, capital of Stafford county Virginia, 76 miles North from Richmond.

Stanardsville, a post village, capital of Greene county, Virginia, 92 miles N. W. from Richmond, and five miles S. E. from the Blue Ridge. The village has been much improved within a few years. It became the county seat in 1838.

Staunton, a river in the South part of Virginia, rises in Montgomery county, among the Alleghany mountains; flowing eastward and south-eastward, it passes through the Blue Ridge, falling nearly 1,000 feet in a distance of 20 miles. After a very rapid and tortuous course of about 200 miles, it unites with Dan river at Clarkesville, Mecklenburg county, constituting the Roanoke. The latter name is also applied by highly respectable writers to the whole stream just described. See Roanoke River.

Staunton, a flourishing town, capital of Augusta county, Virginia, is situated on a small branch of Shenandoah river, near its source, and on the Central railroad of Virginia, 120 miles W. N. W. from Richmond. The Central railroad, which is completed from Richmond to Staunton, and will be extended to the Ohio river, and bring large accessions to the trade and population of this place. Staunton is the seat of the Western Lunatic Asylum, and of the Virginia Institution for the Deaf and Dumb and Blind. The blind are in the same building with the deaf and dumb, but under a separate instructor. It contains five or six churches, two academies, 3 female seminaries and 2 banks. Four newspapers are published here. The surrounding country is highly productive, and beautifully diversified, forming part of the great valley of Virginia. In the limestone formation of this region extensive caverns occur, among which the most celebrated is Weyer's cave, about 18 miles N. E. from Staunton. Population, about 5,000.

Steel's Tavern, a post office of Augusta county, Virginia, 138 miles W. N. W. from Richmond.

Steer Creek, a post office of Gilmer county, Virginia.

Stephenson's Depot, a post office of Frederick county, Va.

Stevensburg, a post office of Culpepper county, Virginia, on the road from Fairfax to Fredericksburg, about 95 miles N. W. from Richmond, contains one or two churches, a hotel and several stores.

Stevensville, a post village of King and Queen county, Virginia, 31 miles N. E. from Richmond.

STEWART'S DRAFT, a post office of Augusta county, Virginia.

STEWARTSTOWN, a small post village of Monongalia county, Va.

STILLWELL, a post office of Wood county, Virginia.

STOCK CREEK, a post office of Scott county, Virginia.

STONER'S STORE, a post office of Roanoke county, Virginia.

STONEWELL MILLS, a post village of Appomattox county, Virginia, on James river, 108 miles West by South from Richmond.

STONY CREEK, a post office of Scott county, Virginia.

STONY FORK, a post office of Amherst county, Virginia.

STONY HILL, a small village of Madison county, Virginia, on the Blue Ridge turnpike.

STONY MOUNT, a post office of Brunswick county, Virginia.

STONY POINT MILLS, a post village of Cumberland county, Virginia, 61 miles W. S. W. from Richmond, contains a flouring mill.

STRASBURG, a thriving post village of Shenandoah county, Virginia, on the North fork of the Shenandoah river, and on the Manassas Gap railroad, 18 miles S. W. from Winchester. It has three churches. Population, about 650.

STROUD'S GLADES, a post office of Nicholas county, Virginia.

STURGEONVILLE, a post village of Brunswick county, Virginia, about 60 miles S. S. W. from Richmond.

SUBLETT'S TAVERN, a post office of Powhatan county, Virginia.

SUGAR GROVE, a post office of Pendleton county, Virginia.

SUGAR RUN, a post office of Wetzel county, Virginia.

SUGAR TREE, a post office of Pittsylvania county, Virginia.

SUMMERS, a post-office of Rockbridge county, Virginia.

SUMMERVILLE, a post village, capital of Nicholas county, Virginia, 286 miles West by North from Richmond.

SUMMIT POINT, a post office of Jefferson county, Virginia.

SUNRISE, a post office of Bath county, Virginia.

SURRY, a county in the S. E. part of Virginia, has an area of 340 square miles. James river forms the boundary on the N. E., and Blackwater river on the S. W. The surface is moderately uneven; the soil is generally sandy. Indian corn is the staple product. In 1850 there were raised 204,975 bushels of corn. There were 5 saw mills and 11 churches. Formed in 1652, and named from Surry, a county in England. Capital, Surry Court House. Population, 5,679, of whom 3,200 were free, and 2,479 slaves.

SURRY COURT HOUSE, a small post village, capital of Surry Co., Va., 5 miles from James river, and 60 miles S. E. from Richmond.

JAMES McCLINTOCK, M. D.

Late Professor of Anatomy and Surgery in the Philadelphia College of Medicine,

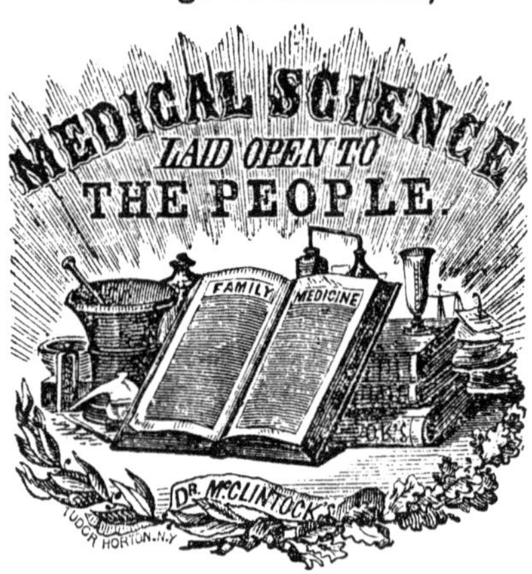

And Acting Professor of Midwifery; one of the Consulting Physicians of the Philadelphia Hospital, Blockley; late member of the National Medical Associations; member of the Philadelphia Medical Society; member of the Medico-Chirurgical College of Philadelphia; formerly President and Professor of Anatomy and Surgery in Castleton Medical College, Vermont; and also late Professor of Anatomy and Physiology in Berkshire Medical Institution, Pittsfield, Mass., &c.

Has lately introduced in a popular form several of his favorite prescriptions for the principal diseases of this climate. We give below a list of the remedies; the name of each article will imply the disease for which it is intended to be used

DR. McCLINTOCK'S PECTORAL SYRUP. Price $1.

DR. McCLINTOCK'S COLD AND COUGH MIXTURE—for Colds, Coughs, &c. Price 25 cts.

DR. McCLINTOCK'S ASTHMA AND HOOPING COUGH REMEDY. Price 50 cts.

DR. McCLINTOCK'S TONIC ALTERATIVE SYRUP.—For Purifying the Blood. Price $1.

DR. McCLINTOCK'S DYSPEPTIC ELIXIR. For giving tone to the stomach, relieving pains after eating, heart-burn, and all disagreeable symptoms arising from indigestion. Price $1.

DR. McCLINTOCK'S RHEUMATIC MIXTURE—A Purely Vegetable Remedy for internal use. Price 50 cents.

DR. McCLINTOCK'S RHEUMATIC LINIMENT—For Rheumatism, Sprains, Swellings, &c. &c. Price 50 cents.

DR. McCLINTOCK'S ANODYNE MIXTURE—For Pains, Toothache, Headache, Neuralgia, &c., &c. Price 50 cents.

DR. McCLINTOCK'S FEVER and AGUE SPECIFIC.—A certain cure for all Intermittents. Price $1.

DR. McCLINTOCK'S DIARRHŒA CORDIAL and CHOLERA PREVENTIVE—A safe Remedy.

DR. McCLINTOCK'S VEGETABLE PURGATIVE PILLS—For Costiveness, Headache, &c. Price 25 cents.

DR. McCLINTOCK'S ANTIBILIOUS PILLS—For Irregularity in the Functions of the Liver and Bowels—the best Liver Pill made. Price 25 cents a box.

For sale by JAMES McCLINTOCK, at his Medical Depot, N. W. corner NINTH and FILBERT streets, Philadelphia, and at all Druggists and Dealers in Medicines. All Druggists and Dealers in Medicines who wish to be agents, will please address Dr. McCLINTOCK, furnishing reference, name of Post-Office, county and State.

The Doctor may be consulted daily from 10 to 12 A. M. at his Depot.

SUSSEX, a county in the S. S. E. part of Virginia, has an area of 400 square miles. It is intersected by the Nottaway river, and bounded on the N. E. by Blackwater river. The surface is moderately uneven; the soil produces cotton, Indian corn, and forests of pine. In 1850 there were raised 356,171 bushels of corn, 35,133 of wheat, and 780 bales of cotton. There were 20 flour, grist and saw mills, two coach manufactories and one tannery. It contained 24 churches, and 249 pupils attending academies and other schools. The railroad from Petersburg to Weldon passes through the county. Formed from Surry in 1754. Capital, Sussex Court House. Population, 9,820, of whom 3,828 were free, and 5,992, slaves.

SUSSEX COURT HOUSE, a post village, capital of Sussex county, Virginia, 50 miles South by East from Richmond.

SUTTON, or BRAXTON COURT HOUSE, a small post village, capital of Braxton county, Virginia, on the Elk river, 289 miles W. N. W. from Richmond.

SWANSONVILLE, a post office of Pittsylvania county, Virginia.

SWEEDLINHILL, a post office of Pendleton county, Virginia.

SWEET SPRINGS, a post village of Monroe county, Virginia, is pleasantly situated near the foot of the Alleghany mountain, 204 miles West from Richmond. This is one of the oldest and most fashionable watering-places of the State.

SWINEYARD, a post office of Charles City county, Virginia.

SYDNORSVILLE, a post village in Franklin county, Virginia, 160 miles S. W. by West from Richmond.

TACKETT'S MILLS, a post office of Stafford county, Virginia.

TANGIER'S ISLANDS, of Virginia, in Chesapeake bay, nearly opposite the mouth of the Potomac river.

TANNER'S STORE, a post office of Mecklenburg county, Virginia.

TAPPAHANNOCK, a port of entry and capital of Essex county, Virginia, on the right bank of the Rappahannock river, 50 miles N. E. from Richmond. It contains a custom house, one church, two flourishing seminaries, and 5 stores. The shipping of this port June 30, 1852, amounted to an aggregate of 5,621 tons, of which 5,039 were employed in the coasting trade. Population, about 350.

TAYLOR, a county in the N. N. W. part of Virginia, has an area of 130 square miles. It is intersected by the Tygart's Valley river, a branch of the Monongahela, and also drained by Sandy and Elk creeks. The surface is hilly The soil in some parts fertile. Indian corn, wheat, oats, hay, butter and live stock are the staples.

STANDARD FAMILY MEDICINES,

PREPARED UNDER THE IMMEDIATE CARE OF

DR. SWAYNE,

AT HIS LABORATORY,

No. 4 NORTH SEVENTH STREET, ABOVE MARKET,

PHILADELPHIA.

DR. SWAYNE'S COMPOUND SYRUP OF WILD CHERRY.

Read the following Certificate of Thomas Dixon and the Testimony of Rev. J. R. Durborrow.

POINT OF ROCKS, Frederick county, Md., June 9th, 1852.

DR. SWAYNE: *Dear Sir*,—Believing it a duty I owe to the public, and in justice to you, I have thought proper to make known one of the most extraordinary cures in my own case, that has ever been truly recorded. In the month of October last, I was afflicted with a severe gathering in my breast, which formed a large abscess, and also communicated to my lungs and very much afflicted them, and discharged large quantities of corruption, external and internal. My breath could also pass through my lungs and out through the cavity of the breast with apparent ease, attended with a violent cough, day and night, loss of appetite and extreme debility, so that my physician thought my case entirely hopeless and beyond the power of medicine. I remained in this wretched condition for a long time until I was wasted to a mere skeleton and there seemed to be no hope for me; but having read in the public papers of the many wonderful cures performed by your COMPOUND SYRUP OF WILD CHERRY, I immediately sent for five bottles and commenced its use, and to my great satisfaction and the joy of my anxious family, the abscess or opening in my lungs began to heal, and the cough to subside, and on using ten bottles I was restored to perfect health. I feel very grateful, and firmly believe that to your valuable medicine, under the blessing of Divine Providence, I am indebted for this great change, and am happy to say that I am now enjoying as good health as I ever have.

Yours, very respectfully, THOMAS DIXON.

The subscriber is well acquainted with Thomas Dixon, and can testify that he has been afflicted as above represented. I regard the recovery as almost a miracle. He is a worthy member of society.

JAMES R. DURBORROW,
Pastor of Berlin Circuit, Baltimore Conference.

LOOK WELL TO THE MARKS OF THE GENUINE.

☞ Remember no preparation of Wild Cherry is genuine except the original article as prepared by DR. SWAYNE. See that his PORTRAIT is on the wrapper around each bottle. Until you obtain this Compound you will never know the real virtues of the Wild Cherry.

DR. SWAYNE'S

VERMIFUGE,

An effectual remedy for Worms, Dyspepsia, Cholera Morbus, Delicate, Sickly or Dyspeptic Children, Convulsions, &c. None genuine except in SQUARE BOTTLES.

DR. SWAYNE'S SUGAR-COATED SARSAPARILLA

And Extract of Tar Pills.

☞ These valuable Pills are the result of *medical knowledge combined with long experience.* Having used them many years in my private practice, I therefore have had ample opportunity in testing their power to relieve and cure those diseases for which they are designed.

AGENTS.

TODD, HINTON & TRAYLOR, Petersburg, Va.; ADIE & GRAY and PEYTON JOHNSTON, Richmond, Va.; KING & TOY, Norfolk, Va.; A. LEWIS, Weston, Va.; W. S. WOOD, Waterford, Va.; A. M. KRIDLER, Harper's Ferry, Va.; PATTERSON & CO., Wheeling, Va.; J. & W. GOSHORN, Kanawha C. H., Va., and by most Druggists and Storekeepers throughout the United States.

In 1850 this county produced 101,118 bushels of corn, 23,995 of wheat, 41,499 of oats, 4,051 tons of hay, and 87,110 pounds of butter. There were five flour and grist mills, four saw mills, five tanneries, one manufactory of cabinet ware, and one of earthen ware, and eleven churches. The county contains iron ore and stone coal. It is intersected by the Baltimore and Ohio railroad, and the North-western railroad has its eastern terminus near the county seat. Formed in 1844, out of parts of Harrison, Barbour and Marion, and named in honor of John Taylor, of Caroline county. Capital, Pruntytown, sometimes called Williamsport. Population, 5,367, of whom 5,199 were free, and 168 slaves.

TAYLOR'S STORE, a post office of Franklin county, Virginia, 173 miles W. S. W. from Richmond.

TAYLORSVILLE, a post village in Hanover county, Virginia, on the Richmond, Fredericksburg and Potomac railroad, 20 miles north from Richmond.

TAYLORSVILLE, of Patrick county, Virginia. See PATRICK COURT HOUSE.

TAZEWELL, a county in the S. W. part of Virginia, bordering on Kentucky, is 60 miles in length, and has an area of 1,300 square miles. The Clinch and Bluestone rivers rise in the county; the Tug fork of Sandy river forms part of its northern boundary, and it is also drained by the Dry fork of the latter stream, and by Wolf creek. Clinch mountain extends along the S. E. border, and other mountain ridges pass across the county. The highlands produce good timber and pasturage; the soil of the valleys is highly productive. Indian corn, wheat, oats, butter, cattle, horses and swine are the staples. In 1850 there were raised 235,126 bushels of corn; 21,327 of wheat; 125,214 of oats, and 135,910 pounds of butter were made. There were 6 tanneries, 3 cabinet ware manufactories and 1 saddlery. It contained 15 churches, and 654 pupils attending public schools. Limestone, iron ore, and stone coal are abundant in the county; the mines of the latter are thought to be inexhaustible. The county is plentifully supplied with water-power. Formed in 1799, and named in honor of Henry Tazewell, who represented Virgina in the United States Senate about that period. Capital, Jeffersonville. Population, 9,942; of whom 8,882 were free, and 1,060 slaves.

TAZEWELL COURT HOUSE, Virginia. See JEFFERSONVILLE.

TEAZE'S VALLEY, a post office of Kanawha county, Virginia.

Temperance, a post office of Amherst county, Virginia.

Temperanceville, a post office of Accomack county, Virginia.

Templeton, a post village of Prince George county, Virginia, 36 miles S. E. from Richmond.

The Glades, a post office of Carroll county, Virginia.

Theological Seminary, a post office of Fairfax county, Va.

The Plains, a post office of Fauquier county, Virginia.

Thompson's Cross Roads, a post office of Louisa county, Virginia, 45 miles N. W. from Richmond.

Thompsonville, a post village of Culpepper county, Virginia, 104 miles N. N. W. from Richmond. It has two churches.

Thornburg, a post village of Spottsylvania county, Virginia, on the Po river, 69 miles North from Richmond

Thorn Hill, a post office of Orange county, Virginia, 92 miles N. W. from Richmond.

Thorton's Mills, a post office of Rappahannock county, Va.

Thornton's River, in the N. E. part of Virginia, rises from the Blue Ridge, near the West border of Rappahannock county, and flowing south-eastward through Culpepper county, unites with Hedgman's river, forming the North fork of the Rappahannock.

Thoroughfare, a post village of Prince William county, Virginia, 124 miles North from Richmond.

Three Forks, a post office of Taylor county, Virginia.

Three Springs, a post office of Washington county, Virginia.

Timber Grove, a post office of Washington county, Virginia.

Timber Ridge, a post office of Rockbridge county, Virginia.

Timberville, a post village in Rockingham county, Virginia, about 150 miles N. W. from Richmond.

Tinker Knob, a post office of Botetourt county, Virginia.

Tobacco Row, a post office of Amherst county, Virginia.

Todd's, a post office of Spottsylvania county, Virginia.

Tolersville, a post village in Louisa county, Virginia, on the Virginia Central Railroad, 45 miles N. W. by North from Richmond.

Tomahawk Spring, a post office of Berkely county, Virginia.

Tom's Brook, a post office of Shenandoah county, Virginia.

Town House, a post office of Smyth county, Virginia.

Traveler's Repose, a post office of Pocahontas county, Va.

Traylorsville, a post village of Henry county, Virginia, 200 miles W. S. W. from Richmond.

TREVILLIAN'S DEPOT, a post village of Louisa county, Virginia, on the Central Railroad, 67 miles from Richmond.

TRIADELPHIA, a post office of Ohio county, Virginia.

TUG RIVER, a post office of Tazewell county, Virginia.

TUMBLING CREEK, a post office of Tazewell county, Virginia.

TURKEY COVE, a post office of Lee county, Virginia.

TURNER'S STORE, a post office of Caroline county, Virginia.

TUSCARORA, a creek in the N. N. E. part of Virginia, flows through Berkely county, passes by Martinsburg, and falls into the Potomac, or some small affluent of that river. It affords fine water-power.

TWO MILE BRANCH, a post office of Smyth county, Virginia.

TWYMAN'S STORE, a post office of Spottsylvania county, Va.

TYE RIVER, a small stream in the S. E. central part of Virginia, rises at the base of the Blue Ridge, flows south-eastward through Nelson county, and enters James river. It furnishes motive-power, for mills.

TYE RIVER MILLS, a post office of Nelson county, Virginia, 128 miles West from Richmond.

TYE RIVER WAREHOUSE, a post office of Nelson county, Va.

TYGART'S VALLEY RIVER, in the north-west part of Virginia, rises in Randolph county, among the Greenbrier mountains, passes through Barbour and Taylor counties, and unites with the West fork of the Monongahela, one mile south from Fairmount, in Marion county. Its general direction is northward; its whole length is estimated at 150 miles. It is navigable by small boats in the lower part of its course.

TYLER, a county in the N. W. part of Virginia, is situated on the Ohio river, some fifty miles below Wheeling: area 390 square miles. The Ohio river forms its north-western boundary, separating it from the State of Ohio, and is intersected by Middle Island creek. The surface is hilly and broken, and partly covered with forests of good timber. The soil is excellent, well watered, and adapted to wool growing. Indian corn, wheat, oats, hay and live stock are the staples. In 1850 this county produced 130,014 bushels of corn, 15,100 of wheat, 27,544 of oats, and 1,737 tons of hay. There were nine saw mills, four flour mills, three tanneries, seven churches and 145 pupils attending public schools. The county contains abundance of stone coal, iron ore, and good building stone; limestone is one of the principal rocks. Large quantities of ore resembling zinc are found. Middle Island creek is a fine mill stream. The county is

WM. H. HORSTMANN & SONS,

PHILADELPHIA.

Manufactory, Fifth & Cherry Sts.

Store, 51 North Third Street.

HAVING completed the erection of the Largest Manufacturing Establishment of its class in the United States, the advertisers are prepared to execute with promptness orders for any of the following articles:

Military Goods,

OF EVERY DESCRIPTION,

LADIES' DRESS TRIMMINGS,

CARRIAGE LACES & TRIMMINGS,

MASONIC AND OTHER REGALIA,

CURTAIN TRIMMINGS,

TAILORS' TRIMMINGS,

THEATRICAL DECORATIONS,

VENETIAN BLIND TRIMMINGS, HATTERS' BINDINGS, SOCIETY GOODS, KYLES.

They also offer at the lowest prices, a Choice Stock of

Hosiery, Gloves and Fancy Goods,

OF THEIR OWN IMPORTATION.

intersected by three good turnpike-roads. Organized in 1814, and named in honor of John Tyler, governor of Virginia in 1810. Capital, Middlebourn. Population, 5,498,—5,460 free, and 38 slaves.

TYLER MOUNTAIN, a post office of Kanawha county, Virginia.

UFFINGTON, a post office of Monongalia county, Virginia.

UNION, a handsome post village, capital of Monroe county, Virginia, 208 miles W. from Richmond. It contains two or three churches. Population, about 500.

UNION GROVE, a post office of Prince George county, Virginia.

UNION HALL, a small post village of Franklin county, Virginia, 200 miles W. S. W. from Richmond.

UNION LEVEL, a post office of Mecklenburg county, Virginia.

UNION MILLS, a post village of Fluvanna county, Virginia, on the Rivanna river, 75 miles N. W. from Richmond. The river affords water power, which is used for a cotton factory and several mills.

UNION VILLAGE, a post village in Northumberland county, Virginia, 88 miles E. N. E. from Richmond.

UNISON, a post village of Loudoun county, Virginia, 16 miles S. W. from Leesburg, contains three churches and several stores.

UNIVERSITY OF VIRGINIA, a post office of Albemarle county, Virginia. See CHARLOTTESVILLE.

UPLAND, a post office of Mason county, Virginia.

UPPER FALLS OF COAL, a post office of Kanawha county, Virginia.

UPPER TRACT, a post office of Pendleton county, Virginia.

UPPERVILLE, a post village of Fauquier county, Virginia, is situated at the foot of the Blue Ridge, on the turnpike from Winchester to Alexandria, 135 miles N. by W. from Richmond. It is surrounded by a fine farming district, and contains three churches and about 700 inhabitants.

UPSHUR, a new county in the N. W. central part of Virginia, on the West fork of the Monongahela river.

URBANNA, a post village, capital of Middlesex county, Virginia, on Urbanna creek, about 84 miles E. by N. from Richmond.

VALLEY, a post office of Tazewell county, Virginia.

VALLEY FALLS, a post office of Marion county, Virginia.

VALLEY HEAD, a post office of Randolph county, Virginia.

VAN BUREN FURNACE, a post office of Shenandoah county, Va.

VAN CLEVESVILLE, a post office of Berkely county, Virginia.

VARIETY MILLS, a post office of Nelson county, Virginia, 112 miles W. by N. from Richmond.

JAS. B. M'FARLAND, WM. R. EVANS, } JAMES P. TATMAN, { HENRY BERGHAUSER, JAS. R. C. OLDHAM.

M'FARLAND, EVANS & CO.

IMPORTERS AND WHOLESALE DEALERS IN

FOREIGN & DOMESTIC

DRY GOODS,

No. 105 MARKET STREET,

And No. 34 CHURCH ALLEY,

BETWEEN SECOND AND THIRD STREETS,

PHILADELPHIA.

YARD, GILLMORE & CO.

No. 12 NORTH THIRD STREET,

PHILADELPHIA,

WHOLESALE DEALERS IN

SILK GOODS,

RIBBONS IN GREAT VARIETY,

GLOVES, MITTS AND DRESS TRIMMINGS,

SHAWLS, MANTILLAS AND SCARFS.

ALSO,

DRESS GOODS

Of every description,

TOGETHER WITH

Embroideries, White and Lace Goods,

To which they invite the attention of Buyers.

VERDIERVILLE, a post office of Orange county, Virginia.

VERDON, a post village of Hanover county, Va., on Little river, 30 miles North from Richmond. It has a cotton factory.

VICKSVILLE, a post office of Southampton county, Virginia.

WADE'S, a post office of Bedford county, Virginia.

WADESTOWN, a post office of Monongalia county, Virginia.

WADESVILLE, a post office of Clarke county, Virginia.

WAGRAM, a post office of Accomack county, Virginia.

WALKER'S CHURCH, a post office of Appomattox county, Va.

WALKER'S CREEK, in the S. W. part of Virginia, rises in Wythe county, flows north-eastward, and enters New river in Giles county.

WALKER'S MOUNTAIN, Virginia.

WALKERTON, a post office of King and Queen county, Virginia, on the Mattapony river, 30 miles N. E. from Richmond.

WALLACE, a post office of Harrison county, Virginia.

WALNUT GROVE, a post office of Kanawha county, Virginia, 330 miles W. by N. from Richmond.

WALNUT HILL, a post office of Lee county, Virginia.

WALTON, a post office of Kanawha county, Virginia.

WARDENSVILLE, a post office of Hardy county, Virginia.

WARMINSTER, a small post village of Nelson county, Virginia, on the James river, 100 miles West from Richmond.

WARM SPRINGS, called also BATH COURT HOUSE, a post village, capital of Bath county, Virginia, 170 miles W. N. W. from Richmond, is situated in a narrow valley, between two mountain ridges. The springs are much frequented during the summer season by invalids and others. The temperature of the water at all seasons is 98°, without the slightest change. The largest spring is 40 feet in diameter. Fine buildings have been erected for the accommodation of visiters. These improvements, together with the salubrity of the air, and the romantic character of the scenery, render this one of the most attractive watering-places in the State. The water contains muriate of lime, sulphate of lime, carbonate of lime, and sulphate of magnesia.

WARREN, a county in the N. E. part of Virginia, has an area of about 250 square miles. It is intersected by the Shenandoah river, and also drained by the North fork of the same. The county occupies part of the great valley bounded on the S. E. by the Blue Ridge. The surface is hilly ; the soil mostly good and well watered. Wheat, Indian corn, oats, hay and live stock are the staples. In 1850 it

WM. A. DROWN,

UMBRELLA & PARASOL MANUFACTURER,

86 MARKET STREET,

PHILADELPHIA.

Umbrellas and Parasols from this Manufactory cannot be excelled in beauty of style and finish, or durability of workmanship.

Particular care given to the manufacture of Goods adapted to a Fine and Stylish Trade.

WM. A. PEARSON,

(FORMERLY OF RICHMOND, VA.)

IS STILL ENGAGED IN THE SALES DEPARTMENT.

Buyers are solicited to examine the stock before purchasing.

B. A. FAHNESTOCK & CO.

WHOLESALE DRUGGISTS,

AND IMPORTERS OF

ENGLISH, FRENCH & GERMAN

DRUGS, CHEMICALS AND PERFUMERY,

DEALERS IN

Medicines, Paints, Oils, Dye Stuffs, Patent Medicines, Glassware and Druggists' Ware.

MANUFACTURERS AND PROPRIETORS OF

B. A. FAHNESTOCK'S VERMIFUGE,

No. 209 Market Street, North side, above 5th,

PHILADELPHIA.

Particular attention paid to the purity and freshness of every article. All orders packed with security and care. Having extensive and unusual facilities for purchasing, we are enabled to offer goods at such prices as cannot fail to give satisfaction to our customers.

produced 145,354 bushels of wheat, 128,875 of corn, 25,906 of oats, 2,119 tons of hay, and 64,185 pounds of butter. There were 40 flour, grist and saw mills, six distilleries and three tanneries. It contained 13 churches, and 484 pupils attending academies and schools. Limestone, copper, iron and manganese are abundant. It is amply supplied with water-power. The wealth of the county has recently been increased by several public works, viz : the Manassas Gap railroad, extending to Alexandria ; a plank-road from the county seat to Winchester, and two or three turnpikes. Organized in 1836. Capital, Front Royal. Population, 6,607, of whom 4,859 were free and 1,748 slaves.

Warren, a post village of Albemarle county, Virginia, on James river, about 88 miles above Richmond.

Warrenton, a beautiful town, capital of Fauquier county, Virginia, on the turnpike from Alexandria to Charlottesville, 100 miles N. by W. from Richmond. It is surrounded by a beautiful and productive country, and has an active business. A branch railroad connects the town with the Orange and Alexandria railroad, 10 miles distant. Warrenton contains a handsome court house, three or four churches, 2 academies, and 2 newspaper offices. Population, about 1,500.

Warrenton Springs, a post office of Fauquier county, Virginia.

Warsaw, a post village, capital of Richmond county, Virginia, 70 miles N. E. from Richmond, about three miles from the Rappahannock river. It contains several stores and about 30 dwellings.

Warwick, a county in the S. E. part of Virginia, containing about 50 square miles, is situated on a peninsula between Chesapeake bay and the mouth of James river, the latter of which washes its Western border. The surface is slightly diversified ; the soil is alluvial. The productions are wheat, Indian corn, and sweet potatoes. In 1820 there were raised 61,340 bushels of corn, 10,252 of wheat, and 9,844 of sweet potatoes. It contained two churches, and 54 pupils attending public schools. Oysters and firewood (oak and pine) are important articles of export. Capital, Warwick. Population, 1,546, of whom 641 were free, and 905 slaves.

Warwick, a small and handsome village, capital of Warwick county, Virginia, is situated near the mouth of James river, about 80 miles E. N. E. from Richmond.

Washington, a county in the S. S. W. part of Virginia, bordering on Tennessee, has an area of 484 square miles. It is intersected

by the North, Middle, and South forks of Holston river, dividing it into three fertile valleys, branches of the great valley of Virginia. The Clinch mountain forms the N. W. boundary, and the county is traversed by Walker's mountains. Indian corn, wheat, oats, grass, and maple sugar are the staples. In 1850 this county produced 438,900 bushels of corn, 69,264 of wheat, 249,674 of oats and 153,-044 pounds of butter. There were 25 flour, grist and saw mills, five salt works, two iron furnaces, and two tanneries. It contained 33 churches, 1,512 pupils attending public schools, and 194 attending academies or other schools. This county is no less remarkable for its valuable minerals than for its fertile soil and excellent pastures. Limestone, gypsum, iron, and stone coal are abundant, and large quantities of salt are procured on the N. E. border. The Virginia and Tennessee railroad is now in progress through the county. Capital, Abingdon. Population, 14,612, of whom 12,481 were free, and 2,131 slaves.

WATERFORD, a thriving post village of Loudoun county, Virginia, on Kittoctan creek, 156 miles North from Richmond, contains two churches and several mills. Population estimated at 500.

WATERLOO, a post village of Fauquier county, Virginia, on the Rappahannock river, 63 miles W. S. W. from Washington. It contains two stores and one mill.

WATKINSVILLE, a small village of Goochland county, Virginia, 36 miles West from Richmond.

WATTSBOROUGH, a post office of Lunenburg county, Virginia, 97 miles S. W. from Richmond.

WAYLANDSBURG, a post village of Culpepper county, Virginia, on Crooked creek, 102 miles N. N. W. from Richmond. It contains two mills.

WAYNE, a county in the West part of Virginia, has an area estimated at 500 square miles. The Ohio river forms its boundary on the North, separating it from Ohio, and the Sandy river separates it from Kentucky on the West; it is also drained by Twelvepole creek. The surface is broken by numerous hills or ridges, and mostly covered with forests. The soil is productive. Indian corn, oats, and grass are the staples. The highlands abound in stone coal. Ginseng is one of the articles of export. In 1850 the county produced 226,800 bushels of corn, 27,785 of oats, and 36,555 pounds of butter. There were six saw mills, one wool-carding mill and two tanneries. It contained nine churches, and 203 pupils at-

tending public schools. Formed in 1842, out of part of Cabell county. Capital, Wayne Court house. Population, 4,760, of whom 4,571 were free and 189 slaves.

WAYNE COURT HOUSE, capital of Wayne county Virginia, 275 miles in a direct line West from Richmond. Laid out in 1842.

WAYNESBOROUGH, a post village of Augusta county, Virginia, on or near the Central railroad, and on the South river, at the West base of the Blue Ridge, 108 miles W. N. W. from Richmond. The village contains two or three churches, and an academy. Population estimated at 600.

WEAVERSVILLE, a post office of Fauquier county, Virginia, 114 miles N. by W. from Richmond.

WEBB'S MILLS, a post office of Ritchie county, Virginia.

WELLSBURG, a thriving post village, capital of Brooke county, Virginia, is beautifully situated on the Ohio river, 16 miles above Wheeling. It contains five churches, two academies, one bank, two newspaper offices, 1 manufactory of cotton, two of glass, one of woolen goods, two of stone ware, six flour mills, and one paper mill. Rich mines of coal are worked in the vicinity. Population in 1853, about 3000.

WELLVILLE, a post-office of Nottoway county, Virginia.

WEST COLUMBIA, a thriving post-village of Mason county, Virginia, on the Ohio river, 160 miles below Wheeling. It owes its growth and importance to the valuable salt springs recently found here: 5 or 6 wells have been sunk, and several furnaces put in operation. Laid out about 1850.

WESTERN FORD, a post-office of Randolph county, Virginia, 210 miles N. W. from Richmond.

WESTHAM LOCKS, a post-office of Henrico county, Virginia.

WEST LIBERTY, a post-village in Ohio county, Virginia, about 10 miles N. E. from Wheeling.

WEST MILFORD, a post-office of Harrison county, Virginia.

WESTMORELAND, a county in the E. part of Virginia, bordering on the Potomac river, which separates it from Maryland, has an area of about 170 square miles. It occupies part of the northern neck, a peninsula formed by the Potomac and Rappahannock rivers, the former of which washes the county on the N. E., and the latter on the S. W. It is penetrated by inlets from the Potomac, named Nomini bay, and Pope's and Monroe creeks. The surface is somewhat diversified by hills, and partly covered with forests of pine and cedar.

C. B. ROGER'S

SEED AND AGRICULTURAL WAREHOUSE,

No. 29 Market Street,

PHILADELPHIA,

MANUFACTURER OF

Mowing and Reaping Machines, Ammoniated Super Phosphate Lime, Chemical Fertilizer, Bone Dust,

Dealer in Guano, &c.

ALL THE MOST APPROVED

AGRICULTURAL AND HORTICULTURAL IMPLEMENTS

MADE TO ORDER.

Dealer in Imported and American Field and Garden Seed, &c. &c.

INVENTOR AND MANUFACTURER OF THE

Cast Steel Extending Point Surface & Subsoil

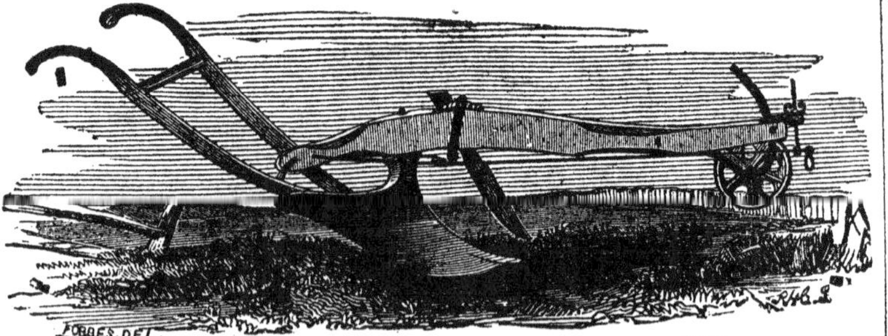

PLOUGHS.

The soil near the rivers is fertile. Indian corn, wheat, and oats are cultivated. The waters abound with fish and oysters, and firewood is one of the chief exports. In 1850 this county produced 269,115 bushels of corn; 82,774 of wheat, and 7897 of oats. It contained 1 wheelwright establishment, 2 coach and 1 saddle manufactory, and 1 tannery; 13 churches, and 300 pupils attending public schools. Westmoreland county is distinguished as the birth-place of two

Presidents of the republic, Washington and Monroe, and also of Richard Henry Lee. The spot on which Washington was born, half a mile from the Potomac, is marked with a stone bearing this inscription, "Here, on the 11th of February, (O. S.,) 1732, George Washington was born. Capital, Westmoreland Court House. Population 8,080; of whom 4,523 were free, and 3,557 slaves.

WESTMORELAND COURT HOUSE, a village, capital of Westmoreland county, Virginia, 65 miles N. E. from Richmond.

WESTON, a post village, capital of Lewis county, Virginia, on the West fork of Monongahela river, 278 miles N. W. from Richmond. The hills in this vicinity abound in coal. Weston is connected by turnpike with Fairmont. The village has one bank. Population about 300.

WEST UNION, a post village of Doddridge county, Virginia, on Middle Island creek, and on the turnpike from Winchester to Parkersburg, 300 miles N. W. from Richmond. Lumber is exported from this vicinity by flat-boats and rafts.

WEST UNION, a village of Marshall county, Virginia, 12 miles S. E. from Wheeling.

WEST VIEW, a post village of Augusta county, Virginia, six miles West of Staunton. It has two stores.

WEST WARREN, a small village of Monongalia county, Virginia.

WETZEL, a new county in the N. W. part of Virginia, bordering on Pennsylvania, and on the Ohio river, which separates it from the State of Ohio; area, about 250 square miles. It is drained by Fishing creek and branches. The surface is exceedingly hilly; the soil of the river bottoms is excellent, and of the uplands moderately fertile. Indian corn, wheat, oats, hay, cattle and pork are the staples. In 1850 this county produced 124,198 bushels of corn, 12,162 of wheat, 22,266 of oats; 1,440 tons of hay, and 46,327 pounds of butter. It contained five saw mills, two saddlery shops, and 78 pupils attending public schools. The county contains stone coal. The Baltimore and Ohio railroad passes along the N. E. border. Formed a few years ago out of part of Tyler county. Capital, New Martinsville. Population, 4,284 of whom 4,267 and 17 slaves.

WHEATLAND, a post office of Loudoun county, Virginia.

WHEATLEY, a post office of Fauquier county, Virginia.

WHEELING, a city and port of entry of Virginia, and capital of Ohio county. The sight now occupied by the city of Wheeling was first settled by white men in 1770, five years after the treaty with the Indians at Fort Pitt, effected by the Military expedition of Colonel Boquet to the Muskingdom. The settlement was made during the tranquillity and friendly intercourse between the whites and Indians, which succeeded that treaty, and almost simultaneous with several other settlements in this region and along the borders of the Alleghany and Monongahela rivers, which were then free from Indian depredations. In 1774 the hostility of the Indians was renewed, awakened afresh at that time, it is generally conceded, by

the cruel massacre at Yellow Creek, between Fort Pitt and Wheeling, of the family of Logan, a chief of the Mingo tribe. The bloody alliance of the Indians with the British followed soon after, and with it that protracted border warfare which made almost every hill and valley along the Ohio the scene of some sanguinary conflict.

The first settlement was made here by Colonel Ebenezer Zane and his brothers, Jonathan, Isaac and Silas. Prominent also among the early pioneers and settlers were Lewis Wetzel, Samuel McColloch, Adam Poe and his brother. The hardships and dangers encountered by these men deserve an abiding place in the annals of our country. I have incidentally obtained portions of their history that for thrilling interest have rarely been surpassed, but which, if at all appropriate to this work, would swell it far beyond its allotted limits. It is to be hoped that the historian will yet do justice to their memories. Suffice it to say that some of them lived to see the haunts of the savage and the fields of their heroic courage converted into abodes of civilization and refinement; and many of their descendants, who have long been among our most worthy citizens, have seen the "waste places made glad, and the desert blossom as the rose."

The city is finely situated on the East bank of the Ohio river, and on both sides of Wheeling creek, 92 miles below Pittsburg, 365 miles above Cincinnati, 350 miles N. W. from Richmond, and about 630 feet above the level of the sea. Lat. 40° 7′ N., lon. 80° 42′ W. The site is a narrow alluvial tract, overlooked by precipitous hills, and extending about two miles along the river. Wheeling is the most important place on the river between Petersburg and Cincinnati, and in respect to trade, manufactures and population, the most considerable town of Western Virginia. It contains a fine court house, about 14 churches, two academies, three banks, aggregate capital above $1,400,000, and a savings institution. Four or five newspapers are published here. The town is supplied by water raised from the river by machinery. The National road crosses the river at Zane's Island, opposite the city, by a beautiful wire suspension bridge, the span of which is one of the longest in the world, measuring 1,010 feet. The height of the towers is 153 feet above low-water mark, and 60 feet above the abutments. The bridge is supported by 12 wire cables, each 1,380 feet in length and 4 inches in diameter. The cost of this structure is estimated at $210,000. Wheeling is the Western terminus of the Baltimore and

Ohio railroad, 380 miles long, finished in 1853, and of the Hempfield railroad, which joins the Pennsylvania railroad at Greensburg. The Cleveland and Pittsburg railroad is to be extended from Wellsville to this city, and the Central Ohio, and the Cincinnati and Marietta railroad, are now finished, and will open a more direct communication with the Western States. In 1852 38 steamboats were owned in this place, with an aggregate tonnage of 6,843 tons. During the same year, 10 steamboats and two other vessels were built, with a burthen of 1746 tons. The hills which rise in the immediate vicinity contain inexhaustible beds of coal, which supply fuel at a small expense to the numerous manufactories of Wheeling. In 1850 it contained four iron foundries, three forges, three manufactories of nails, five of glass ware, two or three of cotton goods, three of paper, 1 of steam engines, one of silk goods, and two of wire. Flour, woolen goods, whitelead, and other articles are produced here. Wheeling became the capital of the county in 1797. In 1802 it contained about 70 houses. Population in 1820, 1567; in 1830, 5221; in 1840, 7885; in 1850, 11,391, exclusive of West Wheeling, which had 438 inhabitants; and in 1854 about 20,000.

DESCRIPTION

Of the line of the Baltimore and Ohio Railroad from Baltimore to Wheeling.

The Mount Clare Station of the Baltimore and Ohio Railroad was established in 1829, at what was then the extreme western end of Pratt street, (Baltimore,) and indeed some distance beyond the paved part of the street. Here, surrounded by some rough sheds, was planted the little box at which tickets were sold for an excursion to the Carrollton Viaduct, one mile out; this being the length of the road when business began to be done upon it, and a revenue to be collected from those who visited a Railway as an object of curiosity, to be seen and *felt* for the first time. The station has since grown to be a vast area of some forty acres, a large proportion of it covered by buildings of every size and shape, and a reticulation of tracks of which it would puzzle the eye to pursue the numerous lines and intersections. When the track was extended into the city and carried through many of its principal streets by numerous branches, the Mount Clare (at first the *only*) became the "outer"

station, and the "inner station" was located upon Charles street, between Pratt and Camden streets, and within a few steps of the head of the Basin. It was afterward removed to Pratt street, below Charles, where it remained until the opening of the road to Wheeling. It was here also for a number of years that the Passenger station of the Philadelphia Railroad was located, the two lines meeting under a common roof. The Philadelphia has sometime since removed towards the eastern section of the ctiy, and the Baltimore and Ohio Railroad has also removed its inner station to the spacious grounds recently purchased between Camden and Lee streets on the North and South, and Howard and Eutaw streets on the East and West.

The new station is reached through the "Locust Point Branch," which leaves the original Main Stem of the road near the Carrollton Viaduct, at the western boundary of the city. The branch will henceforward become the trunk, as the transportation business of the Company will be chiefly concentrated at the new station, and the Mount Clare will be devoted principally to the machinery department.

Leaving the city, we cross the Carrollton Viaduct, a fine bridge of dressed granite, with an arch of eighty feet span, over Gwyn's Falls; after which the road soon reaches the long and deep excavation under the Washington Turnpike, which is carried over the Railroad by the "Jackson Bridge." Less than a mile further the "deep cut" is encountered, famous for its difficulties in the early history of the road. It is seventy-six feet in extreme depth and nearly half a mile in length, and the traces of the slides and gulleyings of twenty odd years are to be seen upon its furrowed sides, tinted with various ochrous colors of the richest hue. Beyond this the road crosses the deep ravine of Robert's Run, and, skirting the ore banks of the old Baltimore Iron Company, now covered by a dense forest of cedar trees, comes to the long and deep embankment over the valley of Gadsby's Run and the heavy cut through Vinegar Hill immediately following it. The "Relay House," eight miles from the inner station, is then reached, where, as the name imports, there was a change of horses during the period which those animals furnished the motive power of the road.

At this point the open country of sand and clay ends, and the region of rock begins at the entrance to the gorge of the Patapsco river. In entering this defile you have a fine view of the "Thomas

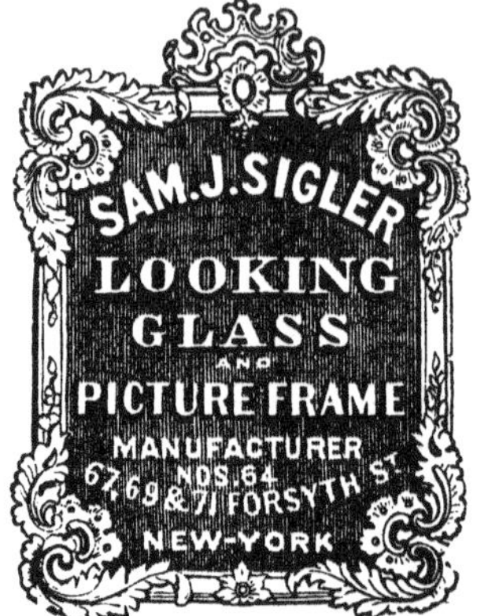

LOOKING GLASS
AND
PICTURE FRAME
MANUFACTORY.

This Establishment, by far the largest in the U.S., possesses many advantages in variety and extensiveness of Stock over all others, and from the long established and continued increase of trade from all parts of the Union, enables the proprietor to dispose of his articles at less prices than any other in his line of business, and respectfully requests his friends and the public to call and examine his large stock of LOOKING GLASSES AND PICTURE FRAMES, previous to going elsewhere, as the subscriber assures them that they will find it to their decided advantage in so doing. Gilding in all its branches. On hand, Rosewood, Walnut, Gilt and Mahogany Mouldings. ☞ Particular attention given to all orders. **Nos. 64, 67, 69 & 71 Forsyth street, New York.** Communications by mail.

S. J. SIGLER.

THIS PREPARATION IS PRONOUNCED BY ALL WHO HAVE TRIED IT as the best in use. It has received from the *American Institute* Two Silver Medals and Six Diplomas, when in competition with Blacking from all parts of the Union. The

common articles cause the leather to rot and crack in a very short time, while this, on the contrary, softens, improves and preserves it, making a saving in Boots and Shoes more than sufficient to pay for twice the quantity used.

As some Manufacturers in Philadelphia claim on their show-bills to have received Premiums at the Fairs in New York, held 1850 and 1851, the following Certificate has been obtained:

AMERICAN INSTITUTE, March 29, 1854.

This is to certify that Mr. JOHN VAN DEVENTER received the First Premium for Paste Blacking at the 23d and 24th Annual Fairs of the American Institute in the City of New York, in the years 1850 and 1851. JOHN W. CHAMBERS, *Secretary of the Premium Committee.*

The following testimonial was received from Dr. JAMES R. CHILTON, Chemist, New York:

Having for several years past used the **OIL PASTE BLACKING**, manufactured by John Van Deventer, and having tested its properties as compared with many other kinds of Paste Blacking which have come under my notice, while acting as one of the judges of the Fairs of the American Institute, I can with confidence recommend it as the best article of the kind which I have yet examined.

NEW YORK, March 10, 1852. JAMES R. CHILTON, M. D.

JOHN VAN DEVENTER, DEALER IN OILS, PAINTS, DRUGS, &c. Also, Wholesale Agent for Hyatt's Celebrated Matches. Wholesale Agents: **E. H. Stabler & Co.,** Baltimore; **A. D. Grief & Co.,** New Orleans; **Davison, Cavanagh & Co.,** Mobile; **Warren Bryant,** Buffalo; **Mathieson & Smith,** Hamilton, C. W.; and most other prominent Merchants and Dealers throughout the United States and Canadas.

Viaduct," (named after the first President of the Company,) a noble granite structure of eight elliptic arches, each of about sixty chord, spanning the stream at a height of sixty-six feet above the bed, and of a total length of some seven hundred feet. This bridge belongs to the Washington Branch Road, which departs from the Main Line at this place. The pretty village of Elkridge Landing is in sight, and upon the surrounding heights are seen a number of country seats belonging to men of business who reside here during the summer, tempted by the beauty of the spot and the facilities of access which the Railroad affords.

The road now pursues its devious course up the river, passing the Avalon Iron Works a mile beyond the Relay House, and coming in a couple of miles farther, to the Patterson Viaduct, a fine granite bridge of two arches of fifty-five, and two of twenty feet span. This bridge crosses the river at the Ilchester Mill, situated at a very rugged part of the ravine. The Thistle Cotton Factory appears immediately beyond, and soon after Gray's Cotton Factory, and then the well known and flourishing town of "Ellicott's Mills," fourteen miles from Baltimore, covering the bottom and slopes of the steep hills with dwellings and their tops with churches and other public edifices. The Frederick Turnpike road passes through the town here, and is crossed by the railroad upon the "Oliver Viaduct," a handsome stone bridge of three arches of twenty feet span. Just beyond this bridge is the Tarpeian rock, a bold insulated mass of granite, between which and the body of the cliff the Railroad edges its way. Half a mile further we see the extensive buildings of the Union Cotton Factory scattered over the opposite hill side, and from between two of the mills a fine cascade pouring incessantly down from the race into the river.

The road next comes in sight of the Elysville Factory buildings, where at a circuitous bend it crosses the river upon a viaduct of three timber arches, each of one hundred and ten feet span, and almost immediately recrosses it upon one of two arches of one hundred and fifty feet span. Thence it follows the windings of the stream to the "Forks," twenty-five miles from Baltimore, where, by a deep cut through a narrow neck, it turns the western branch of the river, and thus crosses its former channel twice without a bridge. Passing the Marriottsville limestone quarries, the road then crosses the Patapsco by an iron bridge fifty feet span, and dashes through a sharp spur of the hill by a tunnel four hundred feet long, in mica slate rock,

Excelsior!—World's Fair Premium!

DANIEL D. WINANT,

BILLIARD TABLE MAKER,

(The oldest and most Extensive Manufactory of the kind in America,)

71 GOLD STREET,

BETWEEN BEEKMAN AND SPRUCE STREETS,

NEW YORK.

EVERY THING IN THE LINE FURNISHED AT TEN PER CENT. LESS THAN ANY OTHER ESTABLISHMENT IN THE CITY.

☞ TABLES, BALLS, MACES, CUES; CLOTHS by the Piece or Yard; GIBB'S ADHESIVE CUE WAX, SICK AND WORSTED POCKETS, FRINGES, FRENCH AND AMERICAN PATENT CUE POINTS, CORD, POOL BOARDS, RULE BOARDS, SPANISH PINS, &c. In short, every thing in the Trade always to be had.

☞ ORDERS by Letter, for New Articles or Repairs, attended to as promptly as if given in person.

IMPORTANT TO BILLIARD PLAYERS.

FOR SALE AT THE OFFICE OF PUBLICATION,

71 GOLD STREET, NEW YORK,

PRICE $3.00.

BILLIARDS WITHOUT A MASTER,

By Michael Phelan.

The above-named work, the first American publication of the kind, is illustrated by fifty fine copper-plate diagrams, each containing from one to twenty-four shots, from which sufficient knowledge may be acquired to enable the player to accomplish any possible stroke on the billiard table, all of which are fully explained on the pages opposite to the respective plates. The work contains an invaluable and original invention in the shape of a chart or scale of strengths necessary to be used in making each shot, of an arrangement so simple that it can be comprehended by all, and will be found of the highest importance to the novice and amateur, as every shot there delineated has been graduated by it, and the quantity of strength necessary to be used is given in the description annexed to each plate. It contains, also, a full and complete set of rules for the government of the game of billiards, and the various games of pool; hints to players; advice to amateurs, with a variety of explanations, interesting to all connected with billiards or billiard playing. To keepers of billiard rooms, the "Rules" are worth more than the price of the work, and the hints and the advice are invaluable. Accompanying the work is a treatise on the origin, rise, and progress of the game. It is also embellished by a fine steel plate frontispiece, showing a billiard table and players in position. The above work is the most complete one of the kind ever produced in any part of the world, and the only one in which the theoretical science and philosophy of the game has ever been explained.

which forms a substantial roof without other support. For a mile or two beyond this the road runs along pretty meadow lands, but soon re-enters a crooked gorge, which it follows with many diversions of the stream from its original bed, as far as Sykesville, a village prettily situated at an opening in the valley and showing a mill and cotton factory. This point is thirty miles from Baltimore, and the road after leaving it encounters some rough cutting through points of hard rock, after which it again emerges upon a comparatively open country, and after passing one or two rocky hills at Hood's Mill, it leaves the granite region and enters upon the gentle slopes of the slate hills, among which the river meanders until we reach the foot of "Parr's Ridge," dividing the waters of the Patapsco from those of the Potomac. The road crossed this ridge at first by four inclined planes, (two on each side of the ridge,) intended to be worked by stationary power, which was however never applied, as before the trade of the road would have justified its use a new location was made in 1838, and a grade of eighty-two feet per mile with a cut of fifty feet at the summit was substituted for the planes, the steepest of which had upon it an inclination of about three hundred and sixty feet per mile. The new road of about five miles in length, crosses the ridge north of the old and is but little longer.

From the summit of the ridge at the Mount Airy Station, forty-four miles from Baltimore, is a noble view Westward across the Fredericktown Valley, and as far as the Catoctin Mountain some fifteen miles distant. The road thence descends the valley of Bush Creek, a stream of moderate curves and gentle slopes, with a few exceptions, where it breaks through some ranges of trap rocks, which interpose themselves among the softer shales. The Monrovia and Ijamsville Stations are passed at Bush Creek. The slates terminate at the Monocacy River, and the limestone of the Fredericktown Valley commences. That river is crossed by a bridge of three timber spans one hundred and ten feet each, and elevated about forty feet above its bed. At this point, fifty-seven miles from Baltimore, the Frederick Branch, of three miles in length, leaves the Main Road and terminates at the city of that name, the centre of one of the most fertile, populous, and wealthy sections of Maryland.

From the Monocacy to the Point of Rocks, the road having escaped from the narrow winding valleys to which it has thus far been confined, bounds away over the beautiful champaign country lying between that river and the Catoctin Mountain. This rolling region

ENAMELED FURNITURE.

BRIGGS & VICKRERE,

No. 6 SULLIVAN STREET,

NEW YORK,

MANUFACTURERS OF THIS STYLE OF

FURNITURE,

Would respectfully invite the attention of the trade and purchasers generally, to the substantial and beautiful productions of their manufacture. They have quite a variety of styles and patterns, and in the Ornamental Department endeavor to produce a pleasing variety. The

FLOWERS AND LANDSCAPES

On our Furniture are executed by Artists of superior merit. We will make to order one or more suits of furniture in a style to assimilate with the peculiar architecture of a house.

We received from the American Institute, 1853, a

FOR A SUIT OF

FURNITURE

Of our own Manufacture,

ALSO A

Diploma from the New York State Agricultural Fair,

HELD AT HAMILTON SQUARE, 1854.

Orders solicited, and articles carefully boxed and shipped to any part of the United States.

BRIGGS & VICKRERE,

No. 6 SULLIVAN STREET, N. Y.

N. B. SUITS $25 TO $150.

of rich limestone land is the garden of the State, and contains the celebrated Carrollton Manor. The line for upwards of eleven miles consists of long straight stretches and fine sweeping curves, and lies near the gently rolling surface of the ground with little cutting or filling. On approaching the "Point of Rocks," it passes by a cut of some extent through the ridge of breccia marble, from which the beautiful material of the columns in the Senate Chamber and Hall of Representatives of the Capitol at Washington was obtained.

The "Point of Rocks," celebrated in the contest between the Railroad and Canal Companies, is formed by the bold profile of the Catoctin Mountain, against the base of which the Potomac River runs on the Maryland side, the mountain towering up on the opposite, Virginia, shore, forming the other barrier of the pass. Here, sixty-nine miles from Baltimore and forty-eight from Washington, the Canal and Railroad first came side by side, and a village has arisen. There is also a bridge over the river, which is about a quarter of a mile wide. The Railroad turns the promontory by an abrupt curve, and is partly cut out of the rock precipice on the right, and partly supported on the inner side of the Canal on the left by a stone wall of considerable length. Two miles further another cliff occurs, accompanied by more excavation and walling. From hence the ground becomes comparatively smooth, and the Railroad, leaving the immediate margin of the river to the Canal, runs along the base of the gently sloping hills, passing the villages of Berlin and Knoxville, and reaching the "Weverton Factories" in the pass of the South Mountain.

From this point to Harper's Ferry the road lies along the foot of a precipice for the greater part of the distance of three miles, the last of which is immediately under the lofty cliffs of Elk Mountain, forming the north side of this noted pass. The Shenandoah river enters the Potomac immediately below the bridge over the latter, and their united currents rush rapidly over the broad ledges of rock which stretch across their bed. The length of the bridge is about nine hundred feet, and at its western end it divides into two, the left hand branch connecting with the Winchester and Potomac Railroad which passes directly up the Shenandoah, and the right hand carrying the Main Road, by a strong curve in that direction, up the Potomac. The bridge consists of six arches of one hundred and thirty, and one arch of about seventy-five feet span over the river, and an arch of about one hundred feet span over the canal; all of which are of

timber and iron and covered in, except the western arch connected with the Winchester and Potomac Railroad, which is entirely of iron,* excepting the floor. This viaduct is not so remarkable for its length as for its peculiar structure, the two ends of it being curved in opposite directions and bifurcated at the western extremity. Harper's Ferry and all its fine points of scenery are too well known to need description here. The precipitous mountains which rise from the water's edge leave little level ground on the river margin, and all of that is occupied by the United States Armory buildings. Hence the Baltimore and Ohio Railroad has been obliged to build itself a road in the river bed for upwards of half a mile along the outer boundary of the Government Works, upon a trestle work resting on the side next the river, upon an insulated wall of masonry, and upon the other side upon square stone columns placed upon the retaining wall of the Armory grounds. After passing the uppermost building, the road runs along upon the outer bank of the Canal which brings the water of the river to the works, and soon crosses this Canal by a stone and timber bridge one hundred and fifty feet span. Thence the road passes up the river on the inner side of the Canal, and opposite the dam at its head, about one and three-quarters of a mile from the mouth of the Shenandoah, pierces a projecting rock by a tunnel or gallery of eighty feet in length.

The view down the river through this perforation is singularly picturesque, and presents the pass through the mountain at the confluence of the rivers in one of its most remarkable aspects. A short distance above the tunnel, where the river sweeps gradually round to the eastward in the broad smooth sheet of water created by the dam, the Railroad leaves the Potomac and passes up the ravine of Elk Branch which presents itself at this point in a favorable direction; this ravine, at first narrow and serpentine, becomes wider and more direct until it almost loses itself in the rolling table land which characterizes the "Valley of Virginia." The head of Elk Branch is reached in about nine miles, and thence the line descends gradually over an undulating champaign country, to the crossing of the "Opequa" Creek, which it passes by a stone and timber viaduct of one hundred and fifty feet span and forty feet above the water surface. Beyond the crossing the road enters the open valley of Tuscarora Creek which it crosses twice and pursues to the town of Mar-

*The "Winchester Span," (which is of iron,) is one of Bollman's Patent Rail Road Bridges.

tinsburg, eighteen miles from Harper's Ferry. At Martinsburg the Tuscarora is again bridged twice, the crossing east of the town being made upon a viaduct of ten spans of forty-four feet each, of timber and iron, supported by two abutments and eighteen stone columns in the Doric style, and which have a very agreeable achitectural effect. The Company have erected here large engine houses and workshops, and have made it one of their principal stations for the shelter and repair of their machinery, a measure that has greatly promoted the prosperity of the town, which like many of the old Virginia villages had previously been in a stagnant state for an almost immemorial period.

Westward from Martinsburg the route for eight miles continues its course over the open country, arternately ascending and descending until it strikes the foot of the North Mountain and crossing it by a long excavation, sixty-three feet deep, in slate rock, through a depression therein, passes out of the "Valley," having traversed its entire breadth upon a line twenty-six miles in length. The soil of the valley is limestone, with slight exceptions, and of great fertility. On leaving these rich and well tilled lands we enter a poor and thinly settled district, covered chiefly with a forest in which stunted pine prevails. The route encounters heavy excavation and embankment for four or five miles from the North Mountain, and crosses Back Creek upon a stone viaduct of a single arch of eighty feet span and fifty-four feet above the stream. The view across and up the Potomac valley is magnificent as you approach this bridge, and extends as far as the distant mountain range of Sideling hill twenty-five miles to the West. The immediate margin of the river is reached at a point opposite Fort Frederick on the Maryland side, an ancient stronghold, erected a hundred years ago and still in pretty good preservation.

From this point, thirty miles from Harper's Ferry, the route follows the Virginia shore of the river upon bottom lands, interrupted only by the rocky bluffs opposite Licking Creek, for ten miles to Hancock. The only considerable stream crossed in this distance is Sleepy Creek, which is passed by a viaduct of two spans of one hundred and ten feet each. Hancock is in Maryland, and although a town of no great size or importance, makes some show when seen across the river from the station at the mouth of Warm Spring Run.

The route from Hancock to Cumberland pursues the margin of the Potomac river, with four exceptions. The first occurs at *Doe Gul-*

ley, eighteen miles above Hancock, where by a tunnel of 1,200 feet in length, a bend of the river is cut off, and a distance of nearly four miles saved. The second is at the Paw Paw Ridge, where a distance of nearly two miles is saved by a tunnel of 250 feet in length. The third and fourth are within six miles of Cumberland, where two bends are cut across by the route with a considerable lessening of distance.

In advancing westward from Hancock the line passes along the western base of Warm Spring Ridge, approaching within a couple of miles of the Berkely Springs, which are at the eastern foot of that ridge. It then sweeps around the termination of the Cacapon Mountain, opposite the remarkable and insulated eminence called the "Round Top." Thence the road proceeds to the crossing of the Great Cacapon River, nine and a half miles above Hancock, which is crossed by a bridge about 300 feet in length. Within the next mile it passes dam No. 6 of the Chesapeake and Ohio Canal, and soon after, it enters the gap of Sideling Hill, that famous bugbear of the traveler, which on the National Turnpike opposes such a formidable barrier to his journey, but which here is unnoticed except in the fine profile which it exhibits on each side of the river, as it declines rapidly to the water level.

In the gap of this mountain are the coal veins which the late R. Caton, Esq., with that zeal which always distinguished his researches in this branch of practical geology, endeavored to turn to profitable account. The slack water of the Canal dam extends some two miles above Sideling Hill.

The next point of interest reached is the Tunnel at Doe Gulley. The approaches to this formidable work are very imposing, as for several miles above and below the tunnel they cause the road to occupy a high level on the slopes of the river hills, and thus afford an extensive view of the grand mountain scenery around. The tunnel is, as before mentioned, about a quarter of a mile in length, through a compact slate rock, which is arched with brick to preserve it from future disintegration by atmospheric action. The fronts or facades of the arch are of a fine white sand-stone, procured from the summit of the neighboring mountain. The width of the opening within the brick work of the arch is 21 feet, and the height 20½, affording room for two tracks. The height of the hill above the roof of the tunnel is 110 feet. The excavation and embankments adjacent are very heavy, and consist of the slate rock through which the tunnel is cut.

M. W. KING. W. H. HALLICK.

M. W. KING & SON,

PATENT

CHAIR MAKERS,

466 & 468 BROADWAY, NEW YORK.

Pivot Revolving Chairs,

RECUMBENT REVOLVING CHAIRS,

SELF-ACTING EXTENSION

RECUMBENT CHAIRS,

DENTIST CHAIRS,

Improved Invalid Wheel Chairs,

BRANCH READING AND WRITING DESKS,

And every variety of Mechanical Chairs for comfort and convenience.

☞ Also, by permission, manufacturers of MAJOR SEARLE'S (U. S. A.) TRAVELING INVALID CHAIR.

☞ Fashionable Cabinet Furniture made to order.

WONDERFUL DISCOVERY!

HAIR! HAIR! HAIR!

KNIGHT & CO.

CHEMISTS,

341 BROADWAY, NEW YORK,

Have prepared a wash for the Hair, called HAIR REGENERATOR, which they will warrant to restore the grey hair of any person, old or young, to the natural and original color, and produce an entire *new growth*, even where the head is bald. The above has been fully tested and needs no *long puffing*, but will *do its work*, which is the best recommendation it can have; try it, and you will then acknowledge that you have at last found something besides *humbuggery*. **Price $1 per bottle; $5 for six bottles. Sold only by us, 341 BROADWAY, NEW YORK.**

The following are testimonials from numerous New York newspapers:

"We are very skeptical as to the merits of Hair Regenerators, and have studiously avoided recommending any nostrums emanating from perfumers; but we are open to conviction, and having witnessed in our own families the extraordinary virtues of Knight & Co's Regenerator, we embrace this opportunity of making a public avowal of its excellence as a permanent restorer. No person, with weak or grey hair, or bald pate should neglect securing so inestimable a prize—remembering that Knight & Co. are Chemists as well as Perfumers."—*Mercantile Guide.*

"Being personally acquainted with Mr. Knight, we have had many opportunities of observing the operation of his Regenerator, have used it in our own family, and have seen it used among our friends in numerous instances, and in every case it has proved entirely satisfactory."—*New York Dutchman.*

"The above remark is decidedly true respecting the properties of the HAIR REGENERATOR, as the writer of this knows from experience. It should be remembered that it does not act as a *dye* to the hair, but restores the original color, after repeated applications. In fact, it will not fail of success if the directions of the renowned Chemist be implicitly followed."—*New York Day Book.*

"Among the many preparations in market for the preservation of the hair. there is one which stands pre-eminent as actually performing what is claimed for it. It does restore grey hair to its original color; there is no mistake about it—we have seen a dozen instances of its use on the old and the young, and in no instance has it ever failed of producing a perfect cure. We allude to the Hair Regenerator sold by Knight & Queru, 341 Broadway."—*New York Atlas.*

"The reputation of the well known Chemists that manufacture this Hair Regenerator, and the fact that it has been used by several of our friends to their entire satisfaction—leads us to place great reliance on its efficacy as a permanent restorer of the hair."—*National Democrat*

Above this point the line pursues the very sinuous part of the river lying between Sideling Hill on the east, and Town Hill on the west. The curves are not however abrupt, but form fine sweeping circuits, passing sometimes along beautiful alluvial bottoms and again at the foot of precipitous cliffs.

The Paw Paw Ridge Tunnel is next reached, thirty miles from Hancock, and twenty-five miles below Cumberland. This tunnel is through a soft slate rock, and is curved horizontally with a radius of 750 feet. It is of the same sectional dimensions with the Doe Gulley Tunnel, and is completely arched with brick, and fronted with white sand stone. Thence the route reaches Little Cacapon Creek, 21½ miles from Cumberland. At the mouth of this stream there are fine flats, and a beautiful view of the mountains to the eastward.

The viaduct over the creek is 143 feet long. About five and a half miles further on, the south branch of the Potomac is crossed on a bridge 400 feet long. This is in fact the main Potomac, and would have been (as the story runs) so treated by the Commissioners who determined the boundary of Maryland and Virginia, but that the north branch has the appearance, at the *confluence*, of being the larger stream. The river bottoms are here wide and exceedingly fertile, and the scenery very beautiful. The *arching* of the strata in the section of the South Branch Mountain, just above the junction, is most remarkable and grand.

Some two miles above is a fine straight line, over the widely expanded flats opposite the ancient village of Old Town, in Maryland. These are the finest bottom lands on the river, and from the upper end of them is obtained the first view of the Knobly Mountain, that remarkable range which lies in a line with the town of Cumberland, and is so singularly diversified by a profile which makes it appear like a succession of artificial mounds. Dan's mountain towers over it, forming a fine back ground to the view. Soon after, the route passes the high cliffs known by the name of Kelly's Rocks, where there has been very heavy excavation.

Patterson's Creek, eight miles from Cumberland, is next reached. Immediately below this stream is a lofty mural precipice of limestone and sand-stone rock, singularly perforated in some of the ledges by openings which look like Gothic loop holes. The valley of this creek is very straight and bordered by beautiful flats. The viaduct over the stream is 150 feet long. Less than two miles above, and six miles from Cumberland, the north branch of the Po-

SANCTIONED BY THE FACULTY OF MEDICINE.

TARRANT'S PREPARATIONS.

TO THE MEDICAL PROFESSION AND THE PUBLIC.

The attention of the Medical Profession and the Public is invited to the following preparation:

TARRANT'S EFFERVESCENT SELTZER APERIENT—Prepared on an entirely new principle, from a late and accurate analysis of the celebrated SELTZER SPRING in Germany, combining efficacy, economy and portability, with such additions and improvements as will be found materially to increase its efficacy. This much esteemed and highly valuable preparation will not fail to effectually remove Dyspepsia or Indigestion, Bilious Affections, Headache, Heartburn, Acidity of the Stomach, Costiveness, Gout, Rheumatism, Loss of Appetite, Gravel, Nervous Debility, Nausea of Vomiting, Affections of the Liver, &c., &c.

FAMILY MEDICINE.

TARRANT'S CORDIAL ELIXIR OF TURKEY RHUBARB—Takes its place as the best remedy for dyspepsia or indigestion, of the present day; and for its efficacy and safety, deserves the name of being in truth a Family Medicine. Those who suffer from excessive fatigue, mental anxiety, or intellectual application of wnatsoever kind, will find it to be a medicine of extreme value. It is particularly recommended to those suffering from Bilious and Nervous Headache, Diarrhœa, Constipation, Flatulency, Indigestion, Summer Complaints, Cholera Morbus, &c., &c., the utmost reliance can be placed on it both as to its innocent nature and highly curative qualities.

TARRANT'S INDELIBLE INK,—A superior article, warranted by the proprietor, and acknowledged by all who have tested it to be the best article of the kind now in use.

TARRANT'S COMPOUND EXTRACT OF CUBEBS AND COPAIBA,—Sanctioned by popular opinion and the high authority of the most distinguished of the medical faculty, it offers to the afflicted a remedy whose success has in every instance supported its deserved reputation. Being convenient and agreeable in its use, experience has proved that it retains in every climate its desirable and truly valuable character. It is in the form of a paste, is tasteless, and does not impair the indigestion. It is prepared with the greatest possible care, upon well tested principles. To persons following the sea, or going long voyages, this preparation possesses qualities far surpassing any other—neat and portable in its form, speedy and efficacious in its operation, successful both in the earliest and worst stages of the severest disease, while the usual and nauseous taste and unpleasant odor of copaiba is wholly avoided in this preparation. Prepared and sold wholesale and retail by JOHN A. TARRANT, successor to James Tarrant, 278 Greenwich, corner of Warren street, New York; and sold by E. M. Carey, Druggist, Charleston, S. C.; P. H. McGraw, Natches; J. B. Moore, Savannah; M. A. Santos & Son, Norfolk; W. S. Reese, Baltimore; Joseph Tucker, Mobile; Sickles & Co., New Orleans; Z. D. Gillman, Washington, D. C.; T. W. Dyott & Sons, Philadelphia; Joseph T. Brown, Boston; Weeks & Potter, Boston; Rothmahler & Anderson, Georgetown, D. C.; Clements & Bloodgood, Flushing, L. I.

THORN'S COMPOUND EXTRACT OF COPAIBA AND SARSAPARILLA—Possesses a few advantages not enjoyed by any other medicine for the cure of the afflicted, and which must, with an enlightened public, render it assuredly highly popular, and a desideratum long sought for in the medical world. It needs no confinement or change of diet. In its approved form, that of paste, it is entirely tasteless, and causes no unpleasant sensation to the patient.

It has acquired the utmost fame in every part of Europe, where it has been examined, approved of, and sanctioned by the faculty of medicine, and recommended by the most eminent of the profession. Prepared by J. B. Thorn, Chemist, London, and for sale, wholesale and retail, by J. A. TARRANT, sole agent for the United States, 278 Greenwich street, New York.

IMPORTANT CAUTION.

The increased reputation and great demand for THORN'S COMPOUND EXTRACT OF COPAIBA AND SARSAPARILLA, have been inducements for others to offer an imitation of this valuable medicine. Venders are particularly warned of this fact, that they may be on their guard, and not dispose of an impure article calculated to injure their reputation, and destroy the merits of the original preparation: to obviate which the subscriber, (by whom it was first introduced into the United States,) has attached his signature to this caution, to counterfeit which is forgery.

JOHN A. TARRANT,

Successor to JAMES TARRANT.

tomac is crossed by a viaduct 700 feet long, and rising in a succession of steps—embracing also a crossing of the Chesapeake and Ohio Canal. This extensive bridge carries us out of Virginia and lands us once more in Old Maryland, which we left at Harper's Ferry, and kept out of for a distance of 91 miles.

The route thence to Cumberland is across two bends of the river, between which the stream of Evett's Creek is crossed by a viaduct of 100 feet span.

The entrance to the town of Cumberland is beautiful, and displays the noble amphitheatre in which it lies to great advantage—the gap of Will's Mountain, westward of the town, being a justly prominent feature of the view.

The Company's depot in Cumberland is in a central position at the intersection of the Rail Road and National Turnpike.*

The brick and stone viaduct over Well's Creek at Cumberland, is entitled to particular notice. It consists of fourteen elliptical arches of fifty feet span and thirteen feet rise, and is a well built and handsome structure.

From Cumberland to Piedmont, twenty eight miles, the scenery is remarkably picturesque—perhaps more so than upon any other section of the road of similar length. For the first twenty-two miles to the mouth of New Creek, the Knobly mountain bounds the valley of the North Branch of the Potomac on the left, and Wills and Dan's mountains on the right; thence to Piedmont the river lies in the gap which it has cut through the latter mountain.

The following points may be specially noticed:

The general direction of the road is south-west, for twenty-two miles, to the mouth of New Creek.

The cliffs which occur at intervals during the first ten miles.

The wide bottom lands extending for the next four miles, with some remarkably bold and beautiful mountain peaks in view.

* The Baltimore American of November 5th, 1842, in its editorial notice of the opening of the road to Cumberland on the 3d of that month, says:

"We cannot conclude our notice this morning without referring to the excellence of construction by which the new portion of the road (between Hancock and Cumberland) is distinguished. Every improvement which science has brought to this department of engineering, has been successfully used by the Chief Engineer, BENJAMIN H. LATROBE, Esq., under the judicious dictation of his own genius and well matured experience. The President and Directors expressed the utmost satisfaction at the evidences of skill and masterly execution afforded throughout the whole route."

THE GREAT
PIANO & MUSIC
ESTABLISHMENT OF
HORACE WATERS,
333 BROADWAY,
NEW YORK.

The most celebrated PIANOS and MELODEONS in the United States, in LARGER assortment and at a LESS price than can be found elsewhere, consisting of every variety of Modern Style, from the most richly Carved Case, Carved Legs, Carved Lyre, and Case Inlaid with Pearl and Pearl Keys, to those of the plainest finish.

T. GILBERT & CO'S PREMIUM PIANOS, with or without the celebrated ÆOLEON, with IRON frames, (adapting them to any climate,) and Circular Scales.

HALLETT & CUMSTON'S PIANOS, (of the old firm of Hallett & Co.)

HORACE WATERS' MODEL PIANOS, pronounced by the HIGHEST musical authorities in the Union to be equal to any of American manufacture, in Power, Brilliancy and Richness of Tone, Elasticity of Touch, Beauty and Durability of Make.

PIANOS of several other celebrated BOSTON AND NEW YORK manufacture.

☞ SECOND-HAND PIANOS at great bargains. Prices from $40 to $150.

MELODEONS.

S. D. & H. W. SMITH'S well known MELODEONS, (tuned the equal temperament,) beautifully adapted to the use of the PARLOR, CHURCH, SCHOOL OR CLUB ROOMS, &c.

MELODEONS of all other styles and prices.

PRICES of Different Makes $45, $60, $75, $100, $115, $125, $130, $150, $200.

☞ Each Instrument guaranteed to give entire satisfaction.

☞ Clergymen, Churches, Schools, Clubs, &c., supplied with Pianos and Melodeons at a LARGE DISCOUNT.

☞ All forwarding their orders for Instruments will be as well and fairly dealt by as though personally present.

MUSIC.

The Choice Musical productions of the first EUROPEAN and AMERICAN COMPOSERS published daily. A large assortment of all Foreign and American MUSIC, constantly in Store.

THOMAS BAKER, LEADER OF JULLIEN'S BAND, and Arranger of Jullien's Popular "Repertoire" of Dance Music for the Piano, and for a number of years Manager of the publishing department of the great Music House of JULLIEN & CHAPPELLS, LONDON, and at present Musical Director and Conductor at the English Opera at Niblo's, has assumed the charge of the Publishing Department of this House, and the musical public have the assurance of being enabled to procure the CHOICEST MUSICAL GEMS, published in the most approved and perfect manner.

☞ Music sent by mail post paid. General and Select CATALOGUES and Schedule of Retail Prices of Instruments sent to any address free of charge.

The high rocky bluffs along Fort Hill, and the grand mural precipice opposite to them, on the Virginia shore, immediately below the "Black Oak Bottom," a celebrated farm embracing five hundred acres in a single plain, between mountains of great height.

The "Chimney Hole Rock," at the termination of Fort Hill, a singular crag, through the base of which the Railroad Company have driven a tunnel under the road to answer the purpose of a bridge for several streams entering the river at that point.

The crossing of the Potomac from the Maryland to the Virginia shore, twenty-one miles from Cumberland, where the railroad, after passing through a long and deep excavation, spans the river by a bridge of timber and iron, on stone abutments and a pier. The view at this point, both up and down the river, is very fine. The bridge is a noble structure, roofed and weather-boarded. It has two spans of one hundred and sixty feet each, making the total length three hundred and twenty feet. On the west end are the words "Potomac Bridge, 1851; designed by B. H. Latrobe, Chief Engineer; Executed by A. Fink, Assistant Engineer; J. C. Davis, Carpenter."

The "Bull's Head Rock," a mile beyond this point the Railroad, having cut through the *neck*, has left the *head* standing, a bold block of rock breasting the river, which dashes hard against it. Immediately on the other side of the cut made by the Railroad through the neck, rises a conical hill of great height. The mouth of New Creek, where there is a beautiful plain of a mile or more in length, and opposite to which is a long promontory of "Pine Hill," terminating in "Queen's Cliff," on the Maryland side of the river. The profile and pass of Dan's Mountain is seen in bold relief to the north-west, to which direction the road now changes its course. The road skirts the foot of "Thunder Hill," and winds along the river margin, bounded by Dan's Mountain and its steep spurs, for seven miles, up to Piedmont. The current of the river is much more rapid here than below, and islands are more frequent.

Piedmont—a flat of limited extent, opposite the small but ancient village of Westernport, at the mouth of George's Creek. The plan of the engine house at this point was suggested by the Chief Engineer, Mr. Latrobe, and the design admirably carried out by Mr. Albert Fink, Assistant Engineer. It is shaped very much like a marquee and is arranged to hold sixteen engines, and cost between $12,000 and $13,000.

West of Piedmont the road ascends seventeen miles by a grade, of which eleven miles is at the rate of one hundred and sixteen feet per mile, to the "Altamont" Summit. The points worthy of notice in this distance are:

The stone viaduct of three arches, of fifty-six feet span, over the Potomac river, where the road re-crosses into Maryland. It is a substantial and handsome structure, and elevated fifty feet above the water. The road then winds, for five miles, up the valley of Savage River, passing the "Everett" Tunnel, of three hundred feet in length, and thirty-two miles from Cumberland. This tunnel is secured by a brick arch. To this point the line was completed in July, 1851, and opened on the occasion of the "Piedmont" celebration. The winding of the road up the mountain side, along Savage river, gradually increases its elevation until it attains a height of two hundred feet above the water, and placing us far above the tops of the trees growing in the valley, or rather deep ravine, on our right, presents a grand view.

The mouth of Crab-Tree Creek, where the road turns the flank of the Great Back-bone Mountain—from this point the view up Savage River to the north, and Crab-Tree Creek to the south-west, is magnificent; the latter presenting a vista of several miles up a deep gorge gradually growing narrower—the former a bird's-eye view of a deep, winding trough bounded by mountain ridges of great elevation.

Three miles up Crab-Tree Creek is an excavation one hundred and eight feet deep, through a rocky spur of the mountain.

About five miles from its mouth, Crab-Tree Creek is first crossed by the road on an embankment of sixty-seven feet in height, and after that several times at reduced elevations, until in two miles more the forks of the creek are reached at the "Swanton" level, where are the remains of an abandoned clearing and an old mill. Here also the old Cumberland and Clarksburg road crosses, the first wagon road of the country after the pack-horse had given place to the wheeled vehicle.

All the way up Savage River and Crab-Tree Creek, eleven miles to this point, the road is hung upon the rugged and uncultivated mountain side—but from Swanton to the Altamont Summit, three or four miles, it ascends along the flat bottom of a beautiful valley of gentle slopes, passing one or two pretty farms.

"Altamont," the culminating point of the line, at a height of

LAUNDRY STARCH POLISH.

Transparent Soap,

IN BARS, BALLS AND CAKES,

IN IMMENSE VARIETY.

JOHNSON'S TRANSPARENT HONEY SOAP, NEW YORK.

MYRTLE SHAVING SOAP,

THE BEST IN USE.

Original Walnut Oil Soap,

INVENTED BY WM. JOHNSON.

The above are the most popular and salable articles now in use, and in demand in every town and village in the United States; the quality and extreme low price places them within the reach of the strictest economy.

Manufactured by William Johnson,

59 FRANKFORT ST., NEW YORK.

☞ AGENTS in Richmond—PURCELL, LADD & CO.

2,626 feet above tide water at Baltimore—the dividing ridge between the Potomac and Ohio waters—is passed by a long open cut of upwards of thirty feet in depth. The great Back-Bone Mountain, now passed, towers up on the left hand, and is seen at every opening in that direction.

The "Glades," which reach from "Altamont" to "Cranberry Summit,"—nineteen miles—the "Glades" are beautiful, natural meadows, lying along the upper waters of the Youghiogheny River, and its numerous tributaries, divided by ridges generally of moderate elevation and gentle slope, with fine ranges of mountains in the back-ground. The glades have numerous arms which make charming expansions of their valleys, and afford beautiful vistas in many directions. Their verdure is peculiarly bright and fresh, and the streams watering them are of singular clearness and purity, and abound in fine trout. The forest foliage was at the date of the Fairmont opening (June 22, 1852,) still imperfectly developed, giving an idea of the lateness of the Spring in this high country. Numerous herds of cattle were observed feeding on these natural pastures, here and there a house, at long intervals, breaking the monotony of the scene.

Oaklands is a promising village fifty-four miles West of Cumberland. It is newly laid out, and already shows a respectable number of good frame houses. From this point a magnificent view of the broad Glade eastward and the mountain beyond it is obtained.

The crossing of the great Youghiogheny River is by a viaduct of timber and iron—a single arch of one hundred and eighty feet span resting on stone abutments. The site of this fine structure is wild; the river running here in a woody gorge.

The crossing of the Maryland and Virginia boundary line is sixty miles from Cumberland.

The falls of Snowy Creek where three branches come together, making a broad valley west of the pass just described.

The Cranberry Swamp Summit, (sixty-three and a half miles from Cumberland,) at the head of Snowy Creek, falling into the Youghiogheny, also of Salt Lick Creek emptying into Cheat River. A village shows its beginnings here. The ground on the margin of the road is flat, (as its name imports,) yet its elevation above tide water is 2,550 feet, and but 76 feet lower than Altamont Summit.

The descent, of twelve miles, to Cheat river, presents a rapid succession of very heavy excavations and embankments and two tun-

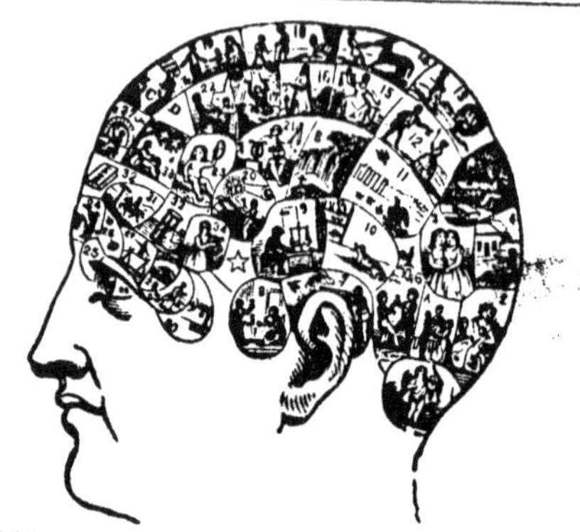

nels, viz: the McGuire Tunnel of five hundred, and the Rodemer Tunnel, four hundred feet in length, secured by heavy timbers preparatory to arching with brick. There is also a stone and iron viaduct over Salt Lick Creek fifty feet span and fifty feet high. The creek passes through a dense forest of fir trees in its approach to the river.

Cheat river is a dark rapid mountain stream, whose waters are of a curious coffee colored hue, owing, it is said, to its rising in forests of laurel and black spruce on the highest mountain levels of that country. This stream is crossed by a viaduct consisting of two arches one hundred and eighty and one hundred and thirty feet span, of timber and iron on stone abutments and pier. The masonry, built from a fine free-stone quarry close at hand, is remarkably substantial and well looking.

The ascent of the Cheat River hill comes next. This is decidedly the most imposing section of the whole line—the difficulties encountered in the four miles West of the crossing of the river being quite appalling—the road winding up the slope of Laurel hill and its spurs, with the river on the right hand, first crosses the ravine of Kyer's Run, seventy-six feet deep, by a solid embankment,—then, after bold cutting, along a steep, rocky hill side, it reaches "Buckeye hollow," the depth of which is one hundred and eight feet below the road level, and four hundred feet across at that level—some more side cutting in rock ensues, and the passage of two or three coves in the hill side when we come to "Tray Run," and cross it one hundred and fifty feet above its original bed by a line of trestling 600 feet long at the road level. Both these deep chasms have solid walls of masonry built across them, the foundations of which are on the solid rock one hundred and twenty and one hundred and eighty feet respectively below the road height. These walls have been brought, at Buck-Eye hollow, to within forty-six feet, and at Tray Run, fifty-eight feet of the grade, and the track is for the present carried over them by a substantial frame of timber securely footed upon the walls, and bolted and braced in every way conducive to strength and safety. They have been tested by constant use with the heaviest engines and trains. They are, however, to be replaced by cast iron viaducts, now being built alongside, and which when finished will be among the most beautiful architectural structures of the road. They are from the designs of Mr. A. Fink.

After passing these two tremendous clifts in the mountain side,

the road winds along a precipitous slope with heavy cuting, filling and walling, to "Buckhorn Branch," a wide and deep cove on the western flank of the mountain. This is crossed by a solid embankment and retaining wall, ninety feet high at its most elevated point. Some half a mile further, after more heavy cuts and fills, the road at length leaves the declivity of the river, which, where we see it for the last time, lies five hundred feet below us, and turns westward through a low gap, which admits it by a moderate cutting, followed soon, however, by a deep and long one through Cassidy's Summit Ridge to the table land of the country bordering Cheat River on the west. Here, at eighty miles from Cumberland, we enter the great western coal fields, having passed out of the Cumberland field at thirty-five miles from that place. The intermediate space, although without coal, will be readily supplied from the adjacent coal basins.

Desending somewhat from Cassidy's Ridge, and passing by a high embankment over the Brushy Fork of Pringle's Run, the line soon reaches the Kingwood Tunnel, of 4,100 feet in length, the longest finished tunnel in America, and which was built by Messrs. Lemmon, Gorman, and Clark & McMahon, contractors. It is through a compact slate rock, overlaid in part by a good limestone roof, and for the rest of its length it is supported by timbering preliminary to brick arching. There are two long deep cuts at each end of the tunnel. It was worked from the two ends, and from three shafts fifteen by twenty feet square and one hundred and eighty feet deep. The greatest height of the ridge over the tunnel is two hundred and twenty feet. The time employed on the work was about two years and eight months, and the number of cubic yards removed from the tunnel was about 90,000, together with about 110,000 yards of earth and rock outside the tunnel, making some 200,000 yards in all. The tunnel has been named from Kingwood, the county seat of Preston county, Virginia, which stands a few miles off on the same ridge. The tunnel not having been finished in time to permit the transportation of the iron rails through it, a track was laid over the top of the hill, *at a grade of upwards of five hundred feet per mile*, over which the materials were taken by a locomotive engine, which propelled a single car at a time, weighing with its load thirteen tons, at a speed of ten miles per hour and upwards. When the track was rendered slippery, however, by moisture, the engine and its load occasionally slid backward, and more than once

E. R. DURKEE,

PROPRIETOR AND MANUFACTURER OF

DURKEE'S

CHEMICAL YEAST OR BAKING POWDER,

AND

FLAVORING EXTRACTS.

WHOLESALE DEALER IN

BLACK LEAD AND BRITISH LUSTRE,

SAL SODA, CREAM TARTAR, SUPER CARBONATE OF SODA,

REFINED PEARLASH, SALERATUS,

CORN STARCH,

AND ARTICLES OF DRUGS USUALLY SOLD BY GROCERS.

Offices, 137 & 139 Water Street,

NEW YORK.

THOMAS H. BATE,

FIRST PREMIUM AWARDED

FOR

NEEDLES,

FISH HOOKS AND FISHING TACKLE,

No. 35 Maiden Lane,

NEAR NASSAU STREET,

NEW YORK.

ran in this way, with locked wheels, nearly half a mile down to the bottom of the grade—without damage however. This, we believe, is the most extraordinary display of locomotive steam power on record.

Leaving Kingwood Tunnel, the line for five miles descends along a steep hill-side to the flats of Raccoon Creek, at Simpson's. In this distance, it lies high above the valley, and crosses a branch of it with an embankment one hundred feet in elevation. There are two other heavy fills further on. Two miles west of the Kingwood Tunnel, is Murray's Tunnel, two hundred and fifty feet long, a regular and beautiful semi-circular arch cut out of a fine solid sand-stone rock, overlaying a vein of coal six feet thick, which is seen on the floor of the tunnel.

From Simpson's, westward, the route pursues the valleys of Raccoon and Three Forks Creeks, which present no features of difficulty to the mouth of the latter, one hundred and one miles from Cumberland, at the Tygart's Valley River, where the railroad to Parkersburg will diverge from that to Wheeling. The distance to these two places (which are ninety miles apart on the Ohio river) will be nearly equal, being one hundred and four miles to the former, and ninety-nine to the latter.

Fetterman, a promising looking village, two miles west of the last point, and one hundred and three and a half miles from Cumberland. Here the Turnpike to Parkersburg and Marietta crosses the river. The route from Fetterman to Fairmont has but one very striking feature. The Tygart's Valley River, whose margin it follows, is a beautiful and winding stream, of gentle current, except at the Falls, where the river descends, principally by three or four perpendicular pitches, some seventy feet in about a mile. A mile and a half above Fairmont the Tygart's Valley River and the West Fork River unite to form the Monongahela, the first being the larger of the two confluents.

A quarter of a mile below their junction, the railroad crosses the Monongahela, upon a viaduct six hundred and fifty feet long and thirty-nine feet above low water surface. The lofty and massive abutments of this bridge support an iron superstructure of three arches of two hundred feet span each, and which forms the *largest iron bridge in America.* It is designed by Mr. Fink, whose name deserves such favorable mention in connection with the architecture of the road, and whose works are alike worthy of him and his able preceptor, Benjamin H. Latrobe.

☞ For Recommendations, see page 448.

The road, a mile and a half below Fairmont, leaves the valley of the beautiful Monongahela and ascends the winding and picturesque ravine of Buffalo Creek, a stream some twenty-five miles in length. The creek is first crossed five miles west of Fairmont, and again at two points a short distance apart, and about nine miles further west. The bridges are of timber stringers, trussed with cast-iron posts and cross-ties, and wrought iron bars, and, lying under the rails, make no show from the cars as you pass, but when examined are found to display a remarkable combination of lightness and strength. About eleven miles beyond Fairmont we pass the small hamlet of Farmington, and seven or eight miles further is the thriving village of "Mannington," at the mouth of Piles' Fork of Buffalo. There is a beautiful flat here on both sides of the stream, affording room for a town of some size, and surrounded by hills of a most agreeable aspect. Thence to the head of Piles' Fork, the road traverses at first a narrow and serpentine gorge, with five bridges at different points, after which it courses with more gentle curvatures along a wider and moderately winding valley, with meadow land of one or two hundred yards broad on one or other margin. Numerous tributaries open out pretty vistas on either hand. This part of the valley, in its summer dress, is singularly beautiful. After reaching its head at Glover's Gap, twenty-eight miles beyond Firmont, the road passes the ridge by deep cuts, and a tunnel three hundred and fifty feet long, of curious shape, forming a sort of Moorish arch in its roof. From this summit, (which divides the waters of the Monongahela from those of the Ohio,) the line descends by Church's Fork of Fish Creek,—a valley of the same general features with the one just passed on the eastern side of the ridge. Passing the "Burton" Station, where there is an engine house and dwelling, and a reservoir dam a little way off for supplying the water-tanks in the dry season, the route continues down stream, and at the crossing of a tributary called "Cappo Fork," four miles from Glover's Gap, is the residence of Mr. Church, from which the creek derives its name. This place has been appropriately called "Old Hundred," from the age of its proprietor, who has just turned his 102d year, and is still enjoying good health and the powers of locomotion.

The road now becomes winding, and in the next four miles we cross the creek eight times by bridges of a pattern similar to those described above. We also pass Sole's Tunnel, one hundred and twelve feet, Eaton's Tunnel, three hundred and seventy feet, and

WHAT IS SAID OF RIDER'S PATENT VULCANIZED GUTTA PERCHA GOODS.

[From the New York Daily Express.]

Gutta Percha—The use of which has been hitherto restricted by its non-elasticity, rigidity, and too great susceptibility to heat—can now, under the patent of Mr. Rider, owned by the North-American Gutta Percha Company, be endowed with permanent elasticity and flexibility, rendered unsusceptible to heat and cold, and applied to all the purposes for which India Rubber has heretofore enjoyed the exclusive monopoly. Few inventions more strikingly illustrate the ingenuity of man.

[From the Buffalo Republican, Buffalo, N. Y.]

Gutta Percha has come into the field, and is already having a great run, with every prospect of entirely superseding the use of India Rubber. The advantages of this wonderful material over India Rubber are, that it is more durable, free from disagreeable smell, and does not decompose and become sticky. From the vast variety of water-proof clothing and other articles being made by the North-American Gutta Percha Company of New York, it is plainly seen that Rubber must give way to Gutta Percha.

[From the Whitehall Chronicle, Whitehall, N. Y.]

The manufacture of water-proof clothing, and many other articles, from Gutta Percha, under Rider's patent, by the North-American Gutta Percha Company, of New York, is carried on extensively. These articles do not get sticky like India Rubber when exposed to heat or friction, which certainly is very desirable to the consumer, and which must give Gutta Percha the preference as it becomes known.

[From the United States Argus, N. Y.]

Gutta Percha.—When India Rubber became an article of clothing, etc., there was no idea but that the ultimatum had been arrived at. Not so, however; for hardly had the article got well into notoriety, than it was immediately superseded by Gutta Percha, because there were evident inconveniences in the former which the latter is free from. Gutta Percha now stands pre-eminent, and Rider's Patent Vulcanized Gutta Percha is ahead of every thing in the line.

[From the Republican and Argus.]

We never expected to find a substitute for India Rubber, but one has been recently found in the article of Gutta Percha. A mode of manufacture has been discovered by Mr. Rider, of New York, which gives Gutta Percha all the pliability and elasticity of India Rubber, without its unpleasant and objectionable qualities.

[From the Westchester Herald, Sing Sing.]

The manufacturers of India Rubber goods are having a formidable rival in Vulcanized Gutta Percha, under Rider's patent. The North-American Gutta Percha Company own this patent exclusively, and are making large quantities of clothing and other articles.

[From the Memorial, Plymouth, Mass.]

The Messrs. Riders, of New York, long engaged in the Rubber manufacture, have discovered a mode of preparing Gutta Percha, which gives it all the pliability and elasticity of India Rubber—it converts Gutta Percha, which before was as hard as wood, and little more than a curiosity, into one of the most beautiful of known water-proof substances. The discovery has been patented, and is now being worked, in the manufacture of clothing and other goods, very extensively by the North-American Gutta Percha Company of New York.

TESTIMONIALS may be seen at the Warehouse of the Company, highly approving of these goods, from Col. J. H. Eaton, U. S A.; Capt. H. D. Hunter, U. S. N.; Lieut. J. M. Fraily, U. S. N.; Capt. Marcy, U. S. A.; Col. Gray, of Mexican Boundary Survey; Capt. G. L. Smith, of clipper-ship Vulture; Lieut. Fox, U. S. N., and hundreds of others, who have actually tested the goods in actual wear in different climates.

Martin's Tunnel, one hundred and eighty feet long—the first a low-browed opening, which looks as if it would knock off the smoke pipe of the engine; the next a regular arched roof, and the third a tall narrow slit in the rock, lined with timbers lofty enough to be taken for part of a church steeple.

The "Littleton" Station is reached just beyond, and here upon a long side track are ranged the ten locomotives designed to carry cars* over the Board Tree Tunnel, now close at hand. The road having thus far pursued the margin of the South Fork of Fish Creek, now gradually leaves it and winds upwards along the steep hill, slopes for about a mile and a half, constantly increasing its height above the stream and crossing the rocky chasm of Cliff Run, upwards of fifty feet above its bed. Shortly after, the route turns up the ravine of the "Board Tree Run," after passing through a high spur at its mouth by a formidable cut more than sixty feet deep through slate rock. Thence it ascends the eastern bank of the run just named, cutting and filling heavily along a precipitous hill side until it reaches the point forty-three miles West of Fairmont, where the temporary road leaves the permanent grade. You here see before you the latter entering the approach cut at the eastern end of the tunnel, while the former begins to climb the hill on the East side of the cut, crossing several branch ravines and rising every moment higher and higher on the flank of the main ravine until you perceive the eastern portal far below you, and presenting a yawning chasm penetrating the bowels of the mountain, over the top of which you are being lifted by the tremendous power of the engine, which pushes the two passenger cars, (on one of which you are standing,) up the steep incline. The temporary road after leaving a point opposite the mouth of the tunnel, turns into a hollow on the side of the ridge and soon reaches the first switch. Here the movement of the train is reversed, the engine pulling the cars backwards instead of pushing them forward as before. The second switch is soon arrived at, and the direction of the train again reversed—and the engine, with its train once more ahead, advances steadily to the summit of the hill by a line winding around the head of the hollow just mentioned. There is a short level upon the summit, after passing which the road makes a notch in the sharp edge of the hill top at a

* This part of the description of the road was written on the occasion of the opening to Wheeling, (January, 1853;) at this time (April 1st, 1853,) the tunnel is constructed, and the mountain crossing avoided,

little depression therein, and descends on the western side to the third switch. The view from this summit is very grand, looking right down to the termination of the approach cut at the western portal of the tunnel, into which you think you could leap at a single bound.

The temporary road now runs downwards on the West, backing to and fro upon the western escarpment of the ridge and passes in these zig-zags, the 4th, 5th, 6th and 7th switches, the direction of the train being reversed, and the engine pulling and pushing alternately at each of them. The last switch being passed, the road descends by a very direct line along the western side of the approach cut of the permanent grade, which it reaches at length in the bed of Raccoon Run, the stream falling into the North Fork of Fish Creek, from the western side of the summit. There are two switches on the East and five on the West side of the ridge, the latter being the most precipitous, and requiring therefore the most manœuvring to descend. The distance over the mountain by the temporary road is 12,000 feet, just twice the distance through the hill by the Permanent grade. The length of the tunnel is 2,350 feet. The ascent of the different planes varies from two hundred and ninety-three to three hundred and forty feet per mile according to the curvature, and their grades were so arranged as to permit the engine to propel two loaded cars (or twenty-five tons gross) upon them. At the crossing of the mountain over the Kingwood Tunnel previous to the completion of that work in 1853, the grade was upwards of five hundred feet per mile, and but one car, or twelve and a half tons, was the load. The engines and car on this latter grade were moreover liable to the risk of sliding down the grade with locked wheels, an accident which could not happen on the Board Tree Tunnel grades. Hence, although the total height of the hill at the latter place is three hundred feet, being eighty feet more than at the other, the use of the switches has permitted the reduction of the grades so as to double the loads carried, and diminish the risk correspondingly.

The crossing of this ridge, in the manner described, is a great achievement in engineering science. It was made necessary by the delay in the completion of the tunnel, occasioned by sundry causes beyond control, and has thus been the means of illustrating a mode of surmounting ridges, which has been heretofore employed, but never under circumstances such as the present. The sight of so many locomotives toiling up the hill, one after another, upon the dif-

ferent levels, was novel and exciting in a high degree, and not the less so from the darkness of the night, (on the opening trip 11th January, 1853,) which made their changing position visible only by the clouds of fire and steam which marked their tracks. The passage over the tunnel by daylight is equally interesting.

Leaving Board Tree Tunnel, the line descends along the hill side of the North Fork of Fish Creek, crossing ravines and spurs by deep fillings and cuttings, and reaching the level of the flats bordering the creek at Bell's Mill; soon after which it crosses the creek and ascends Hart's Run and Four Mile Run to the Welling Tunnel, fifty miles west of Fairmont, and twenty-eight from Wheeling. This tunnel is 1,250 feet long, and pierces the ridge between Fish Creek and Grave Creek. It is through slate rock like the Board Tree Tunnel, and is substantially propped with timbers.

From the Welling Tunnel the line pursues the valley of Grave Creek seventeen miles to its mouth at the Flats of Grave Creek on the Ohio River, eleven miles below Wheeling. The first five miles of the ravine of Grave Creek is of gentle curvature and open aspect, like the others already mentioned. Afterwards it becomes very sinuous, and the stream requires to be bridged eight times. There are also several deep cuts through sharp ridges in the bends of the creek, and one tunnel four hundred feet long at Sheppard's, nineteen miles from Wheeling.

The approach to the bank of the Ohio River at the village of Moundsville, is very beautiful. The line emerging from the defile of Grave Creek, passes straight over the "flats" which border the river, and forming a vast rolling plain, in the middle of which looms up the "great Indian mound," eighty feet high and two hundred feet broad at its base. There is also the separate village of Elizabethtown, half a mile from the river bank, the mound standing between two towns and looking down upon them both. The "flats" embrace an area of some 4,000 acres, about three-fourths of which lies on the Virginia, and the remaining fourth on the Ohio side of the river. The soil is fertile and well cultivated, and the spot possesses great interest, whether for its agricultural richness, its historic monuments of past ages, or the beauty of its shape and position as the site for a large city.

About three miles up the river from Moundsville, the "flats" terminate, and the road passes for a mile along rocky narrows washed by the river, after which it runs over wide, rich and beauti-

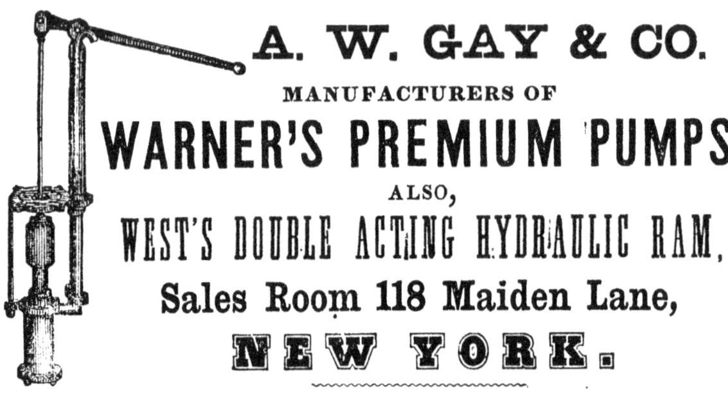

Where a farmer desires to have a pump in his well, which besides supplying his family and stock with water, will answer for a fire-engine when connected with a hose and pipe; he cannot have a pump better suited to his purposes than this one.—*Report of the Committee at the N. Y. State Agricultural Fair, Saratoga*, 1853.

I believe it to be the best force pump for vessels that I have ever seen.—C. H. Mallory, *Mystic, Conn.*

We have Warner's Patent Force Pumps on the Steamers "Hero," and "Buffalo," and after a thorough trial for one season, we can cheerfully recommend them for steamboat use, and believe them to be as good and cheap a pump as can be found.—J. W. Hancox, *Owner of Steamboats "Hero," and "Buffalo." May* 7, 1854.

For mining purposes, I cheerfully certify that it is as good as the best, and much cheaper than any other of the capacity and power.—Charles H. Scott, *Machinist and Engineer.*

Bedstead Factory

AT YONKERS,

17 miles from New York.

OFFICE & STORE

IN COLLINS' HOTEL BUILDING,

FOOT OF CANAL STREET, (North River,)

NEW YORK.

R. BARNES.

ful bottom lands all the way to Wheeling. Two and a half miles below Wheeling Creek the Company's "outer station" is located, and is graded ready for the erection of the required buildings. For the present an engine house and work shops are being built at a suitable spot, about a mile below the creek, where the line reaches the immediate bank of the river and thence follows it along "Water street" to the "inner station." This last is on the north bank of Wheeling Creek as required by the charter. The "inner station" comprises a height house with four tracks, ninety-four feet wide and 340 feet long, a passenger hall of sixty feet front and forty-five depth, with a shed roof extending back over the bridge, and making the entire length of the passenger building 360 feet; all these buildings being on the North side of the creek. On the South side of the creek and adjoining the abutments of the bridge, will be a house for the shelter of passenger engines and cars, which will complete the establishment of this Station. Although well planned and possessing a considerable capacity for business, this "inner station" is not expected to accommodate the whole trade, which will be carried on at the warehouses of the merchants of the city, to which tracks can be conveniently extended, and where the cars will be loaded and unloaded--thus diffusing the benefits of the road through the commercial part of the city, and along the full water front which is commanded by the Railroad for upwards of a mile. The live stock seeking the Wheeling terminus for transportation will be received into the trains at the "outer station," where it can be most conveniently loaded.

The whole length of the road to Wheeling is seventy-eight miles from Fairmont, two hundred and one miles from Cumberland, and three hundred and eighty miles from Baltimore.

The fact that the Baltimore and Ohio Railroad is one of the greatest and most important iron thoroughfares in the country is no longer questioned, while it is becoming as noted for the skill and superiority of its management generally; and it may not be going too far to say, that in such hands as William G. Harrison, John H. Doane, W. P. Smith, and others, the Company will continue to prosper and gain the confidence of the traveling public and a reputation for themselves. We rejoice to note the prosperity and unsurpassed management of this great enterprise, and had we time and space we would with pleasure say more.—[Editor.

www.ingramcontent.com/pod-product-compliance
Lightning Source LLC
LaVergne TN
LVHW021149110826
845150LV00005B/1164

* 9 7 8 1 4 2 5 5 4 6 5 8 8 *